BREAD FROM HEAVEN

SACRA DOCTRINA SERIES

BREAD FROM HEAVEN

AN INTRODUCTION TO THE THEOLOGY OF THE EUCHARIST

Bernhard Blankenhorn, OP

The Catholic University of America Press
Washington, D.C

The paper used in this publication meets the minimum requirements of
American National Standards for Information Science—Permanence
of Paper for Printed Library Materials, ANSI Z39.48-1984.
∞

Library of Congress Cataloging-in-Publication Data

Names: Blankenhorn, Bernhard, 1973– author.
Title: Bread from heaven : an introduction to the theology of the Eucharist /
Bernhard Blankenhorn.
Description: Washington, D.C. : The Catholic University of America Press, [2021] | Series:
Sacra doctrina series | Includes bibliographical references and index.
Identifiers: LCCN 2021021004 | ISBN 9780813233949 (paperback) | ISBN 9780813233956 (ebook)
Subjects: LCSH: Lord's Supper—Catholic Church. | Lord's Supper—Real presence.
Classification: LCC BX2215.3 .B58 2021 | DDC 234/.163—dc23
LC record available at https://lccn.loc.gov/2021021004

To Richard Schenk, OP
Confrere, teacher, mentor, and friend

CONTENTS

ACKNOWLEDGMENTS

Several theologians and exegetes helped to sharpen this manuscript, above all Emmanuel Perrier, OP, who carefully commented on the whole of it and gave me precious insights. This work would look very different without his wisdom. The biblical sections were strengthened thanks to the feedback of Fr. Mauro Gagliardi, Anthony Giambrone, OP, and Gregory Tatum, OP. The last chapter benefited from comments by Serge-Thomas Bonino, OP, and Gilles Emery, OP. Two anonymous readers for CUA Press offered constructive critiques that allowed me to improve the style and theological arguments in various places. Many thanks also to John Martino of CUA Press for his invaluable help and consistent encouragement.

Every chapter integrates the fruits of my annual lectures on the Eucharist for the undergraduate students at the Angelicum and echoes of graduate seminars on the Eucharist. The students' many questions, insights, and deep curiosity shaped this work in various ways. My research advanced thanks to the fantastic library resources of the Angelicum and its reference librarian, Joanna Kryjak. During the periods of intense writing, I enjoyed the fraternal hospitality of several Dominican communities, especially the Couvent de saint Hyacinthe in Fribourg, Switzerland; Blackfriars in Oxford; La Clarté Notre Dame monastery of Dominican nuns in Taulignan, France; and my province's house of studies, St. Albert's Priory, in Oakland, California. To my brothers and sisters in these delightful places, I am most grateful.

Finally, this book is the long-term fruit of the Eucharistic wisdom, faith, and devotion of many Dominican brothers, sisters, and lay members, of loved ones and parishioners, friends and treasured acquaintances.

ABBREVIATIONS

CCSL	Corpus Christianorum Series Latina
DH	Denzinger
PG	Patrologiae Cursus Completus: Series Graeca, ed. J.-P. Migne (Paris)
a.	article
ad	answer to an objection
d.	distinction
q.	question

BREAD FROM HEAVEN

INTRODUCTION

In the beginning of his first teaching on the Eucharist, a young Thomas Aquinas states: "All things that are in the Eucharist pertain to representing the same reality, namely, the death of the Lord, and to effecting the same, namely, the grace by which the human being is incorporated into the mystical body."[1] Here we find in dense summary form the heart of Eucharistic theology. Since the Eucharist is a sacrament, it is a sign. The Eucharistic liturgy, especially the consecration, signifies or represents Christ's saving death. Because the prayers and gestures at Mass are fruitful, they bring to us what they represent: Jesus' sacrifice on the Cross, with his body and blood given for the life of the world, and the graces that flow from it. When we celebrate the Eucharist and partake of his body and blood, we are joined ever more closely to the Church, Christ's mystical body. Contact with the crucified and risen Christ corporeally present entails communion with the Church, and vice versa.

Aquinas offers the most developed Eucharistic theology of any classical theologian, and has rightly enjoyed much influence on ecclesial doctrine and piety. The present study synthesizes Aquinas's Eucharistic theology with contemporary biblical exegesis, the history of the liturgy and

1. Thomas Aquinas, *Commentary on the Sentences*, book IV, d. 8, q. 1, a. 1, quaestiuncula 2, sed contra 2, in idem, *Commentary on the Sentences, book IV, distinctions 1–13*, trans. Beth Mortensen, Latin/English Edition of the Works of St. Thomas Aquinas 7 (Green Bay, Wisc.: Aquinas Institute, 2017), 326.

the doctrine contained in the Eucharistic prayers, as well as the doctrine expressed by the councils of Florence, Trent, and Vatican II.

Three themes guide the present study. First, the Eucharist is a celebration of the Paschal Mystery. That is, we enter into the double-mystery of his Passion and Resurrection. In the sacred liturgy, the dying and risen Christ prays with us. He consecrates the gifts through the priest and intercedes for us, as the whole Church joins her prayer to his. As a result of his priestly, dynamic presence, the Lamb's own body and blood come upon the altar. The blessings of his saving Passion flow out of the pierced side of the Lamb corporeally present in our midst. On our altars, we encounter his risen body. When we eat and drink the body and blood of the glorified Christ, he renders us immortal, as he conforms us to himself, body and soul. Communion with him also brings us ever closer to the heavenly liturgy, that perpetual worship of the saints before the ascended Lord, the celestial ritual in which every Mass on earth already participates.

Second, as our way of entering into Christ's Paschal Mystery, we are called to see the Eucharist as the perpetuation of the New Passover. This calls for special attentiveness to the Last Supper and its link with the Jewish Passover. Furthermore, we want to see the continuity between Christ's Passover celebration and the Christian Eucharistic liturgy, especially in the liturgical practices of the early Christians. The Church celebrates the sacrifice and sacrament instituted at the Last Supper, a teaching found in the writings of the Fathers and the early Eucharistic prayers. The Church's diverse rites have a common historical and spiritual origin in Christ's Passover. Consequently, the Eucharistic liturgy is not a ritual that the Church primarily constructs, but a gift that she receives from her Lord, and that develops organically over the centuries under the Spirit's guidance.

Third, the corporeal, substantial presence of the paschal lamb is essential for a Passover celebration. This presence should be understood in light of the Gospel of John, chapter 6, as well as the doctrine of transubstantiation. Proper exegesis of John 6 prevents theology from engaging in abstract speculation, and also holds much promise for Christian unity. John 6 offers the most powerful biblical teaching on the mode of Christ's presence in the gifts on the altar and a central revelation of the spiritual fruits offered to us in this, the new manna. This Gospel text also leads us to understand the Eucharist in light of Christ's hypostatic union and the relation between Christ's humanity and the Holy Spirit. The theology of transubstantiation, especially as developed by Aquinas and taught at the Council of Trent, gives the Church a clear way to exclude spiritualizing tendencies in theologies of Eucharistic presence, to protect the ancient and perpetual liturgical practice of adoring the gifts on the altar, and to give a theological account of biblical, liturgical, and patristic affirmations about the mode of Christ's presence in the Eucharistic gifts.

This study begins with Holy Scripture, for Scripture is the soul of theology. The biblical sections primarily employ contemporary critical exegetical studies, without ignoring the contributions of classical exegesis. The first two chapters focus on two Eucharistic images in the Bible: the gift of manna, which culminates in Christ as the true bread of life in John 6, and then, the Last Supper, especially in relation to Passover.

In the third chapter, I ponder the ancient Eucharistic prayers and patristic witnesses to the Eucharist in antiquity in view of their link with the Last Supper, with the purpose of recognizing biblical and ecclesial testimony to Christ's way of instituting the Eucharist. Among these sources, I look for the place of the institution narrative in the liturgies, common sacrificial terms in the liturgical texts, and the use of bread and wine, to see how the Church remains faithful to Christ's will for this sacrament, amidst a diversity of liturgical practices.

Chapter 4 takes up essential Christological and ecclesiological foundations of Eucharistic theology. Here, the image of the Church as a sacrament of communion will be key. I take up the "descending and ascending" aspects of Christ's mediation of salvation: first, the manner in which he brings life and grace to us through his humanity (instrumentality), and second his "upward mediation," wherein he makes sacrifice and satisfaction for us, so as to reconcile us with the Father. Next, I explore several Old Testament images of sacrifice, which are fulfilled at Calvary. Finally, I present a brief discussion of satisfaction for sins, a much-misunderstood doctrine.

Chapters 5 and 6 form the heart of this book. Chapter 5 ponders the Eucharist as sacrifice, a neglected doctrine in contemporary catechesis and preaching. After a brief biblical study of the Eucharist as a sacrificial offering, I turn to the ancient liturgy and Church Fathers to explore a range of sacrificial themes: the sacrifice of Christ as victim, the sacrifice of praise and thanksgiving, sacrifice for sins and reconciliation, and others. The proper balance between these themes is crucial: theologians and preachers in various periods in the Church's history have overemphasized one at the expense of another. I also seek a balance between the Eucharist as sacrifice and as meal, ultimately arguing that there is no competition between these. The systematic part of chapter 5 takes Aquinas and various Thomists as its guide, to explore difficult questions such as the unity of the sacrifice of the Mass with the sacrifice of Christ at Calvary. Next, I look for ways to honor the priority of Christ's priestly action in the liturgy without diminishing the proper role of the Church. Chapter 5 takes the relation between the interior and exterior sacrifice (of Christ and of his members) as a guiding theme. This chapter also presents Martin Luther's critique of Eucharistic sacrifice and responds to it.

Chapter 6 ponders the manner of Christ's presence in the gifts on the altar and how those gifts are transformed. I explore the Eucharistic realism of the Church Fathers, that is, their manner of affirming Christ's corporeal presence in the gift on the altar, without the technical notions of transubstantiation or substantial presence. Against the background of the great medieval western Eucharistic controversy, this chapter analyzes in some detail Aquinas's theology of how the gifts of bread and wine are changed and how Christ abides therein. I seek to make this doctrine more accessible, partly by providing an excursus on the general notions of substance and accident. The loss of a classical philosophical formation among theology students and even many scholars of liturgy risks rendering a large part of Catholic Eucharistic theology unintelligible. Christ's Eucharistic presence cannot be grasped properly without a metaphysical theology, just as the relation of his divinity and humanity cannot be grasped well without the notions (such as person and nature) that were employed by the ancient Christological councils. Scripture alone, or appeals to history, the liturgical texts, or spiritual experience, simply cannot suffice on matters such as these. Chapter 6 follows up on the study of Aquinas with an analysis of Trent, in light of three Protestant critiques of transubstantiation (in the writings of Luther, Zwingli, and Calvin). Finally, two alternative contemporary Catholic theologies of presence are explored: trans-signification (Schillebeeckx) and symbolic presence (Chauvet).

Chapter 7 takes up the theology of the consecration, or the prayer by which the bread and wine become Christ's body and blood. Here, east and west have taken somewhat divergent approaches: the east places greater emphasis on the epiclesis or calling upon the Spirit for the change of the gifts on the altar, while the west focuses on the words of institution ("This is my body.... This is the chalice of my blood"). This difference, as well as recent theological proposals to recognize the entire Eucharistic prayer as consecratory, lead to a deeper consideration of the particular role of the priest and the Church within the liturgy.

Chapter 8 presents a theology of the minister or celebrant of the Eucharist. I show the biblical, patristic, and early liturgical foundation for the doctrine that an ordained minister is the proper presider at the Eucharist. Next, I consider how the priest represents both Christ and the Church, a key notion, since Christ and the Church act through the priest by representation. Here, the priest's relation to Christ as Bridegroom of the Church deserves special attention. The priest's manner of assisting the laity in bringing their perfect, personal offering to the Father is also taken up. The chapter concludes with a brief study of the history and theology of concelebration.

The ninth and final chapter is dedicated to Eucharistic communion, a topic of much controversy in recent years. In reliance on Scripture, the teaching of the Fathers, and early liturgical practice, as well as a series of systematic arguments rooted in Aquinas, I focus on two key issues: who may or may not receive Communion, and what are the unique spiritual fruits of Communion? In an age when a call for "inclusivity" or "a welcoming Church" can easily cut theological reflection short, clear and careful reflection on the reasons for and intelligibility of longstanding liturgical practice becomes crucial. I consider the question of Communion for non-Catholics and for the divorced and civilly remarried. The fruits of Eucharistic Communion are manifold. Here, I ponder the Eucharist as the sacrament of friendship that increases charity, as spiritual medicine, as protection against evil, as an intensification of ecclesial unity, as a source of forgiveness for venial and forgotten sins, and as a means to bodily immortality. We will see how the Eucharist is especially spiritual food and drink, whose consumption can provoke a spiritual experience or taste of joy and divine sweetness. Eucharistic doctrine should find its finality in mystical contact with Christ.

This work provides an introduction to Catholic Eucharistic doctrine from a dogmatic perspective. It does not pretend to offer a complete Eucharistic theology. Thus, not all Old Testament figures of the Eucharist can be given adequate attention. I do not offer detailed analyses of entire Eucharistic prayers. One reason for these lacunae is simply a lack of space. Another reason is the deliberate choice to accentuate metaphysical considerations of the most mysterious and controversial aspects of Catholic Eucharistic doctrine. Today's academic literature and manuals for students abound with liturgical studies that place the liturgical texts and the history of liturgy in the foreground. On the one hand, the present handbook presumes that the reader takes advantage of these resources. On the other hand, these studies tend to lack a coherent philosophical and metaphysical account of Eucharistic sacrifice and Christ's presence in the Eucharistic gifts. For example, I find that some authors do not adequately face the question of how the Mass is one with the sacrifice of Calvary. Thus, some scholars make a quick appeal to the idea that a collapse of the space-time continuum occurs in the Eucharistic liturgy, so that the event of the Cross becomes present now (more on that below). Here, we might draw an analogy with Christology. While our historical understanding of the Christology of the Scriptures has advanced much in recent decades, today, greater attention is needed to doctrines such as the hypostatic union and Christ's two wills, explored both historically and systematically, to show their foundation in Scripture, their philosophical coherence and their fruitfulness in preaching and pastoral care. Eucharistic theology has benefited greatly from the renewal of biblical and liturgical studies. These sources can bear their full fruit in the life of the Church only when complemented by an appropriation of the Church's dogmatic Eucharistic teachings and the metaphysical theologies that undergird them. For just as the biblical narrative and classical, metaphysical Christology do not stand in opposition but enrich each other, so the liturgical sources and a metaphysical Eucharistic doctrine should enrich each other. The quest for a synthesis of liturgical studies and dogmatic Eucharistic theology remains an unfulfilled desire of our age, and will likely be achieved only by a team of exegetes, systematic theologians, and historians of liturgy.

Translations of Thomas Aquinas are my own. For Scripture, I use the Revised Standard Version, the most literal English translation available today, with occasional modifications. For Vatican II documents, I use the English translation from Austin Flannery.[2] Regarding the Councils of Florence and Trent, I employ the translation given in the most recent edition of Denzinger. Translations of non-Roman liturgical texts come from varying sources, at times from recent scholarly literature. As for the new Roman rite, I follow the 2011 English edition (which is based on the 2008 Latin edition).

2. *Vatican Council II*, vol. 1, *The Conciliar and Post Conciliar Documents*, rev. ed., ed. Austin Flannery (Dublin: Dominican Publications, 1996).

CHAPTER 1

BREAD FROM HEAVEN

We cannot understand the Eucharist without the Old Testament. Already, here, the divine pedagogue begins to illumine us about his greatest gift to the Church. The Book of Exodus contains the two most powerful Old Testament figures of the Eucharist, a first revelation of this gift. We find the Eucharist prefigured in the Israelites' celebration of Passover and in the miracle of the manna in the desert. The next chapter will present the Last Supper and its link to the Passover. The present chapter ponders the manna and its New Testament fulfillment. The biblical narrative first presents the manna in Exodus 16. We also find it in Deuteronomy 8, the Psalms, and Nehemiah 9. The Book of Wisdom offers an elaborate teaching on the manna. My study will focus on Exodus and Wisdom as a foundation for a reading of John 6, where Jesus reveals the new manna.

The Manna in the Old Testament

From the start of Israel's pilgrimage through the desert, God fed his people with manna. Exodus 16 recounts the beginning of this wonder. The manna was a bread-like substance that fell from the heavens in the morning, while quail (or bird meat) fell in the evening. Now this double miracle was also accompanied by a third, namely, the appearance of the glory cloud, a great sign of God that is leading the people to the Promised Land. Israel was fed daily, except on the Sabbath, and so the people were allowed to gather only as much as they could eat: nothing edible could be conserved for the next day. Each day, Israel had to look to God for food. A double portion was gathered on Friday, and this would suffice for two days, including the Sabbath (or Saturday). All the Israelites received the same gift, yet according to the need of each person, so that each was nourished and satisfied. The gift was not generic, but personal. In this way, God's people learned that only he can nourish them, as he fed them by the manna and his word (through Moses).[1] The miracle of the manna was utterly new: no one had seen anything like it. Their first question was, "what is it?" (*man hu* in Hebrew), and so, it was called *manna*. This miracle was an utter surprise, a gift that did not fit into any existing category in Israel's knowledge and experience.[2] It lasted all through the Exodus: N. T. Wright points out that it was given neither in Egypt nor in the Promised Land. This was God's daily bread for his people on pilgrimage, away from the place of sin and toward the land flowing with milk and honey.[3] The manna was for Israel, not for the Egyptians, meaning it was the food of the righteous, whereas God sent the oppressive Egyptians plagues.[4] This was bread without leaven, like the bread eaten at Passover. Some of it may have been preserved in the sanctuary of Israel's temple (Num 17:2–5; Heb 9:4).[5]

In the past two centuries, some exegetes have proposed that the man-

1. Claudio Arletti, "La manna, cibo rivelatore del patto tra YHWH ed Israele," in *Il Verbo si è fatto 'pane': l'Eucaristia tra Antico e Nuovo Testamento*, ed. Giacomo Violi (Assisi, Italy: Cittadella Editrice, 2009), 36.

2. R. W. L. Moberly, *Old Testament Theology: Reading the Hebrew Bible as Christian Scripture* (Grand Rapids, Mich.: Baker Academic, 2013), 80.

3. N. T. Wright, "The Lord's Prayer as a Paradigm for Christian Prayer," in *Into God's Presence: Prayer in the New Testament*, ed. Richard N. Longnecker (Grand Rapids, Mich.: William B. Eerdmans, 2001), 139–40, cited in Brant Pitre, *Jesus and the Last Supper* (Grand Rapids, Mich.: William B. Eerdmans, 2015), 161.

4. József Zsengellér, "'The Taste of Paradise', Interpretation of Exodus and Manna in the Book of Wisdom," in *Studies in the Book of Wisdom*, ed. Géza G. Xeravits and József Zsengellér, Supplements to the Journal for the Study of Judaism 142 (Leiden: Brill, 2010), 207.

5. Pitre, *Jesus and the Last Supper*, 153–54.

na was a natural phenomenon, perhaps the resin that comes from desert flowers or the excretion of desert insects. But such readings have no basis in the text of Exodus. They also presume an Enlightenment philosophy that excludes *a priori* any miracles as impossible.[6] Instead, the Book of Wisdom presents the manna as the central sign of a new order of salvation that simply goes beyond the natural order of the world. Strikingly, the same book simultaneously affirms the beauty and stability of the natural order (Wis 5:17–20). In short, there is no conflict or contradiction between nature and miraculous deeds. Indeed, the biblical account of the manna stands or falls with its supernatural character.[7]

Wisdom 16 contrasts the manna with another miracle, the seventh plague that God sent against the Egyptians. This last plague (before the death of the first-born) was extraordinary, for God sent hail that contained fire (Wis 16:16): hail and fire are signs of God's judgment of the sinner, of those who persecute his people. In this way, Wisdom highlights the extraordinary docility of creation's elements to God's will.[8]

This brings us to Wisdom 16:20–26:

20 Instead of these things [plagues] you gave your people the food of angels, and without their toil you supplied them from heaven with bread ready to eat, providing every pleasure and suited to every taste. 21 For your sustenance manifested your sweetness toward your children; and the bread, ministering to the desire of the one who took it, was changed to suit every one's liking. 22 Snow and ice withstood fire without melting, so that they might know that the crops of their enemies were being destroyed by the fire that blazed in the hail and flashed in the showers of rain; 23 whereas the fire, in order that the righteous might be fed, even forgot its native power. 24 For the creation, serving you who have made it, exerts itself to punish the unrighteous and in kindness relaxes on behalf of those who

6. Pitre, *Jesus and the Last Supper*, 155. For an excellent response to David Hume's famous argument against miracles, see Anselm Ramelow, "Not a Miracle: Our Knowledge of God's Signs and Wonders," *Nova et Vetera* (English Edition) 14 (2016): 659–73. For the broader issue of miracles and contemporary physics, see Michael J. Dodds, *Unlocking Divine Action: Contemporary Science and Thomas Aquinas* (Washington, D.C.: The Catholic University of America Press, 2012), 247–58.

7. Pierre Dumoulin, "La manne dans le livre de la Sagesse: Synthèse de traditions et préparation au mystère eucharistique," Dissertation of the Gregorian University (Rome: Pontificia Universitas Gregoriana, 1994), 89–93, 112–13, 134.

8. Chrysostome Larcher, *Le livre de la Sagesse ou La Sagesse de Salomon*, vol. 3, Études bibliques, New Series 5 (Paris: J. Gabalda, 1985), 917–18.

trust in you. 25 Therefore at that time also, changed into all forms, it served your all-nourishing bounty, according to the desire of those who had need, 26 so that your sons, whom you did love, O Lord, might learn that it is not the production of crops that feeds man, but that your word preserves those who trust in you.[9]

The plagues destroyed the earthly food of the Egyptians (e.g., the plague of locusts), while God sent his people food from heaven. This pattern can be found again in Paul's teaching on the Eucharist, which brings life to the just but condemnation to sinners.[10]

But what was this heavenly food, and why is it called "the food of angels," since angels have no bodies? Here, one could mention two ancient Jewish sources. The Jewish Targum on this text interprets the manna as bread descending from the realm of the angels. A Jewish Midrash proposes a reference to bread that renders men strong like angels. Wisdom 16 evokes the paternal care of God, he who gives nourishment to his children, and shows Israel's total dependence on God. Verses 20–23 indicate a food that is utterly marvelous, with extraordinary properties, something that escapes the normal conditions of matter, and evokes life in a supernatural world. In this sense, manna is "the nourishment of angels" or "angelic food," since it is not natural.[11] With this gift, the eschaton has already begun.

The maker of the manna does not tire in preparing it, for he is omnipotent. The end of verse 20 mentions the delight that this food produces. The manna virtually contains every flavor, so that it can satisfy anyone, according to his or her preference. This is not a miracle that God works in the receiver's sense perception, but in the food itself: he does not cause an impression of a certain taste, rather, he makes the food itself taste a certain way. Such a theme has a precedent in the ancient Palestinian Midrash on Exodus 16:31, where we learn that the manna tasted like milk for children, bread for adults, honey for aging persons, and barley dipped in honey and oil for the sick.[12] Albertus Magnus, the teacher of Thomas Aquinas, mentions oil and manna as he explains 2 Kings 4:1–7 and the miracle of the oil in the poor widow's jar: "The oil signifies the Eucharist

9. Translation taken from the RSV, with stylistic modifications.

10. Dumoulin, "La manne dans le livre de la Sagesse," 159.

11. Larcher, *Le livre de la Sagesse*, 922–24.

12. Larcher, *Le livre de la Sagesse*, 924–26 (brackets in the original).

well, of which the manna is a figure because it was said that it had the taste of anointed bread, or oiled bread [Ex 16:31]."[13]

Now the manna is also a symbol of something greater. It signifies divine wisdom. The manna is the Word of God received and tasted, according to the dispositions of the hearer of the Word.[14] Verses 25–26 manifest a strong link between the manna and God's Word: both sustain the believer in his very existence, giving him life. Indeed, the manna offers a concrete, physical experience of what the divine word does in an invisible mode.[15] Verse 26 evokes Deuteronomy 8:3: "He humbled you and let you hunger and fed you with manna, which you did not know, nor did your fathers know; that he might make you know that man does not live by bread alone, but that man lives by everything that proceeds out of the mouth of the Lord." Here, Deuteronomy primarily refers to the word of God found in the Law that he has given to Israel. But this word is neither simply a set of written words, nor just a past revelation of God, for it is also a present, living reality. Israel must remain disposed to receive God's word today, and ought to trust that he continues to guide history and orders all of nature. We see that the terms "word" or "word of God" designate God's activity in the midst of creation, an activity that even modifies the normal course of natural causes. The miracles recounted, whether the plagues or the descent of the manna, reinforce Israel's faith that God is all powerful, present, and acting everywhere.[16] Indeed, both gifts can only be received rightly with faith and gratitude. The fruit of this reception includes a transformation of human desire, a new hunger for God's word, a thirst for wisdom. Gradually, the Israelites should learn to detach themselves from the fleshpots of Egypt and look for the food that God provides, both physical and spiritual nourishment. They sought the manna early in the morning, and thus man should pray: "I rise before dawn and cry for help, I hope in your words" (Ps 119:147). Such purification and

13. Albertus Magnus, *On the Body of the Lord*, trans. Albert Marie Surmanski, The Fathers of the Church: Mediaeval Continuation 17 (Washington, D.C.: The Catholic University of America Press, 2017), d. 1, chap. 2, p. 36.

14. Larcher, *Le livre de la Sagesse*, 926, 931.

15. Dumoulin, "La manne dans le livre de la Sagesse," 112–13.

16. Larcher, *Le livre de la Sagesse*, 938–39.

elevation of desire leads to petitionary prayer. The manna symbolizes the wisdom for which believers ought to hunger.[17]

Two other themes from Wisdom 16 deserve mention. First, verse 21a highlights how the gift of manna reveals the sweetness and tenderness of God in his whole relation with his children.[18] This passage is all the more striking when we compare it with the recounting of the seventh plague. Second, the text offers teaching on the mysterious, miraculous mingling of the material elements in the manna. Verse 24 reinforces this point: "For creation, serving you who have made it, exerts itself to punish the unrighteous and in kindness relaxes on behalf of those who trust in you." God's influence makes the elements within the manna change their effects instantaneously. This is how the first century Jew Philo expounds on the manna (in his book, *The Life of Moses*): only God's sovereign mastery over matter can account for this event.[19]

Looking back, we can see that the manna is food for God's people. This food provides essential sustenance, for without it, the people would die in the desert. This gift is wholly supernatural: it manifests God's extraordinary power over creation. It is bodily nourishment as well as a sign of spiritual nourishment. Both kinds of food are linked: the word that nourishes spiritually is also at work in creation, as it makes the manna descend. We thus find a manifestation of God's sovereignty over creation, of his immanence, and his radical transcendence. All of these teachings are essential if one is to contemplate the Eucharist.

The Manna in the Gospel of John

Perhaps no part of the New Testament appropriates the theme of the manna as extensively as the sixth chapter of John's Gospel. Here, we find a miraculous food that both feeds the bodies of God's people and points

17. Dumoulin, "La manne dans le livre de la Sagesse," 119–22.

18. Larcher, *Le livre de la Sagesse*, 929. See also Albertus Magnus, *On the Body of the Lord*, dist. 1, chap. 2, p. 41, where he glosses Wisdom 16:21: "In his sweetness, God sweetly thinks of us. Nothing can be thought or desired sweeter or better than that God should be in us in his divinity and humanity, as sustenance for life invigorating us, and as spiritual food perfecting in us all union with himself."

19. Larcher, *Le livre de la Sagesse*, 930.

to a greater gift. The proper understanding of the true manna is a matter of life and death. John 6 ends with a Petrine confession that harkens back to Wisdom 16.[20]

John 6 begins with the multiplication of the loaves.[21] The time is close to the feast of Passover. This accentuates the manifestation of Jesus as the new Moses: the first Moses was present at the first Passover and interceded with God so as to feed the people in the wilderness. The setting in John evokes the first Passover mentioned in the Gospel, when Jesus changed water into wine at the wedding in Cana (Jn 2:13), and points the reader toward a third Passover, the Crucifixion (Jn 19:14). The Passover theme sets the whole of chapter 6 in relation to the paschal lamb.[22]

As John's Gospel continues, five thousand men have followed Jesus, for he has been healing the sick. Ancient Jewish tradition looked forward to the Messiah as a new Moses who would renew the miracle of manna in the future.[23] After the feeding, Jesus crosses the Sea of Galilee by walking on the water. This event confirms his extraordinary power over creation. Jesus' body can exceed the limits of nature's laws, for divine power is at work in him.

There has been some debate about the internal unity of chapter 6. Many Scripture scholars today hold that Jesus' discourse on the bread of life (Jn 6:25–71) is internally coherent and thematically unified.[24] But some exegetes consider verses 51–58 a later addition. They identify a teaching on faith as the central theme of verses 31–50, and contrast it with a teaching on Christ's flesh and blood in verses 51–58. For example, Rudolf Bultmann holds that verses 51–58 are too Eucharistic to have come from the evangelist. Bultmann refers this passage and the teaching on baptism in chapter 3 to a later redactor. He also sees the redactor adding sacramental themes to verses 39, 40, and 44 of chapter 6.[25]

Bultmann's claim is based on a theological *a priori*, for he assumes

20. Dumoulin, "La manne dans le livre de la Sagesse," 157.

21. Already by the third century, popular Christian exegesis gave this miracle a Eucharistic reading, as can be seen in the art of the Catacombs of St. Callixtus in Rome.

22. Craig S. Keener, *The Gospel of John: A Commentary*, vol. 1 (Peabody, Mass.: Hendrickson, 2003), 665.

23. See 2 Baruch 29:3–8; see also Pitre, *Jesus and the Last Supper*, 198–99.

24. Keener, *The Gospel of John*, 1:675.

25. Rudolf Bultmann, *Das Evangelium des Johannes*, Kritisch-exegetischer Kommentar über das Neue Testament (Göttingen, Germany: Vandenhoeck & Ruprecht, 1968), 161–63.

that the evangelist could not have had a robust doctrine of the Eucharist. Bultmann hypothetically reconstructs the evangelist's theology, perhaps partly on the basis of his own. In fact, verses 31–58 fit well together. Verses 32–58 essentially expound on verse 31, which reads: "He God gave them bread from heaven to eat."[26] Bultmann misses this link. The theme of manna stands out at the beginning of the bread of life discourse, and returns in verses 49 and 58. Indeed, the manna theme frames verses 31–58.[27] This theme connects verses 49–58 with the multiplication of the loaves. We will soon see other links between verses 31–50 and 51–58.

Raymond Brown identifies the following structure for Jesus' discourse: an introduction (verses 25–34) is followed by three parts: (a) Jesus as the bread of life (verses 35–51a), (b) a Eucharistic section (verses 51b–59), and (c) the listeners' reaction to Jesus (verses 60–66).[28] However, the exegesis of Augustine and Thomas Aquinas may be more illuminating here: they see the manna (and thus the miracle of the loaves in verses 1–15) as a sign of spiritual food, which takes two forms: Christ's word and his flesh. This reading manifests well the internal unity of the whole of chapter 6 and its link with the Old Testament manna: the Israelites who consumed the word of God spiritually also attained life.[29] In this interpretation, verses 25–59 show how Jesus seeks to guide his audience's hearts and minds from the visible manna to the invisible, spiritual manna in its various forms: the person of Christ himself, his word or wisdom, and his Eucharistic flesh and blood. As a good pedagogue, Jesus will expound on the various aspects of the true manna, one after the other, where each part of his explanation prepares for the subsequent one.

After the multiplication of the loaves, the people follow Jesus across the sea to Capernaum. He exhorts them: "You seek me not because you

26. Keener, *The Gospel of John*, 1:675, 678.

27. Pitre, *Jesus and the Last Supper*, 198.

28. Raymond E. Brown, *The Gospel according to John*, Anchor Bible Commentary 29 (New York: Doubleday, 1966), vol. 1, 293–94.

29. See Augustine, *Tractates on the Gospel of John*, tractate 26, no. 12, in Augustine, *Tractates on the Gospel of John 11–27*, trans. John W. Rettig, The Fathers of the Church 79 (Washington, D.C.: The Catholic University of America Press, 1988); also Thomas Aquinas, *Commentary on the Gospel of John*, chapter 6, lectio 2, no. 881; lectio 3, no. 895; lectio 6, no. 954, in Thomas Aquinas, *Commentary on the Gospel of John, Chapters 1–8*, ed. the Aquinas Institute, trans. F. R. Larcher, Latin/English Edition of the Works of St. Thomas Aquinas 35 (Lander, Wyo.: The Aquinas Institute for the Study of Sacred Doctrine, 2013).

saw signs, but because you ate your fill of the loaves. Do not labor for the food which perishes, but for the food which endures to eternal life, which the Son of man will give you" (Jn 6:26–27). The manna in the desert and the miracle of the bread in Galilee both primarily aim to offer a lesson about the word of God. Aquinas sees the food that endures as "God himself, inasmuch as he is the truth to be contemplated, and the goodness loved, which refreshes the spirit; [as in] Proverbs 9:5: 'Eat my bread.'"[30] This food is divine wisdom, imperfectly contemplated here below, and perfectly enjoyed in the vision of God face to face. Christ offers food that has a permanent effect of nourishing, unlike earthly food, which nourishes for a day. The ultimate effect of this food that Christ is offering is the gift of eternal life. Christ himself gives this food, and we receive it by faith. Verse 29 explains that working for the food that endures means believing in Jesus.[31]

At John 6:30–31, the Jews demand yet another miracle. Their mentality is earthly or fleshly: they are interested in free food, not in Jesus' word, nor in eternal life.[32] He needs to raise their minds to a higher way of perceiving the manna. Jesus responds to their request for food by commenting on Psalm 78:24, which they just quoted to him: "He [God] gave them bread from heaven to eat." The Father gives the true bread from heaven: "For the bread of God is that which comes down from heaven and gives life to the world" (Jn 6:33). Jesus here alludes to the Incarnation: he is the eternal Word who has become flesh (1:14). Because he is the eternal Word, he brings the ultimate wisdom, the definitive revelation. We find the same theme of Christ as the bread descending from heaven later, in verses 38, 41–42, 50–51, and 58. This theme unites various parts of the discourse on the bread of life.[33]

The Old Testament wisdom imagery is evident. Jesus uses it to show the excellence of his person and his teaching. Sirach 24:21 has wisdom declare that whoever eats and drinks her will hunger and thirst for more. The ancient rabbis identified this wisdom with the Torah.[34] But the wis-

30. Thomas Aquinas, *Commentary on the Gospel of John*, chap. 6, lectio 3, no. 895.

31. André Feuillet, "Les thèmes bibliques majeurs du discours sur le pain de vie (Jean 6)." *Nouvelle revue théologique* 82 (1960): 810–14.

32. Keener, *The Gospel of John*, 1:678.

33. Feuillet, "Les thèmes bibliques," 923.

34. Keener, *The Gospel of John*, 1:679–81.

dom of Jesus is greater, for "he who comes to me shall not hunger, and he who believes in me shall never thirst" (Jn 6:35). This is an astounding claim. It evokes the messianic banquet promised in the Old Testament, a banquet which God himself prepares for his people, so that they might no longer hunger and thirst.[35] Later verses also take up this theme of the messianic banquet, at which God himself will teach his people.[36]

Jesus has come down from heaven to do the Father's will (Jn 6:38). He thus looks forward to the Passion, for the Cross is the means whereby the Father wills to bring life to the world. The finality of Jesus' coming in the flesh is our resurrection from the dead on the last day, that is, bodily resurrection (Jn 6:39–40, 54). Eating spiritual food makes our bodies immortal, giving them the fullness of life. Jesus will participate in the Father's work of raising the dead. Christ thus points to his divine identity.[37] He will enable us to enter into the eschatological banquet where he will also feed us. In this teaching about our future resurrection, we see another indication of Jesus' extraordinary sovereignty over material creation. Such power recalls one of the major themes of the Book of Wisdom and its teaching on the Old Testament manna. This will be important when we consider the change of the Eucharistic gifts.

At John 6:41, the Jews murmur, like the disgruntled Israelites in the desert who murmur and rebel against Moses (Ex 16). The Jews do not understand Jesus' origin, for they think that he is only a man. They do not recognize his divine origin. For this reason, they cannot understand how Jesus himself can be the manna, nor how he can come from heaven. Jesus' self-description as the bread of life defies human reasoning. The person of Christ cannot be understood without revelation: the same applies for the Eucharist.

John 6:32–50 dwells at length on the mystery of Christ's person, his wisdom, and the reception of both through faith. We see that this faith has a specific object, namely, the Incarnate Word, he who has come down from heaven. Faith implies clinging to all that Christ is with complete trust. The theme of faith in Christ does not exclude a Eucharistic interpretation of John 6. This will have implications for our understanding of

35. Is 48:21, 48:9–10, 65:13.

36. Jn 6:45; Is 54:13–55:1; Jer 31:31–34; Feuillet, "Les thèmes bibliques," 817–20.

37. Keener, *The Gospel of John*, 1:684.

Eucharistic communion and the importance of faith when one partakes in the Eucharist.

We now come to the most disputed part of John 6, namely, verses 51–63. As we seek to make sense of the text, we should recall that there is no Catholic dogma that requires a Eucharistic reading of this passage. A non-Eucharistic interpretation was adopted by some early ecclesiastical writers, such as Clement of Alexandria and Origen.[38] The Council of Trent abstained from excluding such readings of John 6.[39] Thus, we can ask: In John 6, does Jesus speak of his flesh and blood metaphorically or in another way?

First, let us look at the text of John 6:48–63 and 66.

48 "I am the bread of life. 49 Your fathers ate (*ephagon*) manna in the wil-
derness, and they died. 50 This is the bread that comes down from heaven, that
a man may eat (*phagē*) of it and not die. 51 I am the living bread which came
down from heaven; if anyone eats of this bread, he will live forever; and the bread
which I shall give for the life of the world is my flesh (*sarx*)."

52 The Jews then disputed among themselves, saying "How can this man give
us his flesh to eat?" 53 So Jesus said to them, "Amen, amen, I say to you, unless you
eat (*phagēte*) the flesh of the Son of man and drink his blood, you have no life in
you; 54 he who eats (*trōgōn*) my flesh and drinks my blood has eternal life, and I
will raise him up at the last day. 55 For my flesh is real food, and my blood is real
drink. 56 He who eats (*trōgōn*) my flesh and drinks my blood remains in me, and I
in him. 57 As the living Father sent me, and I live because of the Father, so he who
eats (*trōgōn*) me will live because of me. 58 This is the bread which came down
from heaven, not such as the fathers ate and died; he who eats (*trōgōn*) this bread
will live forever." 59 This he said in the synagogue, as he taught at Capernaum.

60 Many of his disciples, when they heard it, said, "This is a hard saying.
Who can listen to it?" 61 But Jesus, knowing in himself that his disciples mur-
mured at it, said to them, "Do you take offense at this? 62 Then what if you were
to see the Son of man ascending to where he was before? 63 It is the spirit that
gives life; the flesh is of no avail; the words that I have spoken to you are spir-
it and life.... 66 After this many of his disciples drew back and no longer went
about with him.[40]

38. Rudolf Schnackenburg, *Das Johannesevangelium*, vol. 2 (Freiburg im Breisgau: Herder, 1971), 97.

39. F.-M. Braun, "L'eucharistie selon saint Jean," *Revue Thomiste* 70 (1970): 6.

40. Translation from RSV, modified by Pitre, *Jesus and the Last Supper*, 195.

Verse 51 transitions from the language of the "bread of life" to "flesh and blood." The same verse also identifies these. The evangelist thus presents a link with the preceding verses and also introduces a new theme.

Verses 51 and 53 probably echo the Last Supper traditions that underlie the Synoptic Gospels. First, Raymond Brown points to the proximity with the words of institution in Matthew 26:26–28. Even more important is the likely parallel with Luke (or the tradition behind Luke), which reads: "This is my body which is given for you" (Lk 22:19). John seems to echo this phrase when Jesus says: "the bread that I shall give is my flesh for the life of the world" (Jn 6:51).[41] As Brown notes, regardless of the fact that John's account of Jesus' last meal before his Passion is vastly different from that of the Synoptic Gospels, John's Gospel comes from Asia Minor, a crossroad which would hardly have ignored the primitive Eucharistic liturgical tradition to which the Synoptic authors and St. Paul witness.[42] Second, at verse 53, we have the combination of eating flesh and drinking blood, which is highly unusual.[43] This combination would seem to echo the Last Supper as well. Overall, verses 51–53 provide excellent reasons to read verses 51–58 eucharistically.

Verse 52 recounts the Jews' reaction to Jesus' invitation to eat his flesh, and suggests a violent dispute. Deuteronomy 28 forbids the consumption of human flesh. Jesus responds to the Jews' perplexity by taking the language even further: (a) he repeats the term "flesh," (b) makes the verb used for "eating" more graphic, and (c) adds the consumption of his blood: "unless you eat (*phagēte*) the flesh of the Son of man and drink his blood, you have no life in you; he who eats (*trōgōn*) my flesh and drinks my blood has eternal life" (Jn 6:53). The Book of Leviticus forbids the drinking of any blood, even that of other animals: it was the place of man's and the animal's life, which belong to God alone (Lev 17:10–12). Jesus therefore appears to contradict a strict Torah prohibition in a very direct way.

We have seen Jesus switch from one verb for eating to another. The use of the Greek term *trōgein* seems to be provocative. We could also translate

41. Brown, *The Gospel according to John*, 1:285.

42. Brown, *The Gospel according to John*, 1:247.

43. Rudolf Bultmann, *The Gospel of John*, trans. G. R. Beasley-Murray (Philadelphia: Westminster, 1971), 235; Feuillet, "Les thèmes bibliques," 821.

it as "to munch," "to gnaw" or "to chew." Jesus uses it no less than four times in verses 54–58. Now James D. G. Dunn argues that John's preference for this term may tell us little. He holds that John may be following a typical stylistic trend of the era, in which the verb *esthiein* ("to consume, to devour," standard in the LXX) is replaced by *trōgein* as the present tense of *phagein* (used by the Jews in Jn 6:53).[44] In this way, it was becoming a more standard, generic term for "eating." Now it is true that John never uses the word *esthiein*. However, John never uses *trōgein* elsewhere, except to modify a citation of the Greek Old Testament (the Septuagint) in John 13:18.[45] That is, he uses it only in chapter 6 and in the narrative of Jesus' last meal with his disciples before the Passion. Both Brown and Pitre have signaled important Passover motifs in John 13.[46] This further points to a Eucharistic meaning of *trōgein* in John 6. Thus, Dunn's objection falls short.

Other clues in the text call for a literal reading of the verb. John 6:55 uses the term "real food" to indicate that Jesus' body and blood have real value.[47] The essential background text remains the gift of manna in the desert, which was accompanied by quail or bird meat. While the manna is also consumed spiritually, it was not only metaphorical food. Hence, it is reasonable to argue that the new manna is also corporeal food.[48]

The language of eating in verses 54–68 is therefore intended to be graphic, and this deserves explanation. The object to be consumed is Christ's flesh, *sarx* in Greek. This term recalls the prologue of John's Gospel: "And the Word was made flesh." John 19:38 refers to the dead body of Christ as *sōma*, not *sarx*. This does not signal a denial of a link between the gift of his flesh and his crucified body (John 6:51 already established that link). Rather, Christ's discourse on munching his flesh (*sarx*) indicates that his living body, and not his cadaver, should be eaten.[49] The theme of *sarx* gives a first indication that Christ does not intend any form

44. James D. G. Dunn, "John VI—A Eucharistic Discourse?," *New Testament Studies* 17 (1970–71): 334.

45. Brown, *The Gospel according to John*, 1:283.

46. Raymond E. Brown, *The Gospel according to John*, Anchor Bible Commentary 29A (New York: Doubleday, 1970), vol. 2, 576; Pitre, *Jesus and the Last Supper*, 346–50.

47. Brown, *The Gospel according to John*, 1:283.

48. Pitre, *Jesus and the Last Supper*, 201, 210.

49. Braun, "L'eucharistie selon saint Jean," 8–9.

of cannibalism, which is precisely what the Torah forbids. But what does Jesus mean when he says that we should eat his flesh?

Christ's own disciples now begin to grow restless. He responds with perhaps the most debated verses of the entire chapter: "Do you take offense at this? Then what if you were to see the Son of man ascending to where he was before? It is the spirit that gives life; the flesh [*sarx*] is of no avail; the words that I have spoken to you are spirit and life" (Jn 6:61–63). For scholars such as Craig Keener, verse 63 confirms that Jesus' entire discourse has been metaphorical: we are to eat Jesus by faith, thus attaining life through the power of Christ's Spirit at work in those who believe.[50] Dunn's reading is similar but goes further, as he detects a negative sacramental view in John: the language of eating describes the effect of union with the ascended Jesus through his Spirit, not the effect of the sacrament, for "the flesh is useless." Furthermore, Jesus himself remains in the earthly realm of *sarx*: only once he rises and ascends will he give the Spirit to his disciples.[51]

There are several problems with these interpretations. First, Keener essentially reduces the meaning of verses 51–58 to the teaching of verses 27–50. If the passages on eating Christ's flesh say little more than the preceding verses, why does Jesus spend so much time repeating himself? Were verses 27–50 not challenging enough? Furthermore, this misses the way in which Jesus' discourse progresses thematically: he moves from the offer of the food that endures, with its wisdom imagery (v. 27), to an exhortation to faith (v. 29), a teaching on the Incarnation (v. 33), the food that satiates every hunger and thirst (a theme that was not explicit before) (v. 35), and the promise of resurrection (v. 40). In a Eucharistic reading, verses 51–59 build on these themes without repeating the same lesson. Second, Keener says nothing about the graphic language of munching on Christ's flesh.[52] He sidesteps the realism of the text, without explanation.

Keener acknowledges that many early Christian interpreters, such as St. Ignatius of Antioch and St. Justin Martyr, gave this text a Eucharistic reading. Yet he rejects their interpretation as unreliable. Keener argues that, since Ignatius's and Justin's teachings on the episcopate go beyond Scrip-

50. Keener, *The Gospel of John*, 1:690.

51. Dunn, "John VI—A Eucharistic Discourse?," 332, 334–37.

52. Keener, *The Gospel of John*, 1:687–91.

ture, we need not accept their reading of John 6.[53] Keener thereby seeks to justify his refusal to engage in the details of a nineteen-hundred-year-old exegetical tradition.

Brown and Pitre have laid out several arguments for a positive Eucharistic reading of John 6:51–59. First, when the Old Testament speaks of eating someone's flesh and drinking his blood, it always refers to a violent situation. That is, the Old Testament never uses such imagery as a metaphor for believing in someone or accepting their teaching.[54] Second, Pitre notes the link between the consumption of Jesus' flesh and blood and believers' future bodily resurrection.[55] This suggests that, in each case, we have a nonmetaphorical reference to a body. Third and more importantly, Augustine and others have noted that the words "the flesh is useless" cannot possibly signify that Jesus' human body is useless for salvation, for it would contradict the teaching of John's prologue on the Incarnation.[56] Yet Dunn makes precisely that perplexing claim. On the contrary, much of John's Gospel highlights the astounding value of Jesus' humanity. In addition to these three arguments, we can say that the use of *trōgein*, the invitation to drink his blood and the reference to Jesus' flesh as "real food" encourage a literal, Eucharistic reading of verses 51–59. Consequently, we should look to interpret verse 63 in a way that stands in harmony with the positive references to Christ's flesh in verses 51–59.

There are at least four additional reasons to give John 6:62–63 a positive Eucharistic sense. First, the phrase "the flesh is useless, the Spirit gives life," signals the refusal of a cannibalistic interpretation of Jesus' words, an interpretation that his audience assumes.

Second, Pitre argues that verse 62 contains a widely overlooked Old Testament allusion, namely to Daniel's Son of Man. Verse 62 reads: "what if you were to see the Son of man ascending to where he was before?" Here, Jesus fulfills a mysterious prophecy of Daniel 7:13–14, where one like a Son of man comes on the clouds, is presented to God and given dominion over all peoples. In other words, Christ will ascend to heaven, to "where he was before," but in a glorified state. Hence, in verse 62, he iden-

53. Keener, *The Gospel of John*, 1:689.

54. Brown, *The Gospel according to John*, 1:284; Pitre, *Jesus and the Last Supper*, 206–7.

55. Pitre, *Jesus and the Last Supper*, 208.

56. Augustine, *Tractates on the Gospel of John*, tractate 27, no. 5.

tifies himself with a celestial figure, though not in order to diminish the value of his human flesh.[57] In this way, John signals that the flesh Christ will give for food is heavenly flesh, and not earthly. His flesh will truly come from heaven, like the manna in the desert. Because he will ascend to heaven, the glorified Christ will be consumed in the Eucharist, so that those eating the new manna will not do violence to him, nor will those consuming him become cannibals.

The allusion to Daniel 7 (Jn 6:62) helps to explain why Christ's words are "spirit and life" (v. 63). The entire discourse can be understood as a teaching on the coming resurrection and ascension of Jesus, on the transformation of his very body and blood into a state of immortality.[58] Yet this does not mean that we have entered the realm of pure metaphor: Jesus' disciples will really eat his body and drink his blood. However, they cannot yet fully grasp his teaching on the Eucharist, for they must still come to believe in his glorification, when his body will be Spirit-filled, and when they will grasp his teaching by the help of the Spirit given at Pentecost.

A third reason is offered by Cyril of Alexandria in his *Commentary on the Gospel of John*, composed between 425 and 428. Cyril acknowledges a Eucharistic reading of John 6, yet much of his exposition of verses 50–63 focuses on the person of Christ, and not on the Eucharist. Cyril explains that, by becoming man, the Son of God, who is life by nature, renders his human body life-giving. Cyril argues that Christ's activity of raising the dead comes not just by his powerful word but also by his body: he is the Incarnate Word.[59]

These considerations undergird Cyril's interpretation of John 6:63. The Egyptian patriarch notes that, considered in itself, the flesh is of no benefit, for it cannot give life. Mere human flesh can nourish a body, but it cannot transmit eternal life. Yet the mysterious union between Christ's body and his life-giving Word changes everything. The Johannine phrase "the flesh is of no avail" applies to other flesh or bodies, but not to Christ's

57. Pitre, *Jesus and the Last Supper*, 214–19; Brown, *The Gospel according to John*, 1:299

58. Pitre, *Jesus and the Last Supper*, 215–19.

59. Cyril of Alexandria, *Commentary on the Gospel of John*, vol. 1, trans. David R. Maxwell, ed. Joel C. Elowksy, Ancient Christian Texts (Downers Grove, Ill.: IVP Academic, 2013), bk. 4, chap. 3, John 6:51 (Patrologiae Cursus Completus: Series Graeca, ed. J.-P. Migne (Paris) [hereafter PG] 73:520), p. 232; John 6:52–53 (PG 73:529–30), pp. 236–37.

flesh, because his is the flesh of the Only-Begotten Son. When considered *by itself*, flesh is useless and cannot give eternal life. Yet Christ's flesh does not exist by itself, it is not merely the body of a man: "Because his whole flesh is utterly united to him [the Logos] and clothed with life giving power, it now ought to be called 'spirit' as well."[60] It is therefore the hypostatic union that ensures that Christ's flesh is not useless. Cyril's exegesis reminds us that Christology is crucial for any reading of verses 51–63.

Finally, a fourth reason, which is similar to Cyril's and which draws inspiration from Augustine, can be found in Thomas Aquinas. According to the Bishop of Hippo, verse 63 highlights the power of the Spirit because Eucharistic communion leads to ecclesial union, which is the work of the Holy Spirit.[61] Augustine also reads verses 51–63 in reference to Jesus' Eucharistic body, with a focus on its fruitfulness in believers. Aquinas follows Augustine and notes that the flesh of Christ is joined to the Word and the Spirit, that is, to the eternal Son (the Logos) and to the Holy Spirit. For this reason, the flesh of Christ cannot be without benefit, for otherwise the Incarnation would not be fruitful in bringing us salvation. If we ponder Christ's body in abstraction from his divinity and from the Holy Spirit that fills his humanity, then we cannot perceive the benefit of his flesh. But in doing so, we mentally separate what cannot be separated in reality. Those who commune in the Eucharistic body of Christ derive much benefit, because the Spirit and Christ's divinity come to the believer through the Eucharistic body and cause him or her to remain in Christ. His flesh gives life, but only because it is joined to the divinity of the Logos, whereby we are given access to the Spirit.[62] In the background stand the *Filioque*: The Son gives the Spirit, for the Spirit proceeds from the Son (and the Father) from all eternity.

Let us note that these four ways of reading verse 63 as a reference to the Eucharist do not exclude each other. John often speaks at multiple levels, and his text remains open to further meanings that arise in the tradition.

60. Cyril of Alexandria, *Commentary on the Gospel of John*, vol. 1, bk. 4, chap. 3, John 6:63 (PG 73:552), p. 247. Compare Thomas Aquinas, *Commentary on the Gospel of John*, chap. 6, lectio 4, no. 914 (on John 6:35); lectio 6, no. 959 (on John 6:51 in modern Bible editions).

61. Augustine, *Tractates on the Gospel of John*, tractate 27, nos. 5–6.

62. Thomas Aquinas, *Commentary on the Gospel of John*, chap. 6, lectio 8, no. 993.

Now let us consider a theological consequence of John 6. This biblical text does not directly teach the doctrine of the substantial presence of Christ's body and blood. However, it calls for a Eucharistic theology that goes beyond the alternatives of Christ's merely symbolic presence or a hyper-realistic vision that borders on cannibalism. Communion in Christ's flesh goes beyond a purely spiritual communion. Also, Eucharistic doctrine needs to account for some type of corporeal union with Christ that transcends the limits of nature's laws, and thus also transcends cannibalism. The close link between the Eucharist and the manna theme calls for nothing less. A theology of communing in Christ's body and blood in a corporeal way is the route that the early Church takes, centuries before invoking the notion of transubstantiation. The doctrine of transubstantiation continues and develops this patristic theology.

Let us summarize the effects or fruits of the Eucharist that John 6 proposes, either explicitly or implicitly. First, the multiplication of the loaves shows an innumerable crowd that is hungry and then satiated. The Eucharist is a gift whose power to nourish knows no limits and fills the desires of the human heart. Second, the Eucharist gives life, starting here and now, and continuing for eternity (verse 51), which is to say that the sacrament imparts grace. Third, the Eucharist leads to the Resurrection of the body at the end of time (verse 54). Christ will resurrect us, which is fitting given that he is the immortal, risen Christ who already lives within us by his flesh and blood received in the Eucharist. Fourth, eating Christ's flesh and drinking his blood leads to a new or deeper mutual indwelling of Christ and the believer, which imitates Christ's dwelling in the Father and the Father's dwelling in him (verse 56). Fifth, the Eucharist imparts a more intense participation in the Holy Spirit (verse 63). Indeed, we should never separate Christ and the Spirit. Finally, the Eucharist as spiritual food should be understood in light of the whole discourse: we are to feed on the wisdom of Christ received in faith, and also on his flesh and blood. In other words, the Liturgy of the Word and the Liturgy of the Eucharist go together: the first opens us to a fuller share in the blessings of the second, and the second heightens our hunger for the wisdom of Christ.[63] We find

63. Emmanuel Perrier, "Le Pain de Vie chez Louis-Marie Chauvet et saint Thomas d'Aquin: Représentation de l'inconnaissable ou terme de l'union spirituelle?" *Revue Thomiste* 113 (2013): 216.

the same pattern in Jesus' appearance to two disciples on their way to Emmaus (Lk 24).

Looking back at John 6, we can see how Jesus' life-giving flesh is at once the body offered up at the Cross (verse 51), risen (verse 62), glorified and overflowing with the Spirit (verse 63). Right after his death, the body of the crucified Lord was opened and water burst forth (Jn 19:31–36). For John, water is a powerful sign of the Spirit (see 7:37–39). All of this points to Christ's Eucharistic body, a body at once spiritual (full of life) and corporeal.[64]

64. Roch A. Kereszty, *Wedding Feast of the Lamb: Eucharistic Theology from a Biblical, Historical and Systematic Perspective* (Chicago: Hillenbrand Books, 2007), 61.

CHAPTER 2

THE LAST SUPPER

The theology of the manna reaches its apex in John 6: it is our first biblical pillar for the doctrine of the Eucharist. The Last Supper constitutes the second pillar. This is evident from our own Eucharistic celebration today.

A fierce exegetical debate has taken place over the last few decades on whether the Last Supper was a Passover meal. This question is crucial for Eucharistic theology, as we will see in subsequent chapters. We need to consider both the date of the Last Supper and the internal clues about its paschal identity. Finally, we look at other details of that sacred event.

The Date of the Last Supper

Crucial to the question of whether the Last Supper was a Passover meal is the date on which it took place. The Synoptic Gospels affirm that it was a Passover meal (Mk 14:12–16, Lk 22:7–13), while the Gospel of John apparently places Jesus' Crucifixion on the Day of Preparation for the Passover (Jn 19:14). In other words, John seems to place Jesus' last meal with his disciples on a Thursday, but seems to present Friday evening as the vigil of Passover, and Saturday as the day of Passover.

A first group of interpreters (led by the great Lutheran exegete Joachim Jeremias) have argued that John's chronology is theological: John wants to show Jesus as the true Passover Lamb who is sentenced at the same time that the lambs are being slaughtered in the temple in preparation for the evening of Passover.[65] This theory says that, chronologically, Friday was the day of Passover. The Synoptic Gospels are historically accurate in making the Last Supper a Passover meal, while John does not intend to give a historical chronology. Leading exegetes such as Martin Hengel, Craig Keener, and E. P. Sanders support this approach. It is also called "The Synoptic hypothesis."[66]

A second approach, favored by Raymond Brown and other scholars, argues that John's timing is historically accurate and that the Synoptic Gospel writers are confused. Therefore, the Last Supper occurred before the lambs were slaughtered in the temple and was not a Passover meal.[67] This approach is also called "the Johannine hypothesis."[68]

A third approach modifies the second and finds support with N. T. Wright as well as Joseph Ratzinger's second Jesus book.[69] According to this approach, Jesus knows that his death is coming, and that he will not be able to celebrate the Passover according to the standard, majority calendar, which would place the Passover meal on Friday evening. Jesus knows that he will already be dead by Friday evening. Therefore, he cel-

65. Joachim Jeremias, *The Eucharistic Words of Jesus*, 3rd ed. (Minneapolis, Minn.: Fortress Press, 1966), 1–61.

66. Martin Hengel and Anna Maria Schwemer, *Jesus und das Judentum* (Tübingen, Germany: Mohr Siebeck, 2007), 582–86; Craig S. Keener, *The Historical Jesus of the Gospels* (Grand Rapids, Mich.: William B. Eerdmans, 2009), 372–74; E. P. Sanders, *The Historical Figure of Jesus* (London: Penguin, 1993), 285–86.

67. Raymond E. Brown, *The Gospel according to John*, Anchor Bible Commentary 29A (New York: Doubleday, 1970), vol. 2, 555–57.

68. Such exegesis gives support for liturgical studies that read the early Christian Eucharist not in relation to the Passover but rather as modeled on the Jewish festive meal, including the *qiddush* prayer. This theory has inspired multiple liturgists to propose hypothetical reconstructions of the liturgy in the early centuries of the Church in abstraction from the Passover meal. For example, Enrico Mazza uses this approach in an extensive way as he hypothesizes about the nature of the early Christian liturgy. See Mazza, *The Celebration of the Eucharist: The Origin of the Rite and the Development of Its Interpretation*, trans. Matthew J. O'Connell (Collegeville, Minn.: Liturgical Press, 1998), 19–34.

69. N.T. Wright, *Jesus and the Victory of God* (Minneapolis, Minn.: Fortress Press, 1996), 556–59; Joseph Ratzinger, *Jesus of Nazareth, Part Two: Holy Week, from the Entrance into Jerusalem to the Resurrection*, trans. Vatican Secretariat of State (San Francisco: Ignatius Press, 2011).

ebrates a New Passover meal with his disciples, but he does so on Thursday, the day before the Passover, as recounted in John. This would give John priority in the chronology of days while also partly accounting for the Synoptic Gospels, which identify the Last Supper as a Passover meal. Ratzinger argues that it is highly unlikely that the high priests and Pharisees would have participated in Jesus' trial on the eve of Passover and sought his execution on the day of Passover, because of Jewish purity laws. But this would be the case if we were to follow the Synoptic chronology instead of John's chronology.[70] In other words, Jesus instructs the disciples to prepare a new Passover meal and celebrates it early. This approach is also called "The Anticipatory Passover Meal hypothesis."

Other exegetes favor a fourth approach and argue that the evangelists followed different calendars: John followed the official lunar calendar used by the Jerusalem priests in 30 A.D., while the Synoptics followed a calendar used in Galilee and Qumran.[71] In other words, Jesus celebrated the Last Supper on the Passover according to an alternative Jewish priestly calendar (a calendar transmitted via ancient Jewish texts, the Book of Jubilees, and the Qumran community). According to this theory, Jesus would have celebrated the Passover meal on Tuesday, been arrested on Wednesday and died just before the Passover as dated by the Jerusalem priests' calendar. Such an interpretation finds support in an ancient tradition about the date of Jesus' Last Supper: the third-century Christian text, the *Didascalia of the Apostles*, states that Jesus celebrated his Last Supper on a Tuesday. This fourth approach is also called "the Essene hypothesis" (after the calendar of Qumran).

Brant Pitre has offered some insightful critiques to these ways of understanding the timing of the Last Supper. First, the Johannine hypothesis maintains that no Passover lamb is mentioned in the Synoptic accounts of the Last Supper.[72] Pitre responds that it was Jewish custom to refer to the lamb simply by using the term *Passover* (*pesah* in Hebrew, *pas-*

70. Ratzinger, *Jesus of Nazareth, Part Two*, chap. 5, section 1.

71. Annie Jaubert, *The Date of the Last Supper*, trans. I Rafferty (Staten Island, N.Y.: Alba House, 1965).

72. Raymond E. Brown, *The Death of the Messiah: From Gethsemane to the Grave, a Commentary on the Passion Narratives in the Four Gospels*, vol. 2, The Anchor Bible Reference Library (New York: Doubleday, 1994), 1364.

cha in Greek). He cites Mark 14:12 and Luke 22:7–8, 14–15 as evidence.[73] Second, the Johannine hypothesis maintains that the Jewish leaders could not have entered Pilate's palace and participated in a trial on the day of Passover, since this would have violated the Torah (e.g., Lv 23).[74] Pitre responds by distinguishing between the Sabbath rest and certain activities permitted for special Jewish feasts, including Passover. Following E. P. Sanders, Pitre points out that the question of which activity was permitted on such feasts was highly debated by the Pharisees in Jesus' time.[75] Thus, rabbinic tradition called for the execution of false prophets during feasts, and the prohibition of sitting in judgment pertained only to daily matters.[76] Third, Pitre takes up an objection from Raymond Brown, who holds that, in John, the lambs were already being sacrificed at noon on the day of Christ's Crucifixion. Pitre responds that there is no historical evidence for this claim. Instead, all ancient Jewish sources that refer to the timing of the slaughter (e.g., the Book of Jubilees, Qumran texts, and Philo) place it between three and five o'clock in the afternoon. But John's Gospel never mentions this time. All that John 19:14 says of Jesus' trial before Pilate is the following: "it was the day of Preparation of the Passover; it was about the sixth hour." Now John does not mention the sacrifice of the lambs, while Josephus (who served as a priest in the Jerusalem temple) states that any such sacrifice before three o'clock was unlawful.[77] Yet the Synoptic accounts tell us that Jesus died at three o'clock, and in their chronology, this would be twenty-four hours after the slaughter of the lambs.[78] We should note that John does not mention the time of Jesus' death.[79] Fourth, regarding the Anticipatory Passover Meal hypothesis, Pitre points out that there is no precedent in Second Temple Judaism (i.e., Jesus' historical era) for an anticipated Passover without a lamb.[80]

In my view, some version of the first theory (the Synoptic hypothesis) would seem to offer the best solution. For example, Craig Keener main-

73. Brant Pitre, *Jesus and the Last Supper* (Grand Rapids, Mich.: William B. Eerdmans, 2015), 291.
74. Brown, *Death of the Messiah*, 2:1358.
75. Pitre, *Jesus and the Last Supper*, 296.
76. Pitre, *Jesus and the Last Supper*, 300–302; Jeremias, *The Eucharistic Words of Jesus*, 78–79.
77. Pitre, *Jesus and the Last Supper*, 325–28, referencing Josephus, *Questions on Exodus*, 1.11.
78. Mt 27:46, Mk 15:34, Lk 23:44–46.
79. Pitre, *Jesus and the Last Supper*, 330.
80. Pitre, *Jesus and the Last Supper*, 306–8.

tains that Mark's Gospel is generally more dependable in its historical details than John's. In Mark, Jesus is executed on the day of Passover, just before the eve of the Sabbath. One can easily find theological motives for John to describe Jesus' trial and death as occurring just before the eve of Passover (even if it is not simultaneous with the sacrifice of the lambs). Keener also signals that the Last Supper recounted in the Synoptics seems to presuppose that the slaughter of the lambs has already begun, because a Passover lamb is being eaten.[81] Thus, Keener does not espouse a lamb-less Last Supper. I would add that it is wrong to see John as pure theology, yet the historicity of the Synoptics should not be underplayed, especially when they conflict with John (e.g., on the chronological duration of Jesus' ministry).[82]

Was the Last Supper a Passover Meal?

The debate just mentioned evidently touches on the question of whether the Last Supper was a Passover meal. For if the historical death of Jesus took place while or before the lambs were slaughtered in the temple, then the Last Supper recounted in the Synoptics could (at best) have been a modified (lamb-less) Passover meal, so that Jesus anticipated the feast with his disciples. Yet some scholars go further and hold that the Last Supper was not a Passover meal at all. They argue that the lamb is never mentioned in the narrative, and that key elements of the Passover ritual are missing in those accounts.[83]

And yet, several exegetical arguments show that the Last Supper was indeed a Passover meal. First, the theme of remembering (such as: "Do this in memory of me") points to the Passover.[84] Second, in 1 Corinthians 11,

81. Craig S. Keener, *The Gospel of Matthew: A Socio-Rhetorical Commentary* (Grand Rapids, Mich.: William B. Eerdmans, 1999), 622–23.

82. A theological gloss is not "invented theology," but the work of the Holy Spirit, in the sense that (1) the Spirit illumines the apostles in their preaching to bring out the hidden significance of God's saving work, and (2) the Gospel writers never intended to follow the standards of modern historiography, even if their genre as ancient biography takes them well beyond the genre of un-historical or mythological writings.

83. See, for example, James D. G. Dunn, *Christianity in the Making*, vol. 1, *Jesus Remembered* (Grand Rapids, Mich.: William B. Eerdmans, 2003), 772.

84. Roch A. Kereszty, *Wedding Feast of the Lamb: Eucharistic Theology from a Biblical, Historical and Systematic Perspective* (Chicago: Hillenbrand Books, 2007), 29.

Jesus speaks of his body given for others and his blood poured out for sins, two images of his expiatory death. These words fit well with the role of the presider or father of the family at the Passover meal. At this ritual meal, the presider explains the meal's elements and the events remembered, as he designates an instrument of redemption by taking some food, such as bread, fruits, or nuts.[85] Third, the Last Supper took place at night, while the main daily meal in Jewish culture took place in the afternoon. Fourth, both the Last Supper and Passover concluded with a hymn, likely from Psalm 118, or perhaps Psalms 114–117 (Mk 14:26, Mt 26:30).[86] Fifth, as noted above, the Passover lamb is mentioned indirectly, using Jewish custom of the time, simply by referring to the *pascha*.[87] Sixth, the fact that some elements of Passover ritual are missing in the New Testament accounts of Jesus' Last Supper need not be fatal: the evangelists need not mention every detail. An omission does not mean that something did not occur. The absence of evidence is not the evidence of absence.

Finally, even if historical exegesis cannot give absolute certitude about the nature of the Last Supper, other texts and early tradition offer a precious witness. At 1 Corinthians 11:26–34, Paul describes Jesus' Last Supper precisely by terms taken from the Jewish Passover.[88] This finds support in second century Christian authors. Justin Martyr's *Dialogue with Trypho* places Jesus' arrest on the day of Passover, which allows the Last Supper to be celebrated on the eve of Passover.[89] St. Irenaeus of Lyon describes Jesus as eating the Passover and suffering his Passion on the next day.[90]

85. Leo Scheffczyk, *Die Heilszeichen von Brot und Wein: Eucharistie als Mitte christlichen Lebens* (Munich: Don Bosco Verlag, 1973), 29.

86. Anthony C. Thiselton, *The First Epistle to the Corinthians: A Commentary on the Greek Text*, The New International Greek Testament Commentary (Grand Rapids, Mich.: William B. Eerdmans, 2000), 871.

87. Mk 14:12, Lk 22:7–8, 14–15; Pitre, *Jesus and the Last Supper*, 291.

88. Pitre, *Jesus and the Last Supper*, 440.

89. Justin Martyr, *Dialogue with Trypho*, chapter 111, no. 3, in *The Apology, The Second Apology, Dialogue with Trypho*, ed. Michael Slusser, trans. Thomas B. Falls, rev. Thomas P. Halton, Fathers of the Church 6 (Washington, D.C.: The Catholic University of America Press, 2003).

90. Irenaeus of Lyon, *Against the Heresies*, book 2, chapter 22, no. 3, in *Against the Heresies*, vol. 2, trans. Dominic J. Unger and John J. Dillon, Ancient Christian Writers 65 (New York: Paulist Press, 2012); Pitre, *Jesus and the Last Supper*, 323.

The Last Supper in Detail

The Last Supper account was transmitted by four witnesses: Matthew, Mark, Luke and Paul. These four recitations of the Last Supper have many common elements, for they witness to Jesus' historical deeds. The same four texts also contain some noteworthy differences. Many scholars agree that these reflect the emerging first-century liturgical traditions.[91] For example, Mark's version, whose Greek echoes various Semitic phrases, probably has roots in the Jerusalem liturgy, while Paul's smoother Greek reflects the Greek-speaking Antioch liturgy.[92] The Last Supper accounts give a precious witness to the content of the Christian liturgy in the first decades of the Church, to what the first Christians commonly practiced by the 40s and 50s. This is a good example of how historical-critical scholarship can be at the service of faith. The Spirit guided the composition of the Scriptures and the liturgical developments of different communities so as to reveal the truth of the New Passover. Revelation is richer with these multiple texts than it would be if we had four identical accounts, which reflected only the precise historical deeds and words of Jesus on Holy Thursday.

We have seen why the Last Supper was a Passover meal. The structure and meaning of the Passover are crucial to understand the Last Supper itself. No New Testament account gives a complete description of all details. Rather, each narrative is a summary that focuses on just some of Jesus' words and deeds.[93] No evangelist needs to say everything. Yet this also means that we can arrive at only a probable reconstruction of some elements of the meal.

Both Mark (14:12–16) and Luke (22:7–13) tell us that the disciples prepared the Passover in the afternoon, at the time when the lambs were being slaughtered in the temple. The Torah (Dt 12:5–6, 13–14) and an-

91. Dunn, *Christianity in the Making*, 1:229–30; Jacques Dupont, "'Ceci est mon corps', 'Ceci est mon sang'," *Nouvelle revue théologique* 80 (1958): 1028; Otfried Hofius "The Lord's Supper and the Lord's Supper Tradition: Reflections on 1 Corinthians 11:23b–25," in *One Loaf, One Cup: Ecumenical Studies of 1 Cor 11 and Other Eucharistic Texts*, ed. B. F. Meyer, New Gospel Studies 6 (Macon, Ga.: Mercer University Press, 1993), 75–77; Kereszty, *Wedding Feast of the Lamb*, 22–23, 26.

92. Pierre Benoit, *Exégèse et théologie*, vol. 1, Cogitatio fidei 46.1 (Paris: Cerf, 1960), 212.

93. Benoit, *Exégèse et théologie*, 1:212.

cient Jewish literature such as the Book of Jubilees stipulated that it must be celebrated in the city of Jerusalem. At the Jerusalem temple, between three and five o'clock in the afternoon, the disciples would have found thousands of priests offering an immense number of lambs.[94] The disciples would have left the temple with a sacrificed lamb. The lamb could be eaten only at night, which explains why the Last Supper took place in the evening.[95] Jesus gathered with the twelve (Mt 26:20, Mk 14:17). Luke mentions the apostles, by which he means the twelve (6:13, 22:14).[96]

We do not have absolute certitude about all the elements and progression of a first century Passover meal. Yet if the second century Jewish *Mishna* reflects first century practice, then we can say that Jesus' last Passover probably would have looked as follows.

The disciples would have reclined on cushions next to the table, that is, not as slaves, but as free men. The celebration opened with a blessing (*quiddus*) over the first cup said by the father of the family or the presider (in this case, Jesus), and it begins in this way: "Blessed are you, our Lord, king of the world, Creator of the fruit of the vine."[97] All drank from the cup and then washed their hands. The presider took celery with salt and vinegar and said: "Blessed are you, Lord our God, king of the world, Creator of the fruit of the earth." All ate of the same dish. Then some unleavened bread was broken, though without consuming it right away. With this introductory rite completed, one proceeded to the main part of the meal.[98] The paschal lamb was brought to the table and left whole for the moment. A second cup was distributed but not yet consumed. Raising a dish of unleavened bread, the presider then said: "This is the bread of misery, which our fathers ate in the land of Egypt." Here usually followed a dialogue between the father and his sons on the meaning of the elements of the ritual: the unleavened bread, the bitter herbs, and the lamb. The first part of the Hallel (Psalm 113 or 113–114) was sung. The second cup

94. Pitre, *Jesus and the Last Supper*, 390–94.

95. E. P. Sanders, *Judaism: Practice and Belief, 63 BCE–66 CE* (Philadelphia: Trinity Press International, 1992), 134–37.

96. Kereszty, *Wedding Feast of the Lamb*, 24.

97. In this paragraph, I translate from Cesare Giraudo's reconstruction of the rite. See his *In unum corpus: Traité mystagogique sur l'eucharistie*, trans. Éric Iborra and Pierre-Marie Hombert (Paris: Cerf, 2014), 112–24.

98. Giraudo, *In unum corpus*, 108–11, 165.

was raised, and the presider prayed: "Blessed are you Lord our God, king of the world, who have redeemed us and who have redeemed our fathers from Egypt." All drank of the cup and again washed their hands, while saying a prayer. Then the presider broke a whole piece of unleavened bread and said: "Blessed are you, Lord our God, king of the world, who have brought this bread from the earth."[99] It was normal for the presider to insert other words here. Perhaps at this point, Jesus would have added a new blessing: "This is my body." The mention of Jesus breaking the bread at the Last Supper helps us to see its possible location within the progression of the Passover ritual. This blessing was completed before the participants ate the unleavened bread, or, in this case, Christ's body. The eating of bitter herbs and unleavened bread would have followed, each accompanied by a blessing. If Jesus retained the ritual order of the Passover, then the lamb would have been eaten at this point as well.[100] Next came a prayer of thanksgiving over a third cup. In the Passover ritual, this prayer included an introductory dialogue followed by an elaborate triple blessing, for the gift of creation, for the gift of the covenant, and a plea for the restoration of the house of David. If we take Luke and Paul as witnesses to the historical order of the Last Supper's celebration, then Jesus' words over the cup were probably uttered over this third cup, though the matter is disputed.[101] This cup very likely contained red wine. During the blessing, Jesus would have elevated it by about the width of a hand.[102] Then came the concluding rite. The second part of the great Hallel was sung, namely, Psalms 115–118, the last of which is a Psalm of thanksgiving. The blessing and consumption of a fourth cup normally would have followed, but it is not clear whether Jesus completed this part of the ritual at that time.[103] The Last Supper accounts end abruptly, as Jesus and the disciples depart for Gethsemane. The next time we see him drink is when he consumes vinegar from a sponge just before his death, just after having refused the cup of vinegar mixed with frankincense to numb the

99. Giraudo, *In unum corpus*, 124–25.
100. Giraudo, *In unum corpus*, 125–26, 166–67.
101. Pitre, *Jesus and the Last Supper*, 483n124.
102. Jeremias, *The Eucharistic Words of Jesus*, 177, 221–24.
103. Pitre, *Jesus and the Last Supper*, 483n124.

pain.[104] This may signify that the new Passover ritual was completed on the Cross.[105]

Overall, the Passover meal celebration essentially employed the basic structure of the Jewish meal ritual, while adding special prayers and dishes.[106] Louis Bouyer has shown that the early Christians recognized the importance of this meal ritual: the ancient Eucharistic prayers integrated and developed various Jewish table blessings, as well as blessings used in the synagogue service (*berakah* or thanksgiving).[107] I will return to this theme in chapter 5.

Now we can look more closely at the meaning of two phrases: Jesus' words over the bread and cup, and the command to do this in his memory.[108] In the phrase "This is my body," the pronoun "this" (*touto*) is neuter, not masculine. The Greek term for "bread" is masculine. Therefore, Jesus does not intend to say: "This bread is my body." Xavier Léon-Dufour proposes that Christ thereby indicates a gift. With the benediction or blessing of the presider in the Passover ritual, the unleavened bread becomes a gift from God. Thus, Jesus essentially says: "This [gift of God] is my body."[109] This seems correct, yet it was evident to ancient Jews celebrating the Passover, with its many blessing prayers, that all of the elements were gifts from God. Max Thurian rightly argues that "this" also indicates the entire action of taking bread, giving thanks, breaking and giving it, while saying "Take, eat, this is my body."[110] Yet Scripture's meaning is often multi-valent. We should not lose sight of the striking simplicity of Jesus' expression. He essentially tells us: "This thing, that which is in my hands,

104. Mt 27:31–36, 48; Mk 14:36, 15:23; Lk 23:36; Jn 19:29–30.

105. On this theme, see Scott Hahn, *The Fourth Cup: Understanding the Mystery of the Last Supper and the Cross* (New York: Image, 2018).

106. Louis Bouyer, *Eucharist: Theology and Spirituality of the Eucharistic Prayer*, trans. Charles Underhill Quinn (Notre Dame, Ind.: University of Notre Dame Press, 1968), 80.

107. Bouyer, *Eucharist*, 106ff.

108. I do not adopt part of Cesare Giraudo's analysis of these key phrases, as he proposes to read the details of the Last Supper strictly in light of Jewish ritual and theology of memorial (*In unum corpus*, 179–81). In my view, the gift of the Eucharist is too new, so the Jewish categories offer a necessary but not sufficient foundation for the interpretation of Christ's words.

109. Xavier Léon-Dufour, *Le partage du pain eucharistique selon le Nouveau Testament* (Paris: Seuil, 1982), 140.

110. Max Thurian, *The Eucharistic Memorial, Part 2: The New Testament*, trans. J. G. Davis, Ecumenical Studies in Worship 8 (Richmond, Va.: John Knox Press, 1961), 34–35.

is in fact my body." This is precisely how Catholic tradition has understood him.

In all four accounts of the Last Supper, Jesus refers to his body, *soma* in Greek. In the Synoptic Gospels, this term refers not just to the physical aspect of the human being, but to the whole person, with an emphasis on human fragility.[111] The ancient Jewish use of the word already pointed to man's mortality (e.g., Eccl 14:17, 17:31). Now Jeremias argues that this holistic understanding of "body" is not as important in this context. Rather, he maintains that we should primarily see the mention of "body" in relation to the other key term, "blood." In ancient Judaism, the couplet "body/blood" signals the two main parts of the sacrificial animal, which are separated when it is slain, so that it can be offered to God. The body/blood couplet, taken together with other sacrificial allusions (such as "for you") means that Jesus is evoking his coming sacrificial death.[112] Yet the usual sense of *soma*, as a reference to the whole person, can still be honored. Hence, the phrase "This is my body which is for you" also has the meaning, "This is me, who will die."[113] This theme is echoed when Matthew and Mark mention the blood that "will be poured out." By these words, Jesus indicates his own person in the act of dying. It is a prophecy of his coming, violent death.[114]

The Synoptic authors and Paul mention the covenant in relation to the cup. The phrase "this is my blood of the covenant" and "this cup is the new covenant in my blood" evoke the blood of the covenant in Exodus 24. At the foot of Mt. Sinai, God establishes a covenant with Israel by an offering of animals, whose blood is sprinkled on the people. The scene culminates with Moses, Aaron, Nadab, Abihu, and seventy elders ascending the mountain to eat and drink in God's presence. Now Jesus institutes a new covenant by a new sacrifice. We find the same combination of sacrifice and meal in the Passover tradition: the eating of the Passover lamb completed the Passover sacrifice.[115]

111. Bernard Dupuy, "Pâque juive et Pâque chrétienne: à l'origine de la différence herméneutique," *ISTINA* 48 (2003): 350.

112. Jeremias, *The Eucharistic Words of Jesus*, 221–22.

113. Léon-Dufour, *Le partage du pain*, 141–43; Pitre, *Jesus and the Last Supper*, 409.

114. Giraudo, *In unum corpus*, 187–88.

115. Pitre, *Jesus and the Last Supper*, 94, 410.

We now come to a key question: Does Scripture itself call for a literal reading of the words, "This is my body," "This is my blood"? Does Christ thereby signify what theology will later call the Real Presence? Here, we should distinguish two levels of interpretation. The first level considers only the Last Supper accounts, in abstraction from John 6 and the Christian tradition. The second level integrates these three sources. From the perspective of the former, phrases such as "This is my body" could be a reference to the Real Presence, but it is not absolutely certain that, taken by itself, the phrase needs to have this sense. Why is this so? Jesus' gesture and words at the Last Supper have a prophetic character, for they point to the Cross, to his coming death. The Old Testament prophets use expressions whose style comes close to that of Jesus' phrase at the Last Supper. Thus, God tells Ezekiel to cut off his hair and throw it into a fire before the people, while saying "This is Jerusalem." The prophet signifies that Israel or Jerusalem is surrounded by the pagan nations (who are signified by the fire) (Ezek 5:1–5). Now Ezekiel does not mean that the hair surrounded by fire literally is Jerusalem or the people of God. Scripture sometimes uses prophetic expressions with the structure "This is ..." without a literal sense. Therefore, when read in isolation, Jesus' words at the Last Supper need not signify the Real Presence.[116]

Yet we should also note two crucial differences between Christ's and Ezekiel's words. First, Ezekiel's use of the phrase "this is" involves a parable, in which he presents a symbol in order to teach the Israelites. But at the Last Supper, Jesus does not speak in parables. Nor is he primarily teaching. Rather, he invites his disciples to eat, to do something, and he is concerned with offering them a share in the power of his sacrifice, in his sacrificial body and blood, which are very concrete realities. The genre of parable hardly fits the Last Supper narrative.[117] Second, such parabolic prophecies have efficacy in the moment, and not the future. But Jesus' deed at the Last Supper is destined to be efficacious throughout the future: "do this in memory of me."[118]

There is another reason to opt for a literal reading of Christ's words: The Last Supper accounts contain multiple references to sacrifice. In an-

116. Dupont, "'Ceci est mon corps'," 1033–34.

117. Benoit, *Exégèse et théologie*, 1:228–29.

118. Giraudo, *In unum corpus*, 179n47.

cient Judaism, it was essential to commune in the victim being sacrificed, especially the Passover victim, so as to receive the saving power of the sacrifice. Now if Jesus is the New Passover Lamb, then communing in a mere symbol of Jesus is not enough.[119] Therefore, on the basis of the Last Supper accounts, one can make a probable argument in favor of a literal reading for the words of institution. That argument attains certitude when we combine it with John 6 and ancient tradition.

We can now look at the subsequent words of Jesus at the Last Supper. When Mark and Matthew witness to this sacred event and recount that Jesus refers to "many," they mean neither "some" nor "many, but not all." Rather, the word "many" points to a multitude that could include all.[120] Jesus also describes his suffering and death in a way that evokes Isaiah's Suffering Servant.[121] In Isaiah 52:14–15, the "many" for whom the Servant suffers include the Gentiles, and not just Israel (who are indicated by "the many" in Is 53:4–8). "The many" therefore has a potentially broad meaning, as it evokes a vast, undetermined multitude.[122] Isaiah's Christological prophecy ultimately directs our gaze toward two crucial teachings: God's universal salvific will in Christ and the actual reception of salvation by faith. That is, Christ died in order to save all and offers that gift to each person (Jn 6:51), yet the gift's reception comes by faith, which entails the person's free entry into the Covenant sealed in the blood of the lamb. The paschal setting of the Last Supper implies that "the many" being addressed are God's people. In this way, "the many" mentioned in the Last Supper narratives of Matthew and Mark neatly parallels the "for you" recounted by Luke and Paul in 1 Corinthians. The preceding interpretation further helps to explain the later and constant liturgical tradition of translating the *hyper pollon* of the Last Supper Narrative as "for many" in the Eucharistic prayers.[123]

Luke and Paul report Jesus' commandment: "Do this in memory of

119. Dupont, "'Ceci est mon corps,'" 1038.

120. Giraudo, *In unum corpus*, 191n62; Helmut Moll, *Die Lehre von der Eucharistie als Opfer* (Cologne: Peter Hanstein, 1975), 59. See also Hebrews 2:9.

121. Jeremias, *The Eucharistic Words of Jesus*, 226–29; Pitre, *Jesus and the Last Supper*, 100–104.

122. Ben F. Meyer, "The Expiation Motif in the Eucharistic Words: A Key to the History of Jesus?," in Meyer, *One Loaf, One Cup*, 25–26.

123. See Manfred Hauke, *"Versato per molti:" Studio per una fedele traduzione del "pro multis" nelle parole della consecrazione* (Siena, Italy: Cantagalli, 2008).

me." This precept echoes the divine commandment in Exodus 12, that the Passover ritual is to be celebrated in the future. Jesus commands not an exact repetition of the entire Last Supper, but of the particular rite that he has celebrated with the bread and the single cup, which is "a covenant in my blood."[124] It is a command to eat the body and drink the blood in a ritual manner.[125]

Some scholars argue that the command to celebrate this ritual in Jesus' memory is a later addition, and not a saying of the historical Jesus. They point to the absence of the phrase in Mark and Matthew and argue that it would not have been deleted.[126] But this reading remains unconvincing.[127] For an omission is not a deletion. Each Gospel writer worked with a wealth of material about the Last Supper and had to choose some elements. Also, Mark and Matthew knew the importance of following Jesus' example in the life of the Church, something that Matthew's recounting of the great commission at Jesus' Ascension makes explicit.[128] Furthermore, Mark and Matthew reflect liturgical practices that have applied the command to "do this" in Jesus' memory: for the communities linked with Mark and Matthew regularly celebrated the liturgy by imitating part of Jesus' Last Supper. Strikingly, the entire ancient liturgical tradition has retained the phrase "do this."[129]

The same command seems to contain another, very specific meaning: it is not simply an ordinance for the community. Jesus' command to "do this" (*touto poieite* in Greek) likely evokes a cultic action. In Exodus 29:31–35, God explains to Moses an ordination ritual, and then tells him to "do this" (*poieseis … houtōs* in the Septuagint) to Aaron and his sons, that is, to anoint them as priests. In Numbers 15:8–11 and 15, we find God's instructions on how the priests are to perform a peace offering with the sacrifice of a bull, flower and wine. They are to "do this" (*houtōs … poiēseis*). Here, "doing" means "to sacrifice." The language of remembering only reinforces this sense, for it points to the ritual repetition or reenact-

124. Scheffczyk, *Die Heilszeichen*, 45.
125. Kereszty, *Wedding Feast of the Lamb*, 29.
126. Jeremias, *The Eucharistic Words of Jesus*, 128
127. Benoit, *Exégèse et théologie*, 1:221.
128. Giraudo, *In unum corpus*, 193.
129. Giraudo, *In unum corpus*, 192.

ment of the Passover sacrifice. Thus, at the Last Supper, Jesus commands the repeated, cultic celebration of the New Passover.[130]

To conclude this chapter, let us notice the presence of two major themes in the biblical accounts of the Last Supper: (1) the theme of sacrifice is omnipresent; and (2) the meal theme is present, but it does not dominate over the theme of sacrifice. Rather, we find a balance of both themes.

130. Pitre, *Jesus and the Last Supper*, 417–20.

CHAPTER 3

THE INSTITUTION OF THE EUCHARIST

The previous two chapters gave us the beginning of a biblical foundation for a systematic doctrine of the Eucharist. We now turn to a historical and theological study of the institution of the Eucharist, with a focus on liturgical practice in the ancient Church. This theme is intimately linked with the Last Supper.

The current topic offers a veritable theological key to the rest of Eucharistic doctrine. Our answer to the question of what the Eucharist's institution concerns will largely shape the rest of our work. The issue of institution is crucial, for the Eucharist is a gift from Jesus, a gift that assures the Church's unity and fidelity to him. As Bruce Marshall notes: "Conformity to his words and deeds, doing what he did, is not a matter of mere historical accuracy or obsessive primitivism, but of grateful submission to the design of God for our salvation."[1] In short, we have the privilege of celebrating the New Passover.

1. Bruce Marshall, "What Is the Eucharist? A Dogmatic Outline," in *The Oxford Handbook*

This chapter's treatment is guided by contemporary historical debates on the nature of the early Christian liturgy. Did the early Christians celebrate the Eucharist in a way that consistently manifests a link with and imitation of the Last Supper? Do we find a consistent memorial celebration of Christ's Passion in the ancient liturgies, expressed in sacrificial language, as Jesus did at the Last Supper? How much freedom did the Church have in developing the liturgy? The first sections of this chapter take up these issues. Then follows a systematic section, where I will integrate the results of the historical study and our previous biblical analyses within a scholastic framework, guided by the teaching of the ecumenical councils. After proposing an overall theology of the Eucharist's institution, I will turn to the more specific issue of the material signs of bread and wine used for the Eucharist, from a biblical, historical, and theological perspective.

The historical section of this chapter gives much attention to the use of the institution narrative in the ancient liturgies. The aim of this study is not to demonstrate that, throughout the Eucharistic prayers of the early Church, this narrative constituted the sacramental "form" whereby bread and wine become body and blood. Rather, this study seeks to trace the early Church's expression of the link between her Eucharistic practice and the foundational event of the Last Supper. Hence, I will not look for evidence of patristic theologies that posit the words of institution as the effective means to change the gifts instantaneously: in most cases, such an answer cannot be found.

Biblical and Historical Considerations

The First-Century Christians on the Institution of the Eucharist

In the previous chapter, I mentioned that the New Testament accounts of the Last Supper differ somewhat among themselves partly because they already reflect the liturgical practice of various primitive Christian communities. This practice developed under the guidance of the apostles, in

---

of Sacramental Theology, ed. Hans Boersma and Matthew Levering (Oxford: Oxford University Press, 2015), 505.

the age when revelation was still open. The Synoptics and 1 Corinthians combine two elements: first, they recount Jesus' historic deeds and words on the night of the Last Supper, and second, they retell the words and deeds of Jesus in a way that partly reflects the way the earliest Christian communities celebrated the Last Supper in memory of Jesus.[2] While we cannot reconstruct the exact gestures and (Aramaic) words that Jesus used, the Last Supper accounts present a consistent meaning that he communicated. The four accounts of the Last Supper can be divided into two main strands of tradition: Paul recounts one established tradition, and it is close to Luke, while Matthew and Mark have the most in common. In chapter 1, we saw how John 6:51 links with this tradition, as it echoes the words of institution: "the bread which I shall give for the life of the world is my flesh."

Thanks to consistent and multiple attestation, we can say that the historical Jesus himself celebrated the Last Supper in a way very similar to the New Testament accounts. Furthermore, the only substantial first-century witness to the liturgy celebrated by the first two generations of Christians is found in the four explicit Last Supper accounts and in John 6. For no other New Testament reference to liturgy comes close to the amount of detail offered here. The other key witness to the Eucharist of the first Christians comes in the Book of Acts, as it recounts the "breaking of the bread." As Keener notes, the passages on the rite of breaking bread tell us little, except that it occurred frequently, was linked to an *agape* meal, and was celebrated in the homes of Christians.[3]

On the basis of these considerations and our analyses in chapters 1 and 2, we can draw the following conclusions. First, the first-century Christians recognized that the Last Supper of Jesus was intended by him as a liturgical ritual to be repeated in his memory. Like the first Passover, the New Passover was to be celebrated as a memorial of Jesus' exodus to the Father. The first Christians knew that they were to "do this," like

2. For the second point, see Maxwell E. Johnson, "The Apostolic Tradition," in *The Oxford History of Christian Worship*, ed. Geoffrey Wainwright and K. B. Westerfield Tucker (Oxford: Oxford University Press, 2006), 44–46; Daniel Sheerin, "Eucharistic Liturgy," in *The Oxford Handbook of Early Christian Studies*, ed. David G. Hunter and Susan Ashbrook Harvey (Oxford: Oxford University Press, 2008), 713.

3. Craig S. Keener, *Acts: An Exegetical Commentary*, vol. 1, *Introduction and 1:1–2:47* (Grand Rapids, Mich.: Baker Academic, 2012), 1003–4.

Aaron and the Old Testament priests offering sacrifice. Second, the same Christians were faithful to Jesus' intention, so that the most basic words, gestures, and material elements used in the ritual reflect Jesus' example, even as they manifest slight modifications. Indeed, we find no clear New Testament evidence that the first Christians celebrated the Eucharist in another way.

My approach to the theme of institution clashes with that of the liturgical historian Paul Bradshaw. He and other scholars have emphasized the radical diversity of the early Christian liturgies. The idea is not wholly objectionable, yet Bradshaw pushes it very far. Because of his influence, I will devote some space to Bradshaw's position. I will first take up his treatment of Scripture and the second-century witnesses. The next section will prolong my response to Bradshaw.

First, Bradshaw minimizes the Passover theme in first-century Christian worship. His doubts about the date and paschal nature of the Last Supper are largely based on mid-twentieth-century biblical and liturgical scholarship. My study above shows that such doubts are exaggerated.[4]

Second, Bradshaw holds that John the evangelist likely did not know of an institution of the Eucharist at the Last Supper, while the Eucharistic passages of John 6:51–59 are probably the addition of a later redactor.[5] But we saw above that John 6 has a strong literary unity: the idea that verses 51–59 were inserted later is no longer tenable. Bradshaw sees the omission of the Eucharist in John 13 as significant. Yet he fails to account for three things. First, as Brown and Pitre have shown, the end of chapter 13 of John's Gospel contains five allusions to a Passover ritual: (a) Jesus and the disciples reclined instead of sitting (Jn 13:23–25), (b) Jesus dipped a morsel in a dish (13:26–27), (c) there was a custom of giving to the poor at Passover (13:29), (d) the preparations for the meal took place just before (13:29–30), and (e) the Last Supper took place at night (13:30).[6] We find

4. Paul F. Bradshaw, "Worship in the New Testament" in *The Search for the Origins of Christian Worship: Sources and Methods for the Study of Early Liturgy* (Oxford: Oxford University Press, 1992), 47–55. Similarly, Enrico Mazza holds that the Last Supper was not a Passover meal. This mistake renders part of his overall narrative on the history of the early liturgy fragile. See his *The Celebration of the Eucharist: The Origin of the Rite and the Development of Its Interpretation*, trans. Matthew J. O'Connell (Collegeville, Minn.: Liturgical Press, 1998), 25–26.

5. Paul F. Bradshaw, "Did Jesus Institute the Eucharist at the Last Supper?," in *Reconstructing Early Christian Worship* (London: SPCK, 2009), 3–4.

6. Raymond E. Brown, *The Gospel according to John*, vol. 2, Anchor Bible Commentary 29A

some echoes of the Last Supper in John 13, because it was a Passover meal. John was not only aware of the Last Supper tradition, but also recognized its importance. Second, nothing in the Synoptics matches the rich Eucharistic doctrine of John 6. This gives the fourth evangelist the liberty to focus on other themes in chapter 13, especially given the foreshadowing of the words of institution in verse 51. In other words, the (relative) silence on the Eucharist in John 13–17 hardly demonstrates that John did not consider Jesus' last meal with his disciples to have been Eucharistic. Third, as was noted previously, John and his readers in Asia Minor would have been deeply aware of the Last Supper event through the Gospel of Mark and the oral tradition. But Bradshaw takes the absence of evidence to indicate the evidence of absence. This is a fundamental exegetical mistake.

Bradshaw's third important move is to argue from the evidence in second-century Christian writers. He proposes that Ignatius of Antioch's description of the Eucharist as the flesh of Jesus (*sarx*) instead of body (*soma*) suggests that Ignatius follows John but knows nothing of the Synoptic tradition. Furthermore, Bradshaw points out that Ignatius does not directly describe the Eucharistic cup as Jesus' blood.[7] Yet John 6:51 precisely gives us a bridge between the Eucharistic *sarx* and the Last Supper of Jesus. I already noted why John would prefer the language of flesh to that of *soma*. In his study of Justin Martyr, Bradshaw signals the absence of the language of the "breaking the bread." Here, Bradshaw takes the absence of an explicit reference to one part of the Last Supper ritual as decisive, even though Justin clearly echoes one formulation of the words of institution (more on that below). Finally, Bradshaw argues that, when Irenaeus mentions the phrases "This is my body" and "he declared his blood," he betrays no awareness of the Last Supper or Passover setting for these Eucharistic words.[8] I will evaluate this last argument in the next section.

(New York: Doubleday, 1970), 556, 576; Brant Pitre, *Jesus and the Last Supper* (Grand Rapids, Mich.: William B. Eerdmans, 2015), 346.

7. Bradshaw, "Did Jesus Institute the Eucharist at the Last Supper?," 5.

8. See Bradshaw, "Did Jesus Institute the Eucharist at the Last Supper?," 7. He refers to Irenaeus of Lyon, *Treatise Against Heresies*, bk. 4, chap. 17, no. 5, which I will cite below.

The Last Supper in the Second and Third-Century Liturgy: The *Didache*, Justin Martyr and Irenaeus

Bradshaw and other historians appeal to an ancient work called the *Didache* (or Teaching) as a witness to a primitive Eucharistic liturgy that lacks an institution narrative. This collection of moral and liturgical instructions dates to the late first or early second century. It may come from Egypt or Syria.[9] The work contains two possible references to the Eucharistic liturgy: in chapters 9–10, and in chapter 14. Chapter 9 and the first five verses of chapter 10 probably describe an *agape* meal that is perhaps followed (at chapter 10, verse 6) by an introduction to the Eucharistic liturgy in the strict, sacramental sense of the term.[10] Already in chapter 9, the meal is described as a "eucharist." The prayers mentioned echo Jewish table blessings, which the Jews also called "eucharist" or "thanksgiving." The document insists that only the baptized may partake of the meal. Similarly, festive Jewish meals restricted those who could partake of it.[11] In chapter 9 of the *Didache*, a blessing is said over a cup before it is said over the bread, which is unusual, and again suggests an *agape*. There are no references to the Last Supper or to Christ's Passion. Nor is it clear if the gifts shared are Christ's body and blood. Chapter 10 begins with a prayer of thanksgiving for the meal just shared. Verse 6 gives the following prayer, perhaps a transition in the ritual: "May grace come, and may this world pass by. Hosanna to the God of David! If anyone is holy, let him come. If anyone is not, let him repent. Maranatha! Amen." Then the author adds: "Allow the prophets, however, to give thanks as much as they like."[12] An *agape* meal followed by a sacramental celebration would imitate the pattern described in 1 Corinthians 11. We learn that the "prophets" can preside at this liturgy. While chapters 9–10 of the *Didache* describe a weekday liturgy, chapter 14 speaks of a Sunday sac-

9. Kurt Niederwimmer, *The Didache: A Commentary*, trans. Linda M. Maloney, Hermeneia: A Critical and Historical Commentary on the Bible (Philadelphia: Fortress Press, 1998), 52–54.

10. Willy Rordorf, introduction to *La doctrine des douze apôtres (Didachè)*, ed. W. Rordorf and André Tuilier, Sources Chrétiennes 248 (Paris: Cerf, 1978), 38–41; Niederwimmer, *The Didache: A Commentary*, 142–43.

11. Willy Rordorf, *Liturgie, foi et vie des premiers chrétiens: Études patristiques*, Théologie historique 75 (Paris: Beauchesne, 1986), 195–97.

12. *Didache*, 10.6–7. I use the edition of Niederwimmer, *The Didache: A Commentary*, 155.

ramental liturgy, where a bishop of the local church apparently presides (he is mentioned just before and just after). Chapter 14 calls this Sunday liturgy a sacrifice, but does not indicate the content of the Eucharistic prayer.

Bradshaw and others appeal to chapter 9 of the *Didache* as a Eucharistic celebration in the strict sense, without any reference to the Last Supper, an interpretation that remains debatable. In fact, the text may contain no more than a one-verse reference to a sacramental prayer, at the end of chapter 10. Overall, the *Didache* does not offer a clear witness to radical liturgical diversity in the second century.

St. Justin Martyr gives a summary account of the Eucharist in mid-second-century Rome:

> And this food is called among us *eucharistia* [thanksgiving], of which no one is allowed to partake except one who believes that the things which we teach are true, and has received the washing that is for the remission of sins and for rebirth, and who so lives as Christ handed down. For we do not receive these things as common bread and common drink; but in like manner as Jesus Christ our Savior, having been made incarnate by God's logos, took both flesh and blood for our salvation, so also have we been taught that the food eucharistized *through the word of prayer that is from Him*, from which our blood and flesh are nourished by transformation, is the flesh and blood of that Jesus who became incarnate. For the apostles, in the memoirs composed by them, which are called Gospels, thus handed down what was commanded them; that Jesus took bread, and having given thanks, said, "Do this for my memorial, this is my body;" and likewise, he took the chalice and having given thanks said, "This is My blood."[13]

Justin notes the essential conditions for receiving the Eucharist, namely, acceptance of Christ's teachings in faith, baptism, and right living. He also reports a tradition that he has received, much as Paul does in 1 Corinthians 11. Finally, Justin seems to link the presence of Christ's body and blood to "the word of prayer that is from Him," meaning, from Christ. This prayer is said over bread and wine, but which prayer might this be?

Just after discussing "the word of prayer" and the identity of the gifts, Justin mentions the institution narrative at the Last Supper. His primary

13. Justin Martyr, *First Apology*, chap. 66, in *First and Second Apologies*, ed. and trans. Leslie William Barnard, Ancient Christian Writers 56 (New York: Paulist Press, 1997), 70–71 (emphasis added).

intention is not to specify which prayer is uttered, but to show what kind of gift is present on the altar. Scholars have noted that Justin's recitation of the Last Supper does not perfectly match either the Synoptic Gospels or 1 Corinthians. This means that he probably reports the liturgical practice of his community.[14] Further analysis by Othmar Perler supports this judgment.[15] He argues that the "word of prayer" should be seen in parallel to the phrase "word of God," found earlier in the passage just cited.[16] That is, Justin refers to both (1) the words of institution as the way in which the presider gives thanks, and (2) the transformative power of Christ.[17] The liturgical prayer is a word or logos, a word uttered by the Incarnate Logos at the Last Supper. It would seem that the word of prayer takes part in the divine, creative power of God's word. The doctrine of Christ as the Logos with creative power stands at the heart of Justin's theology.

This means that we are likely dealing with the beginnings of a Logos epiclesis in the second-century Roman liturgy. This epiclesis is a prayer addressed to the Logos asking for his descent into the gifts, similar to a Spirit epiclesis that begs the Spirit to come down upon the gifts on the altar during Mass. Justin is the first historical witness of a particular liturgical prayer directly addressed to the eternal Logos, a prayer that seeks the descent of God's power onto the gifts for their sanctification and conversion. Notice also the striking parallel between the Incarnation of the Logos and the change of bread and wine into the flesh and blood of the Logos. Justin attributes the fructifying of Mary's womb not so much to the Holy Spirit as to the Logos (though we would say that it is both).

14. A theory held by G. J. Cuming, as noted by Mazza, *The Celebration of the Eucharist*, 110.

15. Othmar Perler, "Logos und Eucharistie nach Justinus I Apol. 66," *Freiburger Zeitschrift für Philosophie und Theologie* 18 (1940): 296–316. Bradshaw thinks that Justin probably ignores the Last Supper tradition. Bradshaw never mentions the work of Perler (Bradshaw, "Did Jesus Institute the Eucharist at the Last Supper?," 6–7). Giraudo takes Justin's omission of the words of institution in his direct description of the Eucharistic prayer as evidence of the absence of any institution. Cesare Giraudo, *In unum corpus: Traité mystagogique sur l'eucharistie*, trans. Éric Iborra and Pierre-Marie Hombert (Paris: Cerf, 2014), 260–62. This type of argument does not hold.

16. Perler, "Logos und Eucharistie," 300–302.

17. Perler also compares the phrase "*we have been taught* that the food eucharistized *through the word of prayer that is from Him* … is the flesh and blood," with another, "the apostles … have handed down what was commanded to them" concerning the memorial celebration of the Last Supper ("Logos und Eucharistie," 302). See also Ansgar Santogrossi, "Anaphoras without Institution Narrative: Historical and Dogmatic Considerations," *Nova et Vetera* (English Edition) 10 (2012): 31.

By analogy, the Logos brings to us his divine power, to change bread and wine into flesh and blood.[18] Overall, Justin is the most important, precise witness to the Christian liturgy as celebrated in the second century.

In his *Treatise Against Heresies*, Irenaeus follows up a discussion of Old Testament sacrifices with an explanation of the Christian Eucharist:

> To his disciples also, he [the Lord] counseled to offer God the first fruits of his own creatures, not that he had need of them, but that they might not be sterile or ungrateful. He took the bread, which comes from creation, gave thanks saying (Mt 26:26): "This is my body." And likewise [he took] the cup, which comes from creation, of which we are, and he declared it to be his blood and taught that it [the cup] was the new oblation of the New Covenant. It is this very oblation that the Church has received from the apostles, and which in the whole world she offers to God who has given us nourishment, as the first fruits of God's own gifts, under the New Covenant.[19]

Against the Gnostics, who despise material creation and material sacrifices, Irenaeus holds for continuity between the Old and New Covenant: both have an offering of the first-fruits of creation. Christ himself taught his apostles how to make this offering. The Church receives the new oblation directly from the apostles, who received it directly from Christ. Irenaeus marshals a typical argument against the Gnostics: the true Christians inherit the authentic tradition. The Church celebrates the Eucharist according to the instructions of Jesus, as transmitted by the apostles.[20] The reference to such instructions shows that Irenaeus does more than offer a catechesis: he also reflects second-century liturgical practice. Finally, in chapter 18 of the same work, Irenaeus considers Jesus to be personally instituting a new sacrifice when he declares the bread to be his body and the cup to be his blood in the new covenant. Irenaeus clearly evokes the Last Supper as the Eucharist's origin, in contrast to Bradshaw's claim

18. Perler, "Logos und Eucharistie," 303–8.

19. Irenaeus of Lyon, *Treatise Against Heresies*, bk. 4, chap. 17, no. 5. Translation by the author, based on the critical edition in Irenaeus of Lyon, *Contre les hérésies, livre IV*, ed. Adelin Rousseau, Sources chrétiennes 100.2 (Paris: Cerf, 1965), 590–93.

20. Helmut Moll, *Die Lehre von der Eucharistie als Opfer* (Cologne: Peter Hanstein, 1975), 168–69; Antonio Orbe, *Teología de San Ireneo IV: Traducción y comentario del libro IV del "Adversus haereses"* (Madrid: Biblioteca de Autores Cristianos, 1986), 235–36.

mentioned above.[21] Irenaeus's insistence on the apostolic roots of the Eucharistic liturgy could not be stronger.

Valuable testimony about the ancient liturgy comes from the third-century North African bishop and martyr, Cyprian of Carthage. In "Letter 63," Cyprian states that, in the liturgy, God has commanded the Christians to do nothing else than what the Lord himself did at the Last Supper.[22] This applies even to details such as mixing water and wine in the chalice. Furthermore, Cyprian states that the sacrifice of the Lord is not legitimately celebrated if our oblation and our sacrifice do not correspond to the Passion, that is, to the Last Supper.[23] For Cyprian, the Last Supper constitutes not just the origin of a sacred ritual, but the source of norms for the correct use of bread and wine.[24] The martyr shows that imitation of the Lord's Supper is an essential liturgical principle in third-century northern Africa.[25] We will see that the oriental liturgical families will propose a different accent, without ever separating themselves from the Last Supper tradition.

21. Antonio Orbe, *Introduction à la théologie des IIe et IIIe siècles*, trans. Joseph M. López de Castro, Agnès Bastit, and Jean-Michel Roessli, Patrimoines: Christianisme (Paris: Cerf, 2012), vol. 1, 691–92.

22. Cyprian of Carthage, "Letter 63," no. 2, in Cyprian of Carthage, *Epistularium: Epistulae 58–81*, ed. G. F. Diercks, CCSL 3C (Turnhout, Belgium: Brepols, 1996), 391, ll. 22–30. For an English edition, see Cyprian of Carthage, *Letters 55–66*, trans. G. W. Clarke, Ancient Christian Writers 46 (New York: Paulist Press, 1986).

23. Cyprian of Carthage, "Letter 63," no. 9, in *Epistularium*, ed. Diercks, 400–401, ll. 141–160.

24. Michel-Yves Perrin, "Pratiques et discours eucharistiques dans les premiers siècles (des origines jusqu'à la fin du IVe siècle): Considérations introductives," in *Eucharistia: Encyclopédie de l'eucharistie*, ed. Maurice Brouard (Paris: Cerf, 2002), 111.

25. Bradshaw maintains that Cyprian's view presents an evolution in liturgical practice. The Anglican scholar argues that (1) the New Testament was becoming authoritative Scripture in the third century, thus overriding oral traditions, and (2) the threat of martyrdom called for a link between Jesus' self-offering and the celebration of the Eucharist, so that it could be a source of strength in times of persecution (Bradshaw, "Did Jesus Institute the Eucharist at the Last Supper?," 10). However, the New Testament was already authoritative with St. Irenaeus around A.D. 180, several decades before Cyprian wrote. Finally, the link between the Eucharist and martyrdom can already be found in the New Testament (see chapter 2). It is evident in the works of Ignatius of Antioch and Polycarp in the early second century, long before Cyprian. See Luc de Bellescize, "L'eucharistie chez Ignace d'Antioche et Polycarpe de Smyrne," *Nouvelle revue théologique* 132 (2010): 197–216. Bradshaw therefore fails to explain the shift. Indeed, if there was no such evolution, then there is no need to account for a new teaching in Cyprian.

The Last Supper in the Liturgies of the Third and Fourth Centuries

We now turn from the oldest post-biblical witnesses for the Eucharistic liturgy to the oldest Eucharistic prayers (or anaphora). Here, the place of the institution narrative will take center stage. Our attention turns mostly to the east, source of the oldest anaphora.

An ancient witness that is often invoked as an example of a Eucharistic liturgy without the words of institution is the mid-third-century *Apostolic Tradition* by Hippolytus. The liturgical scholar Enrico Mazza argues that the text of the *Apostolic Tradition* includes two irreconcilable structures for the liturgy (meaning, it fuses two different traditions), of which one has an institution narrative, while the other lacks that narrative.[26] Let us note that the version of the *Apostolic Tradition* that has come down to us contains an institution narrative. Mazza thinks that this part of the manuscript represents only one tradition behind the text. This proposal remains very hypothetical.[27] Also, scholars still dispute whether this text reflects any actual liturgy of the third century.[28]

The *Barcelona Papyrus* dates from the middle of the fourth century. It is the oldest manuscript that contains an entire Eucharistic prayer, which gives the document immense historical importance. The text probably comes from a Pachomian monastic community in Spain. It is not a copy of a liturgical book, but a scholarly report of the community's liturgical practice.[29] The Eucharistic prayer has multiple links with the character-

26. Mazza, *The Celebration of the Eucharist*, 52.

27. There would appear to be a parallel between some liturgists' attempts to reconstruct the sources of various ancient texts on the Eucharist with the nineteenth and twentieth century exegetical enterprise of reconstructing the written sources of the Pentateuch (the four-source theory) or of the Synoptic Gospels (the "Q document"). In recent decades, more and more exegetes have recognized the highly tentative and fragile nature of such projects. Indeed, scholarly consensus on the sources of the Pentateuch no longer exists, while efforts to reconstruct the whole of "Q" and the belief of the hypothetical community that stands behind it have been met with more and more skepticism in the academy. Liturgical studies would benefit from exercising similar caution and skepticism when it comes to reconstructing hypothetical liturgical sources or claiming what these sources did or did not contain.

28. Louis Bouyer, *Eucharist: Theology and Spirituality of the Eucharistic Prayer*, trans. Charles Underhill Quinn (Notre Dame, Ind.: University of Notre Dame Press, 1968), 168; Daniel G. Van Slyke, "The Study of Early Christian Worship," in *T&T Clark Companion to Liturgy*, ed. Alcuin Reid (London: T&T Clark, 2016), 48.

29. Michael Zheltov, "The Anaphora and the Thanksgiving Prayer from the Barcelona Papyrus:

istics of pre-fourth-century liturgies. For example, the addressee switches between God the Father and Jesus Christ, and the text once calls Jesus "God's child." The prayer in the *Barcelona Papyrus* includes a threefold structure that also was clearly practiced in Egypt in the fourth century: sanctus, epiclesis, institution narrative (in that order). The latter reads thus:

> He Himself, when He was about to hand Himself, having taken bread and given thanks, broke it and gave it to His disciples saying: "Take, eat, this is My body." Likewise after the supper, having taken a cup and given thanks, He gave it to them saying: "Take, drink the blood, which is shed for many for remission of sins." And we also do the same in Your remembrance.[30]

The text does not mention the words "This is my blood," but simply invites those present to drink it. However, since this manuscript is not the reproduction of a liturgical book but a discussion of the liturgy for theological purposes, there are likely some gaps in the text.[31]

Two other ancient Egyptian sources should be noted. The so-called euchologion of Serapion, bishop of Thmuis (d. 359) contains the institution narrative. Between the blessing over the bread and the cup, it begs God to gather the Church out of every land and people. This prayer for unity, in imitation of the *Didache*, alludes to the multiplication of the loaves. The text makes abundant use of the language of similitude (*homoiōma*), which has the meaning of sacrament and memorial: the Church offers the similitude of Christ's body and blood, but also of his death.[32] Serapion thus accentuates the link with the Last Supper, which is precisely a sacramental celebration of Christ's death. After the institution narrative, the presider calls upon the Logos to descend upon the gifts.[33] Overall, Serapion posits a smooth link between the Last Supper and John 6, makes frequent use of sacrificial language, and manifests belief in the change of the gifts.

An Underestimated Testimony to the Anaphoral History in the Fourth Century," *Vigiliae Christianae* 62 (2008): 468–69, 497.

30. The translation is by Zheltov, "The Anaphora and the Thanksgiving Prayer," 490–91.

31. Zheltov, "The Anaphora and the Thanksgiving Prayer," 489–96, 502.

32. Giraudo, *In unum corpus*, 359–65.

33. Johannes Betz, *Die Eucharistie in der Zeit der griechischen Väter*, vol. 1.1: *Die Aktualpräsenz der Person und des Heilswerkes Jesu im Abendmahl nach der vorephesinischen griechischen Patristik* (Freiburg im Breisgau: Herder, 1955), 178–80.

Finally, we can mention the Liturgy of St. Mark, for which our extant text probably comes from after the year 380, shortly after the time of Serapion. The Anaphora of Mark includes an institution narrative as well as multiple references to sacrifice, especially in relation to the theme of memorial. It is strongly influenced by 1 Corinthians.[34]

The Egyptian tradition, exemplified in the texts just discussed, was one of the sources for the Roman liturgy. We have no complete text for the Roman canon of the third or fourth centuries. We have only partial witnesses to its content before the sixth century, for example, in the catechesis of St. Ambrose of Milan.[35] Ambrose witnesses to the Eucharistic prayer in his diocese in the late fourth century. Not only is it very similar to the later Roman canon (e.g. that of St. Gregory the Great), but the prayer that Ambrose mentions was already close to the fourth-century Roman canon and might even have drawn upon it as a source.[36] The following comes from Ambrose's *On the Sacraments*, likely composed about 380 or 390:

> The priest speaks. He says: "Perform for us this oblation written, reasonable, acceptable, which is a figure of the body and blood of our Lord Jesus Christ. On the day before He suffered He took bread in His holy hands, looked toward heaven, toward you, holy Father omnipotent, eternal God, giving thanks, blessed, broke, and having broken it gave it to the Apostles and His disciples, saying: 'Take and eat of this, all of you; for this is my body, which shall be broken for many.'" Take note. "Similarly, also on the day before He suffered, after they had dined, He took the chalice, looked toward heaven, toward thee, holy Father omnipotent, eternal God and giving thanks He blessed it, and gave it to the Apostles and His disciples, saying: 'Take and drink of this, all of you; for this is my blood.'"[37]

34. Bouyer, *Eucharist*, 192, 212–13.

35. D. M. Hope, "The Medieval Western Rites," in *The Study of the Liturgy*, rev. ed., ed. Cheslyn Jones, Geoffrey Wainwright, Edward Yarnold and Paul Bradshaw (Oxford: Oxford University Press, 1992), 267.

36. Uwe Michael Lang, "Rhetoric of Salvation: The Origins of Latin as the Language of the Roman Liturgy," in *The Genius of the Roman Rite: Historical, Theological, and Pastoral Perspectives on Catholic Liturgy*, ed. U. M. Lang (Chicago: Hillenbrand Books, 2009), 29; Hans Bernhard Meyer, *Eucharistie: Geschichte, Theologie, Pastoral*, Gottesdienst der Kirche 4 (Regensburg: Friedrich Pustet, 1989), 114.

37. Ambrose of Milan, *The Sacraments*, bk. 4, chap. 5, nos. 21–22, in Ambrose of Milan, *Theological and Dogmatic Works*, trans. Roy Deferrari, The Fathers of the Church 44 (Washington, D.C.: The Catholic University of America Press, 1963).

The liturgies of Milan and Rome placed great emphasis on the institution narrative, especially by adding various details about Christ's gestures to that narrative.[38]

It is likely that all third- and fourth-century Eucharistic prayers known to us contained an institution narrative, with the possible exception of Addai & Mari. These include Addai and Mari's liturgical cousins Sharar and Theodore (I discuss all three anaphora below), book eight of the Apostolic Constitutions, the Anaphora of St. James, the Anaphora of St. Basil, and the Anaphora of St. John Chrysostom.[39] Let us note that the inclusion of the institution narrative does not constitute proof that it was considered a sufficient prayer (or complete sacramental form) to effect the change of the gifts. Rather, it manifests an awareness that the Last Supper was the foundational event for the Eucharist: the liturgy is a renewal of the memorial that Christ himself celebrated.

The Rite of Addai and Mari: A Eucharist without the Institution Narrative?

I now come to the most debated ancient Eucharistic prayer, Addai and Mari, used by the Assyrian Church of the East, a community that lost full communion with the West following the Council of Ephesus in 431.[40] That rupture was caused by poor communication rather than heresy, as the Assyrian community was no longer within the borders of the Byzantine empire. The anaphora belongs to the Eastern Syrian liturgical family. At least in its modern form, it has no institution narrative. The Chaldean Catholics, who have been in communion with Rome for centuries, also pray the Addai and Mari, but with an explicit institution narrative. In 2001, with the approval of John Paul II, the Pontifical Council for Promoting Christian Unity recognized the use of the Addai and Mari without an institution narrative in the Assyrian Church of the East.[41]

38. Another witness that could be invoked here is Cyril of Jerusalem. Edward J. Yarnold explains why one cannot appeal to Cyril as a reliable witness to a Eucharistic Prayer that lacked an institution narrative. On the contrary, it seems more likely that he employed that narrative. See Yarnold's essay, "Anaphoras without Institution Narratives?," *Studia Patristica* 30 (1997): 401–6.

39. See Meyer, *Eucharistie: Geschichte, Theologie, Pastoral*, 108–9, 138–39.

40. William Macomber, "The Ancient Form of the Anaphora of the Apostles," in *East of Byzantium: Syria and Armenia in the Formative Period*, ed. Nina Gargoian, Thomas Mathews and Robert Thomson (Washington, D.C.: Centre for Byzantine Studies, 1982), 79–80.

41. The English text of the Guidelines of "Admission to the Eucharist between the Chaldean

The oldest manuscripts of Addai and Mari go back to the tenth century. Scholars have attempted to reconstruct earlier versions of the rite, but we do not know its exact content in the first few centuries.[42] In recent decades, a majority of liturgists, including Robert Taft and Nicholas Russo, have argued that Addai and Mari prayer is a major ancient witness to a Eucharistic liturgy without the institution narrative.

The text of the anaphora contains scattered allusions to the institution narrative, but the words of institution are not found together in one place. Here is the heart of the prayer, preceded by the line numbers of the critical edition:

> 51 And we also, O my Lord, thy unworthy, frail and miserable servants, who are gathered [in thy name] and stand before thee,
> 52 and have received by tradition the example which is from thee,
> 53 rejoicing and glorifying and exalting and commemorating
> 54 and celebrating this great and awesome mystery
> 55 of the passion and death and resurrection of our Lord Jesus Christ.[43]

There are several arguments that, in ancient practice, the institution narrative was not used in Addai and Mari. First, all the manuscripts for this liturgy are missing the words of institution. Now liturgical texts usually contain markers at places where secret prayers are to be inserted from memory, but we seem to have no such indications for an institution narrative.[44] Second, it is perplexing how the use of this narrative would have disappeared in recent centuries, if it was originally present. Third, the lack of an institution narrative is said to prolong or mirror a similar lacuna that was commonly found in the Eucharistic liturgy of the first three centuries (one supposedly also reflected in the *Didache*).[45] This last argument

---

Church and the Assyrian Church of the East" by the Pontifical Council for Christian Unity is found at: www.vatican.va/roman_curia/pontifical_councils/chrstuni/documents/rc_pc_chrstuni_doc_20011025_chiesa-caldea-assira_en.html.

42. Uwe Michael Lang, "Eucharist without Institution Narrative? The Anaphora of Addai and Mari Revisited," in *Die Anaphora von Addai und Mari: Studien zu Eucharistie und Einsetzungsworten*, ed. Uwe Michael Lang (Bonn: Nova & Vetera, 2007), 31–37.

43. Anthony Gelston, *The Eucharistic Prayer of Addai and Mari* (Oxford: Clarendon Press, 1992), 55. I give the line numbers from Gelston's edition.

44. Nicholas Russo, "The Validity of the Anaphora *Addai and Mari*: Critiques of the Critique," in *Issues in Eucharistic Praying in East and West: Essays in Liturgical and Theological Analysis*, ed. Maxwell E. Johnson (Collegeville, Minn.: Liturgical Press, 2010), 37–39.

45. Russo, "The Validity," 27. Russo's reading of the *Didache* contradicts the analysis of Rordorf

is the weakest, as it is mostly based on hypothetical reconstructions of the sources for surviving liturgical texts.

One can mention four arguments in favor of the thesis that, from early on and over many subsequent centuries, the words of institution were part of an oral tradition and were added by the celebrant from memory. First, the main paragraph of Addai and Mari begins in an odd way: "And we also O my Lord" (line 51). This sentence also lacks a verb, which may suggest a deliberate lacuna in the text. This would be an ideal place to add a memorized phrase. Also, the subsequent lines contain terms such has "having received by tradition" and "commemorating," which likely evoke 1 Corinthians 11 and its account of the Last Supper.[46]

Second, the last phrase of the main paragraph of the Eucharistic prayer (lines 51–55) parallels the conclusion of the heart of another major Eucharistic prayer in the ancient eastern Syrian tradition, called Theodore (attributed to Theodore of Mopsuestia). The institution narrative directly precedes the conclusion of that section in Theodore.[47] Perhaps Theodore preserved in writing what Addai and Mari possessed by oral tradition.[48]

Third, Addai and Mari bears strong resemblances to the Eucharistic prayer of the ancient Maronite rite, called the Third Anaphora of St. Peter, or Sharar. Addai and Mari and Sharar may share a common ancestor, one that predates the Council of Ephesus.[49] Interestingly, Sharar does have an institution narrative. It comes at the part of the Eucharistic prayer that is very similar to Addai and Mari (before line 47 in the critical edi-

---

and Niederwimmer, which I employed above (Russo, "The Validity," 27–28). Yarnold rightly recalls the highly fragmentary nature of pre-fourth-century liturgical texts ("Anaphoras without Institution Narratives?," 395–410).

46. These arguments were proposed by Bernard Botte. See Russo, "The Validity," 44–45.

47. Stephen B. Wilson, "The Anaphora of the Apostles Addai and Mari," in *Essays on Early Eastern Eucharistic Prayers*, ed. Paul F. Bradshaw (Collegeville, Minn.: The Liturgical Press, 1997), 23–24, 34.

48. Bouyer, *Eucharist*, 151–52. In fact, the Chaldean Catholic Church preserves three ancient anaphora: (1) Addai and Mari (or the Anaphora of the Apostles), still used today, with the words of institution; (2) Theodore; and (3) and Nestorius. The latter two prayers date from the late fourth or early fifth centuries, and each includes the institution narrative. Interestingly, ancient liturgical commentators such as Narsai give no indication that Theodore and Nestorius have innovated in using the words of institution. See *Missel chaldéen: L'ordre des mystères avec les trois anaphores, selon le rite de la sainte Eglise de l'Orient*, ed. Francis Alichoran and P. Perrier (Paris: Eglise chaldéenne, 1982), 12, 16–17, 82–83.

49. Macomber, "The Ancient Form," 79–80.

tion).[50] Thus, Addai and Mari has two cousins, and both have an institution narrative.

Fourth, there is some modern evidence of this kind of insertion from memory. In the nineteenth century, Chaldean Catholic priests who celebrated the Addai and Mari rite told Anglican missionaries that the institution narrative was always said from memory, and thus was part of the lived rite.[51] Their report of the place of insertion matches well with the clues that Gabriel of Qatraya, a seventh-century Syrian commentator on the liturgy, seems to give on the place of the institution narrative in the rite.[52]

Where does this leave us? The historical question remains open. Still, a word of caution is in order: while, today, many historians of the liturgy maintain that the ancient rite of Addai and Mari had no institution narrative, fifty years ago, the majority of liturgists (including Louis Bouyer) held the exact opposite opinion.[53]

Beyond the issue of the words of institution, other features of Addai and Mari should be indicated. Before the passage cited above, the prayer mentions the memorial of Christ's body and blood, which are offered on a pure and holy altar. This memorial is celebrated as God has taught, a teaching transmitted by the forefathers in the faith. By tradition, the "figure" has been received, a reference to the body and blood present in sacramental mode.[54] The entire Paschal Mystery is the object of the memorial: The Passion, Death, and Resurrection of Christ. Then follows an epiclesis, asking the Spirit to bless and sanctify the oblation. Thus, Addai and Mari appeals to revelation as the source of the Eucharist, received by tradition. The sacrificial language is clear, while the theme of memorial tends to dominate. Hence, even considered without the institution narrative, Addai and Mari manifests a strong awareness of the Last Supper as the origin of the Eucharist.

50. Russo, "The Validity," 45.

51. Santogrossi, "Anaphoras without Institution Narrative," 44.

52. Lang, "Eucharist without Institution?," 61. We might also note a general feature of early Christian liturgical practice that provides an important principle in the interpretation of ancient witnesses and texts on the liturgy: before the fourth century, celebrants regularly recited parts of the Eucharistic prayer from memory (see Sheerin, "Eucharistic Liturgy," 716). Bouyer notes that ancient liturgical manuscripts without the words of institution are legion, yet we know from various sources that the very same rites did include those words (*Eucharist*, 152).

53. Bouyer, *Eucharist*, 151–52.

54. Giraudo, *In unum corpus*, 355–56.

Scripture and Early Tradition on the Institution of the Eucharist: A Summary

We can now synthesize what Scripture and the witnesses of the first four centuries tell us about the institution of the Eucharist, directly or indirectly. First, the Scriptures, Justin Martyr, Irenaeus, and Cyprian, as well as each of the early Eucharistic prayers mentioned above, recognize that the Eucharistic ritual that they celebrate has its historical origin with Jesus of Nazareth. Second, the same sources identify this origin with the Last Supper. The Synoptic Gospels, 1 Corinthians, Irenaeus, and Cyprian are most explicit on this matter. Yet even Addai and Mari has references to the Last Supper. Third, our sources recognize that Christ determined some of the specific elements for celebrating the Eucharist.

We can recognize Christ's intention of instituting the following elements as part of the Eucharistic liturgy. First, Jesus instituted the New Passover for the Church. The Synoptic accounts, Paul, and later witnesses (such as Irenaeus) testify to this. This also means that Christ established a sacrifice (as a memorial celebration of the Passion): the allusion to sacrifice is strong in the Last Supper accounts. Irenaeus saw this beautifully, while Serapion makes abundant use of sacrificial language in his version of the institution narrative.[55] Second, the most radically new aspect of the ritual is that Jesus' body and blood now take the place of the Passover lamb. Of course, this calls for a transformation of the gifts. In other words, the Eucharist exceeds the miracle of the Old Testament manna (Jn 6), and is not unlike the Incarnation of the Son of God in Mary's womb (Justin Martyr). The anaphora consistently point to a mysterious change of the gifts. I will take up that issue again in the chapter on Eucharistic presence. Third, all of the first-century evidence points to the inclusion of the words of institution in the liturgy celebrated by the first Christians, whose prayers are echoed in the slightly different New Testament versions of the Last Supper. The ancient anaphora also consistently use the institution narrative, while Addai and Mari (at the very least) makes allusions to the Last Supper event. Appeal to other Eucharistic prayers in antiquity that supposedly lacked an institution narrative is based on

55. Chapter 5 will include a study of sacrificial language in other Eucharistic prayers.

fragmentary evidence or the hypothetical reconstruction of sources for actual liturgical documents. Fourth, like the Passover, the Church has a sacred obligation to continue this celebration: "do this in memory of me." Two of the biblical witnesses explicitly mention this, yet all the New Testament accounts of the Last Supper reflect the liturgical practices of their respective communities. Irenaeus and Cyprian clearly saw the importance of continuing this memorial. The command to celebrate the memorial fits perfectly with the Passover setting. Fifth, the command involves no mechanical repetition.[56] For example, already in the first century, Christians celebrated the New Passover without a lamb, and did so not annually but frequently. The manner of celebration was to follow the apostolic tradition, which continues to be handed down, an emphasis found especially in Irenaeus and in Addai and Mari.[57]

A Systematic Theology of the Institution of the Eucharist

Scripture, several early Church Fathers, and the oldest Eucharistic Prayers thus give valuable indications of Christ's work of instituting a sacrament at the Last Supper. My next step is to take a brief look at the theology of the institution of sacraments. Here, I take a scholastic approach rooted in medieval theology and confirmed by the Councils of Florence and Trent. I take up a systematic view, that is, an organized view of particular theological themes that seeks to integrate Scripture, liturgical practice, and the teaching of the councils, popes, and great theologians.

56. Later theologians understood this well. See, for example, Thomas Aquinas, *Commentary on the Sentences*, bk. 4, d. 8, q. 1, a. 4, quaestincula 1, ad 1, in *Commentary on the Sentences, Book IV, Distinctions 1–13*, trans. Beth Mortensen, Latin/English Edition of the Works of St. Thomas Aquinas 7 (Green Bay, Wisc.: Aquinas Institute, 2017), 346.

57. The recent statement on the unity of Catholic-Lutheran Eucharistic doctrine by a German ecumenical working group bases much of its proposal on historical claims of differing and partly contradictory traditions in the New Testament witness to ancient Eucharistic celebrations, differences that the document traces into the first centuries of the Church, partly by relying on the *Didache*, chapter 9 (105). The ecumenical paper goes well beyond the historical data as it bases its ecclesial and pastoral program on debatable scholarly hypotheses. See Volker Leppin and Dorothea Sattler, eds., *Together at the Lord's Table: A Votum of the Ecumenical Working Group of Lutheran and Catholic Theologians* (Freiburg im Breisgau: Herder, 2020), 89–105.

General Principles for a Theology of the Sacrament's Institution

I begin with some general principles of the institution of the sacraments, so that we can more fruitfully consider the institution of the Eucharist. First, sacraments are means of grace, and grace is a gift of God. Therefore, only God can institute sacraments: only the giver of grace determines the means of grace.[58] Now Catholic theologians ancient and modern, from east and west, continue to debate the meaning of grace. Yet the Catholic understanding is that we are dealing especially with an intrinsic transformation of the human being that is beyond the order of nature (the east prefers to speak of divinization). Second, the Eucharist's institution comes through a revelation. For some sacraments, this revelation emerged especially in tradition and only vaguely in Scripture, as the Church reflected over the centuries on the order inscribed within God's plan of salvation (e.g., Paul's teaching on the spousal bond between Christ and his Church implies the sacramentality of Christian matrimony). Other sacraments (especially baptism) were instituted through a more explicit revelation of Christ and transmitted by the apostles. Third, to institute a sacrament does not always mean determining the specific rite to be used. For example, Jesus need not have instructed the apostles to ordain priests by laying hands on the candidate and then saying a prayer of ordination.[59] It is one thing to institute a sacrament, it is another to fix the precise words and material sign used. Here, we must distinguish between the substance of a sacrament and its outward expression, between the meaning and the expression of meaning, between signification and particular signs that are the vehicles or means of signification.[60] I will come back to this distinction shortly. Fourth, the Church's power over the sacrament is limited.[61] As the *Constitution on the Sacred Liturgy* (*Sacrosanctum Concilium*) states, "the liturgy is made up of unchangeable elements divinely instituted, and of el-

58. Bernard Leeming, *Principles of Sacramental Theology* (London: Longmans, 1956), 385.

59. Leeming, *Principles of Sacramental Theology*, 416, 421.

60. This distinction was especially developed by the seventeenth-century theologian John of Saint-Thomas. See Jean-Philippe Revel, *Traité des sacrements*, vol. 1, *Baptême et sacramentalité*, part 1: *Origine et signification du baptême* (Paris: Cerf, 2004), 148.

61. Leeming, *Principles of Sacramental Theology*, 397, 417.

ements subject to change."[62] The Church can determine and make explicit the sacramental forms only implicitly contained in the New Testament.[63] Here, the Church can determine the signs, but not the signification. The latter needs to have its foundation in Christ's revelatory work.[64] A sacrament's signification is instituted by Christ, even if that institution was only *recognized* after many centuries of reflection on revelation. However, Jesus' use of a sign does not, in and of itself, indicate that he intended to determine that sign as the sacramental form of the whole Church.

Let us return to the third principle mentioned above. The distinction between signification and signs helps us to understand how Jesus instituted the Eucharist, what he determined and what he left undetermined. This will also allow us to account for the legitimate diversity found among the various venerable liturgical rites.

By the term *signification*, I refer to a meaning that is to be communicated. When that meaning is expressed through a sign that is apt to express it, then (given other factors) we have a sacrament that effects what it signifies. The baptismal formula joined to the pouring of water over the forehead expresses the meaning that the Trinity is saving and purifying the person being baptized. Signification is universal: it can be transmitted to all cultures. It therefore transcends any particular language.

Words and gestures are vehicles for signification. Words joined to gestures such as the act of pouring water over the forehead of a catechumen are a means to indicate meaning. The sacramental signs are a synthesis or unity of these parts: word and gesture. In the case of the Eucharist, the gesture is performed with material gifts. We can recall Augustine's famous phrase: "The word is added to the elemental substance, and it becomes a sacrament."[65] The signification occurs through what are called the form and matter of a sacrament. Form and matter are a composite sign that

62. *Sacrosanctum Concilium*, no. 21.

63. Perrin, *L'institution des sacrements dans le Commentaire des Sentences de saint Thomas*, Bibliothèque de la Revue Thomiste (Paris: Parole et Silence, 2008), 388, 591.

64. Thomas Aquinas, *Summa theologiae* III, q. 60, a. 7, ad 1; Edward Schillebeeckx, *L'économie sacramentelle du salut*, trans. Yvon van der Have, Studia Friburgensia 95 (Fribourg, Switzerland: Academic Press, 2004), 312.

65. Augustine, tractate 80, no. 3, in *Tractates on the Gospel of John, 55–111*, trans. John W. Rettig, The Fathers of the Church 90 (Washington, D.C.: The Catholic University of America Press, 1994), 117. The doctrine of sacramental form and matter is a development of patristic theology. See Schillebeeckx, *L'économie sacramentelle du salut*, 290–304.

expresses a sacramental intention. The words uttered by the right minister with the proper intention are the form, while the gesture done is the matter (e.g., taking bread and wine). The sign is attained only by joining these together.[66]

Our consideration of the signification-sign distinction, form and matter, and related themes gives insight on how the institution of the sacraments works. It gives us a framework for the historical portion of our study, while that history in turn brings content to the framework. The witnesses to the Eucharist's historical origin in Jesus' celebrating the Last Supper with his disciples show us the divine origin we need if the Eucharist is to be a means whereby grace is given. Jesus intentionally instituted a new ritual, a New Passover. The Last Supper's many references to his coming death show that he instituted a memorial celebration of his sacrifice on the Cross. He instituted the gift of his very self, his body and blood: a sacrament, that is, a visible means of grace. He intended this ritual to be continued in the Church, and the Church understood this. We will soon see that history also supports the claim that Jesus intended to institute the matter of bread and wine for the Eucharist.

Did Christ establish the words of institution as the sacramental form, as the means to change bread and wine into body and blood? Based on our study above, we cannot give a definitive answer. First, with the exception of Ambrose and the liturgical tradition of the west (to be studied again in chapter 7), it is not clear whether the early Church Fathers and anaphora employed the institution narrative *with the particular intention* of converting the gifts by that precise prayer and in that moment. Second, the possible absence of the institution narrative in the ancient practice of Addai and Mari would argue against the institution of this specific form by Christ. Third, Trent deliberately refused to define whether Christ changed bread and wine at the Last Supper with these words or by some other means.[67] That omission signals the need for caution.

However, in uttering the words of institution, Christ did establish the signification, or essential meaning, of the sacrament of the Eucharist. These words show that he gives his very body and blood, that he gives

66. Leeming, *Principles of Sacramental Theology*, 409, 417; Schillebeeckx, *L'économie sacramentelle du salut*, 310–12.

67. Giraudo, *In unum corpus*, 552.

them in a sacrificial mode (as he prophetically signifies the separation of his body and blood at Calvary), and that this sacrifice is inseparable from his offering on the Cross. The Church's task is to determine the form and matter (or specific words and gestures) that aptly express the signification established by Christ for the Eucharist. This is precisely what the Council of Florence did in the fifteenth century for the Latin Church (as we will see in chapter 7).

The Council of Trent has left us a teaching on the institution of the Eucharist. In her *Decree on the Sacrament of the Eucharist* (from the year 1551), Trent taught that Christ instituted the Eucharist at the Last Supper. He becomes truly present in these gifts after his blessing.[68] In the *Decree on the Sacrifice of the Mass* (from the year 1562), Trent proclaims that, at the Last Supper, Jesus instituted a sacrifice.[69] The Council also teaches that Jesus instituted the apostles as priests at the Last Supper by saying, "Do this in memory of me." He thus ordered them to perpetuate his sacrifice.[70] Finally, Vatican II reaffirms that, at the Last Supper, Christ instituted the Eucharistic sacrifice.[71]

The Material Signs Used for the Eucharist

Jesus instituted the Eucharist as spiritual nourishment for God's people. He gave the Church particular signs of this nourishment, in fulfillment of Old Testament figures of the Eucharist. Scripture and the early liturgical tradition manifest the institution of the signs of bread and wine. We will study their significance and also consider the divergent eastern and western uses of leavened and unleavened bread.

In ancient Palestine, bread was the basic daily food, and wheat bread was the most common type of cereal.[72] We have seen that the Last Supper was a Passover meal. Perhaps starting with the reform brought by the Book of Deuteronomy, Passover was closely bound to the Feast of Un-

68. Chapters 1–2, DH 1636–38.

69. Chapter 1, DH 1740. For an excellent study of Trent and the Eucharist, see Florent Urfels, *Pâque du Messie: Introduction à une théologie eucharistique du judaïsme*, Collège des Bernardins 20 (Paris: Parole et Silence, 2013), 358–59.

70. Canon 2, DH 1752.

71. *Sacrosanctum Concilium*, no. 47; see also no. 7.

72. Roger Gaïse, *Les signes sacramentels de l'eucharistie dans l'église latine: Études théologiques et historiques*, Studia Friburgensia 89 (Fribourg, Switzerland: Éditions universitaires, 2001), 48–49.

leavened Bread. This feast occurred at the beginning of the barley harvest, when the new bread was consumed. Matthew and Mark report that the Last Supper happened on the first day of the Feast of Unleavened Bread. Some scholars hold that Jesus and the apostles could have eaten barley bread at the Last Supper.[73] The mingling of the two feasts (Passover and Unleavened Bread) and the uncertainty about how these feasts were fused in practice in the time of Jesus entail the following consequence: we cannot say with absolute historical certitude whether Jesus used wheat bread at the Last Supper.[74] However, from a strictly historical perspective, it is very probable that Jesus used wheat bread. For the Synoptic and Pauline accounts of the Last Supper all refer to the bread with the Greek term *artos*.[75] In everyday first-century Greek (*koine*), the term *artos* usually referred to wheat bread.[76]

The early tradition confirms the widespread if not universal liturgical use of wheat bread. First, we find no evidence of any common use of barley bread for the Eucharist in the early Church. Second, the early Church controversies about the kind of food and drink used at the liturgy concern items such as cheese, wine, and water, but not the type of bread. Third, whenever early Christian authors refer to the Eucharistic food, they speak of *artos*. Here, we can cite chapter 14 of the *Didache* and Justin Martyr's *First Apology*.[77] Irenaeus refers to the offering of "wheat and grape, bread and wine" as he discusses the sacrifice of the New Covenant.[78] Later on, Augustine speaks of the common use of wheat bread for the Eucharist.[79] At ancient Jewish feasts, wine was always consumed, whereas water was drunk at other meals, at least by the poor. Jesus certainly drank wine at the Passover. We saw that the Eucharistic cup may have been the third cup

73. See Gaïse, *Les signes sacramentels*, 52–54, 58.

74. Bertrand-Marie Perrin, *L'institution des sacrements*, 392.

75. Mt 26:26, Mk 14:22, Lk 22:19, 1 Cor 11:23–24.

76. Ángel García Ibáñez, *L'eucaristia, dono e mistero: Trattato storico-dogmatico sul mistero eucaristico*, Sussidi di teologia (Rome: EDUSC, 2006), 493.

77. Justin Martyr, *First Apology*, chap. 67, nos. 3–5; For an overview, see García Ibáñez, *L'eucaristia, dono e mistero*, 494.

78. Irenaeus of Lyon, *Treatise Against Heresies*, bk. 4, chap. 17, no. 5; Orbe, *Introduction à la théologie*, 1:697, 724.

79. Augustine, Sermon 227. See the collection, Augustine, *Sermons (184–229Z) on the Liturgical Seasons*, trans. Edmund Hill, Works of St. Augustine 3.6 (Hyde Park, N.Y.: New City Press, 1993).

of wine in the Passover ritual.[80] The wine was mixed with water, so as to make its consumption more pleasant (pure wine still had grains).

Apocryphal literature from the second and third centuries shows that some communities seem to have celebrated the Eucharist without wine, meaning, only with bread (see the Acts of John, Acts of Andrew, and Acts of Thomas). These texts are apocryphal, because they incorrectly claim to have an apostle as their author or as their main source. Some of these are Gnostic works that promoted various doctrinal errors. This minority practice seems to have continued in some regions through the sixth century. This explains why the Council of Hippo in 393 and the Council of Orleans in 541 forbid Eucharistic celebrations without wine.[81] Another group in early Christianity celebrated the Eucharist with bread and water, hence their name "The Aquarians." The late-second-century Alexandrian writer Clement of Alexandria and the third-century bishop Cyprian of Carthage mention and reject this practice.[82]

Here, the witness of Cyprian is crucial. In "Letter 63," he states that God has commanded Christians to preserve the tradition of Jesus in their manner of offering the chalice. They are to do nothing else than what the Lord himself did at the Last Supper, that is, to offer wine mixed with water, an offering performed in his memory (a practice already attested by Justin Martyr).[83] There is no offering of the blood of Christ if there is no wine in the chalice. The sacrifice of the Lord is not legitimately celebrated if our oblation and sacrifice do not correspond to the Passion, that is, to the Last Supper.[84]

The use of wine at Mass has been the standard practice since antiquity. We find references to the use of bread and wine of the grape all through the ancient liturgical families. The Church Fathers confirm this. The same practice continued through the medieval and modern eras. The Council of Florence, in its *Decree for the Armenians* (*Exsultate Deo*), determined that the matter or essential material sign of the Eucharist are wheat bread

80. Gaïse, *Les signes sacramentels*, 59–60; A. Bride, "Vin de Messe," *Dictionnaire de théologie catholique*, ed. É. Amann, vol. 15 (Paris: L. Letouzey et Âne, 1950), col. 1315.

81. Gaïse, *Les signes sacramentels*, 68–72.

82. Perrin, *L'institution des sacrements*, 111–12.

83. Justin Martyr, *First Apology*, chapter 65.

84. Cyprian of Carthage, "Letter 63," nos. 2, 9.

and wine of the grape.[85] The same Council accepted the use of leavened bread by the east. In her *Decree for the Greeks* (*Laetentur caeli*), Florence insists that each Church should follow her own venerable custom.[86]

As we consider the Eucharistic signification of bread and wine, we focus on the species or natural identity of the gifts, and not their pure chemical constitution. That is, we are dealing with fruits of the earth whose nature remains intact even if a small amount of other natural products (e.g., other grains) is mingled with them.[87] We are also dealing with man's harvest of nature's gift brought before God.

Bread and wine signify common, daily nourishment. They are associated with feasting, with banquets of fraternal and familial communion. They can signify the unity of those who partake of them: "Because there is one bread, we who are many are one body, for we all partake of the one bread" (1 Cor 10:17). As Augustine explains, "even as men of God knew this before us, our Lord, Jesus Christ, manifested his body and blood in those things which are reduced from many to some one thing. For the one is made into one thing from many grains, the other flows together into one thing from many grapes."[88] The many grains in one bread represent the unity of many believers, as the many grapes in one cup signify the same unity. Bread can be sweet, like manna in the desert. The use of bread evokes Jesus' appropriation of the manna imagery in John 6:35: "I am the bread of life." Wine can inebriate, signifying spiritual joy and ecstasy. The separate use of bread and wine (in the separate consecration) can also signify Christ's death, where the liquid signifies his blood separated from his body. Bread and wine are frequently found in Old Testament sacrifices, as in cereal offerings (Lv 7:9–14) and burnt offerings (Nm 28:11–14). Or again, in Genesis 14:17–18, Melchizedek offered bread and wine in sacrifice. The Letter to the Hebrews (chapter 7) links this mysterious figure with Christ and his priesthood.

We know that, from at least the time of Cyprian of Carthage, the mingling of water and wine, while not absolutely necessary for the valid-

85. Council of Florence, *Decree for the Armenians*, DH 1320.

86. Council of Florence, *Decree for the Greeks*, DH 1303.

87. Thomas Aquinas, *Summa theologiae* III, q. 74, a. 3, ad 3.

88. Augustine, *Tractates on the Gospel of John, 11–27*, tractate 26, no. 17.

ity of the Eucharist, communicates a rich meaning.[89] This gesture recalls that water and blood flowed from Christ's side on the Cross, and thus signifies his Passion, as well as the unity of the sacrifice of the Cross with the sacrifice of the Mass. The water also symbolizes the people, whose unity with Christ is signified by the mixing of water into wine.[90] The offertory prayer in the Roman rite recalls that the Son's taking on of our nature enables us to share in his divine nature. This participation in divine life comes especially through the Eucharistic liturgy.

The western practice of using unleavened bread draws its inspiration from the Synoptic Gospels. It recognizes the Last Supper as a Passover meal. However, in antiquity, the west also often used leavened bread, without controversy. But starting around the ninth century, the west has consistently used unleavened bread. The east has often preferred leavened bread.[91] One reason is the eastern tendency to follow the apparent chronology of John's Gospel instead of that of the Synoptic accounts. From this perspective, Jesus would have anticipated the Passover meal, and thus celebrated it before the Feast of Unleavened Bread began. So, since ancient times liturgical families in both east and west seem to have used both types of bread.[92] All of this illumines a theology of the institution of the Eucharist. Widespread and ancient diversity in the use of leavened and unleavened bread, a historical phenomenon that provoked no controversy until the early Middle Ages, manifests the Church's consciousness that the use or exclusion of leaven was not part of Christ's intention for the institution of this sacrament, even if, historically, Jesus used unleavened bread. The Eucharist's institution is not about a mechanical imitation of the Last Supper. In the Middle Ages, an unfortunate dispute arose about this issue. Yet east and west lived in peace with a legitimate diversity of practice for one thousand years. This should be no cause for division among us.

89. Cyprian of Carthage, "Letter 63," no. 13. See also Thomas Aquinas, *Summa theologiae* III, q. 74, a. 6–7; Council of Trent, *Decree on the Sacrifice of the Mass*, chapter 7, DH 1748; Joseph Pohle, *Lehrbuch der Dogmatik in sieben Büchern*, 7th ed., vol. 3., Wissenschaftliche Bibliothek, Series 1: Theologische Lehrbücher 22 (Paderborn, Germany: Ferdinand Schöningh, 1922), 244.

90. Thomas Aquinas, *Summa theologiae* III, q. 74, a. 6; Council of Trent, *Decree on the Sacrifice of the Mass*, chapter 7, DH 1748.

91. Joseph A. Jungmann, *The Mass of the Roman Rite: Its Origin and Development*, trans. Francis A. Brunner, vol. 2 (Notre Dame, Ind.: Christian Classics, 2012), 31–34.

92. Perrin, *L'institution des sacrements*, 394–97.

Aquinas explains that, when it comes to leaven, the priest should follow the practice of his own rite.[93] An eastern Orthodox priest sins by consecrating unleavened bread, and a Roman Catholic priest sins by consecrating leavened bread. In this example, each priest acts against the tradition and common practice of his ecclesial rite, thus disobeying his bishop and causing confusion among the faithful. But Aquinas thinks that when a priest celebrates the Byzantine rite with unleavened bread or the Latin rite with leavened bread, the bread being consecrated still becomes a true sacrament. In each case, the Eucharist is valid but illicit.

In recent years, some theologians and pastors have expressed the desire to use elements other than wheat bread for the Eucharist, for example, rice cakes. The Magisterium has remained consistent in its appeal to Scripture and tradition: only wheat bread and wine of the grape are valid matter for the Eucharist. Why is this so? First, bread and wine evoke a large range of biblical texts that foreshadow or express the Eucharist, from Melchizedek and the manna to the Jewish Passover and the Last Supper. Our liturgy diminishes its symbolic link with these teachings on the Eucharist when we begin to change the sign for motives of inculturation. But the sacramental signs should allow the faithful to make these connections through their liturgical participation and meditation on Scripture. The Eucharist must be seen within God's broader design of salvation, within a great web of revealed symbols. Second, the ultimate signification of the Eucharistic food and drink does not depend on our own regional, temporary cultural categories, but on the signification established by Christ, by the cultural setting that he chose, by the Jewish ritual that he consciously employed to institute the Eucharist, by the words, food, and drink that he decided to use. Attempts to change the Eucharistic food and drink tend to obscure the revealed source of the liturgy: the core of the Eucharistic liturgy comes from Christ, not from us. By remaining faithful to a venerable apostolic tradition, we can also better protect the Jewish roots of the Eucharist.

93. Thomas Aquinas, *Summa theologiae* III, q. 74, a. 4.

CHAPTER 4

CHRISTOLOGICAL AND ECCLESIOLOGICAL FOUNDATIONS FOR THE EUCHARIST

Christ established the Eucharist as the Church's highest act. Now the people of God receive the true manna from heaven as food for their earthly pilgrimage. This manna is Jesus' flesh and blood given at Passover, Israel's great feast, the new Passover that Christ celebrated with the apostles.

The subsequent chapters explore in systematic fashion the central themes of Eucharistic doctrine: the sacrificial identity of the Church's cultic act, the corporeal presence of Christ in her midst, the celebrant who leads the Church in worship, and the fruits of communing in Christ's body and blood, which builds up the Church. But first, we need a survey of some key Christological and ecclesiological themes that ground Eucharistic theology.

As a sacrament and sacrifice, the Eucharist was instituted by Christ as an inherent element of his Incarnation and his way of saving us by his particular historical deeds. Furthermore, as the greatest of the seven sacraments, the Eucharist constitutes the highest self-expression of the Church, she who is the universal sacrament of salvation. In turn, her sacramentality depends on Christ. Our focus thus turns to a theology of how the Incarnate Word saves, and how to contemplate the sacramentality of the Church by which Christ's saving action is made present anew.

I begin with a survey of the Christological ground of the Church's sacramentality. This will allow us to integrate a key element of Vatican II's ecclesiology. I then turn to a crucial Christological theme that underlies sacramental doctrine, namely, Christ's humanity as an instrumental cause of grace. Here we meditate on Christ's "downward mediation" of divine life, which involves the Church's sacraments as instruments of grace. From there, I will hone in on another Christological theme, his "upward mediation," which is his sacrifice on the Cross, an offering renewed at every Eucharistic celebration. This study calls for a sketch of some biblical images of sin, as well as an overview of various kinds of sacrifice in the Old Testament. Christ came to fulfill the whole Torah, and his work climaxed in the Last Supper, Calvary, and his Resurrection.

Christ as the Foundation of Sacramentality

The Incarnation makes possible the sacramental order, from the Church's sacramentality to the seven sacraments, and here we can mention four ways in which the Incarnation does this. First, sacramentality is all about mediating grace. The Word made flesh is the unique mediator of salvation. In turn, the Church and the sacraments are mediations that extend this saving work, always in dependence on Christ's mediation. Second, the Incarnation means that God's salvation comes to us in a visible, concrete, corporeal mode, especially via Christ's Passion and Resurrection. Third, the words, deeds, and sufferings of Christ are simultaneously salutary and revelatory (like God's word in Scripture, which simultaneously creates and communicates). One can even say: Christ revealed by saving and he saved by revealing. For example, he dies out of love on the Cross, thus simultaneously reconciling us with God and revealing the depth of divine love for us. This too is reflected in the Church and her sacraments. The speaking of the words of consecration over the gifts manifests Christ's presence on the altar and simultaneously effects that very presence. Fourth, Christ's saving deeds are at once divine and human: his two natures operate together. By analogy, the Church's proclamation of the Word, her worship, and the celebration of the sacraments are human deeds by which the Holy Spirit acts.

Now some theologians would prefer to speak of Christ's sacramentality.[1] Following Emmanuel Perrier, I will avoid this term, for the following reasons. Sacraments are signs of invisible, saving realities. Now Christ's humanity is a sign not of his divinity, but of his person. His humanity truly belongs to him, being substantially united to the person of the Logos. Furthermore, the reality of salvation is accomplished in his flesh. His visible deeds are not signs of another reality that is saving, but fully participate in the act of salvation. Those deeds are at once human and divine.[2] By contrast, the Eucharistic signs of bread and wine signify and contain a saving reality, but those signs (the accidents) are not themselves a saving reality. The way that Christ saves grounds sacramentality while remaining above it.

Yet sacramentality is clearly rooted in Christ. Also, our need for the Church and sacraments is partly a consequence of Christ's Ascension, as he is no longer visible to us. Henceforth, we can encounter Christ in a concrete, visible mode, via the "extension" of the Incarnation that is the Church.[3] The Book of Acts would seem to call precisely for that extension, for it often presents the disciples and their ministry as mirror images of Jesus as he is portrayed in the Gospel of Luke.

The Church as Sacrament of Communion

In the aftermath of a post-Tridentine ecclesiology, which often focused on the Church as a hierarchical institution, nineteenth-century theologians began to recover a more patristic vision of the Church as a mystery or as

1. Edward Schillebeeckx, *Christ the Sacrament of the Encounter with God* (Kansas City, Mo.: Sheed & Ward, 1963).

2. Emmanuel Perrier, "L'enjeu christologique de la satisfaction (II)," *Revue Thomiste* 103 (2003): 244–47.

3. Schillebeeckx, *Christ the Sacrament of the Encounter with God*, 41.

a sacrament of salvation. This theological movement bore fruit at Vatican II. The key text on this theme is found at the very beginning of the Council's *Dogmatic Constitution on the Church* (*Lumen Gentium*), which states that "the Church, in Christ, is in the nature of sacrament—a sign and instrument, that is, of communion with God and of unity among all men."[4] This passage offers the first description or definition of the Church in the whole document.

Benoît-Dominique de la Soujeole explains that Christ's humanity renders the divine life visible, and Christ's human deeds transmit a share in that life. The Church participates in the gifts imparted to Christ's humanity. For this reason, she can communicate that grace. Because she is joined to her head, she can transmit a share in his life. In other words, the Church does not simply make us holy, she *is* holy, though her members are sinners. The grace she possesses becomes visible by her various acts, such as worship, evangelization, and service of neighbor.[5] Theology can thus account for the Christocentrism of *Lumen Gentium*, including its description of sign and instrument.

Vatican II's revival of the patristic doctrine of the Church as a sacrament of salvation has engendered a long debate on how best to understand the nature of this sacramentality. I will adopt the interpretation of de la Soujeole, who synthesizes biblical, patristic, and scholastic doctrines while avoiding a perilous division between the visible and invisible Church.[6] We should distinguish these two elements of the Church without separating them, much as we distinguish Christ's two natures while seeing their unity in his person.

De la Soujeole recalls that the notion of sacramentality is applied in analogous ways: it must be employed with nuance. He defines the Church primarily as a sacrament of communion. De la Soujeole articulates the Church's sacramental nature not by analogy with a generic definition of sacrament, nor by analogy with all seven sacraments, but in relation to the Eucharist. I will survey his account of the Church's sacramentality and

4. *Lumen Gentium*, no. 1.

5. Benoît-Dominique de la Soujeole, *Introduction to the Mystery of the Church*, trans. Michael J. Miller, Thomistic Ressourcement 3 (Washington, D.C.: The Catholic University of America Press, 2014), 320–22.

6. Guy Mansini, "Lumen Gentium," in *The Reception of Vatican II*, ed. Matthew L. Lamb and Matthew Levering (Oxford: Oxford University Press, 2017), 66–68.

then turn to the theme of communion. As an entryway to the topic, we need an overview of the Eucharist's sacramentality.

Starting with medieval theology, the Eucharist has been fruitfully analyzed via a threefold structure: it is a sign (bread and wine, and the prayer of consecration), it contains a reality immediately signified (Christ's body and blood), and an ultimate reality that is given (grace). The articulation of this threefold structure in sacramental theology finds its origins in Augustine's theology of baptism, whence the scholastic theologians applied it to the other sacraments. In Latin, this triple structure is called *sacramentum tantum*, *res et sacramentum*, and *res tantum*. The sign, or *sacramentum tantum*, involves the visible aspect of the sacrament. The sign is fruitful: under the signs of bread and wine consecrated by the priest, Christ's body and blood are brought to us. The same body and blood are the *res et sacramentum*. The sign contains a hidden, sacred reality: it is a mystery. The sign directly signifies the presence of Christ's body and blood. Yet these gifts in turn signify and grant a share in divine life or grace, the *res tantum*. Jesus' body and blood also signify the body that is his Church, and they impart a deeper share in her unity by an outpouring of charity (the *res*). The *res et sacramentum* abides, while the *res tantum* is given in a particular moment to those who receive the Eucharist with the proper disposition (a distinction which I will explore more fully in subsequent chapters).

This threefold structure beautifully summarizes the Eucharistic mystery. De la Soujeole argues that the same structure offers the most fruitful entryway into a theology of the Church's sacramentality. She is a communion of divine life—of knowing, loving, and hoping in God—a share in supernatural life that is at once personal and communal. This life of grace is hidden yet also manifested through deeds. Here we have the Church's *res tantum*, which is the invisible element, wherein the Church militant and the Church triumphant are one.

De la Soujeole notes that the Church is a visible sign of communion with God and one another (*sacramentum tantum*). We find this visibility of grace in the Church's rites, her moral discipline, and various aspects of her culture. The shared life of the Church (worship, service, and evangelization) are the manifestation of her life of grace. The Church's visible actions draw unbelievers to conversion, and, for those who have faith, these same actions can be perceived as signs of God's presence in the world. All of the Church's activity, from her prayer to the simplest service of neighbor, should dispose persons to an encounter with God and a share in his life. The Church is a fruitful sign: her deeds communicate salvation.

De la Soujeole proposes that the Church's *res et sacramentum* are the Gospel and the celebration of the sacraments. The act of sharing the Word and the sacramental rites signify the mystery of God's saving plan. At the same time, the transmission of the Word and the sacramental liturgies offer the grace signified thereby. The *res et sacramentum* both signifies and is a holy reality. The Gospel and sacraments are abiding, permanent realities. They remain with us, regardless of the holiness of the Church's pilgrim members. But we also need faith in order to see the Gospel as God's word and the sacraments as means of his grace.[7] The Church's *res et sacramentum* is a mystery of faith.

The Church as a sign possesses a *res et sacramentum*, which in turn causes a share in grace (the *res tantum*).[8] De la Soujeole therefore takes the heart of the Church's visibility and places it first under the *res et sacramentum*. Her other activities may or may not offer a share in divine life, but the Gospel and the sacraments do this by their very nature. Feeding the poor may or may not be an occasion of a new outpouring of grace for those accomplishing this good deed (or those receiving it), depending on the charity and the intention of the moral agent, but the Word and the sacraments always offer grace to those properly disposed.

The Church is a sacrament of communion. The latter theme allows an integration of Trinitarian theology, Christology, and the horizontal element of the Church. At its origin, communion is simply the life of the Triune God, the mutual knowledge and love of Father, Son, and Spirit. By the Incarnation, a share in this communion is offered to humanity.[9] That gift is proposed to us in a supreme mode in the Eucharist: "The cup of blessing which we bless, is it not a communion (*koinonia*) in the Blood of Christ? The bread which we break, is it not communion (*koinonia*) in

7. De la Soujeole, *Introduction to the Mystery of the Church*, 439–48.
8. De la Soujeole, *Introduction to the Mystery of the Church*, 448–49.
9. See 1 Jn 1:3–7.

the Body of Christ. Because there is one bread, we who are many are one body, for we all partake of the one bread."[10] Paul recognized that this communion is both vertical and horizontal.[11] The eighth-century theologian John Damascene comments: "It [the Eucharist] is called communion, and truly is so, because of our having communion through it with Christ and partaking both of His flesh and His divinity, and because through it we have communion with and are united to one another."[12]

At the heart of communion, we find charity, the gift that binds the Church's members together. Inspired by St. John and St. Augustine, *Lumen Gentium* describes charity as the origin, life, and aim of the Church: God's love in Christ, the love of Christ in the Church's members, and the perfect beatifying love obtained in the heavenly Jerusalem.[13] The Church as sacrament naturally expresses this communion of charity. De la Soujeole recalls that, for St. Paul, all the good done by the Church's members should be a spiritual sacrifice offered to God (Rom 12:1–3). The simple, daily sacrifices of the faithful culminate in the one perfect sacrifice of the Eucharistic liturgy. Here, we find the primary manifestation of the Church's life, one that is also (and not coincidentally) the most powerful site for the outpouring of grace. The liturgy is both sign and gift, that is, it is a fruitful sign. Here we find the visibility of the Church's life of charity, a visibility that in turn communicates a greater share in charity.[14] In the Eucharistic liturgy, the proclamation of the Word and the celebration of the sacrament is offered for the people's assent, their *Amen*. Here we see the descending aspect of the liturgy, the transmission of God's gifts. Word and sacrament deepen the ecclesial members' communion, for which de la Soujeole proposes a twofold form: a confessing and a celebrating community. Here we find the ascending aspect of the liturgy, our response to the gifts received. The liturgy spurs the faithful on to spread the Word by words and deeds, and to participate in the Church's liturgy with renewed fervor. The acts of confessing and celebrating manifest the ecclesial life of

10. 1 Cor 10:16–17, RSV translation modified.

11. De la Soujeole, *Introduction to the Mystery of the Church*, 453–59.

12. John Damascene, *On the Orthodox Faith*, trans. Frederic H. Chase, The Fathers of the Church 37 (New York: Fathers of the Church, 1958), bk. 4, chap. 13, p. 361.

13. *Lumen Gentium*, no. 5; see also de la Soujeole, *Introduction to the Mystery of the Church*, 464–65.

14. De la Soujeole, *Introduction to the Mystery of the Church*, 471.

grace, the life of communion. Confession means giving witness to God's saving plan in order to make known the saving economy whose center are the Incarnate Word and his Church. By participating again in the liturgy, we find a new participation in the Trinity's life. These considerations help to illumine the meaning of the famous expression of *Lumen Gentium*, that the Eucharist is the source and summit of the Church's life.[15]

The Church's sacramentality especially pertains to the Eucharistic liturgy. *Sacrosanctum Concilium* explains it thus: "the principal manifestation of the Church consists in the full, active participation of all God's holy people in the same liturgical celebrations, especially in the same Eucharist, in one prayer, at one altar, at which the bishop presides, surrounded by his college of priests and his ministers."[16] Here, the Council focuses on the Eucharist as an ecclesial sign, specifically as a sign of unity, which is expressed in the gathering of the local Church around her bishop. The conciliar text references several passages from St. Ignatius of Antioch's letters. The early-second-century martyr explains that the bishop represents Christ in the midst of the Church.[17] This theme is closely linked to another key image employed in *Sacrosanctum Concilium*: "In the earthly liturgy we take part in a foretaste of that heavenly liturgy."[18] Paul McPartlan notes the striking parallel between Ignatius's doctrine of the liturgy and several visions in the Book of the Apocalypse. According to Ignatius, the bishop images the glorified lamb at the center of the heavenly throne room, while the priests and ministers who immediately surround him image the elders who worship the lamb, and the lay faithful image the great multitude that joins in the celestial worship of the risen Lord. "The Eucharist, then, is the primary place where the heavenly mystery which is the Church is brought to bear upon this historical world, indeed it is the *sacrament* of the heavenly mystery, both containing and portraying it."[19]

15. *Lumen Gentium*, no. 11; de la Soujeole, *Introduction to the Mystery of the Church*, 485–87.

16. *Sacrosanctum Concilium*, no. 41.

17. Ignatius of Antioch, *Letters to the Smyrnaeans*, in *The Epistles of St. Clement of Rome and St. Ignatius of Antioch*, ed. James A. Kleist, Ancient Christian Writers 1 (New York: Paulist Press, 1978), no. 8, p. 93.

18. *Sacrosanctum Concilium*, no. 8.

19. Paul McPartlan, *Sacrament of Salvation: An Introduction to Eucharistic Ecclesiology* (Edinburgh: T&T Clark, 1995), 65.

Christ's Humanity Efficaciously Mediates Grace

The Church and the sacramental rites participate in the saving action of the Incarnate Word, and this in the time after the Ascension. The invisibility of the ascended Lord calls for the sacramentality of the Church that renders his dynamic presence visible. I now look more closely at one of two key ways in which the Church and the liturgy participate in Christ's saving action. I refer to the Church's share in Jesus' act of pouring out grace, which is also called Christ's downward mediation. The specific role of his humanity as an instrumental, efficient cause of grace illumines the entire sacramental order, and especially helps us to grasp the power of his Eucharistic body and blood. It also offers a powerful analogy that helps us understand how the bishop or priest presiding at Eucharist acts *in persona Christi*. After considering Christ's downward mediation, I will in turn take up his upward mediation, namely, Jesus' offering to the Father. The Church as sacrament shares in Christ's work of pouring out grace (downward mediation), and she manifests her identity most powerfully when she offers sacrifice together with her head (upward mediation).

The act of sharing or giving grace belongs not only to the Trinity, not only to Christ in his divinity, but also to Christ in his humanity. This theological claim is rooted in the Christology of several Church Fathers as well as the early Christological councils. Here, I set out in summary form Aquinas's theology of the efficacy of Christ's downward mediation.[20] No other theologian has developed this theme as extensively or, in my view, has succeeded as well in linking Christology and sacramentology.

Inspired by St. Athanasius and St. John Damascene, Thomas draws the following analogy: Christ's humanity is the instrument of his divinity somewhat as the body is the instrument of the soul. The body is intimately joined to the soul. In a similar way, Christ's humanity is joined to his divinity, that is, in his divine person. In each case, we find a metaphysical union that grounds an operative synergy. For example, when I communicate, my body and soul act together in harmony. My thoughts and intentions formed in the soul are shared through the body. In Christ, there is a communion of operation between his two natures. His humanity is a

20. I will be following the interpretation of Charles Journet and Jean-Pierre Torrell.

"conjoined instrument," for his humanity is always joined to his divinity (via his person). His divine power comes to us through his humanity. By contrast, the sacraments are "separate instruments" of Christ, more like the artist's paintbrush than a body metaphysically joined to the soul.[21]

Aquinas insists that Christ's humanity shares instrumentally in the act of giving grace. He can make this claim for he firmly holds that, in the activity of pouring out grace, Christ's humanity depends on his divinity for its causal activity: "The human operation of Christ obtains a certain divine efficacy from the union of the divinity, just as the action of secondary [instrumental] agents obtains a certain efficacy from the principal agent."[22] In other words, when grace is poured out, Christ's humanity does not take the place of the divinity, nor operate without it, nor does his humanity stand in competition with his divinity. Aquinas builds on the Christology of the councils of Chalcedon (451) as well as of Constantinople II (553) and Constantinople III (680–681). The Christ's two natures and two operations are distinct yet not separate, and without tension. Also, Jesus' human will is the perfect instrument of his divine will.

Not only does Christ's humanity work together with his divinity, his human action is elevated in a supernatural way, thanks to the hypostatic union: "The human nature assumed in Christ is such that it operates *instrumentally* those things which are operations proper to God alone, such as to purify sins, to illumine minds through grace, and to lead someone to the perfection of eternal life."[23] Here, the key word is "instrumentally." Thus, it is correct to say that God saves, and that God alone (or Christ in his divinity) is the *source* of salvation. But this does not exclude the Son of God's saving us through the operation of his humanity. In this context, the term "to save" signals the giving of grace to man, not an act of sacrifice or merit. Aquinas points to this operative elevation of Christ's humanity when he says that Jesus' "human nature participates in the operation of the divine nature, just as an instrument participates in the operation of the principal cause."[24]

21. Thomas Aquinas, *Summa contra Gentiles*, vol. 3, ed. Ceslaus Pera, Petrus Marc, and Petrus Caramello (Rome: Marietti, 1961), bk. 4, chap. 41, no. 3798.

22. Thomas Aquinas, *Summa contra Gentiles*, bk. 4, chap. 36, no. 3748.

23. Thomas Aquinas, *Summa contra Gentiles*, bk. 4, chap. 41, no. 3798.

24. Thomas Aquinas, *Summa theologiae* III, q. 19, a. 1, corpus.

Following Chalcedon and Constantinople III, Aquinas maintains that each of Christ's two natures remains integral in their being and operation.[25] Each nature is a principle of operation: we can think and love because we act by our human nature. Each nature shapes or specifies the range of actions possible for the being that has the nature. Each nature has an operation proportioned to it. This remains the case, even when something becomes the instrument of a higher agent or cause. Each agent has its *proper* operation, which does not become the proper operation of the higher agent. For example, the proper operation of Christ's humanity is not to give grace, but to think, talk, and sleep. The proper operation of his divinity is to give grace and resurrect the dead. And yet, when his human nature becomes an instrument of the divine nature, that humanity's *instrumental act* can exceed its merely human operative capacity. A paintbrush cannot paint by itself, and my body cannot communicate intelligent thoughts without an action of my soul. Thus, what we murmur in our sleep usually makes no sense, since our minds are not functioning rationally. But a principal cause with a higher nature can act through an instrumental cause with a lower nature. Your body communicates intelligent sounds because it is moved by your soul, but your body does so in a properly corporeal, temporal way. Christ's humanity communicates grace, for this human operation is also that of the eternal Logos. In other words, as man he continues to act according to his proper operation. Christ's human nature continues to contribute something of its own, its "proper operation," even when he saves. We find an operative synergy, so that Christ heals by his physical touch.[26] The latter is a proper operation of his humanity. Christ's saving activity belongs to both natures in distinct modes: as source or as instrument, as principal cause or as a secondary, dependent cause.

The preceding considerations allow us to see how Thomas can make sense of the following claim: Christ saves by particular historical acts (still taking "to save" as a reference to the giving of grace). The flux of grace

25. Thomas Aquinas, *Summa theologiae* III, q. 19, a. 1, corpus. For this development in Aquinas, see Martin Morard, "Une source de saint Thomas d'Aquin: Le deuxième concile de Constantinople (553)," *Revue des sciences philosophiques et théologiques* 81 (1997): 21–56; also Morard, "Thomas d'Aquin, lecteur des conciles," *Archivum Franciscanum Historicum* 98 (2005): 211–365.

26. Jean-Pierre Torrell, *Encyclopédie Jésus le Christ chez saint Thomas d'Aquin* (Paris: Cerf, 2008), 370.

and life does not simply pass through the humanity of the glorified Christ in heaven. Rather, the river of life comes to us primarily through his saving acts carried out during his earthly pilgrimage, especially his Passion and Death, Resurrection and Ascension.[27] I will focus on the Cross here, without excluding Jesus' other saving deeds and sufferings, which we also call the mysteries of the life of Christ.

The notion of instrumentality tells us that the nature of the instrument leaves a trace of itself on the effect. When we closely study Michelangelo's Moses, we can determine, with at least some level of accuracy, the kind of instruments he must have used in sculpting this statue. Thomas holds that something similar happens with the particular events in Christ's life: here, the disposition of his humanity, such as his suffering, but also the interior dispositions of his heart, leave a trace on the grace poured out.

In the middle of the twentieth century, the Swiss theologian (and later cardinal) Charles Journet drew powerful insights from Aquinas's vision of Christ's instrumentality as man. Journet insists that the interior state of Christ's heart, such as his suffering love for us on the Cross, leaves a trace on the grace and charity given to us, so that the Spirit of Christ begins to incline our hearts according to the inclinations of the human heart of Christ. The grace of the Crucified Lord leads his disciples on the path of love, a path along which we grow in our own willingness to suffer, to do penance for the salvation of our neighbor. The same grace inclines us more and more to give courageous witness to Christ.[28]

Thomas especially developed this doctrine of Christo-forming grace in his study of Christ's Resurrection, though the principles we find there also apply to other mysteries of Christ's life. As Journet shows, Thomas teaches that, in Christ's act of rising from the dead, the power to resurrect bodies is present and passes through time, to bring about our bodily resurrection at the end of time. The focus is not simply on the resurrected Christ, but more specifically on *his act of rising*. The spiritual power of this deed (animated by the Spirit who raised Jesus from the dead) passes through time, bringing to us the life that was given to Christ on Easter

27. Thomas Aquinas, *Summa theologiae* III, q. 48, aa. 2–3 & 6; q. 49, a. 3; q. 56, a. 1.

28. Charles Journet, *L'Église du Verbe Incarné: Essaie de théologie spéculative*, vol. 2, *Sa structure interne et son unité Catholique* (Saint Maurice, Switzerland: Éditions Saint-Augustin, 1999), 482–83, 530–50.

Sunday.[29] Something similar occurs at baptism: the power of the Resurrection is present, so that sin is taken away and a share in Christ's new life and his virtues is imparted.[30]

Following Aquinas, we can draw a theological consequence from this Christology. Since Christ's humanity was chosen by the Father to fulfill an instrumental role in the giving of grace, then something analogous can happen with the sacraments: a share in the power of the higher agent, an operative synergy between God and creatures, and no competition between them.[31] This has important implications for the doctrine of Eucharistic sacrifice.

Christ's Upward Mediation: The Sacrifice of Calvary

Christ's mediation of grace goes together with his upward mediation of prayer and intercession, of sacrifice and redemption. These saving actions performed during Jesus' earthly life constitute part of God's visible presence among us. Christ's act of performing the sacrifice at Calvary allows the Church to participate in his offering, and so actualizes her sacramental identity. For if the Cross were not a sacrifice, then the Church could only offer adoration and praise, but no perfect sacrifice. But the Cross was a sacrifice, and its fruits in turn allow us to contemplate the fruitfulness of the Mass, as it makes present here and now Jesus' self-offering at Calvary. Finally, as we saw above, the liturgy also makes present the heavenly sacrifice of love and praise that the glorified Lord offers to the Father with the Church. This last aspect of Christ's upward mediation will be treated in the next chapter.

I will focus the present study on the New Testament teaching about the Cross as a sacrifice, especially in light of its Old Testament background. Along with some key Old Covenant themes of sacrifice, I shall

29. Thomas Aquinas, *Summa theologiae* III, q. 56, a. 1; Jean-Pierre Torrell, "La causalité salvifique de la résurrection du Christ selon saint Thomas," in *Recherches thomasiennes*, Bibliothèque Thomiste 52 (Paris: Vrin, 2000), 233.

30. Thomas Aquinas, *Summa theologiae* III, q. 56, a. 2; Jean-Pierre Torrell, *Christ and Spirituality in St. Thomas Aquinas*, trans. Bernhard Blankenhorn (Washington, D.C.: The Catholic University of America Press, 2011), 98.

31. For this connection between Christology and sacraments, see my essay, "The Instrumental Causality of the Sacraments: Thomas Aquinas and Louis-Marie Chauvet," *Nova et Vetera* (English ed.) 4 (2006): 275–91.

briefly consider some biblical notions of sin. After the biblical study of sacrifice and sin, I will integrate Aquinas's insights on Christ's sacrificial love and his work of satisfying for sins. I begin by considering sacrifice in the Old Testament, an examination that greatly illumines the Cross.

Sacrifice in the Old Testament

The Old Testament sacrifices foreshadow Christ's offering on the Cross. They also illumine the gift of the Eucharist as an offering made to the Father. The Old Testament presents a vast array of sacrifices, from Cain and Abel to the first Passover and the many rituals that shaped Israel's liturgical life. Israel's sacrifices evolved over time. There were festal sacrificial rites, such as Passover, Pentecost, and the Feast of Booths, daily temple sacrifices, as well as offerings for particular desires and needs such as an individual's ritual purity or celebrations of thanksgiving. Contrary to some popular misconceptions, Old Testament sacrifice concerns much more than cleansing ritual impurity or the appeasement of God for an offense committed. For example, burnt offerings were not intended to appease God. In the Old Testament, to sacrifice means to bring gifts into God's presence in order to enter into communion with him, an act that may or may not include the removal of obstacles to communion. In other words, the primary purpose of Old Testament sacrifice is positive, not negative.

We have already studied the first-century Passover ritual. Space does not allow for a comprehensive treatment of Israel's sacrifices as a foundation for the theology of the Cross and the Eucharist. No single book of the Old Testament gives a comprehensive description of that system. In this partial treatment, I will first review the five kinds of sacrifices laid out in the Book of Leviticus (commonly identified with the priestly sources of the Pentateuch). I will briefly mention some practices and interpretations of these offerings in the Second Temple Period. The aim is to attain an overview of Israel's daily liturgical life at Jerusalem in the time of Jesus. Then, I will give particular attention the Day of Atonement (or Yom Kippur), which the Letter to the Hebrews links with the Cross. I conclude with a brief look at some other Old Testament figures of the Cross.

Sacrifices in Leviticus

The Book of Leviticus sets out five major types of sacrifices, and these became central for the cultic life of Israel: (1) the burnt offering, (2) the cereal offering, (3) the purification offering, (4) the well-being offering, and (5) the reparation or guilt offering.

Burnt offerings were made morning and evening in the temple, as a sacrifice on behalf of Israel. Here, a bull or lamb, wine, and cereal were burned or wholly consumed by fire, an act that signified God's abiding presence with his people.[32] Burnt offerings were made with a male animal from the herd (a bull) or the flock (a lamb or goat), or with a bird such as a pigeon. It was an ascending offering because the animal was entirely burned, with the smoke directed to heaven. The burnt offering invoked God's presence or help for a particular occasion or need (Nm 21–24; 2 Kgs 3:26–28).[33] The blood was poured around the altar as a libation. The Jewish Mishna describes how the priests made the sacrifice. Among other things, one priest slit the animal's throat before taking it to the altar, while a second priest let the blood drip from the throat into cups. Some of the blood was then sprinkled on the altar, and the rest around the base of the altar. From the altar, the blood ran in a channel out of the temple area into the Valley of Kidron, where the Garden of Gethsemane is located.[34]

The temple tax that financed (among other things) the daily burnt offering was called "atonement money" (Ex 30:16). From at least the time of Isaiah, atonement meant (among other things) paying God for the debt incurred through sin.[35] This was one of the favors sought by the burnt offering, though Scripture does not make it clear what can be atoned for or expiated by the burnt offering, and the rabbis debated the matter (Lv 1:4). At least with the development of Israel's cultic life, the burnt offering above all became the expression of joy, for example, in fulfillment of a vow (Lv 22:17–19; Nm 15:3).[36]

32. Ex 29:38–42; Nm 15:1–10, 28:3–8; Ezek 46:13–15.

33. Gary A. Anderson, "Sacrifice and Sacrificial Offerings: Old Testament," in *The Anchor Bible Dictionary*, vol. 5, edited by David Noel Friedman (New York: Double Day, 1992), 877–80.

34. E. P. Sanders, *Judaism: Practice and Belief, 63 BCE–66 CE* (Philadelphia: Trinity Press International, 1992), 104–5.

35. Gary A. Anderson, *Sin: A History* (New Haven, Conn.: Yale University Press, 2009), 49 & chap. 4.

36. Jacob Milgrom, *Leviticus 1–16*, The Anchor Bible 3 (New York: Doubleday, 1991), 175.

One could also request or make a burnt offering for an individual person's need. Let us note that the Bible does not require this kind of offering from individuals. Rather, the individual burnt offering was seen as a free gift made to God. Josephus links the individual burnt offering with thanksgiving and atonement. For example, King David made an such an offering after God had stopped a plague that had been inflicted upon Israel because of David's sin. No first-century author thought that such sacrifices provided food for God.[37]

The second Levitical sacrifice is the cereal offering (Lv 2). It accompanied both the daily burnt offering of animals and the peace offering of animals. The cereal offering could also be made on its own, for example, as a sacrifice of thanksgiving (Lv 7:12–14; Nm 15:1–12). It could obtain the benefits of a burnt offering for those who could not afford to sacrifice an animal. It was considered a gift to God, to show reverence and to obtain some favor from him. Like the burnt offering, it was intended as an expression of joy. The independent cereal offering had various functions, including as a purification sacrifice for the poor man. It was used to present to God the first fruits of the barley and wheat harvest (Lv 2:14–16, 23:10–17).[38] The priests could eat of this sacrifice, thus signifying a shared meal with God.[39] Finally, unlike other sacrifices, the cereal offering could be licitly made outside of the Jerusalem temple.[40]

The third Levitical category of sacrifice is the peace offering (*shelem*) (Lv 3), which is an individual offering. Translations of this term vary, as they include "sacrifice of well-being" and "communion sacrifice."[41] The category of peace offering includes (1) thanksgiving offerings (*toda*), (2) vowed or votive sacrifices (*neder*), and (3) freewill offerings (*nedaba*).[42] By the time of Josephus, the peace offering was always done with a four-legged animal (implied by Lv 3:1–16).[43] The three types of peace offerings I mentioned (thanksgiving, votive, free will) were performed on

37. Sanders, *Judaism: Practice and Belief*, 106.

38. Milgrom, *Leviticus 1–16*, 196–200.

39. Mary Douglas, "The Eucharist: Its Continuity with the Bread Sacrifice of Leviticus," *Modern Theology* 15 (1999): 223.

40. Milgrom, *Leviticus 1–16*, 199.

41. Sanders, *Judaism: Practice and Belief*, 110.

42. Anderson, "Sacrifice and Sacrificial Offerings," 873–80.

43. Sanders, *Judaism: Practice and Belief*, 110.

feast days (1 Sam 1:3–4; Dt 12:11–12). Thanksgiving offerings were similar to the Passover ritual. The sacrificed meat of such offerings was eaten on the same day. Peace offerings were not atonement for sin, but celebratory rites.[44] In peace offerings, unlike burnt offering and purification offering, the laymen bringing the sacrifice communed in the victim, which expresses communion with God.

The fourth sacrifice in Leviticus is the purification offering (Lv 4). It is also called a sin offering, but this term can be misleading, as the Levitical description of this ritual involves cleansing from ritual impurity, but not from the guilt of sin (which here essentially refers to grave sins, such as adultery, unjust bloodshed, or idolatry).[45] Only later Jewish developments and New Testament teaching explain how sacrifice can take away the guilt of voluntary sins. Purification offerings were usually made for individuals.[46]

Most purification sacrifices were done with birds, especially when they were brought by the poor. Josephus mentions purification offerings that were made with a lamb and a kid, though this was probably done mostly by wealthy individuals. Following Leviticus 5, a person in extreme poverty could simply bring flour for a purification offering. The flour remained unmixed on the altar, where some was burned, and the rest was left for the priest to eat. The flour became a sacrifice on the altar.[47] Here we may have Eucharistic imagery.[48]

In purification offerings, the greater the offense (or impurity), the closer the blood was brought to the holy of holies (the place where the Ark of the Covenant was kept before its disappearance in the sixth century B.C.). For individual impurity, blood was sprinkled on the altar outside the sanctuary. For the impurity of the community or of the priest, blood was sprinkled on the veil in front of the inner sanctuary.[49]

In contrast to the Cross, the purification offering did not purify grave

44. Anderson, "Sacrifice and Sacrificial Offerings," 873–80.

45. Jonathan Klawans, *Impurity and Sin in Ancient Judaism* (Oxford: Oxford University Press, 2000), 30–31.

46. Sanders, *Judaism: Practice and Belief*, 107–8.

47. Sanders, *Judaism: Practice and Belief*, 108–10.

48. Adrian Schenker, "Les sacrifices dans la Bible," in *Recht und Kultur im Alten Testament: Achtzehn Studien*, Orbis Biblicus et Orientalis 172 (Fribourg, Switzerland: Universitätsverlag, 2000), 15–19.

49. Anderson, "Sacrifice and Sacrificial Offerings," 880.

sinners, such as murderers or adulterers: these lived in a degraded state, or suffered exile or capital punishment.[50] Indeed, the blood of purification offerings did not purify the sinner, because blood was not applied to the sinner, but rather brought near to God (Lv 1).[51] The Eucharistic blood functions very differently.

The fifth Levitical category is the reparation or guilt offering (Lv 5:14–26). It is mainly distinguished from the purification offering by its focus on the profanation of sacred items, such as bringing an animal unfit for sacrifice or taking a false vow. Here too, an animal such as a lamb or bull was normally offered, yet, for economic reasons, one could substitute for these with two birds or even with flour. This offering was also made for violations committed without knowledge. Overall, the reparation offering remains the most obscure among the five categories found in Leviticus.[52] Philo and Josephus go beyond the text of Leviticus, as they hold that this offering provides a remedy for voluntary transgressions.[53]

Yom Kippur

Yom Kippur (the Day of Atonement) was central to the liturgical life of Israel. The Letter to the Hebrews describes this ritual at length and shows its fulfillment in Christ. Yom Kippur is all about expiation or propitiation.[54] God forgives, while man offers reparation for sin. The divine wrath that man's sin provoked has been appeased. Expiation presupposes rupture in the people's relationship with God. Man's very life or existence is at stake, and God provides the means for him to come back to life. An example can be found in Exodus 32: After the sin of the golden calf, Moses makes expiation for Israel, and is even willing to offer himself to save Israel.[55]

On the feast of Yom Kippur, the high priest entered the inner sanctuary, or Holy of Holies, and sprinkled blood on or in front of the mercy

50. Klawans, *Impurity and Sin in Ancient Judaism*, 30.

51. Anderson, "Sacrifice and Sacrificial Offerings," 880–85.

52. Anderson, "Sacrifice and Sacrificial Offerings," 880.

53. Klawans, *Impurity and Sin in Ancient Judaism*, 64.

54. Paolo Garuti, "Espiazione," in *Dizionario teologico sul sangue di Cristo*, ed. Tullio Veglianti (Vatican City: Libreria Editrice Vaticana, 2007), 474–81.

55. Hartmut Gese, *Sulla teologia biblica*, Biblioteca della cultura religiosa 54 (Brescia, Italy: Paideia, 1989), 105–7.

seat of the ark of the covenant. This was a sign that God had made this blood the means of reconciliation. The blood from purification offerings removed the stain of impurity from the sanctuary, so that God would remain there (Lv 15:31, 16:18–19; Nm 19:13).[56]

The Letter to the Hebrews offers an extensive discourse on the limits of Old Testament sacrifices (including Yom Kippur) to show Christ's perfect sacrifice. Yom Kippur brought only ritual purification, while Christ brings full, personal purification from sin (Heb 10). The doctrine of Hebrews need not imply that Old Testament sacrifices were without value. First, as noted in Hebrews, they brought ritual purity of the body. Second, Aquinas explains that, when joined to faith in the coming Messiah, Old Testament sacrifices could be occasions to receive grace and justification, as the Israelites express their faith in the future Messiah in a figurative way, even if a full understanding of the figure was lacking for most ancient Israelites.[57]

Other Old Testament Sacrifices

Beyond the sacrifices prescribed in Leviticus, one should mention three key Old Testament passages that do not prescribe ritual sacrifices yet serve as an important background for the sacrifice of the Cross or for Eucharistic sacrifice. First, Roch Kereszty points to the binding of Isaac as a powerful prophecy of Jesus' saving death. A father offers his own son, he gives everything. He does so at a place that later rabbinic tradition identifies with Mt. Zion, the place of the Jerusalem temple. Abraham states that God promised to provide the sacrificial victim (Gn 22:7–8). The Jewish exegete Jon Levenson points to this event as the root of the Passover sacrifice.[58]

A second passage is the sealing of the covenant between God and Israel at the foot of Mt. Sinai, in Exodus 24. Moses sprinkles the people with blood, a ritual that culminates in a sacrificial banquet on the holy

56. Anderson, "Sacrifice and Sacrificial Offerings," 873–80; Anderson, *Sin: A History*, 22–23.

57. Thomas Aquinas, *Summa theologiae* I-II, q. 103, a. 2.

58. Roch A. Kereszty, *Wedding Feast of the Lamb: Eucharistic Theology from a Biblical, Historical and Systematic Perspective* (Chicago: Hillenbrand Books, 2007), 9; Matthew Levering, *Sacrifice and Community: Jewish Offering and Christian Eucharist*, Illuminations: Theory and Religion (Oxford: Blackwell, 2005), 29–37.

mountain.[59] Unlike Passover or the Last Supper, this ritual was itself not a covenant sacrifice, yet the Last Supper will evoke that text.

A third text concerns Isaiah's Suffering Servant. Here, an innocent man makes an offering of his life for the sins of others. The Suffering Servant bears the guilt of the people in a vicarious way (which does not imply that Christ substitutes for sinners or receives God's wrath on their behalf).[60] Of course, Isaiah does not describe a sacrificial ritual, but rather offers a prophecy of a personal sacrifice to come. The Letter to the Hebrews will manifest the ritual character of Jesus' sacrifice on the Cross.

Biblical Analogies of Sin

Scripture presents numerous, complementary descriptions of sin, for example, sin as an offense against God or sin as impurity. Two other images or analogies of sin, which help to render Eucharistic theology more intelligible, are sin as a weight or burden and sin as debt.[61]

In the Hebrew Old Testament, the notion of sin as a burden predominates (along with sin as impurity). The image of sin as a burden emerges in the ritual of Yom Kippur (Lv 16–17): a scapegoat or beast of burden is sent into the desert, symbolically carrying Israel's sins out of God's sight. Here, sin is a heavy weight, which the people cannot bear.[62]

In first-century Palestine, the notion of sin as a debt to be paid began to gain favor, especially in Aramaic-speaking Jewish circles. The New Testament reflects this, especially in Matthew's version of the Lord's Prayer ("forgive us our debts"). To explain sin and forgiveness, Jesus frequently tells parables that involve the forgiveness of a great debt.[63] In 1 Corinthians 6:20, Paul reminds his readers that they were "bought with a price." Paul here refers to debt-slavery, which is more precise than the notion of debt that emerges in the other passages just mentioned.

The theme of satisfaction for sins gained importance in medieval and

59. Kereszty, *Wedding Feast of the Lamb*, 11.

60. Kereszty, *Wedding Feast of the Lamb*, 9–11.

61. Here, I largely rely on the work of Gary Anderson.

62. Anderson, *Sin: A History*, 6, 23. Christ will bear the debt of sin for us, which does not mean that we need to identify him with the scapegoat. What is important is the notion of sin involved.

63. Anderson, *Sin: A History*, 7, 23, 31–33, 114–15.

modern theologies, both Catholic and Protestant. This notion finds its root in the biblical analogy of sin as a debt to be paid. For example, when the prophet Isaiah announces the end of Israel's exile and return to the Promised Land, he adds that God has redeemed his people, as he releases them from the bond of slavery (Is 40:1–2). God has remitted their debt. Israel's exile was a penalty for her sins, and now she has satisfied for those sins (this brings up the question of how to balance the theme of God freeing the sinner from debt and the sinner repaying the debt by his own penance, to be taken up later). The ancient Aramaic Targum on Isaiah 40:2 reads: "her debt was remitted."[64] Closely linked with the biblical notion of sin as debt is the notion of a heavenly treasure.

Christ's Passion as a Sacrifice in the New Testament

Having studied part of the Old Testament background on sacrifice and sin, we now turn to the sacrifice of the Cross. Several New Testament passages directly and explicitly describe Christ's death as sacrificial. In addition, about thirty other passages signal the sacrificial nature of Jesus' death by using terminology such as "Jesus died for you."[65] One cannot explain such consistent, widespread use of sacrificial categories for the Cross in the New Testament unless this doctrine is rooted in the message of the historical Jesus.[66] That is, interpreters who categorize the sacrificial identity of Christ's suffering and death as a theological construct of first-century Christian authors cannot account for such a massive biblical witness.[67] As Martin Hengel points out, first-century Judaism had no category for a suffering Messiah: this was a great surprise to Jesus' con-

64. Anderson, *Sin: A History*, 44–49.

65. See, for example, Mk 14:24; Lk 22:19–20; Jn 10:11–15; Rom 5:6–8; 1 Cor 15:3; 2 Cor 5:14–15; Gal 2:20; 1 Thes 5:10; Heb 2:9; 1 Pt 2:21; 1 Jn 3:16.

66. Ben F. Meyer, "The Expiation Motif in the Eucharistic Words: A Key to the History of Jesus?," in *One Loaf, One Cup: Ecumenical Studies of 1 Cor 11 and Other Eucharistic Texts*, New Gospel Studies 6 (Macon, Ga.: Mercer University Press, 1993), 16–20.

67. Here, I oppose the thesis of René Girard, *Violence and the Sacred* (Baltimore, Md.: John Hopkins University Press, 1984).

temporaries.[68] Thus, many clues point to the antiquity of the doctrine of Christ's sacrificial death as going back to the historical Jesus himself.

The New Testament takes a series of Old Testament sacrificial images and applies them to the Cross. For example, Christ's Cross brings liberation from sin, but unlike the Old Covenant purification offering, the Cross makes possible the forgiveness of sin. At 2 Corinthians 5:21, Paul says that Christ was made sin for us.[69] The Hebrew term for "sin" is identical to the term for "sin offering," or "purification offering" (*ḥattât*).[70] Paul intends to teach that Christ became a *sin offering* for us. That is, contrary to the claim of theologians such as Hans Urs von Balthasar, Christ was not literally "made sin," as if all that displeases God were now concentrated in him, as an object of divine wrath against sinners.[71]

Romans 3:25 states that God made Christ an instrument of propitiation (*hilastērion*) by his blood, which involves purification from sin. The term "propitiation" may allude to the Day of Atonement or Yom Kippur (Lv 16:14–16; 1 Cor 1:30). The place of atonement is Golgotha, outside of the temple and Jerusalem.[72] The First Letter of John, at verses 2:2 and 4:10, also mentions propitiation or expiation (*hilasmos*). Ephesians 5:2 describes Christ's death on the Cross as a sacrifice pleasing to God, as it compares the Cross to the sweet odor of Old Covenant animal offerings.

The Last Supper accounts include several key allusions to the Cross as a sacrifice. First, Jesus refers to the blood of the covenant, an allusion to Exodus 24:1–10, where Moses sprinkles the people with blood in order to institute the covenant with God.[73] The blood of the covenant presupposes the sacrifice of a victim. Second, in Mark 14:24, Jesus speaks of the blood poured out for the many. The giving of one's life for the many

68. Martin Hengel, *The Atonement: The Origins of the Doctrine in the New Testament* (Philadelphia: Fortress Press, 1981), 40.

69. Hans-Josef Klauck, "Sacrifice and Sacrificial Offerings: New Testament," in *The Anchor Bible Dictionary*, vol. 5, ed. David Noel Friedman (New York: Double Day, 1992), 887–89.

70. Schenker, "Les sacrifices dans la Bible," 12–15.

71. Hans Urs von Balthasar, *To the Heart of the Mystery of Redemption*, trans. Anne Englund Nash (San Francisco: Ignatius Press, 2010), 25.

72. Helmut Moll, *Die Lehre von der Eucharistie als Opfer* (Cologne: Peter Hanstein, 1975), 72–73.

73. Brant Pitre, *Jesus and the Last Supper* (Grand Rapids, Mich.: William B. Eerdmans, 2015), 90–95.

evokes the Suffering Servant (Is 52:14–15; 53:4–8). The blood imagery also alludes to the blood of the sacrificial animals poured out in the temple.[74] Third, Jesus foreshadows his coming sacrificial death when he says that his blood is poured out for the forgiveness of sins (Mt 26:28).[75] Kereszty notes that this Matthean passage finds a strong echo in Hebrews 9–10.[76] In these three allusions to sacrifice, the Last Supper (1) offers a prophecy of the Cross, (2) reveals the power of the Cross, and (3) presents a teaching about the efficacy of the Last Supper celebration. Overall, the events in the Upper Room show that Christ's suffering and death fulfill the sacrifices that God instituted in the Old Testament.

A few New Testament passages refer to Christ as the paschal lamb (Jn 1:29; 1 Cor 5:7). Christ's Passion fulfills the sacrifice prefigured in the slaying of the Passover lambs on the night of Israel's Exodus from Egypt, when God's people were liberated from slavery.

The Letter to the Hebrews includes the most extensive and systematic New Testament reflection on sacrifice. The anonymous author of Hebrews presents Christ as the high priest who unites God and mankind through his priestly offering and mediation. At Hebrews 5:7–8, the author evokes Christ's whole Passion by referring to his tears and supplications made to God.[77] The result of this offering is mentioned in verses 9–10: through the Cross, Christ is perfected (*teleioun*). This seems to be a technical term, for in the Greek Old Testament (or Septuagint), it is used in reference to the consecration of priests. If that reading is correct, then a consecration of Jesus as high priest especially occurs through his Passion and Death. Hebrews 2:10 notes that Christ was made perfect or consecrated through his suffering. This perfection as high priest enabled Christ to mediate salvation to all human beings. As Hebrews 9:24 teaches, Christ thus has the power to make us enter into the presence of the Father, into the heavenly tent.[78] The result of Christ's priestly consecration on the Cross is his own glorification, which includes his Resurrection and Ascension. Hebrews 9:11 refers to a new tent or temple that has been set

74. Pitre, *Jesus and the Last Supper*, 100–104.

75. Klauck, "Sacrifice and Sacrificial Offerings," 887–88; Pitre, *Jesus and the Last Supper*, 413–14.

76. Kereszty, *Wedding Feast of the Lamb*, 72–73.

77. Albert Vanhoye, *Prêtres anciens, prêtre nouveau selon le Nouveau Testament* (Paris: Éditions du Seuil, 1980), 146–50.

78. Vanhoye, *Prêtres anciens*, 152–55.

up by God. This tent is a heavenly archetype of the earthly temple, and its veil is Christ's glorified body (Heb 10:20). Christ's glorification and establishment as an efficacious high priest follow directly from his Passion.

Christ is both victim and priest. Following Aquinas's reading of Scripture, we can say that Christ is a priest in that he voluntarily offers himself for our liberation from sin and our communion with God. He intercedes (1) by his act of love for God and sinners, (2) through his intense psychological and physical suffering, (3) by his prayer for sinners, (4) by his death, and (5) by his priestly prayer in heaven. He sheds his own blood and thus gives up his life for us. Aquinas rightly notes that the heart of Christ's sacrifice is not found in his physical suffering or death, though both are essential in God's saving plan. Rather, love stands at the heart of Jesus' sacrifice. Charity finds its perfect expression in the Passion of Jesus. This sacrifice has infinite value by (1) Jesus' perfect charity, (2) his perfect innocence, and (3) his dignity as the Son of God, a divine person who suffers in his humanity.[79]

Hebrews already points to the first of these doctrines, for it centers the value of Christ's obedience on the Cross, meaning, in Christ's will and his loving obedience. This is how Albert Vanhoye explains Hebrews 5:7: "In the accounts of the passion, the 'piety' of Jesus shows itself clearly.... This attachment to the will of the Father in such dramatic circumstances manifests extreme filial love. The author [of Hebrews] adds that 'by reason of his piety' Christ's supplication was 'heard.'"[80] We can already see this in the binding of Isaac, where Abraham's obedience stands at the center. Christ's offering of perfect love to the Father and the love for mankind carried out by means of his bodily offering are two sides of the same coin.[81] The sacrifice of love and bodily sacrifice go together.

79. Thomas Aquinas, *Summa theologiae* III, q. 48, a. 3. See also Matthew Levering, *Christ's Fulfillment of Torah and Temple: Salvation According to Thomas Aquinas* (South Bend, Ind.: University of Notre Dame Press, 2002), 58–60.

80. Albert Vanhoye, *The Letter to the Hebrews: A New Commentary*, trans. Leo Arnold (New York: Paulist Press, 2015), 103.

81. Vanhoye, *Prêtres anciens*, 217–25.

Christ's Satisfaction for Sins: A Biblical and Systematic Overview

I now return to the theme of sin as a debt, which finds its complement in Christology and the doctrine of satisfaction.[82] This teaching has been much misunderstood, partly as a result of the imbalances found in some Christologies. Here I propose a biblically grounded, Thomistic approach to the topic. This theme illumines a key aspect of the theology of the Mass as a sacrifice.

The New Testament theme of ransom or redemption grounds the theology of satisfaction. Here, Mark 10:45 is crucial: "The Son of Man came not to be served but to serve, and to give his life as a ransom (*lutron*) for many." In the Old Testament, God himself ransomed wayward Israel, but now Jesus ransoms human beings by his Passion, and he does so voluntarily. This fulfills God's promise in the Old Testament. Christ pays the price for our sins, a theme that evokes the image of sin as a debt. Also, the context of Mark 10:45 indicates that human beings can share in the cup of Christ's Passion.[83]

By sinning, man turns away from God, and thus incurs guilt or fault. He offends God, by failing to give to the Lord his due (especially fidelity and love). Hence, sin merits a punishment, for by turning away from the source of life, the human being turns to death. God has inscribed an order of justice in creation, one that reflects his own justice. This justice orders the relation of creatures with God and one another. Sin violates this justice.

The Father sent the Son in order to manifest his own justice or righteousness, and to restore us to right relation with God:

> since all have sinned and fall short of the glory of God, they are justified by his grace as a gift, through the redemption which is in Christ Jesus, whom God put forward as an expiation by his blood, to be received by faith. This was to show God's righteousness, because in his divine forbearance he had passed over former sins.[84]

82. The liturgy includes references to the debt of sin. Thus, in the great *Exsultet* sung at the beginning of the Easter Vigil, the priest or deacon chants: "[Christ] Who for our sake paid Adam's debt to the eternal Father."

83. Perrier, "L'enjeu christologique de la satisfaction (II)," 205.

84. Rom 3:23–25.

Man could not restore justice on his own. Instead, God takes the initiative, which is to say that salvation always remains a gift. The Cross manifests not an angry God unloading his wrath on his innocent Son, but rather God's holiness and mercy toward sinners.[85] We might also recall the importance of the classical doctrine of divine immutability: since sacrifice cannot change the God who is unchanging love, it can only benefit human beings.[86]

Redemption thus includes liberation from the guilt of sin and the punishment due to it, while satisfaction pertains only to punishment. This twofold liberation restores justice. In other words, salvation involves a re-creation, but not a whole new creation. God could have saved us without satisfaction, yet with satisfaction we can recognize more easily the continuity between God's creating and saving work, continuity between nature and grace. God restores the order of justice inscribed within this creation by restoring us to right relationship with him. The term "justice" gives moral expression to this relationship.[87]

Christ satisfies for us by freely going to the Cross. In his human heart, he offers perfect love to the Father and dies for us. In this way, Jesus makes up for the offense that our sin has caused. He suffers and dies for us, not to receive God's wrath in our place, but as a consequence and expression of his loving obedience to the Father. Christ expiates our sins by his blood because of his loving, docile heart. Above all, it is Jesus' love that pleases the Father and reconciles us with him. We receive the benefits of this satisfying work because the Crucified Lord acts as head of the Church, and we are his members.[88]

85. Fernando Ocáriz, Lucas F. Mateo Seco, and José A. Riestra, *The Mystery of Jesus Christ: A Christology and Soteriology Textbook*, trans. Michael Adams and James Gavigan (Portland, Ore.: Four Courts Press, 2011), 272–77. It should be evident that God the Father did not need the Cross to save us, just as he did not need to send his Son in the flesh to redeem us (Thomas Aquinas, *Summa theologiae* III, q. 1, a. 1). Both the Incarnation and the Crucifixion are his free gift.

86. For a fine exposition of divine love and immutability, see Michael J. Dodds, *The Unchanging God of Love: Thomas Aquinas and Contemporary Theology on Divine Immutability* (Washington, D.C.: The Catholic University of America Press, 2008). The liturgy alludes to God's immutability. See, for example, Common Preface IV (weekdays) in the New Roman Rite: "our praises add nothing to your greatness."

87. Perrier, "L'enjeu christologique de la satisfaction (II)," 236–37, 243.

88. Thomas Aquinas, *Summa theologiae* III, q. 48, a. 2; Ocáriz et al., *The Mystery of Jesus Christ*, 274–75, 281–82. The doctrine of satisfaction can also be found in the Greek Fathers, including Maximos the Confessor. See Paul M. Blowers, *Maximus the Confessor: Jesus Christ and the*

But how is this satisfaction to be received among the faithful? Christ's work of satisfaction removed an obstacle to our communion with God. But the fruits of satisfaction must be applied to us, since they are not automatically communicated to everyone. These fruits are received through faith and the sacraments. At baptism, all punishment due to one's past sins are taken away.[89] Other sacraments also enable us to share in Christ's satisfaction. Aquinas links our share in Christ's satisfaction and merit with Christ's Headship.[90]

Sin merits a punishment. We can also formulate this idea in the following way: sin merits some form of penance. We do such penance in Lent and in other moments of the liturgical year (such as days of fasting and prayer). We can make sense of how punishment and penance naturally follow from sin by drawing an analogy with the natural order. A person who misuses his or her natural gifts faces negative consequences. For example, excessive drinking leads to alcoholism, which does grave harm to the body. Or if a husband offends his spouse by ignoring her or by engaging in an adulterous affair, he needs to seek forgiveness and to make up for the offense committed, and he does so by acts of love for his wife through which he expresses contrition.

The sins that baptized believers commit offend God, as did the sins they committed before baptism. These acts harm our relationship with God and diminish our communion with him. Here too, a new share in Christ's work of satisfaction restores right relationship with the Father. Now the grave sinner can do nothing to satisfy for his or her sins, but must simply receive Christ's satisfaction via repentance and reconciliation. Yet once reconciled, the repentant sinner can enact works of penance whereby he or she shares in Christ's satisfying work. This is part of the dignity of believers, namely, to cooperate in their own salvation. Various penances enacted in charity become satisfying acts, for they are joined to the Crucified Lord by faith and love. Such satisfaction, which is always subordinate to and in dependence on Christ the Head, can be done for one's own offenses and those of others.

Transfiguration of the World, Christian Theology in Context (Oxford: Oxford University Press, 2016), 240–44.

89. Thomas Aquinas, *Summa theologiae* III, q. 49, a. 3, ad 2.

90. Thomas Aquinas, *Summa theologiae* III, q. 48, a. 1.

In the next chapter, we will see that the Eucharist as sacrifice allows for a deeper share in Christ's merits and satisfaction for sins. Also, since any merits and satisfaction obtained by the Eucharistic sacrifice are nothing but a share in Christ's merit and satisfaction, a participation in the fruits of Christ's suffering love given to the Father, Eucharistic merit and satisfaction become modes of receiving a divine gift anew. This recognition is crucial if we are to avoid a caricature of the theology of satisfaction.

CHAPTER 5

THE EUCHARISTIC SACRIFICE

The Mass is the Church's daily participation in Christ's Sacrifice on the Cross for the life of the world. In the sacred liturgy, the faithful offer Christ's body and blood to the Father as the victim who gave himself for us in his Passion, and from whom the river of life flows into the Church. The present chapter ponders the link between sacrifice, presence, and communion. For without the offering of the victim's body and blood truly present on the altar, there is no perfect sacrifice, nor can we commune in Christ as victim (*hostia*) without his corporeal presence.

The theology of the Mass as a sacrifice has fallen on hard times, both in the theological academy and in pastoral life. The causes for this change are varied. Karl Rahner's optimistic anthropology presented God's grace as always-already-here. From this perspective, the sacraments primarily (though not exclusively) become signs of the grace that we have already received, and the need to offer sacrifice becomes unclear.[1] In the early

1. Karl Rahner, "Considerations on the Active Role of the Person in the Sacramental Event,"

work of René Girard, Calvary is seen as bringing sacrifice to an end, thus breaking the cycle of humanity's long quest for a scapegoat.[2] Girard's philosophy of sacrifice continues to mark liturgical and sacramental studies. The French Heideggerian theologian Louis-Marie Chauvet prefers to center the theme of Eucharistic sacrifice on the existential offering of our lives and the ethical transformation wrought by liturgical participation (the sacrifice of love), while minimizing other classical sacrificial themes. For Chauvet, the New Testament and second-century Christians authors spiritualized sacrifice because they gave the sacrifice of praise and thanksgiving theological priority.[3]

The Rahnerian deemphasis on sacrifice might be answered by a fuller recovery of Pauline anthropology, especially the doctrine of flesh and spirit in Romans 7. Girard's reading of the Cross already finds an answer in our previous chapter. I will return to Chauvet's theology below. Still, our contemporaries clearly have immense difficulty with a classical approach to sacrifice. This challenge especially surfaced during the Protestant Reformation.

Starting in 1517, Martin Luther issued several strong critiques of the doctrine of the sacrifice of the Mass. On this question, he greatly influenced all subsequent Protestant leaders. As Florent Urfels argues, Luther's exegesis of the Last Supper wholly abstracted from its Passover setting.[4] Instead, he interpreted the Last Supper as a last will or testament, in which Jesus promises the forgiveness of sins, just before going to this death. The faithful receive this promise through faith. For Luther, we are justified by faith alone (*sola fide*), and not by works. Hence, he thought it was erroneous to approach the Mass as a good *work* pleasing to God. Luther

in *Theological Investigations*, vol. 14, trans. David Bourke (New York: Seabury, 1976), 176; Matthew Levering, *Sacrifice and Community: Jewish Offering and Christian Eucharist*, Illuminations: Theory and Religion (Oxford: Blackwell, 2005), 22–24.

2. René Girard, *Violence and the Sacred* (Baltimore, Md.: Johns Hopkins University Press, 1984).

3. Louis-Marie Chauvet, *Symbol and Sacrament: A Sacramental Reinterpretation of Christian Existence*, trans. Patrick Madigan and Madeleine Beaumont (Collegeville, Minn.: Liturgical Press, 1995), 240–60, 290–316, esp. 302, 310–11; Michon M. Matthiesen, *Sacrifice as Gift: Eucharist, Grace and Contemplative Prayer in Maurice de la Taille* (Washington, D.C.: The Catholic University of America Press, 2013), 16–19.

4. Florent Urfels, *Pâque du Messie: Introduction à une théologie eucharistique du judaïsme*, Collège des Bernardins 20 (Paris: Parole et Silence, 2013), 312–17.

also denied the sacramental priesthood: Christ alone is the priest. That is, the minister or presider has no particular spiritual power. In the liturgy, Christ alone acts and we receive his grace. As we hear Christ's offer of forgiveness, especially during the praying of the institution narrative, we respond by accepting this gift with faith, an interior act that we express by praise and gratitude. The faithful truly receive Christ's body and blood at communion, but they do not offer it as a victim to the Father. For these reasons, Luther rejects the doctrine of the Eucharist as a sacrifice.[5] Indeed, if it were a sacrifice, then the Mass would be a repetition of the offering of the Cross. But Christ cannot be sacrificed again.[6] Luther thus leaves Catholic theology with a firm challenge.

Vatican II evidently promoted deeper union with our separated brethren. It also re-affirmed the Eucharistic teaching of Trent.[7] Strikingly, the Council integrated the theme of sacrifice with its promotion of the laity's conscious, active participation in the liturgy. *Sacrosanctum Concilium* teaches that the faithful "should take part in the sacred action, conscious of what they are doing, with devotion.... They should give thanks to God. Offering the immaculate victim, not only through the hands of the priest but also together with him, they should learn to offer themselves."[8] The text calls for the laity to make a deliberate self-offering, an act joined to their and the priest's sacramental offering of Christ Crucified. Likewise, the document recommends that the laity receive communion from among the hosts consecrated at Mass, rather than those kept in the tabernacle: "The more perfect form of participation in the Mass whereby the faithful, after the priest's communion, receive the Lord's Body from the same sacrifice, is warmly recommended."[9] In this way, Vatican II promotes

5. Martin Luther, *The Babylonian Captivity*, in *Church and Sacraments*, the Annotated Luther Study Edition 3, ed. Paul W. Robinson (Minneapolis, Minn.: Fortress Press, 2016), 40–51; Francis Clark, *Eucharistic Sacrifice and the Reformation* (Oxford: Basil Blackwell, 1960), 101, 111–19.

6. George Hunsinger, *The Eucharist and Ecumenism: Let Us Keep the Feast*, Current Issues in Theology (Cambridge: Cambridge University Press, 2008), 102–7.

7. *Sacrosanctum Concilium*, nos. 7, 47.

8. *Sacrosanctum Concilium*, no. 48. For the importance of this passage in *Sacrosanctum Concilium*, see Jeremy Driscoll, "Sacrosanctum Concilium," in *The Reception of Vatican II*, ed. Matthew Lamb and Matthew Levering (Oxford: Oxford University Press, 2017), 34–35.

9. *Sacrosanctum Concilium*, no. 55. Vatican II here draws upon Pius XII's encyclical *Mediator Dei*, no. 118, DH 3854.

liturgical reform partly by appeal to a well-established theology of Eucharistic sacrifice. The Council draws consequences from that theology, consequences that previous liturgical practice did not always fully realize. It thus implies that the renewal of Eucharistic practice, which the Conciliar Fathers so ardently desired, should integrate a classical approach to sacrifice. Our study of the Councils of Trent and Vatican II later in this chapter will confirm that claim.

The present chapter begins with the biblical roots of Eucharistic sacrifice. I then survey an array of sacrificial themes in the Church Fathers' teachings on the Eucharist and in some ancient anaphora, with a focus on eastern Eucharistic prayers. The latter constitute the oldest liturgical texts, are more numerous than western prayers, and are, at times, sources for the latter tradition. I also present the central sacrificial themes in the decrees of Trent. Last, on the basis of these biblical and historical analyses, I offer a theology of Eucharistic sacrifice that draws upon the Thomist tradition. I conclude by taking a closer look at Martin Luther.

Scripture, History, and Tradition on Eucharistic Sacrifice

The Sacrificial Offering: Some Biblical Foundations

We have already seen various sacrificial themes in the Last Supper accounts of the Synoptic Gospels and 1 Corinthians, as well as the allusion to the Last Supper in John 6. Our study raises the following question: Are these allusions essentially a prophetic teaching about the sacrificial nature of Christ's coming death, or do they also point to the sacrificial character of the Last Supper celebrated in Christ's memory? Here, I follow up on three clues from our previous study of the Last Supper. I then turn to the historical implications of 1 Corinthians to further my argument.

First, by instituting a New Passover, Christ drew a strong link with the Old Passover celebration. Now, the latter ritual was a sacrifice culminating in a sacrificial meal. Therefore, the New Passover would seem to be a sacrifice as well. Second, Jesus' command to "do this" likely evokes the priestly ordination of Aaron and his sons, as well as their cultic, sacrificial acts. If this exegesis is correct, then Jesus specifically commands the apostles to offer the Eucharist as a sacrifice.[10] Third, the four New Testament accounts of the Last Supper show that the Christians continued to practice the separate blessing over the bread and the cups. This act signifies Christ's death, specifically, by evoking the separation of the blood from the victim's body in temple sacrifices. We thus have a clear sign of the sacrificial nature of the cultic deed in question.

The preceding considerations focused on the early Christian celebration of the Last Supper. We can now turn to 1 Corinthians 10 for additional evidence. In this passage, Paul explains why Christians cannot participate in the worship of idols, a ritual that climaxed in the consumption of sacrificed meat. Christians are to practice covenant loyalty. One of Paul's arguments compares the Last Supper to pagan sacrifices:

> The cup of blessing which we bless, is it not a participation in the blood of Christ? The bread which we break, is it not a participation in the body of Christ? Because there is one bread, we who are many are one body, for we all partake of the one bread. Consider the practice of Israel; are not those who eat the sacrifices partners in the altar? What do I imply then? That food offered to idols is anything, or that an idol is anything? No, I imply that what pagans sacrifice they offer to demons and not to God. I do not want you to be partners with demons (1 Cor 10:16–20).

Through the Eucharist, the faithful commune in the death of Christ, as they share in his body and blood that was offered on the Cross. The focus here is not so much on the precise identity of the gifts (i.e., Christ's corporeal presence), but on the fact that these gifts grant access to the power of Christ's death. Overall, Paul's argument presupposes that a sacred meal enables communion with God, who is worshipped therein. This notion finds parallels in the ancient Mediterranean religious world. Paul also mentions the more important background to his thinking, namely, the logic of Israel's sacrifices. In the Old Testament, a sacrifice enables a shared, sacred meal, which in turn grants spiritual contact with the Lord, the God to whom one sacrifices, the one who is worshipped (Lv 7:6, 7:15; Dt 18:1–4). Hence, when one participates in sacrifices made to demons

10. Brant Pitre, *Jesus and the Last Supper* (Grand Rapids, Mich.: William B. Eerdmans, 2015), 417–20.

(who hide behind the names of idols), one communes with them and breaks covenant loyalty.[11]

Now Paul's argument in 1 Corinthians 10 works only if in fact the Eucharist is a sacrifice.[12] It is this characteristic that allows him to oppose the Last Supper celebration to idolatrous sacrifices. Participation in Christ's body and blood involves a sacred meal, indeed, the completion of a sacrificial meal. Paul contrasts the Lord's cup with the cup of demons, and the Lord's table with the table of demons. George Montague signals that, in verse 18, Paul uses the term "altar" (*thusiastērion*). The terms "altar" and "table" were sometimes interchangeable in the Old Testament, and the central function of Israel's altars was that of sacrifice.[13] Interestingly, Paul never contrasts the Lord's Supper with the worship of idols by calling the latter a sacrifice and the former a sacred meal. Instead, the opposition focuses on the spiritual effect of the two rituals: communion with Christ or with the demons.[14] We will find this theme again in two important second-century Church Fathers.

The Scriptures therefore provide good evidence that the first-century Christians recognized the sacrificial nature of their Last Supper celebration. We find confirmation of our biblical exegesis in the life of the ancient Church.

Jewish Blessings and the Christian Eucharist

As noted in chapter 2, the earliest Eucharistic prayers already imitate the structure of Jewish meal and synagogue prayers. In fact, these blessings have an intrinsically sacrificial nature, and provide the framework through which we can better grasp the doctrine of Eucharistic sacrifice. I will briefly lay out the key themes of Jewish blessings that are directly related to the Eucharist and sacrifice, following Louis Bouyer.

Jewish synagogue and table blessings (*berakoth*) essentially involve a

11. Hans Conzelmann, *First Corinthians: A Commentary on the First Epistle to the Corinthians*, trans. James W. Leitch, Hermeneia: A Critical and Historical Commentary on the Bible (Philadelphia: Fortress Press, 1975), 171–73.

12. I owe this point to my teacher and confrere, Gregory Tatum.

13. Is 65:11; Ezek 41:22, 44:16; Mal 1:7–12.

14. See George T. Montague, *First Corinthians*, Catholic Commentary on Sacred Scripture (Grand Rapids, Mich.: Baker Academic, 2011), 172, 176–78.

response to God's word. Having listened to that word, the community confesses his creative and saving deeds. The blessing centers on God's covenant. In the background stands the doctrine of God's efficacious word as creative and re-creative, a word that brings about what it says.[15]

The ancient synagogue prayers formalized a way of blessing already inscribed in various Psalms that accompanied temple sacrifices (e.g., Ps 39). Jewish table blessings also adopted this structure. The one praying passes from praise and thanksgiving for God's creative, saving deeds to an offering accompanied by intercession. The blessing prayer in turn becomes the means whereby the one who brings the offering consecrates himself to God. The blessing thus expresses the sacrifice of the heart. This is precisely what we find in the sacrifice of praise: the manifestation of one's complete self-giving to God (e.g., Ps 51, Hos 14:2).[16]

The festal meal blessings always enjoyed a special place in Jewish piety. They were likely employed at the Last Supper. The last blessings of the Jewish meal ritual find clear echoes in the early Christian Eucharistic prayers.[17] In the blessing used in the second-century Jewish Passover ritual (and so probably also used at the Last Supper), the theme of memorial dominates.[18] As Bouyer points out, in Jewish piety, the term "memorial" signals a confident supplication that God's powerful word, which worked wonders in the past, may do so again. Here, the people express an objective memorial, showing that God remembers his promises. The focus of this petition lies with the eschatological restoration of Israel.[19]

In this ritual, the meal becomes inseparable from sacrifice.[20] We also find a close link among various forms of sacrifice, as one proceeds from praise and thanksgiving to supplication, with prayers that allow the participants to express their self-offering, in expectation of the eschatological banquet. In the Christian Eucharist, as a memorial of Christ's Passion, the gifts on the altar constitute a sacrifice because they become what they

15. Louis Bouyer, *Eucharist: Theology and Spirituality of the Eucharistic Prayer*, trans. Charles Underhill Quinn (Notre Dame, Ind.: University of Notre Dame Press, 1968), 29–33.

16. Bouyer, *Eucharist*, 45–47, 78–84.

17. Bouyer, *Eucharist*, 89–90.

18. Cesare Giraudo, *In unum corpus: Traité mystagogique sur l'eucharistie*, trans. Éric Iborra and Pierre-Marie Hombert (Paris: Cerf, 2014), 130.

19. Bouyer, *Eucharist*, 85–86.

20. Bouyer, *Eucharist*, 464.

represent, Jesus' body and blood. This perfect offering in turn brings to completion the other sacrifices made, namely, praise, thanksgiving, and each person's self-offering.[21]

The preceding survey shows that the early Christians did not invent prayers *ex nihilo* for their Eucharistic liturgy. Rather, at a time when most Christians were also Jews, they partly drew upon the most obvious sources available to them: Jewish synagogue prayers and the table blessings that made up part of the standard Passover celebration.

The Church Fathers and Ancient Christian Liturgies on the Eucharistic Sacrifice

The Jewish background that we have studied helps us to grasp why the ancient Christian liturgies frequently refer to the whole Eucharistic rite as a sacrifice. Here, the most popular Scripture verse is Malachi 1:11, where God says through the prophet: "From the rising of the sun to its setting my name is great among the nations, and in every place incense is offered to my name, and a pure offering; for my name is great among the nations, says the Lord of hosts." The first use of this passage in a Eucharistic setting is found in chapter 14 of the *Didache*. Apparently, its author sees the whole Eucharistic liturgy as a pure offering.[22]

Another early witness to the theology of Eucharistic sacrifice is Justin Martyr. In his *Dialogue with Trypho*, he presents the wheat offering in Leviticus 14:10 as a prophecy or type of the Eucharistic bread. The Christian offering of the bread and chalice fulfills the prophecy of Malachi 1:10–12: the nations will bring a pure offering to God.[23] Christ himself taught the faithful to make this offering in remembrance of him.[24] For Justin, the Eucharistic celebration as a whole, including the prayers and thanksgiving, constitutes a pleasing offering (*thusia*) to God.[25]

21. Bouyer, *Eucharist*, 465–66.

22. See the summary of different interpretations in Kurt Niederwimmer, *The Didache: A Commentary*, trans. Linda M. Maloney, Hermeneia: A Critical and Historical Commentary on the Bible (Philadelphia: Fortress Press, 1998), 197.

23. Justin Martyr, *Dialogue with Trypho*, chapter 41, in *The Apology, The Second Apology, Dialogue with Trypho*, ed. Michael Slusser, trans. Thomas B. Falls, rev. Thomas P. Halton, Fathers of the Church 6 (Washington, D.C.: The Catholic University of America Press, 2003).

24. Justin Martyr, *Dialogue with Trypho*, chapter 70.

25. Justin Martyr, *Dialogue with Trypho*, chapter 117. For a summary, see Helmut Moll, *Die Lehre von der Eucharistie als Opfer* (Cologne: Peter Hanstein, 1975), 132–36.

We have already seen that Irenaeus of Lyon links the Christian Eucharist with the Last Supper, and that he calls it a sacrifice. In his *Treatise Against Heresies*, he refutes the Gnostics, who separate the New Covenant from the Old. On the contrary, the work of Christ accomplishes the Old Covenant. Irenaeus insists that the Church's sacrifice cannot be simply angelic, cannot simply be a matter of praise and thanksgiving. Rather, human beings also need a material offering, to bring to God the first fruits of his creation, in the form of bread and wine that become the body and blood of Christ. These are offered in thanksgiving to God, for the gifts of his creation. Here, the sacrificial gift of Christ's body and blood and the thanksgiving sacrifice become inseparable.[26]

The oldest Eucharistic prayers tend to combine several sacrificial themes. In the Latin version of Hippolytus's *Apostolic Tradition* the celebrant prays thus after the words of institution:

> Remembering therefore his death and resurrection, we offer to you the bread and cup, giving thanks to you.... And we ask that you would send your Holy Spirit in the oblation of [your] holy church, [that] gathering [them] into one you will give to all who partake of the holy things [to partake] in the fullness of the Holy Spirit, for the strengthening of faith in truth, that we may praise and glorify you.[27]

Within the setting of memorial, the Church makes an offering of the consecrated gifts to God, just as in chapter 41 of Justin Martyr's *Dialogue with Trypho*.[28] This act of offering is also an act of thanksgiving. The petition for the Spirit calls on him to act upon the gifts, which are now identified as an "oblation," though the term may also have a broader sense, and thus include the whole Eucharistic celebration, especially the gifts on the altar.[29]

26. Irenaeus of Lyon, *Contre les hérésies, livre IV*, ed. Adelin Rousseau, Sources chrétiennes 100.2 (Paris: Cerf, 1965), chap. 17, no. 5; Antonio Orbe, *Introduction à la théologie des IIe et IIIe siècles*, trans. Joseph M. López de Castro, Agnès Bastit, and Jean-Michel Roessli, Patrimoines: Christianisme (Paris: Cerf, 2012), vol. 1, 697, 702. Chauvet argues that the second-century theologians essentially spiritualized sacrifice, with a focus on sacrifice as praise, thanksgiving, and moral practice. Chauvet misses the balance that Irenaeus strikes between spiritual and material sacrifice. However, Chauvet does not wholly exclude the themes of redemption or expiation from Eucharistic theology. Chauvet, *Symbol and Sacrament*, 257–59, 311–12.

27. I use the edition of Paul Bradshaw, Maxwell E. Johnson, and L. Edward Phillips, *The Apostolic Tradition: A Commentary*, Hermeneia: A Critical and Historical Commentary on the Bible (Philadelphia: Fortress Press, 2002), 40.

28. Bradshaw et al., *The Apostolic Tradition*, 46.

29. Kenneth Stevenson, *Eucharist and Offering* (New York: Pueblo, 1986), 21.

When the "holy things" and the Spirit bear fruit in the faithful, they can again and more fervently praise the Father, source of all gifts. We find the themes of offering the body and blood, thanksgiving, praise, and the participants' transformation combined in seamless fashion.

Addai and Mari holds together these very themes:

> Do Thou, O my Lord, in thy manifold and ineffable mercies make a good and gracious remembrance for all the upright and just fathers who were pleasing before thee, in the commemoration of the body and blood of thy Christ, which we offer to thee upon the pure and holy altar.... And we ... rejoicing and glorifying and exalting and commemorating and celebrating this great and awesome mystery of the passion, death and resurrection of our Lord Jesus Christ.[30]

Within the setting of praise and memorial, the priest calls for the Spirit to come upon the oblation, so that it may bring forgiveness of sins. The blessings imparted in communion allow the assembly to become a living sacrifice, evoking Romans 12:1.[31] The theme of memorial is pregnant with sacrificial meaning, as it links the celebration with the mystery of Christ's suffering.[32]

The Maronite Sharar liturgy has affinities with Addai and Mari. It maintains the emphasis on memorial, but has more elaborate sacrificial references: "in the commemoration of the body and blood, which we offer to you ... to sanctify the unclean through your sacrifice ... [we] offer this oblation to your divinity ... and may this oblation be acceptable before you."[33] The same anaphora calls the offering a propitiatory sacrifice. Like Irenaeus in his *Treatise Against Heresies*, it employs the language of first fruits.

The language of "bloodless offering" or "bloodless service" is omnipresent in the fourth-century Eucharistic prayers. In general, it refers to the whole Eucharistic celebration, including the gifts on the altar (e.g., Serapion, the Liturgy of St. John Chrysostom).[34] Ambrose uses the same image, but with a more specific reference. His catechesis *On the Sacra-*

30. Anthony Gelston, *The Eucharistic Prayer of Addai and Mari* (Oxford: Clarendon Press, 1992), pp. 51–55, lines 36–40, 51, 53–55.

31. Stevenson, *Eucharist and Offering*, 24–25.

32. Bouyer, *Eucharist*, 156.

33. As quoted by Stevenson, *Eucharist and Offering*, 58–59.

34. See Stevenson, *Eucharist and Offering*, 42–52.

ments recounts the Milanese liturgy. It calls the Eucharistic gifts "this immaculate victim, a reasonable sacrifice, an un-bloody victim, this holy bread, and chalice of eternal life."[35]

For Ambrose and other Church Fathers, the sacrifice of the Mass is one with the sacrifice of the Cross. Writing in the second century, Tertullian refers to communion as a share in the immolated Christ.[36] The notion of sacrament or mystery accounts for the unity of the Mass and the Cross. Preaching in the fourth century, Cyril of Jerusalem calls the Eucharist a propitiatory victim.[37] This doctrine illumines the omnipresence of prayers asking for the participants' purification, reconciliation, or spiritual healing in various ancient anaphora.

Perhaps the classic patristic text on Eucharistic sacrifice is in a homily on Hebrews 9 (verses 24–26) by John Chrysostom.

> What then? Do we not offer daily? Certainly we offer thus, making a memorial (*anamnesis*) of his death. How is it one and not many? Because it was offered once, like that which was carried into the holy of holies.... For we ever offer the same person, not today one sheep and next time a different one, but ever the same offering. Therefore the sacrifice is one. By this argument then, since the offering is made in many places, does it follow that there are many Christs? Not at all, for Christ is everywhere one, complete here and complete there, a single Body.... We do not offer a different sacrifice like the high-priest of old, but we ever offer the same. Or rather we offer the memorial of the sacrifice.[38]

As Gregory Dix points out, for Chrysostom the unity of the Eucharistic sacrifice with that of the Cross is crucial. That unity is explained in three ways: they are joined by having the same offerer (Christ the high priest),

35. Ambrose of Milan, *The Sacraments*, in *Theological and Dogmatic Works*, trans. Roy J. Deferrari, The Fathers of the Church 44 (Washington, D.C.: The Catholic University of America Press, 1963), bk. 4, chap. 6, no. 27.

36. Tertullian, *De Pudicitia*, ed. E. Dekkers, chap. 9, no. 11, in Tertullian, *Opera Montanistica*, vol. 2, CCSL 2 (Turnhout: Brepols, 1954), 1298, ll. 47–49. For an Italian-Latin edition, see *Opere montaniste*, vol. 4.2, ed. A. Capone, S. Isetta, S. Matteoli, A. Persic, R. Uglione, Scrittori Cristiani dell'Africa Romana (Rome: Nuova Città, 2012), 292.

37. Cyril of Jerusalem, "Mystagogical Lecture 5," no. 8. For the Greek text, see Cyril of Jerusalem, *Catéchèses mystagogiques*, ed. Auguste Piédagnel, trans. Pierre Paris, Sources chrétiennes 126bis (Paris: Cerf, 1966), 156–57.

38. John Chrysostom, *Homilies on Hebrews*, "Homily 17," no. 3, quoted in Gregory Dix, *The Shape of the Liturgy* (London: Dacre Press, 1945), 243.

the same offering (his body and blood), and the same benefits (purification from sin).[39]

The early-fifth-century Syrian theologian Theodore of Mopsuestia also sees the Eucharistic sacrifice as one with Christ's Sacrifice on the Cross. He insists that it is neither a new sacrifice, nor the priest's deed alone. Rather, because the Eucharist is a memorial celebration, it is a true sacrifice.[40] The faithful perform a sacrifice along with the celebrant.[41] Theodore refers to the sacrificial ritual as a likeness of heavenly realities, and so signals an intimate connection between the earthly and celestial liturgy. The Christ who suffered, rose again, and ascended to glory is now slain in signs or types (*en tupois*), that is, visibly or sacramentally.[42] Medieval Latin theologians such as Albertus Magnus clung to this mystical notion of signs, as when he refers to "the lamb without spot, which we daily dedicate at the altar by mysteriously slaughtering him."[43]

We can also briefly consider the minister of the sacrifice, a theme to be taken up more fully in chapter 7. Who offers the sacrifice? We saw Chrysostom's answer above. For Ambrose, Christ himself is offered at Mass, and he is the priest who offers as well.[44] Yet the bishop of Milan also refers to the Church as the offering itself (an application of Rom 12:1). Finally, he implies that Christians themselves are the subject making the offering.[45] Christ and the Church are thus both the ones making

39. Dix, *The Shape of the Liturgy*, 244.

40. Theodore of Mopsuestia, "Homily 15," no. 15, in Theodore of Mopsuestia, *Katechetische Homilien*, vol. 1, trans. Peter Bruns, Fontes Christiani 17.1 (Freiburg im Breisgau: Herder, 1994), 399. See also "Homily 15," no. 19, p. 404; Johannes Betz, *Die Eucharistie in der Zeit der griechischen Väter*, vol. 1.1: *Die Aktualpräsenz der Person und des Heilswerkes Jesu im Abendmahl nach der vorephesinischen griechischen Patristik* (Freiburg im Breisgau: Herder, 1955), 195.

41. Khaled Anatolios, "Sacraments in the Fourth Century," in *The Oxford Handbook of Sacramental Theology*, ed. Hans Boersma and Matthew Levering (Oxford: Oxford University Press, 2015), 152–53.

42. Theodore of Mopsuestia, "Homily 15," no. 20, in *Katechetische Homilien*, p. 404.

43. Albertus Magnus, *On the Body of the Lord*, d. 1, chap. 2, trans. Albert Marie Surmanski, The Fathers of the Church: Mediaeval Continuation 17 (Washington, D.C.: The Catholic University of America Press, 2017), 49.

44. Ambrose of Milan, *De officiis*, ed. Mauritius Testard, CCSL 15 (Turnhout, Belgium: Brepols, 2000), bk. 1, chap. 48, no. 239, pp. 88, ll. 61–67.

45. For a Latin-Italian edition, see Ambrose of Milan, *De incarnationis dominicae sacramento*, ed. Claudio Moreschini, Opera Omnia di Sant'Ambrogio 16 (Rome: Nuova Città, 1979), pt. 1, no. 10, pp. 378–79. For an English translation, see Ambrose, *Theological and Dogmatic Works*, 222.

the offering and the victim that is brought to God the Father. As Edward Kilmartin notes, for Ambrose every Mass has a unique sacrificial value. The Latin Father's theology has strong roots in the liturgical prayers used in Milan.[46] His catechesis reflects a well-established belief of the Church's members about the identity and meaning of the Eucharist. Augustine shows Ambrose's influence: the whole Christ, both head and body, offers sacrifice to God in the Eucharist. What the head and his members offer as an oblation is none other than Christ himself, and they offer it daily.[47] Preaching in the same time period, in the eastern Mediterranean, Theodore of Mopsuestia calls the Eucharist an offering brought by the ministers of the New Covenant, who are an image (*eikōn*) of Christ the high priest. Indeed, the heavenly high priest continues to act on earth, precisely through his minister.[48] Thus, the great theologians of the early Church witness to the doctrines of (1) Christ as the priest making the offering in the liturgy, and (2) the Church as the co-subject who offers the sacrifice with her risen Lord.

The ancient Church also witnesses to the doctrine of the Sacrifice of the Mass by its practice and teaching concerning prayers for the dead. Tertullian states that the Christians offer oblations for the sake of the dead on the anniversary of their death.[49] Cyril of Jerusalem notes that the liturgy includes prayers for the dead, especially by presenting Christ who was immolated for our sins to God the Father.[50] The Anaphora of Serapion asks for the sanctification of the deceased.[51] The Syriac Anaphora of the Twelve Apostles begs that the dead may enter into glory on the day of judgment. The prayers for the dead remain neatly distinct from the invocation of the saints in heaven, whose prayers are sought on behalf of the

46. Edward J. Kilmartin, *The Eucharist in the West: History and Theology*, ed. Robert J. Daly (Collegeville, Minn.: Liturgical Press, 1998), 21.

47. Augustine, *De civitate Dei*, ed. Bernardus Dombart and Alphonsus Kalb, CCSL 47 (Turnhout, Belgium: Brepols, 1955), bk. 10, chap. 20, p. 294. For an English translation, see *City of God*, trans. George G. Walsh and Grace Monahan, The Fathers of the Church 14 (Washington, D.C.: The Catholic University of America Press, 1963), 153.

48. Theodore of Mopsuestia, "Homily 15," no. 19, in *Katechetische Homilien*, p. 403. See also no. 21.

49. Tertullian, *De Corona*, ed. Aem. Kroymann, chapter 3, no. 3, in Tertullian, *Opera Montanistica*, vol. 2, CCSL 2, 1043, ll. 19–23.

50. Cyril of Jerusalem, "Mystagogical Lecture 5," no. 10.

51. Stevenson, *Eucharist and Offering*, 52.

pilgrim Church.[52] At this stage in the Church's history and especially in the Orient, we do not yet find a clear doctrine of purgatory, but the Mass clearly brings benefits to the faithful departed who are not yet numbered among the saints.

The Councils of Trent and Vatican II on Eucharistic Sacrifice

These biblical, liturgical, and patristic considerations confirm one of the conclusions of chapter 3, namely, that the Eucharistic liturgy essentially is a sacrifice. In the sixteenth century, in response to Martin Luther and other Protestant leaders, the Council of Trent reached back to liturgical and patristic sources as well as to scholastic theology for inspiration.[53] Trent intended to offer a teaching sufficiently broad so as not to canonize one Catholic theological school's thought over another.

The Council's decrees are divided into two sections: doctrinal chapters and canons. The latter are the most important: they offer dogmatic formula proposed to all the Catholic faithful for their assent. The chapters express the mind of the Council Fathers. They are longer and allow us to interpret the canons well.

In Trent's *Decree on the Sacrifice of the Mass* (from the year 1562), the first canon refuses the notion that the Eucharistic liturgy is not a "true and proper sacrifice."[54] That is, Eucharistic sacrifice is neither simply a metaphor nor a second-class sacrifice. The second canon rejects the notion that, in telling the apostles to "do this in memory of me," Christ did not institute them as priests to offer his body and blood. The third canon proclaims that the Mass is neither simply a sacrifice of praise and thanksgiving, nor a mere commemoration.[55] In other words, it includes the offering of a victim to God. Also, the liturgy does not simply call to mind Christ's words and deeds at the Last Supper. A purely subjective or psychological approach to memorial is unacceptable. Finally, the third canon

52. See Bouyer, *Eucharist*, 205, 285.

53. Erwin Iserloh, "Das tridentinische Meßopferdekret in seinen Beziehungen zu der Kontroverstheologie der Zeit," in *Il Concilio di Trento e la riforma tridentina: atti del convengo storico internazionale*, ed. Convengo storico internazionale 1963 (Rome: Herder, 1965), vol. 2, 404–5, 410–12.

54. Council of Trent, *Decree on the Sacrifice of the Mass*, canon 1, DH 1751.

55. Council of Trent, *Decree on the Sacrifice of the Mass*, canons 2–3, DH 1752–53.

rejects the idea that the Mass has no propitiatory value for the living and the dead. Propitiation is made for the forgiveness of sins and satisfaction for sins.

The canons are strikingly short. The chapters of the decree do much to illumine the reasoning behind the canons. Perhaps the most important passage is found in chapter 1:

> But, because his priesthood was not to end with his death, at the Last Supper, "on the night when he was betrayed," in order to leave to his beloved Spouse the Church a visible sacrifice (as the nature of man demands)—by which the bloody (sacrifice) that he was once for all to accomplish on the Cross would be re-presented, its memory perpetuated until the end of the world, and its salutary power applied for the forgiveness of sins that we daily commit—declaring himself constituted a priest forever according to the order of Melchizedek—he offered his body and blood under the species of bread and wine to God the Father.[56]

The Council reads the Last Supper as an act of the Christ the High Priest. That is, Trent interprets the Gospel accounts in connection with the Letter to the Hebrews.[57] His offering at Calvary was once and for all (Heb 9:12, 10:10), which is to say that its efficacy endures.[58] Because of this efficacy, the Mass cannot be a new sacrifice, nor bring anything not already obtained at Calvary. Still, our constitution as a soul-body composite calls for something more than an invisible sacrifice. The Mass *represents* Christ's historical sacrifice. It is a *memorial* where the saving power of the Cross is "applied," language that signals that the spiritual power of the Mass is wholly derived from the Cross and brought to us via the liturgy. Trent leaves open the precise nature of representation and memorial.[59] Chapter 1 continues:

> he offered his body and blood under the species of bread and wine to God the Father, and under the same signs, gave them to partake of to the disciples (whom he then established as priests of the New Covenant), and ordered them and their successors in the priesthood to offer, saying: "Do this in remembrance of me," etc., as the Church has always understood and taught.[60]

56. Council of Trent, *Decree on the Sacrifice of the Mass*, chap. 1, DH 1740.

57. Urfels, *La Pâque du Messie*, 357

58. Max Thurian, *The Eucharistic Memorial, Part 2: The New Testament*, trans. J. G. Davis, Ecumenical Studies in Worship 8 (Richmond, Va.: John Knox Press, 1961), 7–9.

59. Iserloh, "Das tridentinische Meßopferdekret," 425–26.

60. Council of Trent, *Decree on the Sacrifice of the Mass*, chap. 1, DH 1740.

Trent thus affirms the sacrificial value of the Last Supper, a doctrine that was not part of the Church's dogmatic teaching before Trent, though it finds precedents in the Church Fathers.[61] The Council teaches that the moment in which the Eucharist is instituted should already be a sacrificial ritual. Christ does not just give communion to the apostles and command them to celebrate a sacrifice, he also celebrates that sacramental sacrifice with them on Holy Thursday.[62] Christ institutes the Mass by doing and saying: he offers the sacrifice, and he commands his disciples to perform the same sacrifice. Later in chapter 1, the Council teaches that Christ instituted a new Passover in the context of the old Passover celebration.[63] Here, we find a biblical response to Martin Luther, who had essentially interpreted the Last Supper in complete abstraction from the Passover setting.[64]

In chapter 2 of the same decree, we read:

> In this divine sacrifice that is celebrated in the Mass, the same Christ who offered himself once in a bloody manner on the altar of the Cross is contained and is offered in an un-bloody manner ... the victim is one and the same, the same one now offers himself through the ministry of priests who then offered himself on the Cross; only the way of offering is different. The fruits of this oblation (the bloody one, that is) are received in abundance through this un-bloody [oblation]. By no means, then, does the latter detract from the former. Therefore, it is rightly offered according to apostolic tradition, not only for the sins, punishments, satisfactions and other necessities of the faithful who are alive, but also for those who have died in Christ but are not wholly purified.[65]

The bloody/un-bloody distinction goes back at least to Cyril of Alexandria and is found in various medieval authors.[66] We saw the language of "un-bloody offering" in various ancient Eucharistic prayers. Trent greatly insists on the unity of the Eucharistic sacrifice and Christ's offering on Calvary. This unity ensures the Mass's power of propitiation, and is grounded in (1) the identity of the victim, (2) the different mode of the victim's presence (bloody/un-bloody), (3) the presence of Christ making

61. For the patristic background of this teaching, see Matthiesen, *Sacrifice as Gift*, 66–69.

62. Urfels, *La Pâque du Messie*, 337, 344–60.

63. Council of Trent, *Decree on the Sacrifice of the Mass*, chap. 1, DH 1741.

64. Urfels, *La Pâque du Messie*, 297.

65. Council of Trent, *Decree on the Sacrifice of the Mass*, chap. 2, DH 1743.

66. Urfels, *La Pâque du Messie*, 335.

a priestly offering at Mass, and (4) the difference in the mode of offering (as an act). Consequently, the fruits of the Mass flow in abundance.

Trent deliberately left several issues open, because of ongoing debates among Catholic theologians. The Council did not define whether each Mass has an infinite value (the Thomist position) or is of limited value (the Scotist stance). Instead, chapter 2 simply refers to the "most abundant (*uberrime*) fruit" of the Mass, a compromise formula.[67] Finally, Trent does not appeal to the separate consecration of bread and wine to argue for the Mass's sacrificial character.[68]

The Fathers at Vatican II re-appropriated the rich Catholic teaching on the sacrifice of the Mass, and also reemphasized some liturgical themes present in the tradition, themes that had been somewhat marginalized in ecclesial practice and consciousness. At first, the drafting committee for *Sacrosanctum Concilium* simply assumed the Tridentine teaching on sacrifice and chose not to mention it in the first drafts of the text. The early versions of the constitution emphasized the Eucharist as a Paschal banquet or meal. This focus soon shifted, thanks to the intervention of several Council Fathers.[69] The result of their intervention can be seen in what may be the most doctrinally rich passage in the entire dogmatic constitution:

> At the Last Supper, on the night when he was betrayed, our Savior instituted the eucharistic sacrifice of his Body and Blood. This he did in order to perpetuate the sacrifice of the Cross throughout the ages until he should come again, and so to entrust to his beloved Spouse, the Church, a memorial of his death and Resurrection: a sacrament of love, a sign of unity, a bond of charity, a paschal banquet in which Christ is consumed, the mind is filled with grace, and a pledge of future glory is given to us.[70]

Unlike in previous drafts, the theme of sacrifice now introduces the entire paragraph and offers the framework for the other theological themes.[71]

67. Council of Trent, *Decree on the Sacrifice of the Mass*, chap. 2, DH 1743; Albert Michel, "La messe chez les théologiens postérieurs au Concile de Trente: Essence et efficacité," in *Dictionnaire de théologie catholique*, ed. É. Amann, vol. 10.1 (Paris: L. Letouzey et Âne, 1928), col. 1247.

68. Iserloh, "Das tridentinische Meßopferdekret," 421.

69. Dominic M. Langevin, *From Passion to Paschal Mystery: A Recent Magisterial Development concerning the Christological Foundation of the Sacraments*, Studia Friburgensia 121 (Fribourg, Switzerland: Academic Press, 2015), 116–28, 151–52.

70. *Sacrosanctum Concilium*, no. 47.

71. My reading of this conciliar text finds support in Cipriano Vaggagini, "Fundamental Ideas

By implication, the Eucharist is a banquet precisely as a meal consummating a sacrifice. We see the inspiration behind this teaching when the text, in line with Trent, mentions the historical root of Eucharistic sacrifice. The sacramental meal is our share in Christ's Passover celebration, where the eating of the victim enables the children of Israel to share in God's saving power.[72] The subsequent paragraph supports this reading, for we hear that the faithful should be fed at the Lord's table, and also offer the sacred victim (with the priest) to God the Father.[73] The Council takes the classical term "sacred banquet" from the Office of Corpus Christ composed by Aquinas, and makes it the "paschal banquet." Joris Geldhof explains: "The expression … involves and interweaves meal and mystery, anthropology and theology, assembly and eschaton, the earth and the eternal, togetherness and elevation, bodily pleasures and heavenly joy, etc."[74]

In paragraph 47 of *Sacrosanctum Concilium*, we read that the same sacrifice of the Cross is perpetuated in the Church: we have a unity of sacrifice between Calvary and the Mass. Again, Vatican II echoes Trent. In paragraph 47, the text takes up and develops Trent, as the Eucharist is called a memorial of both Christ's Passion and his Resurrection. Trent had spoken of the former theme but not the latter. The sources of Vatican II for this change include the liturgical texts (the Roman canon, the liturgies of St. Basil and St. John Chrysostom) and several Church Fathers such as Melito of Sardis and Augustine.[75] Echoes of the great Latin doctor appear in the mention of certain Eucharistic fruits: a sacrament and bond of charity, as well as a sign of unity. Both themes were dear to Augustine.

The text refers to one of Aquinas's most famous prayers, which the

---

of the Constitution," in *The Liturgy of Vatican II: A Symposium*, vol. 1, ed. William Barauna, trans. Salvatore Attanasio (Chicago: Franciscan Herald Press, 1966), 115.

72. Langevin, *From Passion to Paschal Mystery*, 151.

73. *Sacrosanctum Concilium*, no. 48. Paragraph 47 reads the Last Supper as a Passover meal. The Council takes this exegesis for granted, against the background of Trent and a massive liturgical tradition. In other words, both Vatican II and constant liturgical tradition supports our exegesis of the Last Supper, which we discussed in chapter 2.

74. Joris Geldhof, "On Interiorizing the Mystery of the Eucharist: A Reflection on *Sacrosanctum Concilium*, no. 48," *Questions Liturgiques / Studies in Liturgy* 97 (2016): 128.

75. Langevin, *From Passion to Paschal Mystery*, 128, 140–42. See also Gérald de Servigny, *La théologie de l'eucharistie dans le concile Vatican II* (Paris: Pierre Téqui, 2000), 147–71; Thurian, *The Eucharistic Memorial, Part 2*, 37–39.

Latin faithful still recite at the beginning of Eucharistic adoration: "O sacred banquet, in which Christ becomes our food, the soul is filled with grace, and a pledge of future glory is given to us."[76] The prayer ends on an eschatological note, one already present earlier in paragraph 47 ("until he should come again"). Here, the Council Fathers allude to St. Paul's instruction to the faithful: "For as often as you eat this bread and drink this cup, you proclaim the Lord's death until he comes" (1 Cor 11:26). The post-conciliar reform of the Roman rite reintroduced this acclamation as a prayer of the people, just as it had been done in the ancient liturgies and in the eastern liturgies over the centuries. This is a strikingly beautiful recovery of a biblical tradition for the Church's liturgy, of the community's confession of Christ's sacrifice.[77]

In the teaching of Vatican II, we find a stunning, compact appropriation of the Catholic tradition of Eucharistic sacrifice, and a theological and pastoral challenge as well. In two paragraphs, the Council Fathers set out a number of tasks for pastors and theologians. First, how can we recover a biblical and traditional vision of sacrifice in which the meal aspect is not minimized but integrated? Second, how can we understand and preach the theme of the Eucharist as a memorial of Christ's Resurrection, and not just as a memorial of his Passion? Third, in what way can we plant the eschatological finality of the Eucharist more firmly in the awareness of the faithful? I shall answer the first and third questions shortly, and the second question in chapter 9.

A Systematic Theology of Eucharistic Sacrifice

A Note on Theological Method

The previous considerations help us to articulate the tasks facing a theology of Eucharistic sacrifice. We see the objections to a classical theology of Eucharistic sacrifice, the biblical and historical data for which systematic theology should account, and the kind of doctrinal balance that should be sought. A Catholic vision of Eucharistic sacrifice should manifest

76. Magnificat Antiphon for Second Vespers, Office of Corpus Christi.

77. The late Msgr. Albert-Marie de Monléon, OP (bishop of Meaux), once told me that the inclusion of this acclamation stands out as one of the most important liturgical reforms instituted by Vatican II.

the complementarity and interplay of various kinds of sacrifices, such as praise, thanksgiving, and the offering of the victim. Such an approach would allow us to make sense of the early liturgy's use of Jewish prayers of blessing (*berakah*) and the various kinds of offerings mentioned in the anaphora. Theology's task is to show how these sacrifices deepen the transformation of the assembly into the body of Christ, a frequent theme in the Eucharistic prayers. Given our findings on the ancient liturgy, the Fathers, and Trent, we also need to seek an account of how the Mass brings reconciliation and affects the souls of the deceased. Finally, theology should provide at least a partial explanation of how the Eucharistic sacrifice remains united with the sacrifice of Calvary, and should illumine the claims of the Catholic theological tradition concerning this unity.

Systematic reflection on how the Eucharist is a sacrifice gradually emerged in the Middle Ages. There was no controversy on this matter in the ancient Church, and little in the medieval period, as everyone accepted the sacrificial character of the Mass. Extensive reflection on the issue began during the Protestant Reformation, when it naturally took on an apologetic aim. One of the more important sixteenth-century Catholic voices was Thomas Vio Cardinal Cajetan. The Italian Dominican took Aquinas's scattered comments on the topic and developed a more explicit synthesis that could respond to the concerns of Martin Luther.[78] Writing shortly before Vatican II, Journet proposed a synthesis on the foundation of Aquinas, Cajetan, and the Council of Trent. Journet would go on to assist at Vatican II as bishop and cardinal.

I center my systematic account of Eucharistic sacrifice on Aquinas's teaching, and this for several reasons. First, his doctrine exercised much influence on Trent, the Council that has left us the most extensive magisterial teaching on sacrifice. Second, Thomas's doctrine enjoys a certain simplicity that was sometimes lost in the subtle Eucharistic theories of

78. For an English translation of Cajetan's responses to Luther on the Eucharist, see his tractates "Errors on the Lord's Supper (1525)" and "The Sacrifice of the Mass: Against the Lutherans (1531)," in Jared Wicks, *Cajetan Responds: A Reader in Reformation Controversy* (Washington, D.C.: The Catholic University of America Press, 1978), 153–74, 189–200. For the Latin of the latter text, see "De Missa Sacrificio et Ritu, adversus Lutheranos, ad Clementem VII," in *Opuscula Omnia* (Venice: Apud Iuntas, 1712), 218–20. For an earlier treatise of his, see "The Celebration of the Mass," in Heiko Augustinus Oberman, *Forerunners of the Reformation: The Shape of Late Medieval Thought*, trans. Paul L. Nyhus (London: Lutterworth Press, 1967), 256–78.

early modern scholastic authors. Third, his thought is tightly interwoven with other doctrinal themes, especially his Christology. Fourth, by looking beyond his formal treatment of the Eucharist in the *Summa theologiae*, we find resources to integrate the theme of interior or spiritual sacrifice so dear to the Fathers and the liturgical tradition. Overall, my aim is to account for Scripture as well as the liturgical and conciliar traditions, without positing rupture in tradition, yet without pretending that Aquinas and Trent solve all theological problems.

In the following pages, I first look at sacrifice in general from an Augustinian-Thomistic perspective. I then turn to a few specific aspects of Eucharistic sacrifice: the Mass as an action that images the Cross and Resurrection; the presence of the victim who suffered for us; Christ the high priest offering himself; the joint priestly action of Christ and the Church in rendering exterior and interior sacrifice; the fruits of the sacrifice as an offering; and finally, communion as completing and sharing in the sacrifice.

Sacrifice in General

We first need to consider some general descriptive definitions (in the plural) of sacrifice. I will not consider an abstract definition that can be applied to the biblical and liturgical data. Starting in the sixteenth century, Catholic theologians have spilled much ink in search of a precise, technical definition that would apply perfectly to the Cross and the Mass. Interestingly, Aquinas provides a rather technical definition of sacrifice in his treatment of the virtue of religion, but he does not use it when he speaks of the Mass. Aquinas employs a descriptive approach, that is, he receives the New Testament description of the Cross as a sacrifice.[79] In fact, he thereby identifies the nature of the primary analogue from which we can in turn find the truth and value of all other sacrifices, including the Old Testament figures.

With Augustine, Aquinas sees sacrifice as an exterior expression of one's interior dedication to God. It signifies interior offering or surrender to God.[80] The relation between external and internal sacrifice is crucial. We already find it at the Cross, where Jesus' perfect charity is the cen-

79. Clark, *Eucharistic Sacrifice and the Reformation*, 446, 464.

80. Thomas Aquinas, *Summa theologiae* II-II, q. 85, aa. 1–3; Matthiesen, *Sacrifice as Gift*, 35, 41.

tral aspect of his sacrifice, while his suffering and death both constitute the external sacrifice and express this charity (they manifest his love in its ultimate realization). The interior/exterior couplet allows us to integrate a holistic anthropology: sacrifice is not just a matter of the heart, while bodily suffering or death alone do not suffice to render a pleasing sacrifice to God. In this way, we link Christian sacrifice (from worship to ascetical practices) with Calvary: in each case, charity holds pride of place.

Sacrifice can also be described as the ritual handing over of a sacred gift to God. It cannot be reduced to making a gift, but rather includes a specific kind of gift. We note four characteristics of sacrifice in this description: (1) a ritual setting, (2) an act of handing over, (3) the sacred character of the gift, and (4) God as the recipient.[81] Now to be a sacrifice, these acts must be freely chosen and intended, for exterior sacrifice is ordered to interior sacrifice and draws its value from it. During his earthly life, Jesus continually gave his love to the Father, yet he made formal sacrifices in particular settings, most especially at the Last Supper and the Cross. Indeed, the Bible never shows Jesus making a temple sacrifice. His Passion, including the Cross, fits well this definition of sacrifice, for the Letter to the Hebrews manifests its ritual or liturgical character. The Cross was a new sacrifice; indeed, it was one of a kind.[82]

The terms *oblation* and *offering* refer to the gift-aspect of sacrifice. In the Scriptures, sacrifice need not include immolation (e.g., Old Testament grain offerings). Offering is essential to sacrifice, but immolation is not necessary in every type of sacrifice. The Eucharist is an offering and includes immolation.[83] To offer something is to bring a gift to God. Immolation means to renounce something, even to destroy a victim: Jesus immolated himself on the Cross.[84] In the Mass, Christ is sacramentally immolated, for he is immolated by means of the signs that make present the fruits of his immolation (on the cross). This is the heart of our offering.[85]

81. Thomas Aquinas, *Summa theologiae* II-II, q. 85, a. 3, ad 3; Matthiesen, *Sacrifice as Gift*, 41.

82. Eugène Masure, *Le sacrifice du chef*, 7th ed. (Paris: Beauchesne, 1944), 299. Michel, "La messe," 1279–83.

83. Matthiesen, *Sacrifice as Gift*, 43–46; also Thomas Aquinas, *Summa theologiae* III, q. 83, a. 1.

84. Masure, *Le sacrifice du chef*, 2–3, 297, 326, 329.

85. Anscar Vonier, *A Key to the Doctrine of the Eucharist* (Eugene, Ore.: Assumption Press, 2013), 160.

A gift or victim is offered to God so that it may be accepted by him. Such acceptance denotes that the favor requested in the sacrifice will be obtained, according to God's will. The Father's acceptance of the Sacrifice of the Cross was signified by the rending of the temple veil at the moment of Jesus' death, and even more so by his Resurrection and Ascension (see the Letter to the Hebrews). God freely obliges himself to enter into a gift exchange. By his acceptance, the gift is returned and we partake in it.[86] Such partaking occurs by communion: the sacred meal consummates the sacrifice and depends on it.

We have seen a series of key themes: interior and exterior sacrifice, a ritual setting, an exchange of gifts, the offering and immolation of a victim, and communion in the offering. Aquinas has a theology of praise and thanksgiving in his study of sacrifice in general, but he does not extensively integrate this with his Eucharistic theology. I shall draw upon twentieth-century theologians such as Charles Journet and Eugène Masure to propose such an integration. This kind of endeavor fits well with Aquinas's Augustinian approach to sacrifice.

As we proceed to the heart of our systematic account, we should keep two distinctions in mind. The first has already been mentioned: the interior and exterior sacrifice. These do not stand in tension, and keeping each of them integrated in our theology of sacrifice will overcome many problems. The second distinction is between the Eucharist as sacrament and as sacrifice. Aquinas explains: "This sacrament is simultaneously sacrifice and sacrament; but it has the nature of sacrifice inasmuch as it is offered up, and the nature of sacrament inasmuch as it is received."[87] As a sacrament, the Eucharist is in the order of sanctification, of God pouring out grace. As a sacrifice, the Eucharist is in the cultic order of our relation to God, our upward movement to him that is made possible by the sacrament.[88] Sacrament and sacrifice are closely linked but not identical: in the first, Christ acts through the priest to bring us his body and blood, while in the second, the Church renders worship to God. There simply is no reason to separate these distinct and central aspects of the Eucharist.

86. Matthiesen, *Sacrifice as Gift*, 47–51.

87. Thomas Aquinas, *Summa theologiae* III, q. 79, a. 5.

88. Thomas Aquinas, *Summa theologiae* III, q. 60, a. 5; q. 79, a. 1.

The Sacrifice as Representation

Thomas's theology focuses on the theme of the Mass as an image of the Cross.[89] In his *Summa theologiae*, he asks whether Christ is immolated in the Eucharist. He answers thus:

> The celebration of this sacrament is called a sacrifice for two reasons. First, because, as Augustine says (*Ad Simplician*, book 2), "the images of things are called by the names of the things whereof they are the images; as when we look upon a picture or a fresco, we say, 'This is Cicero and that is Sallust.'" But, as was said above [q. 79, a. 1], the celebration of this sacrament is an image representing Christ's Passion, which is His true sacrifice. Accordingly, the celebration of this sacrament is called Christ's sacrifice. Hence it is that Ambrose, in commenting on Hebrews 10:1, says: "In Christ was offered up a sacrifice capable of giving eternal salvation; what then do we do? Do we not offer it up every day in memory of His death?" Secondly it is called a sacrifice, in respect of the effect of His Passion: because by this sacrament, we are made partakers of the fruit of our Lord's Passion. Hence in one of the Sunday Secret Prayers (*Ninth Sunday after Pentecost*) we say: "Whenever the commemoration of this sacrifice is celebrated, the work of our redemption is enacted."[90]

Aquinas employs traditional language, yet his terminology can be misleading. A picture of Cicero is not Cicero himself, but rather an artistic creation that recalls Cicero for us. Also, Old Testament rituals likewise were images of the Cross to come, especially the sacrifice of the paschal lambs. Yet Old Testament sacrifices were not the same as the sacrifice of the Cross. Aquinas sees the Mass as something greater. First, he does not say that the Mass is only an image of the Cross. Second, he evokes the doctrine of Augustine, for whom image and the reality imaged are not separate (which is wholly in keeping with the Jewish notion of memorial). Third, Thomas strives to show the unity of the Mass and the Cross. The Eucharist cannot be a separate sacrifice. As Thomas says elsewhere, "it is called a sacrifice insofar as it represents the Passion of Christ."[91] The

89. The next three sections have especially benefited from the insights of Emmanuel Perrier.

90. Thomas Aquinas, *Summa theologiae* III, q. 83, a. 1.

91. Thomas Aquinas, *Summa theologiae* III, q. 73, a. 4, ad 3; Bruce D. Marshall, "The Whole Mystery of Our Salvation: Saint Thomas Aquinas on the Eucharist as Sacrifice," in *Rediscovering Aquinas and the Sacraments: Studies in Sacramental Theology*, ed. Michael Dauphinais and Matthew Levering (Chicago: Hillenbrand Books, 2009), 49. Aquinas's theology of image also emerges

passage provides us with an entryway into Aquinas's theology of Eucharistic sacrifice, yet we need to look elsewhere in his corpus to fill out the picture.

We should recall a basic theological principle: the sacraments of the New Covenant effect by signifying. Through words, gestures, and the use of material realities like water, oil, or bread, we signify or represent a hidden reality, "the sign of a sacred reality inasmuch as it is sanctifying man."[92] What is unique about New Covenant sacraments is their fruitfulness, their spiritual efficacy. Here, sacramental representation is not just a sign, but richly metaphysical, indeed mystical, so that the invisible is rendered present by a visible element, a ritual word and deed. In representing the Passion, we make that very sacrifice present here and now.[93] This does not mean that Old Testament images remain wholly separate from the saving reality that they signify, yet the Mass offers a richer presence of the reality being imaged than the rituals of the Old Covenant did.[94]

We might note that the theme of efficacious representation takes nothing away from the rite's signifying or manifesting function. There is simply no need to oppose the epiphanic or revelatory aspect of the liturgy to the efficacy of the sign.[95] The analogy between the ritual acts of the Eucharist and the mysteries of the life of Christ confirms this claim. Also, the richer the signification, the more marvelous the gift imparted thereby. Indeed, since the many liturgical signs (word and gesture) should be understood in relation to each other and to the revelation attained, we may say that the signification, and so also the gift imparted by those signs, can

in his study of icons, following John Damascene (*Summa theologiae* III, q. 25). I am grateful to an anonymous reviewer for showing me this link.

92. Thomas Aquinas, *Summa theologiae* III, q. 60, a. 2.

93. Marshall, "The Whole Mystery," 57; Masure, *Le sacrifice du chef*, 263–64.

94. For signs and presence, see Robert Sokolowski, *Eucharistic Presence: A Study in the Theology of Disclosure* (Washington, D.C.: The Catholic University of America Press, 1994), chapters 2–3. For an eastern Orthodox approach to the metaphysics of Christian symbols, see John D. Zizioulas, "Symbolism and Realism in Orthodox Worship," in *The Eucharistic Communion in the World*, ed. Luke Ben Tallon (London: T&T Clark, 2011), 83–97.

95. Enrico Mazza sets up a false opposition in Thomas between sacramental sign and sacramental presence, figure and truth, representation and the substantial presence of Christ's body and blood. Where Aquinas distinguishes yet unites, Mazza separates. See Enrico Mazza, *The Celebration of the Eucharist: The Origin of the Rite and the Development of Its Interpretation*, trans. Matthew J. O'Connell (Collegeville, Minn.: Liturgical Press, 1998), 207–14.

never be fully captured by the mind's gaze, much as God's names remain an inexhaustible mystery that we can always ponder anew.

The notion of fruitful representation partly echoes the ancient Jewish vision of Passover: in the memorial of the first Passover, the Jews begged God to once again actualize his saving power that was operative in the Exodus.[96] Still, the rites of the Old Covenant did not contain the power to save or justify (Heb 11:8, 18–19). The Passover ritual is a sign, with its prayers, gestures, and gifts. Christ's Passover is the fulfillment of this sign, and now the sign becomes astoundingly fruitful. He performs the saving deed in the Last Supper ritual and in the Cross that this ritual prefigures.[97] He brings to Israel the power of Passover as he ritually enacts it.

For Thomas, the heart or essence of the sacrifice occurs in the consecration: "The representation of the Lord's Passion is done in the very consecration of this sacrament, in which the body ought not to be consecrated without the blood."[98] For Aquinas, this prayer is the most important liturgical image of the Passion. First, this prayer said over bread and wine effects Christ's bodily presence, so that sacrifice and presence go together. The one who suffered on the Cross comes to us in his body and blood. Second, Aquinas emphasizes the importance of the separate consecration of the bread and wine for sacrifice: "the blood separately consecrated expressly represents Christ's Passion."[99] This twofold act sacramentally represents the separation of Jesus' blood from his body, that is, the shedding of his blood unto death. When I say "sacramentally," I mean by a sign. More precisely, sacramental representation here also refers to a sign that *contains* the hidden, separated substance, the body and blood. Already in Scripture, the separate blessing of bread and wine as body and blood

96. For a helpful overview of Jewish memorial, see David E. Stern, "Remembering and Redemption," and the response by Richard Taylor, both in *Rediscovering the Eucharist: Ecumenical Conversations*, ed. Roch A. Kereszty (New York: Paulist Press, 2003), 1–26.

97. For Aquinas's appropriation of a biblical notion of memorial, see Jean-Pierre Torrell, *Christ and Spirituality in St. Thomas Aquinas*, trans. Bernhard Blankenhorn (Washington, D.C.: The Catholic University of America Press, 2011), 144n43. Here too, Mazza misreads Thomas: see Mazza, *The Celebration of the Eucharist*, 201.

98. Thomas Aquinas, *Summa theologiae* III, q. 80, a. 12, ad 3. See also q. 82, a. 10, ad 1; Manfred Hauke, "What Is the Holy Mass? The Systematic Discussion on the 'Essence' of Eucharistic Sacrifice," in *Celebrating the Eucharist: Sacrifice and Communion*, ed. Gerard Deighan, Fota Liturgy Series 5 (Wells, Somerset, Great Britain: Smenos / Carrigboy, 2012), 123.

99. Thomas Aquinas, *Summa theologiae* III, q. 78, a. 3, ad 2. See also q. 76, a. 2, ad 1.

in the Passover setting has strong sacrificial connotations.[100] As noted previously, the Eucharistic sacrifice is essentially both an oblation and an immolation. The latter is precisely what we see signified, represented and thus realized in the consecratory words and gestures just mentioned. The sacrificial nature of Christ's death finds expression not just by a separate reference to his body and blood, but also in other details of the consecratory prayer: his body is given for us, his blood will be poured out for many.[101] The rite is a sign of the Passion, a sign that contains the reality being represented.[102] The Eucharist as sacrament grounds its sacrificial nature: because of Christ's sacramental presence, we can speak of a sacrifice. Yet there is more to the sacrifice than just the presence of Christ as victim.

The Mass also represents Christ in the acts of celebrating the Eucharist, for the priest says "This is *my* body," not "This is Jesus' body." The Mass images Christ at the Last Supper. The liturgy also represents the crucified Lord offering himself to the Father (as manifested in Hebrews). That is, we have a twofold representation. Clearly, when the Mass signifies, it effects what is being signified. As Bruce Marshall says, "Christ is present in the Eucharist precisely as he is represented by it."[103] The visible priest's act of offering at the altar becomes an efficacious intercession for the world's salvation, because it is part of the representation of the Passion.

Aquinas and Trent focus the language of memorial on the Passion. Here, they continue an ancient tradition (going back to Melito of Sardis) that centered the theme of Christ's Passover on his Passion. Another tradition (which includes Augustine) sees Christ's Passover as his passing to the Father, so that it includes his Passion, Resurrection, and Ascension. The Eucharist is the memorial of all three mysteries, a theme reemphasized in *Sacrosanctum Concilium*.[104] Yet neither the documents of Vatican II nor

100. Thurian, *The Eucharistic Memorial, Part 2*, 51–52.

101. The doctrine that the separate consecration of bread and wine signifies the Passion and Death of Jesus can be found in the writings of Church Fathers and has gained widespread theological acceptance over the centuries. For one patristic example, see Gregory of Nazianzen, "Letter 171," in *Briefe*, ed. Michael Wittig, Bibliothek der Griechischen Literatur 13 (Stuttgart: Anton Hiersemann, 1981). For an overview, see Hauke, "What Is the Holy Mass?," 123; Michel, "La messe," 1247.

102. This likely explains why Aquinas prefers the term "representation" over that of "image" or "sign," even as he employs all three terms. "Image" emphasizes the alterity of the reality imaged, while "sign" might give the theme of memorial a strictly intentional meaning. Representation fits best with a hidden, substantial presence.

103. Marshall, "The Whole Mystery," 50.

104. *Sacrosanctum Concilium*, no. 47.

the conciliar debates tell us much about the intention behind this language.[105] Dominic Langevin fills in this lacuna by applying some principles of Thomistic sacramental theology. The liturgy signifies Christ's Resurrection. For example, in the new Roman rite, the Pauline memorial acclamation after the words of institution have the people "confess your [Christ's] Resurrection, until you come again." Here, Jesus is addressed as risen and ascended.[106] Then, the priest goes on to invoke the memorial of Christ's Resurrection and Ascension. Similar prayers are found in other anaphora, including the Liturgies of St. Basil and St. John Chrysostom: The Passion, Resurrection, and Ascension are indicated together, as a kind of unbreakable unity. By signifying these mysteries, the liturgy becomes a fruitful mediation of their saving power. Christ's self-offering was accepted by the Father at Calvary.[107] This divine acceptance was most powerfully manifested in his Resurrection and Ascension. In the Roman canon, the mention of the memorial of the Passion, Resurrection, and Ascension leads straight to the liturgical prayers asking God to accept our sacrifice today, as the priest begs the Father to send his angel to take our sacrifice to his heavenly altar. Because of the Resurrection, these prayers presume that the sacrifice is already acceptable.[108] The memorial of Christ's Resurrection manifests the efficacy of the Eucharistic sacrifice.

The Paschal Lamb on the Altar

A true Eucharistic sacrifice presupposes the presence of the saving victim. I have already discussed this theme from the perspective of representation. I now ponder the link between Christ's substantial presence and sacrifice in a more direct way.

The Mass makes present the body that suffered on Calvary and the blood that was shed on the Cross.[109] Yet the one whose body is present at Mass is not suffering now. Rather, what is present is the resurrected, glorified Christ. Aquinas accepts the following theological principle: Christ's

105. Langevin, *From Passion to Paschal Mystery*, 128–42.

106. Langevin, *From Passion to Paschal Mystery*, 273.

107. Hence, following a universal ancient and medieval tradition, Christ descends triumphantly to the limbo of the just on Holy Saturday and leads them to heaven. This is possible only if the sacrifice of the Cross was a complete sacrifice, one accepted by the Father.

108. Langevin, *From Passion to Paschal Mystery*, 275–76.

109. Thomas Aquinas, *Summa theologiae* III, q. 73, a. 5, ad 2.

substantial presence in the Eucharist is according to his actual, current existence.[110] Since he now abides in glory, the glorified substance of his flesh and blood are found on the altar. There we have the same body that suffered in the past and is now glorified.[111] That is to say, we are not dealing with time travel.

There is a good biblical reason to hold that the glorified Christ comes to us on the altar. In John 6, Jesus promises the gift of his flesh and blood as food and drink, but in their glorified form. In verses 62–63, Jesus responds to the disciples who are stunned by his invitation to eat his flesh and drink his blood by asking them: "What if you were to see the Son of man ascending to where he was before? It is the Spirit that gives life, the flesh is of no avail." Jesus refers to his future exaltation, to his Resurrection and Ascension, for the Holy Spirit will raise Christ from the dead, rendering him immortal and his body impassible.[112] This passage as well as John 6:54 point to the link between our future bodily resurrection and the consumption of Christ's flesh and blood. By implication, the gift consumed has already been glorified, and so renders our bodies like his.

Still, we can also say that at Mass Christ is present as victim. Indeed, we must say it, for this is how the liturgy refers to the sacrament. Augustine speaks of the liturgy thus: "Has Christ not been sacrificed once in himself, and yet in the mystery he is sacrificed for the people, not only during all the solemnities of Easter, but every day."[113] Augustine's language is perfectly accurate, and this for at least three reasons. First, the one who suffered is corporeally present. It is the same body, for his resurrected body is not a whole new body, as the marks of his Passion remain. Second, he is represented as immolated, as we hear in various Eucharistic prayers, but especially as signified in the separate consecration of the body and blood. Such signification already began in the time of Israel, as Aquinas explains: "in all the sacrifices and offerings of the ancients, the

110. Marilyn McCord Adams, *Some Later Medieval Theories of the Eucharist: Thomas Aquinas, Giles of Rome, Duns Scotus and William Ockham* (Oxford: Oxford University Press, 2010), 85–86; Charles Journet, *The Mass: The Presence of the Sacrifice of the Cross*, trans. Victor Szczurek (South Bend, Ind.: St. Augustine's Press, 2008), 61–71.

111. Thomas Aquinas, *Summa theologiae* III, q. 81, a. 3; Journet, *The Mass*, 62.

112. Pitre, *Jesus and the Last Supper*, 214–15.

113. Augustine, "Letter 98," no. 9, in *Letters 1–99*, trans. Roland Teske, The Works of Saint Augustine 2.1 (Hyde Park, N.Y.: New City Press, 2001). For the Latin, see Augustine, *Epistulae 56–100*, ed. Kl. D. Daur, CCSL 31A (Turnhout, Belgium: Brepols, 2005), 233.

res et sacramentum in the Eucharist was signified, which is also signified by the paschal lamb, namely, Christ himself, who offered himself to God the Father as an offering and victim on our behalf."[114] The priest and the Church immolate Christ, for they offer the separated body and blood to the Father. As this is done in a sacramental mode, the immolation remains un-bloody.[115] Third, the benefits of the immolation are brought to us by the Eucharistic sacrifice, especially a new share in Christ's love, as well as the forgiveness of and satisfaction for sins.

It is important to see that the Eucharist does not involve time travel to Calvary.[116] Christ suffered in his human nature, so that his bloody sacrifice was a temporal act, which has come to an end with Jesus' death. The Passion is not an eternal event, even though the divine person of the Son is the subject that suffers on the Cross.

The High Priest in our Midst

The Eucharistic Sacrifice is carried out today by Christ the High Priest, together with the Church. I have already considered this theme from the perspective of representation. I now take up its other key characteristics. I begin with Christ's priestly offering in the New Testament and then proceed to his priestly act in the liturgy. Here, the theological stakes can be shown well by comparing the approaches of Aquinas and his near-contemporary John Duns Scotus. The aim of our study is to show the unity of Christ's sacrificial act with the Church's. As Aquinas states: "The sacrifice, which is offered daily in the Church, is not other (*aliud*) than the sacrifice that Christ himself offered."[117] This theme leads us to

114. Thomas Aquinas, *Commentary on the Sentences, Book IV*, d. 8, q. 1, a. 2, quaestiuncula 2, ad 6, in *Commentary on the Sentences, Book IV, Distinctions 1–13*, trans. Beth Mortensen, Latin/English Edition of the Works of St. Thomas Aquinas 7 (Green Bay, Wisc.: Aquinas Institute, 2017), 336.

115. Masure, *Le sacrifice du chef*, 325, 329.

116. Inspired by Odo Casel, Cesare Giraudo argues that the Eucharistic sacrifice does not make the past event of Calvary present to us, but rather makes us present to that event, via the liturgy's sacramental representation. He also describes the historical past (Calvary) as being elevated into an eternal present (*In unum corpus*, 532–34). Giraudo derives his understanding of sacramental representation directly from his exegesis of the Old Testament Passover (*In unum corpus*, 87–102). In my view, Giraudo's notions of presence and time remain obscure. His theology of memorial and representation seems to be an interpretation of Scripture, without any philosophical mediation, which may account for the ambiguity of his theory. But Scripture alone does not offer a complete theology of time: for this, we need metaphysical theology.

117. Thomas Aquinas, *Summa theologiae* III, q. 22, a. 3, ad 2.

ponder a twofold representation of Christ's priestly act, at the Last Supper and on the Cross. The latter theme takes us to the question of the suffering Christ's prophetic and beatific knowledge as a means of personal contact with the liturgy today, a contact that includes each believer who participates therein.

At the Last Supper, Christ offered his body and blood to the Father. This un-bloody sacrifice in the Upper Room was a sacramental offering that anticipated his perfect self-offering at Calvary.[118] By separately consecrating bread and wine, Christ signified his coming death. By consecrating these gifts distinctly as his body and blood, he made a sacrifice.[119] For by this act, Christ not only signified his death, he also held the body and blood in his hands and offered it to the Father. The sacrificial sign was filled with the reality signified: the body and blood of the Son about to be given over unto death.

Likewise, the Church's sacrifice presupposes the presence of the victim, which comes about through the consecration. Now at the consecration, the priest is Christ's sole instrument, meaning that the people do not consecrate. But this prayer enables the priest and the people to offer Christ the victim (exterior sacrifice) together with their (and Jesus') love and praise to God (interior sacrifice). In the offertory of the Roman rite, the priest completes the offertory and invites the people: "Pray brethren, that this my sacrifice and yours may be acceptable to God, the almighty Father." The priest and people perform the offering in distinct yet inseparable modes, and Christ's priestly presence enables both.[120]

Aquinas and a long line of medieval and modern theologians identify the heart of the Eucharistic sacrifice with the words of institution: "by the consecration of this sacrament, sacrifice is offered to God."[121] Starting at the consecration, the priest and, through him, the people, can make a perfect offering to the Father. However, Aquinas does not limit the sacrifice to the consecration. Nowhere does he exclusively identify the consecration with the sacrifice. Also, he describes how other parts of the liturgy

118. Vonier, *A Key to the Doctrine of the Eucharist*, 112.

119. Marshall, "What Is the Eucharist?," 515.

120. Journet, *The Mass*, 96–106.

121. Thomas Aquinas, *Summa theologiae* III, q. 82, a. 10; Joseph Pohle, *Lehrbuch der Dogmatik in sieben Büchern*, 7th ed., vol. 3., Wissenschaftliche Bibliothek, Series 1: Theologische Lehrbücher 22 (Paderborn, Germany: Ferdinand Schöningh, 1922), 312–13.

represent the Passion, such as the priest's extension of his arms in prayer and the fraction rite.[122] We can add that communion in the victim is essential for sacrifice, as we will see shortly.[123]

Catholic theology seeks to demonstrate how the sacrifice of the Mass is one with Calvary, and it would give a stronger account if it could show that the sacrificial *act* of offering at Mass is also immediately Christ's priestly act. Such a theological demonstration would illumine or unfold the teaching of Trent, which states: "the same [one] now offers himself through the ministry of priests who then offered himself on the Cross; only the manner of the offering is different."[124] But how does he offer with them? The basis for the unity of the Cross and the Mass is found in the consecration. But how does Christ consecrate at Mass? Two major theological schools have proposed answers, and both are allowed by Trent. I refer to the Scotist and Thomist traditions.

The late-thirteenth-century Franciscan John Duns Scotus does not deny that Christ himself offers the sacrifice of the Mass in some way, but he excludes the notion that Christ is the one who immediately offers the sacrifice. Scotus appeals to Hebrews 9:22, which teaches that Christ offered himself once. The English Franciscan holds that Christ does not offer himself again, except through the Church acting as the principal offerer.[125] In the liturgy, Christ offers mediately or indirectly, in that he instituted the sacrament, and in that the sacrifice is done in his name. The Church in turn delegates this task to the priests.[126] Now, since the priest and the Church make an act of offering that is separate from Christ's, Scotus seems to multiply sacrifices, which is precisely what Hebrews rejects. Yet his account is simpler and metaphysically easier to justify than the Thomist approach.

John Duns Scotus's theology of the priesthood undergirds this ac-

122. Thomas Aquinas, *Summa theologiae* III, q. 77, a. 7; q. 83, a. 5, ad 5.

123. See Thomas Aquinas, *Summa theologiae* III, q. 82, a. 4.

124. Council of Trent, *Decree on the Sacrifice of the Mass*, chapter 2, DH 1743. See also *Sacrosanctum Concilium*, no. 7.

125. John Duns Scotus, *Quodlibet*, q. 20, a. 2, no. 3, in *Opera Omnia*, vol. 2.1, ed. Giovanni Lauriola (Bari, Italy: Alberobello, 1999), 460.

126. Richard Cross, *Duns Scotus*, Great Medieval Thinkers (Oxford: Oxford University Press, 1999), 145. Some Scotists affirm that Christ does principally offer the Eucharistic sacrifice, but in the sense that the Church's and the priest's will are subordinate to Christ's. See Clark, *Eucharistic Sacrifice and the Reformation*, 336–37.

count of Eucharistic sacrifice. He does not see the priest as a metaphysical instrument of Christ. For Aquinas, ordination causes a metaphysical modification of the priest's soul: the sacramental seal or character makes the priest an effective instrument of Christ the high priest. But for Scotus, the sacramental character is simply a modification of the priest's will, as he takes on a moral obligation to do God's will.[127] At the consecration, the priest says the words of institution, and God simultaneously changes the gift, because of a promise that God has made in the New Covenant. Here, Christ does not act through the minister, but in parallel with him. The work of changing the gifts is wholly God's, as the priest performs a strictly exterior act.[128] The priest acts by himself, in obedience to Christ and the Church. Therefore, the spiritual value of each Mass is finite, because of the identity of the one who immediately makes the offering.

Thomists such as Cajetan and Journet argue that each Mass is of infinite value, because of how Christ acts and offers through the priest. For Aquinas, at the consecration Christ is the principal cause moving through the minister as instrumental cause.[129] Christ and the priest act together, not separately, as the power to change the gifts passes through the minister's words, gestures, and intention. The identity of the principal agent of the consecration and subsequent offering accounts for the limitless value of the Church's sacrifice. Aquinas's explanation is harder to conceive than that of Scotus, but it builds on a richer Christology.

Thomas takes a similar approach to sacramental efficacy in general, which he develops by analogy with Christ's humanity as the efficacious instrument of grace. That is, just as Christ's divinity and humanity are both efficient causes of grace, acting together, the human nature in dependence on the divine nature, without competition or tension, so, by analogy, the sacramental acts of the Church are efficient causes of grace, operating in dependence on the Incarnate Word, the principal cause of

127. Jean Galot, *La nature du caractère sacramentel: Étude de théologie médiévale* (Paris: Desclée de Brouwer, 1956), 209–12.

128. Irène Rosier-Catach, *La parole efficace: Signe, rituel, sacré* (Paris: Éditions du Seuil, 2004), 143–44, 155–56. Scotus's position emerges from the "Covenant theology" approach to sacramental efficacy. See my essay, "The Place of Romans 6 in Aquinas' Doctrine of Sacramental Causality: A Balance of History and Metaphysics," in *Ressourcement Thomism: Sacra Doctrina, the Sacraments and the Moral Life*, ed. Reinhard Hütter and Matthew Levering (Washington, D.C.: The Catholic University of America Press, 2010), 136–37.

129. Thomas Aquinas, *Summa theologiae* III, q. 78, a. 4; q. 82, a. 1, ad 1.

grace, without competition between him and his instruments. Aquinas's doctrine of the priesthood flows from his Cyrilian Christology and his way of linking Christology with the sacraments. Interestingly, Scotus's account of Christ's saving work essentially limits itself to the themes of merit and satisfaction. He did not have the kind of access to the Greek Fathers that Thomas enjoyed.[130] Overall, the link between Christology and the sacraments remains fragile in Scotus.

For Aquinas, it is clear that Christ acts through the priest at the consecration. The same cooperative action occurs in the act of offering enabled by the consecration. Without (1) Christ's eternal priesthood and (2) validly ordained priests that are true instruments of Christ, the Mass cannot be the same sacrifice as the sacrifice of the Cross. Because the visible priest that we see at Mass is *only* a minister, Jesus can be the one offering the sacrifice through him.[131] The priest's act wholly depends on that of Christ.

The consecration makes possible the act of offering, so that one instrumental act leads to another. On Holy Thursday, Christ gave to his apostles the power to celebrate the *sacrament* of his body and blood. He also granted them the power to offer with him the same *sacrifice* that he offered on Good Friday to the Father. The one who can (instrumentally) bring the victim to the altar can also offer up that same victim, so that Christ's act of consecrating is prolonged in his act of offering, always via the same instrument.

Christ's offering at Mass has a twofold historical foundation, namely the Last Supper and the Passion. In the Upper Room, Jesus prayed, consecrated, and sacramentally offered himself to the Father. By "sacramentally," I mean a sign by which he gave his invisible body to the Father. In his Passion (especially in his heart, the sacrifice of love that animated the whole offering), Jesus prayed and gave his human life to the Father in a natural, non-sacramental mode ("natural sacrifice" refers to his physical passion and death).

Thus, the liturgical representation is twofold, namely, of Christ cel-

130. Scotus's soteriology focuses on juridical categories, while Thomas balances these with a metaphysical and mystical approach to the humanity of Christ. This enables Aquinas to propose a vision of sacramental efficacy that is much closer to the patristic doctrine of the sacraments as mysteries than is Scotus's vision: for Thomas, God's hidden, saving power is at work within the ritual itself, indeed, within the words, gestures, and material elements.

131. Urfels, *La Pâque du Messie*, 336–37. See also Marshall, "The Whole Mystery," 59–62.

ebrating the sacrament at the Last Supper, and of Christ's self-offering in his Passion. Only this double representation makes it possible for the Eucharistic liturgy to be the sacrifice of Christ. The power to consecrate, which is the power to transubstantiate, flows from Christ's action at the Last Supper. Now taken by itself, the act of transubstantiating bread and wine into body and blood is not a sacrificial act.[132] The making present of a victim is a necessary but not sufficient condition for the sacrificial nature of the Mass. The priest consecrates *in persona Christi*, and he offers the body and blood *in persona Christi*.[133] By representing Christ's offering of charity and his exterior self-offering (by the substantial separation of his body and blood), the sacrifice of the Passion is "substantially" present: no exterior sacrifice without an interior sacrifice. In his Passion, Jesus gives his bodily life to the Father as an offering of love, and enables the faithful to participate in his sacrificial act. All of this is much richer than a simple reenactment of the Passion.

The previous explanation is highly metaphysical. We also need to consider Christ's knowledge or consciousness of the Church's sacrifice. Thomas's Christology allows one to argue that, on Good Friday, the suffering Jesus intentionally offered himself in all Masses. We might see this intention subtly manifested at the Last Supper, with the combination of the sacramental offering (the body "given up for you" and the blood "shed for you") and the command to "do this." On the Cross, Jesus carries out what he promised at the Last Supper. For at the Cross, he consciously gave himself to the Father in union with the Church who would offer the same body and blood to the Father in all ages to come.

The crucified Lord could have obtained knowledge of our future sacramental acts via an abundance of prophetic gifts illuminating his human soul, by his beatific vision, or (more likely) by a combination of both. A venerable theological stream, from Augustine to our time, holds that, all through his earthly pilgrimage, Jesus enjoyed the direct vision of the Father in the depth of his soul. As Aquinas and many medieval as well as modern theologians explain, by this vision and a powerful prophetic gift, he also knew the Church, his disciples to come, and our acts of worship. Perhaps we need not go as far as Aquinas, who held that the suffering

132. Vonier, *A Key to the Doctrine of the Eucharist*, 142.
133. Marshall, "The Whole Mystery," 60.

Christ knew all future events. Instead, we can posit that he foresaw enough future acts to accomplish his saving work, so that he gave himself up personally for each of us, with an intimate knowledge of every human being for whom he died.[134] In his encyclical *Mystici Corporis Christi*, Pius XII affirmed that Christ possessed a personal knowledge of each member of his Mystical Body.[135] And Thérèse of Lisieux exclaims in one of her poems: "Remember on the evening of your agony . . . . An angel showed you this choice harvest and brought joy to your blessed face, Jesus, you who saw me, amidst your flowers, remember me."[136] The suffering Christ knew the Church to come in her many sacramental acts of celebrating the Eucharist, and could thereby intentionally join his act of self-offering on the Cross to hers.[137] Now in addition, the ascended High Priest Christ also offers the Eucharistic sacrifice. By a single interior act of oblation that continues from the Cross into glory, he offers himself to the Father and intercedes for us.[138] This doctrine, grounded in the Letter to the Hebrews, best accounts for the patristic description of Christ's priestly presence at Mass, as the glorified Lord who now celebrates and offers in the midst of the Church.[139]

I have focused on Christ's priestly action through the instrumentality of the priest at the consecration. In addition, Jesus enables the Church to offer the victim to the Father through his minister. The liturgical prayers indicate that Christ's sacrifice has become ours. In the Roman canon, just after the consecration, the celebrant prays: "[we] offer to your glorious majesty, from the gifts that you have given us, this pure victim, this holy victim, this spotless victim, the holy bread of eternal life and the chalice of

134. See Simon Francis Gaine, *Did the Saviour See the Father? Christ, Salvation and the Vision of God* (London: Bloomsbury, 2015); Thomas Joseph White, *The Incarnate Lord: A Thomistic Study in Christology*, Thomistic Ressourcement 5 (Washington, D.C.: The Catholic University of America Press, 2015), chap. 5.

135. Pius XII, *Mystici Corporis Christi*, Encyclical Letter, June 29, 1943, no. 75.

136. Thérèse of Lisieux, *Poésies*, no. 24, in Fr.-M. Léthel, *L'amour de Jésus: La christologie de sainte Thérèse de l'Enfant Jésus*, Jésus et Jésus-Christ 72 (Paris: Desclée, 1997), 235 (translation by the author).

137. Réginald Garrigou-Lagrange, "An Christus non solum virtualiter sed actualiter offerat Missas quae quotidie celebrantur," *Angelicum* 19 (1942): 108, 113.

138. Réginald Garrigou-Lagrange, *De eucharistia, accedunt de paenitentia: Questiones dogmaticae, Commentarius in Summam theologicam S. Thomae* (Paris: Desclée de Brouwer, 1943), 294–98.

139. See Augustine, *City of God*, bk. 10, chapter 20. See also chapter 8, below, on the minister of the Eucharist.

everlasting salvation."[140] The Church's gifts of bread and wine become his body and blood.[141] The Mass is not just the priest's sacrifice done for the Church, but also the whole Church's sacrifice: the universal sacrament of salvation acts through her priest. Now while her sacrifice has its center in the consecration, it is not limited to that moment. For the Church already brings her offering of praise, thanksgiving, and adoration from the very beginning of Mass. The victim on the altar constitutes the ultimate expression of this interior offering that the liturgical prayers and gestures manifest, both before and after the consecration. That the Church can offer the victim is crucial for her sacrifice (enacted all through the liturgy) to be acceptable to God.[142]

I offer one final comment on the unity of the sacrifice. As noted, Christ makes the offering at Mass by way of representation. The Church shares in this act through the minister. The Mass constitutes an application or making present today of Christ's one self-offering. Each Eucharistic liturgy is new, in the sense that Christ's sacrifice becomes present now. We repeat the *representation* of the Passion, which enables the Church to join herself to Christ's offering. Her participation in the act of offering is renewed, but Christ has already completed that offering.[143] What is new is the *sacramental* celebration, as representation makes present the victim and fruits of the one *natural*, non-sacramental sacrifice.

Christ the Head and the Church Offer Love and Praise to the Father

Because Christ's self-offering remains active at Mass today, the Church obtains immense blessings. The Thomist tradition holds that the Eucharistic sacrifice has infinite value, since the power of Christ's self-offering in his Passion becomes operative by the minister at the altar. The reason is that, in the liturgy, the minister and the Church are simply Christ's instruments, so that Jesus' sacrificial act determines the objective value of the Mass. Yet the fruits that the Church actually receives from each Mass

140. New Roman rite. The ancient Roman canon is essentially the same (Bouyer, *Eucharist*, 239).

141. Masure, *Le sacrifice du chef*, 310, 316, 334.

142. Masure, *Le sacrifice du chef*, 308–9, 331.

143. Pohle, *Lehrbuch der Dogmatik*, 3:309.

are measured by the degree of the Church militant's love and devotion.[144] For this reason, the subjective value of the Mass, in the sense of the blessing actually received, remains finite and varies.[145] In addition, the emphasis of Eucharistic prayers (especially the Roman canon) on particular intentions implies that some persons receive greater benefit than others from a single Eucharistic offering. The Mass concretizes and particularizes the saving work of Christ in history.[146]

In his Passion, Jesus gave to the Father the perfect gift of love and praise. This interior sacrifice animated his suffering: his obedience gave his death its salvific value. His passion and death manifested this perfect interior offering. Together, the interior and exterior sacrifice made during his Passion became a single offering of endless value. There, Jesus interceded for all of humanity and obtained all the supernatural blessings which the Father would bestow on us, including forgiveness of sins and satisfaction for the debt of sin. In heaven, Christ the High Priest continues to intercede for us and to give to the Father an offering of love. In the third preface of Easter of the Roman rite, the priest echoes the Letter to the Hebrews as he prays to the Father: "he [Christ] never ceases to offer himself for us, and defends us and ever pleads our cause before you." Jesus' heavenly sacrifice of praise and prayer of intercession obtain no new merit or satisfaction. Rather, they continually render present before the Father and in the Church the saving power of his Passion.

All through the Mass, and in a particular way in the Eucharistic prayer, the Church joins herself to her mystical head in loving adoration of the Father. *Sacrosanctum Concilium* teaches: "every liturgical celebration, because it is an action of Christ the Priest and of his Body, the Church, is a sacred action surpassing all others."[147] Here, we are no longer focused only on the crucified Lord offering himself with the Church, but

144. Devotion is a technical term that signifies readiness to serve God. It is the principal act of the virtue of religion (*Summa theologiae* II-II, q. 83, a. 15).

145. Journet, *The Mass*, 97–98, 126. Journet presents the doctrine of the Thomist school, founded on texts such as Thomas Aquinas, *Summa theologiae* III, q. 79, a. 5 (cited in the next section), which refers to the infinite value of the oblation.

146. The objective value of the Mass should not be determined solely on the basis of the principal cause of the offering, but also on the basis of its instrumental cause: the instrument particularizes the sacrifice, applying it to concrete intentions. Also, one should not presume that Christ's sacrifice is a potential universal cause of salvation that is actualized only through particular Masses.

147. *Sacrosanctum Concilium*, no. 7.

also on the presence of the glorified High Priest at Mass.[148] On Golgotha, Jesus consciously joined his own sacrifice of love, praise, and intercession to ours today (by prophetic insight and his beatific vision). The Mass also allows us to participate in the heavenly liturgy, where Christ and all the saints glorify the Father. It is crucial to keep both elements together, namely, the sacerdotal actions of the crucified Christ and the intercession of the risen Lord.

In the liturgy, the Church's love and adoration constitute part of the great sacrifice, by her hymns, prayers, and gestures. Here, interior and exterior sacrifice become inseparable. The Church's love expresses itself in the offering of bread and wine. The gifts exteriorize and complete this loving submission to God (or devotion in the technical sense): the interior offering reaches completion in the exterior offering, for man is inseparably soul and body. The sign of bread and wine become Christ himself, the perfect exteriorization of the charity of his members. Here, the Church's single offering (interior and exterior) is joined to Christ's one self-offering (interior and exterior). The Church's sacrifice of love and praise are made possible by the power of the rite itself.[149] Now she offers her love and praise only in union with her head. That is, her interior offering must be one with his. The Church brings nothing that is strictly her own to the liturgy, but only a more or less intense participation in Christ's charity. All of her charity is made possible by his gift.

The Church prays with Christ to the Father. Before and after the consecration, the celebrant speaks in the first-person plural, for he acts *in persona ecclesiae*, in the person of the Church. Here, the Bride of Christ speaks, yet the liturgy also continues to represent Christ, thus anchoring the Church's prayer in his sacrifice, for Jesus offers insofar as he is represented.[150] The ancient Church allowed only the baptized to remain for the Eucharistic prayer, a practice that has partly returned since Vatican II, with the dismissal of the catechumens and candidates after the Gospel. All who are present should be disposed to assent to the "we" of the Eucharistic prayer. Through the celebrant, all the baptized present at Mass and the whole Church militant pray to the Father. In the Roman canon,

148. *Sacrosanctum Concilium*, no. 8.

149. Masure, *Le sacrifice du chef*, 308–9, 331–33, 336.

150. *Sacrosanctum Concilium*, no. 33.

before the consecration, the celebrant says: "Lord, we pray, graciously accept this oblation of our service, that of your whole family." In the liturgy, the whole Church, not just those members physically present at Mass, makes an offering of love.

The Church's act of sacrifice always occurs in dependence on Christ the High Priest. Yet he acts in the liturgy in distinct modes. In the priest's consecration and simultaneous offering of the victim to the Father, Christ's act is constant, that is, it simply occurs through the liturgical act. But the Church's sacrifice of charity varies by the degree to which she participates in Christ's sacrifice of charity. Her offering is never autonomous, but the fervor of her charity can be greater or less. That is, she remains Christ's instrument as she makes an offering of love and praise, but in a mode different than that of the priest's offering. The degree to which the Church shares in Christ's offering of love becomes the measure by which she opens herself to the fruits of the sacrifice.[151]

The fervor of the Church's loving adoration depends on the sanctity of her members. Here, the role of all the Church's members comes to the fore. The holiness of all believers, especially as they join their daily prayers, good works, and penances to the prayer of the Mass, intensify the Church's share in Jesus' interior offering. And so, even the sick who are homebound or in hospitals can participate in the Church's offering at Masses that they cannot attend. In this way, the spiritual efficacy of a Mass is neither automatic, nor is it measured by the holiness of the priest who celebrates the liturgy.[152]

Christ's sacrificial act in the Mass has priority, yet the Church's sacrifice of love and praise are crucial as well. Whatever blessings the Church receives through the Mass flow from Jesus' Passion: by his humanity, Christ instrumentally pours out grace, grants a new share in the forgiveness he merited for us, and a deeper participation in Christ's satisfaction. These gifts are made available to the Church in the liturgy, which ap-

151. Journet, *The Mass*, 122. Hunsinger expresses the Protestant concern that the efficacy of God's grace should overcome the limits of our devotion (*The Eucharist and Ecumenism*, 116). In the background stands a longstanding Catholic-Protestant debate on the role of human cooperation in grace. From the perspective of Augustine, Aquinas, and the Council of Trent, God's grace present in the rite precedes our cultic acts and elevates them beyond their present limit (beyond the limits of nature, but also by intensifying the power of grace already present).

152. Thomas Aquinas, *Summa theologiae* III, q. 82, a. 6c.

plies the fruitfulness of Christ's saving work today.[153] But the Church's receptivity to these fruits depends on the fervor of her loving adoration. Christ's saving work takes root via our active, free, personal cooperation with him. God freely wills to make salvation depend on our free cooperation, even as all salvation primarily (and always) depends on the Crucified Lord.

Here, a brief word on the link between the priest's offering for the whole Church and his communion with the bishop also seems *apropos*. The priest offers the Mass on behalf of the Church in virtue of the bishop's power of jurisdiction, which makes the priest's offering a *licit* offering. His bishop in turn dwells in communion with the episcopal college, and so, the priest can act *in persona ecclesiae* as he makes the offering. He can truly represent the Church, so that the whole Church is really involved in the offering of each Eucharist, and not just the faithful who are physically assembled for the celebration. In making the Eucharistic sacrifice, the priest does something that the whole Church intends him to do. Thus, in his juridically regulated action, the whole Church is truly present. Finally, for this reason, we can say that this ecclesial presence can be actualized by those Catholics who prayerfully and consciously join themselves to the sacrifice of the Mass wherever it is being offered.[154]

I have considered Christ's sacrificial act whereby the offering of the body and blood through the priest is always efficacious, as well as the Church's loving adoration of the Father with Christ. Let us note a key difference between these two aspects of Eucharistic sacrifice. With the first aspect, the priority lies with the Incarnate Word acting in the liturgy, as the principal cause that operates via the minister. The second aspect turns our gaze toward the hidden work of the Holy Spirit, whose proper name is Love. The Spirit is the very heart of the mystical body, the hidden source of her holiness, who animates the members of Christ and enables their loving adoration of the Father: Christ's action as head involves his humanity, through whose instrumentality the Spirit is given to us.[155] Here, our gaze shifts from the instrumentality of the priest, which depends on his sacerdotal character, to the whole Church as animated by

153. Thomas Aquinas, *Summa theologiae* III, q. 49, a. 3.

154. I owe this explanation to an anonymous reader, to whom I am most grateful.

155. Thomas Aquinas, *Summa theologiae* III, q. 8, a. 1, ad 1.

the Spirit. We therefore find a balance in the theme of sacrifice, between Christ and the Spirit, between the priesthood as instituted by Christ and the Church as a communion of love. This gives partial confirmation that our account of the Eucharist is on the right path, as it integrates a balanced Trinitarian theology and ecclesiology.

A Sacrifice Overflowing with Blessing

Having considered the dynamic presence of Christ in the liturgy as well as the agency of the priest and Church in the sacrifice, I now turn to the effects or specific fruits of the Eucharistic sacrifice. The normal way for the faithful who are present at Mass to participate in the sacrifice is by their prayers and communion. Indeed, communing in the sacrifice constitutes the most powerful form of sharing therein. Yet the ritual imparts benefits to others as well: to those who are present but do not commune, as well as to those absent. Since the whole Church offers the sacrifice (so that the priest says, "we offer," *offerimus* in Latin), the whole Church benefits by it. Here, I use the scholastic distinction between the fruits of sacrifice and the fruits of communion. I now consider the fruits of the sacrifice available to the whole mystical body. The next section studies sacramental communion as an intense participation in the sacrifice.

The Church's offering is acceptable only if it is joined to Christ. We have seen that this offering includes the Church's gift of charity to the Father. In fact, by the rite, Christ elevates our share in the fruits of his sacrifice, both visible and invisible. Our external and internal offering must be conformed to his.[156] Eugène Masure notes: "Because the body is *our* victim, it is in us that he engenders in this moment the interior immolation of adoration, of love and repentance, of which it [the body] is the efficacious sign."[157] We receive these fruits simply by joining our hearts to the Eucharistic sacrifice, even as partaking of the sacrificial meal of communion intensifies our participation in those fruits. I propose that this is the first and primary effect of the sacrifice. More than any other fruit, charity elevates the power of the Church's share in upward mediation, in her acts of adoration and thanksgiving.

156. Masure, *Le sacrifice du chef*, 334.

157. Masure, *Le sacrifice du chef*, 333 (translation by the author). Masure may at times conflate sacrament and sacrifice, yet his work remains valuable.

It is important to begin a consideration of the fruits of sacrifice with charity. Some classical manuals of theology focus their study of these fruits on sin and satisfaction. This approach leads to an imbalance that gives the theology of sacrifice a primarily negative tone, with a focus on removing obstacles to grace. Yet we need not subordinate the loving glorification of the Father to the sacrificial fruits of reconciliation and satisfaction.[158] The priority of charity matches well Aquinas's doctrine of Christ's Passion: "A sacrifice properly so called is something done to give God the honor that is properly due to him, and in order to please him.... [quoting Augustine] 'Christ offered himself up for us in the Passion,' and this voluntary enduring of the Passion was most acceptable to God, as coming from charity."[159]

That being said, the sacrifice does, indeed, bring reconciliation. Those who live in Christ abide in charity and can thus joins their hearts to his in obedience to the Father.[160] A person whose heart is turned away from God cannot make a pleasing sacrifice. Only the interior offering can animate the exterior offering (hence the harsh polemic of the Old Testament prophets against sinful Israel and its strictly exterior cult). The fruit of joining oneself to Christ's obedient heart is liberation from the power of evil.[161]

We know, because of the Eucharistic prayers, that the liturgy constitutes a sin offering. Also, the Mass is a sin offering, since it is one with Christ's offering at Calvary. Speaking of the Eucharistic sacrifice, Aquinas states: "the effect that Christ's Passion has in the world, this sacrament operates in the human being."[162] This theological principle allows us to say that the Mass constitutes the most powerful form of sacrifice for sins available to us. Following theological tradition, within the category of reconciliation, I shall distinguish three types of effects (which I will categorize as fruits two through four, after charity).

The second sacrificial fruit is the gift of conversion from grave sin or

158. The eastern Orthodox theologian Alexander Schmemann rightly centers the sacrificial act on the Church's love. See David W. Fagerberg, *Theologica Prima: What Is Liturgical Theology?*, 2nd ed. (Chicago: Hillenbrand Books, 2004), 208.

159. Thomas Aquinas, *Summa theologiae* III, q. 48, a. 3.

160. Thomas Aquinas, *Summa theologiae* III, q. 47, a. 2.

161. Thomas Aquinas, *Summa theologiae* III, q. 49, aa. 2 & 4.

162. Thomas Aquinas, *Summa theologiae* III, q. 79, a. 1, corpus.

unbelief. In the offertory of the Tridentine rite, as the priest presents the chalice to God, he prays for the salvation of the whole world.[163] We find similar prayers throughout the new Roman rite, for example, in the third Eucharistic prayer: "May this Sacrifice of our reconciliation, we pray, O Lord, advance the peace and salvation of all the world." Trent teaches that the Eucharistic offering brings even the remission of great crimes.[164] While Eucharistic communion presumes life in Christ, the fruit of the sacrifice can reach those beyond the mystical body.

We can link this insight with the doctrine of the Church as the universal sacrament of salvation. Francis Sullivan has shown the deep harmony between the liturgical prayers for the salvation of the world and the Church's role as not just a sign but also an efficacious instrument of salvation. She is the *universal* sacrament of salvation, bringing to birth all those who come to grace. The extension of her instrumentality should be seen by analogy with the sacred humanity of Christ.[165] Thus, whoever is saved is saved by her prayers, joined to those of the glorified High Priest. Why attribute such importance to the Church? Because she is mother, giving birth to all those in grace, thanks to the loving sacrifice of her spouse.[166]

Let us specify: the sacrifice of the Mass obtains conversion, but it does not constitute a guilt offering for mortal sins: only those alive in God can make a pleasing sacrifice. For otherwise, a person in grave sin could ask for the Mass to be offered for himself and then commune at the same Mass. This would contradict the Church's constant penitential practice. Rather, the Mass begs God to lead the sinner back to life, onto the path to reconciliation, a way that passes through baptism or sacramental confession.[167]

Third, Eucharistic sacrifice brings forgiveness for venial sins: it liberates us from attachment to evil, because we seek to please God. As previously mentioned, many ancient Eucharistic prayers beg for the purification and reconciliation of those who participate at Mass. Similarly,

163. Journet, *The Mass*, 122.

164. Council of Trent, *Decree on the Sacrifice of the Mass*, chapter 2, DH 1743.

165. Francis A. Sullivan, *Salvation Outside the Church? Tracing the History of the Catholic Response* (New York: Paulist Press, 1992), 156–60.

166. For a fine treatment of the controversial axiom "No salvation outside the Church," see Andrew Meszaros, "Yves Congar and the Salvation of the Non-Christian," *Louvain Studies* 37 (2013): 195–223.

167. See Pohle, *Lehrbuch der Dogmatik*, 3:334.

ancient penitential practice shows that such forgiveness was sought in the liturgy for lesser sins. Centuries later, Trent taught that the Cross's "salutary power [is] applied for the forgiveness of the sins that we daily commit."[168] At various moments in the liturgy, the priest and all those present express their desire for forgiveness: in the *Kyrie Eleison*, the *Agnus Dei* and before communion, when the faithful in the Roman rite pray: "Lord, I am not worthy that you should enter under my roof, but only say the word, and my soul shall be healed." Such forgiveness is also mediated by the gift of charity. That is, the sacrifice obtains forgiveness indirectly, by provoking acts of contrition and charity, in those present and in those for whom the Mass is offered.[169] In other words, the sacrifice of the Mass is the means by which the Spirit moves the heart of the believer to bring a more authentic sacrifice. Thus, the rite does not simply wash away one's guilt without any human participation, but rather does so through the human response to grace. Through the liturgy, the Holy Spirit provokes acts of love in us, which in turn lead to acts of sorrow for venial sins committed. In a later chapter, we will see a parallel with charity as a grace of Eucharistic communion, where charity also brings the forgiveness of venial sins. The power of the ritual provokes this charity in the hearts of those who praise and express gratitude to God, so that the rite perfects their interior sacrifice as it cleanses their hearts.

The fourth fruit of the Eucharistic sacrifice (also related to reconciliation) is satisfaction for sins and the punishment due to sin. This doctrine first surfaced in medieval theology, yet the medieval theologians developed a biblical notion of sin as a debt. As we have seen, Cyril of Jerusalem and other ancient witnesses identified the Eucharist as a sacrifice for sins. Yet they did not draw all the implications from this insight. Over time, as the Church's theologians recognized with greater clarity the nature of Christ's saving work, they also better perceived the fruits of the Eucharist.

To grasp how we make satisfaction by the Eucharist, we need to set it in relation to baptism and the sacrament of reconciliation. In baptism, we were freed from all punishment for sins. In sacramental confession, the priest assigns us a penance to assist us in making satisfaction for sins. Vari-

168. Council of Trent, *Decree on the Sacrifice of the Mass*, chapter 1, DH 1740. See also canon 3, DH 1753.

169. Michel, "La messe," 1302–3.

ous good works done in grace also become the means to make satisfaction for sins (e.g., almsgiving). Yet satisfaction is brought to us in a unique way through the Mass, for it is the same sacrifice as the Cross, but in a sacramental mode.

Aquinas describes this fruit of the Eucharistic sacrifice as follows:

> As a sacrifice, the Eucharist has a satisfactory power. But in satisfaction, the love (*affectus*) of the offerer is weighed more than the quantity of the offering; hence, in Luke (21:4), the Lord says of the widow who offered two copper coins that she "has given more than all." Therefore, although by its quantity this oblation [of the Lord's body and blood] suffices to satisfy for all punishment, nevertheless, it becomes satisfactory for those for whom it is offered, or even for those who offer it, according to the measure of their devotion, and not for the whole punishment.[170]

Here, the term "devotion" has the technical sense that was mentioned above. For now, Aquinas focuses only on satisfaction, as he abstracts from other aspects of reconciliation. In the Eucharist, satisfaction can be received for forgiven sins.[171] In other words, the recipient of this gift should be in a state of grace. Thomas signals that we can offer the sacrifice to obtain satisfaction for our sins or those of another. Forgiveness and satisfaction are distinct gifts. However, the same sacrifice can also bring reconciliation for venial sins. Let us add that the Eucharist can obtain satisfaction for mortal sins previously forgiven by the sacrament of penance (whereas baptism brings both reconciliation and satisfaction for all past sins).

On the Cross, Jesus obtained satisfaction for all sins. Because the Mass is the sacrifice of Jesus in sacramental form, Thomas says (in the passage above) that "by its quantity this oblation suffices to satisfy for all punishment." As we saw, considered by itself, Christ's offering on Calvary has limitless value. But this gift comes to us sacramentally, and can be received only if the recipient is properly disposed, meaning, if he or she has faith and charity. Devotion presupposes both virtues. We share in the gift of satisfaction according to the fervor of our devotion. The paying of a debt to God is never an automatic work, without our cooperation. The

170. Thomas Aquinas, *Summa theologiae* III, q. 79, a. 5. See also Council of Trent, *Decree on the Sacrifice of the Mass*, chapter 1, DH 1740; canon 3, DH 1753.

171. Michel, "La messe," 1303; Philippe-Marie Margellidon, "Satisfaction," in *Dictionnaire de philosophie et de théologie thomistes*, ed. Yves Floucat and P.-M. Margellidon (Paris: Parole et Silence, 2011), 479.

sacrifice has its effect according to the disposition of the believer, which in turn limits the gift received. That limit is the person's devotion, or the degree to which the person submits his or her will to God.[172] We benefit from the effects of Calvary only by making an interior offering ourselves.

Last, as a subset of the fourth fruit of sacrifice, the liturgy brings satisfaction for sins to the faithful departed. Trent insists much on the satisfactory function of Mass.[173] The ritual has this effect immediately for the dead, that is, without their active participation (and indirectly for us, via our acts of charity). This is partly because works of satisfaction involve meritorious acts, and the departed are beyond the realm of merit. This gift of satisfaction for the punishment due to sins is distinct from the reconciliation that the souls in purgatory receive for their unforgiven venial sins.[174] At Mass, we also pray for that forgiveness.

Overall, the Mass brings to us the fruits already obtained by the Crucified One, namely, by his perfect charity, his merit in obeying unto death and his physical suffering. The Mass always remains subordinate to and dependent on the Cross.

We have focused on the fruits of Calvary coming to us through the Eucharistic sacrifice, yet we also need to ponder the power of Christ's Resurrection and Ascension active in the liturgical celebration. What kind of spiritual fruit do these mysteries impart through the ritual memorial? First, we have the presence of Christ's glorified body on the altar. I will consider the spiritual effects of communing in his risen body in a later chapter. Second, as Aquinas notes, the blessing of the chalice, with its references to the eternal covenant and the remission of sins, manifests the Eucharist's eschatological end while removing obstacles on the path to it.[175] We have seen that the Eucharistic sacrifice imparts the forgiveness of sins. Here, the power of the Passion stands at the center, with a focus on the negative aspect: the removal of guilt and the spiritual stain. Yet the

172. Thomas Aquinas, *Summa theologiae* II-II, q. 82, a. 2, ad 1.

173. Council of Trent, *Decree on the Sacrifice of the Mass*, chapter 2, DH 1743; Council of Trent, *Decree on Purgatory*, DH 1820.

174. Pohle, *Lehrbuch der Dogmatik*, 3:335.

175. Thomas Aquinas, *Summa theologiae* III, q. 78, a. 3; Langevin, *From Passion to Paschal Mystery*, 276–77.

same divine act of purification has a positive aspect that also comes to us by the power of Christ's Resurrection, namely, a new share in divine life, a deeper imitation of Christ's communion with the Father (Rom 4:25). Both mysteries effectively move us toward heaven.[176] Third, Jesus' heavenly praise and intercession are an un-bloody sacrifice that constitute the full fruition of the Cross, and reveal the finality of all earthly sacrifice, namely, the whole Church's heavenly worship filled with love and praise. That is, each Eucharistic celebration brings us closer to a full sharing in this celestial liturgy, precisely by already participating therein through the earthly liturgy. The fruit of the Resurrection and Ascension are that the glorified Christ and his saints pray with us today, as signified in the liturgical prayers. In the memorial of his Ascension, the ascended Christ joins his prayers to ours. He prays with us because he is thus represented.[177]

Communion as Sharing in the Fruits of Sacrifice

Until now, I have laid out the fruits of Eucharistic sacrifice in abstraction from communion. That is, each of these fruits are available to all the members of the mystical body (more specifically, to the Church militant), whether present at or absent from Mass, whether living or deceased. Still, John Paul II reminds us: "The saving efficacy of the sacrifice is fully realized when the Lord's body and blood are received in communion. The Eucharistic sacrifice is intrinsically directed to the inward union of the faithful with Christ through communion."[178] A future chapter will take up the specific fruits of Eucharistic communion. Here, I briefly consider the importance of communion as the Church's consummation of her sacrifice.

The Passion fulfilled all Old Testament sacrifices, especially the Passover.[179] The Mass renews Christ's offering in an un-bloody mode. Now, it was unthinkable for the devout Jew not to eat the Passover lamb during

176. Langevin, *From Passion to Paschal Mystery*, 276–77.

177. One finds a strong eschatological note in the Office of Corpus Christi, especially the sequence *Lauda Sion*. For an outstanding study of this liturgical corpus, see Jan-Heiner Tück, *A Gift of Presence: The Theology and Poetry of the Eucharist in Thomas Aquinas*, trans. Scott G. Hefelfinger (Washington, D.C.: The Catholic University of America Press, 2018).

178. John Paul II, *Ecclesia de Eucharistia* (Vatican City: Libreria Editrice Vaticana, 2003), no. 16.

179. Thomas Aquinas, *Summa theologiae* III, q. 73, a. 6.

the celebration. The Church fulfills the promise of Passover when her members eat the body and drink the blood of the true Passover Lamb.

I previously noted the importance of sharing in Christ's offering of love. Those present at Mass heighten their participation therein above all in the consummation of the sacrifice at communion. By consuming the offering, we are configured to it.[180] We become like the Christ that we consume, and so our hearts are reshaped in the likeness of his heart, he who gave his love and his whole human existence to the Father on the Cross. "We are thereby configured to the image of his cruciform love and share in the divine communion he enjoys."[181] Eating the victim imparts Christo-forming grace, an imprint of a similitude of Jesus' suffering human love at Calvary. And, by its very nature, charity heightens our communion with the Trinity. The sacrificial meal images this new communion with God. By our eating and drinking, the rite effects what it signifies, as it joins us body and soul to Christ and to the whole Trinity.

Does communion complete the sacrifice? In Latin theology, we find a strong tendency to identify the Eucharistic sacrifice with the act of bringing Christ the victim onto the altar and offering him to God. For example, Augustine tells his congregation that, after the consecration, "when the Sacrifice is finished, we say the Lord's Prayer."[182] Here, he appears to identify the sacrifice with the prayers and deeds that occur during the anaphora, or some part therein: the sacrifice is completed before communion, which follows the Lord's Prayer. Augustine is not perfectly clear on this matter, for elsewhere, he implies that communion is part of the sacrifice.[183] Aquinas holds that the Eucharist is a sacrifice insofar as it is offered, and a sacrament insofar as it is received.[184] That offering is already enacted (and thus apparently perfect) with the completion of the consecration of the separate species, since the consecration efficaciously represents Christ's death and thus enables the priest to bring the victim to the Father.[185] In re-

180. Levering, *Sacrifice and Community*, 89.

181. Levering, *Sacrifice and Community*, 92.

182. Augustine, "Sermon 227," in Augustine, *Sermons (184–229Z) on the Liturgical Seasons*, trans. Edmund Hill, Works of St. Augustine 3.6 (Hyde Park, N.Y.: New City Press, 1993).

183. Augustine, *City of God*, bk. 17, chap. 5. See J. L. van der Lof, "L'eucharistie et présence réelle selon saint Augustin," *Revue des études augustiniennes* 10 (1964), 301–2.

184. Thomas Aquinas, *Summa theologiae* III, q. 79, a. 5, corpus.

185. Thomas Aquinas, *Summa theologiae* III, q. 80, a. 12, ad 3; q. 82, a. 10, ad 1.

cent centuries, most theologians have identified the consecration (and its accompanying act of offering) as the essence of the Eucharistic sacrifice, and made the priest's communion part of the "integrity of the sacrifice," thus distinguishing the heart of the sacrifice from communion.[186] This stance fits well with Pius XII's 1947 encyclical, *Mediator Dei* (as we will see below).[187]

I would propose an expansion of this definition. As an act of offering Christ's body and blood to the Father, the sacrifice is indeed perfected with the completion of the consecration (insofar as it includes the offering). However, the Mass is the New Passover, and thus follows the pattern of the Passover sacrifice. In the Old Passover, the act of offering the lamb did not suffice, for the ritual sacrifice was completed when the Israelites ate the lamb. The priest partaking in the host and the cup signifies and perfects the Church's participation in the offering: her new reception of the sacrificial fruits depends on this act. This better allows us to understand why the priest's communion is an essential part of the Mass from which the Church has never dispensed anyone.[188] Let us note that, in its teaching on sacrifice, *Mediator Dei* seeks to refute at least three errors: (1) that communion, and not the consecration, is the high point of Mass, (2) that the communion of the laity is essential for Mass, and (3) that the priest represents the people in the act of consecration. Pius XII's teaching can be synthesized with an expanded definition of the essence of the Eucharistic sacrifice: it is an offering and a sacrificial eating. The New Passover is a sacrifice of communion.

During the Mass, the minister represents Christ, primarily during the consecration. In other parts of the liturgy, the priest also represents the Church. This illumines the practice whereby the priest always receives the host and the cup offered at Mass. Thomas states that "the priest both offers and consumes the blood on behalf of all."[189] Let us note the reference to both body and blood. The priest offers sacrifice for the whole

186. See, for example, Stepan Martin Filip, "Imago repraesentativa passionis Christi: L'essenza del sacrificio della Messa nella sua parte formale secondo San Tommaso d'Aquino" (Dissertatio ad lauream in Facultatae S. Theologiae apud Pontificiam Universitatem S. Thomae in Urbe, 2007), 188, 197–98; Hauke, "What Is the Holy Mass?" 123; Journet, *The Mass*, 254.

187. Ángel García Ibáñez, *L'eucaristia, dono e mistero: Trattato storico-dogmatico sul mistero eucaristico*, Sussidi di teologia (Rome: EDUSC, 2006), 368–70.

188. Michel, "La messe," 1256–57.

189. Thomas Aquinas, *Summa theologiae* III, q. 80, a. 12, ad 3.

Church and fully enacts the Church's participation therein by sharing in the whole sacrifice. Aquinas explains:

> whoever offers sacrifice must become a participant in it. For the exterior sacrifice that is offered is a sign of the interior sacrifice by which he [the one offering] offers himself to God, as Augustine says (*City of God*, book 10). Hence by participating in the sacrifice, he [the priest] shows that the interior sacrifice pertains to him.... Therefore, it is necessary for the priest to receive this sacrament in its integrity whenever he consecrates.[190]

We can read this text with the help of Aquinas's doctrine that the priest acts *in persona ecclesiae*. The priest communes in the body and blood on behalf of the whole Church, and so he signifies the Church's interior offering at Mass, which culminates in a new union with God. The priest's communion expresses and brings to completion the Church's interior offering of charity, an offering already manifested previously in various gestures and prayers (*offerimus*). That communion signifies and therefore effects the Church's participation in the fruits of the sacrifice, by her union with Christ as victim, including a union of hearts. The Church truly and spiritually communes in the victim because the priest represents her communion with Christ. All others who may commune do so primarily as members of the Church, while the priest communes on behalf of the whole Church militant.[191]

All of this implies that the priest communes in the gifts offered at Mass. That is, he does not simply consume a host taken from the tabernacle, since the latter come from a distinct sacramental offering, from another Mass, and not from the present offering. The priest is called to complete the Church's present sacramental sacrifice, so that it may intensify her present union with Christ. For this reason, he must share in the gifts that he has consecrated and offered up at the present Mass.

As for the lay faithful, while they still participate in the Church's sacrifice when receiving hosts from the tabernacle, they can better signify their participation in the present offering by receiving from the hosts consecrated in this same offering. *Sacrosanctum Concilium* teaches: "The

190. Thomas Aquinas, *Summa theologiae* III, q. 82, a. 4.

191. The key here is not that something be done to the sacrificial victim (as in some early modern theories of Eucharistic sacrifice) but that the Church may receive the victim (corporeal contact) so as to share in Christ's spiritual gifts (as is proper to the sacramental order).

more perfect form of participation in the Mass whereby the faithful, after the priest's communion, receive the Lord's body from the same sacrifice, is warmly recommended."[192] Jeremy Driscoll notes that this is the natural finality of the presentation of the gifts brought by the lay faithful.[193] Indeed, it augments the typological link with Old Testament sacrifices. Also, communion under both species made available to the lay faithful allows them to better symbolize not just their share in the Last Supper (where all present drank of the cup) but also to signify more fully their share in Christ's death, of which the cup is the more potent sign. Several post–Vatican II liturgical reforms allow us to accentuate the sacrificial nature of the Mass, not to diminish it.[194]

Communion is all about sharing in the fruits of sacrifice. In light of the previous sections, we can say that the Mass is fruitful because (1) Christ is represented in his act of offering, (2) Christ the victim is corporeally present, (3) the separately consecrated species are offered to the Father, and (4) the celebrant communes in the oblation *in persona ecclesiae*.

Excursus: The Threefold Application of the Fruits of the Sacrifice

Following a venerable modern scholastic tradition (as represented by Journet), we can further distinguish the different ways in which particular members of the Church receive the fruits of the sacrifice. That is, the Mass applies the fruits of Calvary today in three ways. The fruits are applied (1) to the whole Church, (2) to the person for whom a Mass intention is dedicated, and (3) according to the priest's and the lay faithful's personal intentions. These are called (1) the general fruit, (2) the special fruit, and (3) the particular fruit, respectively.

First, the priest celebrates the Mass on behalf of the Church.[195] In the liturgy, the celebrant often prays in the first-person plural: "We offer you, Father." Here, the "we" refers to the whole Church on earth (or

192. *Sacrosanctum Concilium*, no. 55.

193. Driscoll, "Sacrosanctum Concilium," 36.

194. It is worth recalling that the Council of Trent deliberately left the issue of communion under both kinds open. See John W. O'Malley, *What Happened at Vatican II?* (Cambridge, Mass.: Harvard University Press, 2008), 133.

195. Journet, *The Mass*, 129.

God's pilgrim people) that prays in and with the priest. At every Mass, the Church militant offers sacrifice to the Father, through Christ the High Priest, in the grace of the Holy Spirit (who is "the heart of the Church").

We saw above that the Church attains a share in the fruits of the Mass according to her degree of holiness. This is also called the effect *ex opere operantis*, literally, "from the work of the one operating" (or the work being done), which is the Church's sacrificial deed.[196] The conscious and active participation of the priest and all the faithful who are present at a particular Mass should increase the Church's receptivity to the fruits of the Mass.[197] Because of the link between the liturgical celebration and the holiness of the whole Church militant, the fruits obtained do not depend on the holiness of the priest celebrating or of the lay faithful who are physically present at a particular liturgy.

As Journet points out, each Mass is offered for the whole Church on earth and benefits the souls in purgatory.[198] For this reason, every Mass brings a blessing to all who are in grace, and to all of humanity. This is also part of the general fruits of the Mass. These universal blessings are assured for two reasons: (1) the unity of the Church's members with Christ the head, and (2) the fact that Christ the head principally offers each sacrifice of the Mass.[199] Since the Sacrifice of the Mass is not a separate sacrifice from that of the Cross, it also infallibly merits certain fruits.

Consequently, priests of the Latin rite who do not experience evident growth in personal devotion to Christ and the Eucharist through the celebration of daily Mass should still celebrate it each day, because every Mass brings a blessing to the whole Church, and this via the Church's devotion. The priest is ordained not for his own sake, but for the benefit of the Church: the sacrament of holy orders essentially constitutes the priest as a servant of the Church. Therefore, when a Latin rite priest decides not to celebrate Mass at all on certain days but instead attends the Mass celebrated by another, he falls short in his service to the Church, for he does not bring a distinct sacramental offering to God.

196. Thomas Aquinas, *Summa theologiae* III, q. 79, a. 5, corpus; Michel, "La messe," 1299–1300.

197. *Sacrosanctum Concilium*, no. 33.

198. Journet, *The Mass*, 127.

199. García Ibáñez, *L'eucaristia, dono e mistero*, 548.

Second, the priest has a Mass intention that is prescribed by the parish, shrine, or religious community, which generally comes with a stipend. This intention is linked with what is called the special fruit of the Mass. For centuries, the Church has accepted one stipend per Mass, partly to prevent an obvious source of abuse of the sacraments. The priest's intention must be at least implicit, that is, he intends to say Mass for the intention listed in the sacristy book, even if he forgets the particular intention noted there. If there is no official intention, the priest should form one. This should be done before the consecration.[200] The fruitfulness of the Mass does not depend on the priest's personal holiness. Rather, the fruit comes to the beneficiary *ex opere operato*, that is, by the instrumental efficacy of the rite, for its principal celebrant is Christ himself.

Third, the priest and each of the faithful have a personal intention at Mass, and it is linked with what is called the particular fruit of the Mass. The efficacy of this intention depends on the personal holiness and active devotion of the ones who make the intention. A priest in mortal sin obtains the general fruits of the Mass for the Church militant and the blessing sought in the official Mass intention, but he does not obtain God's favor for his own personal intention. Instead, he finds condemnation. Conversely, the more intense the charity of the priest or the layperson participating at Mass, the more efficacious becomes the offering that they bring for a personal intention. One can bring multiple personal intentions to Mass, since its fruits cannot be limited.[201] The priest and laity should formulate their intention before Mass. The general intercessions that immediately precede the Liturgy of the Eucharist remind us to make this offering.

Evaluating Three Objections to Eucharistic Sacrifice

The theology of Eucharistic sacrifice articulated above must face a series of objections. Earlier, I answered exegetical and historical challenges. There remain at least three major types of objections to this way of envisioning

200. Michel, "La messe," 1305–6.
201. García Ibáñez, *L'eucaristia, dono e mistero*, 550.

sacrifice: (1) theological and pastoral concerns that the meal aspect of the Eucharist will be obscured; (2) Louis-Marie Chauvet's spiritualizing of sacrifice, mentioned at the beginning of this chapter; and (3) Martin Luther's classic objections that have marked much of the Protestant movement.

Sacrifice or Meal?

Should we see the Eucharistic liturgy as primarily a sacrifice or a meal? In recent decades, theologians have placed great emphasis on the Eucharist as a banquet. I maintain that we should not lose sight of the centrality of sacrifice. In the words of Matthew Levering, "In this oblation, the sacrifice and meal mutually interpenetrate and define one another."[202] In other words, we would misunderstand the Eucharist's meal aspect without a proper grasp of its sacrificial nature.[203]

As we saw above see, numerous theological sources demonstrate the importance of sacrifice. Taken together, they show that the Eucharistic meal is best understood as depending on sacrifice, and not vice versa. First, the Last Supper narratives constitute the central biblical locus of a Eucharistic theology, for here Christ enacts the Eucharist as he institutes it. In chapter 3, we saw that all the ancient anaphora maintain a firm reference to the Last Supper. These rites and the Church Fathers witness to that event as the Eucharist's historical and spiritual origin. In other words, the Eucharistic liturgy did not spontaneously emerge from the communal meal practices of the early Christians. Second, we saw in chapter 2 that the Last Supper was a Passover meal. It integrated the Jewish table blessings, which strongly marked the early Eucharistic prayers. In chapter 3, I noted that Christ instituted a new sacramental sacrifice at the Last Supper. Within that institution, he set down a firm link between the gift of his flesh and blood and his saving death on the Cross. He becomes the new lamb, offered on the Cross. His words over the bread and cup

202. Levering, *Sacrifice and Community*, 2.

203. The theme of sacrifice is essentially missing from the biblical analysis of the Eucharist in the recent document of an ecumenical study group in Germany, with an almost exclusive focus on the early Eucharistic celebration as a sacred meal. The document seems to employ a Lutheran hermeneutic that flattens the rich complexity of the biblical and early Church witnesses. See Volker Leppin and Dorothea Sattler, eds., *Together at the Lord's Table: A Votum of the Ecumenical Working Group of Lutheran and Catholic Theologians* (Freiburg im Breisgau: Herder, 2020), 89–104.

contain strong sacrificial images. Also, the eating of his body and blood given up for us fulfills the Passover practice of eating the slain lamb. As Jean Danielou has pointed out, the image of the paschal lamb unites sacrifice and meal.[204] In the context of the Last Supper, eating and drinking are essentially sacrificial acts. Indeed, sacrifice seems to overshadow the act of eating in the biblical Last Supper accounts. For we find only brief indications of or allusions to the apostles' eating and drinking, to the point of causing some exegetes to doubt whether the Last Supper was a Passover meal at all. Instead, Jesus' words and gestures stand in the foreground. Third, our survey of the early Fathers and ancient liturgy in the present chapter manifested a tendency to identify a wide array of prayers and gestures as an offering. In other words, the Eucharistic liturgy is not a ritual that contains some sacrificial elements. Rather, it *is* a sacrifice, one that includes various forms of sacrifice. Fourth, the food and drink that we consume are the flesh and blood of Christ as victim. Our manner of eating depends on the presence of the victim, specifically, the substantial presence of his body and blood. Our eating is a sharing in a sacrifice, and not just the consumption of his glorified humanity. Therefore, the Eucharist as a sacred meal depends on and flows from the sacrificial nature of the Mass. We participate in a banquet because we share in a sacrifice.

We can maintain a vision of the Eucharistic liturgy as a sacrifice consummated in communion while we also avoid numerous theological pitfalls. A doctrine that places much emphasis on the consecration need not minimize the role of the Church in the liturgy, for she offers Christ the victim with and through the priest. The Mass cannot bear fruit in the lives of the faithful without their self-offering, which in turn highlights the role of praise, worship, and thanksgiving. These are forms of exterior sacrifice that express and heighten the interior sacrifice of the participants. The themes of satisfaction and reconciliation are important, yet they need not overshadow other blessings imparted in the liturgy. Indeed, Christo-forming love is the greatest fruit of the Eucharistic sacrifice. There is simply no need to oppose the themes of sacrifice and the communion of love. Finally, a proper understanding of sacrifice gives a strong argument for the importance of the laity's communion, including their

204. Jean Danielou, *The Bible and the Liturgy* (Notre Dame, Ind.: University of Notre Dame Press, 1956), 172.

sharing in the cup, in continuation of Old Covenant sacrificial practice. Abundant gifts may be received by the consumption of the gifts. Sacrifice makes possible the most extraordinary banquet of all.

The heart of the solution seems to be twofold. First, we should recognize the Eucharist as the fulfillment of biblical sacrifices of communion (including Passover), where the oblation of the victim is ordered to its consumption by those who offer it. Eating completes the sacrifice. Second, we ought to refuse any opposition between interior and exterior sacrifice, both of which find their fulfillment in communion.

A Response to Louis-Marie Chauvet on Eucharistic Sacrifice

Louis-Marie Chauvet holds that the New Testament follows a contemporaneous Jewish theological development, in which emphasis shifted from the offering of a victim to the sacrifice of praise.[205] In Chauvet's view, the theme of propitiation remains acceptable, if it is placed within the framework of a communion sacrifice.[206] His biblical exegesis and reading of second-century Christian liturgy lead him to place two themes at the center of Eucharistic sacrifice: the whole people's offering of praise and thanksgiving, and their daily sacrifice of love in service of neighbor, a sacrifice that the liturgy animates (e.g., Heb 13:15–16).[207]

The theology of Eucharistic sacrifice developed above can honor Chauvet's main concerns. The cruciform love received by the sacrifice heightens our concern for our neighbor in need. The gift of reconciliation heals wounded relationships with God and our fellow human beings. Also, the offering of praise is crucial in order for the participants to dispose themselves for a new share in the various gifts that flow from the sacrifice.

However, Chauvet places his theological accents in problematic ways. His account of sacrifice essentially ignores the Last Supper, yet it is here that Jesus himself enacted a sacrificial ritual. Chauvet skips a discussion of the offering of Christ's body and blood, that perfect sacrifice to which our gifts of praise and thanksgiving *must be joined* so as to become one with

205. Chauvet, *Symbol and Sacrament*, 240–44.
206. Chauvet, *Symbol and Sacrament*, 310–11.
207. Chauvet, *Symbol and Sacrament*, 252–59, 311–12.

his self-giving on the Cross. Chauvet exaggerates the spiritualization of second-century sacrificial doctrine, as he overlooks Irenaeus's anti-Gnostic emphasis on bringing the first fruits of material creation. Chauvet insists that the *lex orandi* of the new Eucharistic prayers in the Roman rite should guide sacramental theology, yet we saw how many of these prayers express the Church's act of offering *the victim* to the Father. Finally, Chauvet consistently approaches Eucharistic sacrifice as something that we do, but he says little on how Christ changes the gifts so that we can make an offering through him. The difficulties in Chauvet's account stem not so much from his affirmations as from his omissions.[208] Indeed, the immediate dependence of the Church's sacrificial act on Christ's priestly action seems crucial to avoid the heart of the Protestant objection to a Catholic doctrine of sacrifice.

Evaluating Martin Luther's Critique of the Sacrifice of the Mass

The revised notions of sacrifice presented by Chauvet and other theologians partly respond to the concerns of Martin Luther and his disciples. Here, we can take a closer look at Luther's doctrinal motives for denying Eucharistic sacrifice and give a brief response to him. As we ponder Luther's polemic against the Mass as a sacrifice, we might remember his historical context: a multiplication of private Masses said for the dead, and infrequent communion by the laity. Sixteenth-century Catholic practice limited the experience of the Mass as communion with Christ and as a sacred meal, while placing great emphasis on sacrifice for sins.[209] We should read the Wittenberg theologian with a hermeneutic of charity.

Luther emphasized that the Eucharistic liturgy has the power to elicit and strengthen faith. He considered the liturgical signs and communion with Christ present in the transformed gifts as a true means to grace. He held for a doctrine of the real presence (to be studied in the next chapter),

208. Joris Geldhof rightly points out that Chauvet's hermeneutical approach to the sacraments and the Eucharist brings good insights, yet, due to its link with a (Heideggerian) philosophy of finitude, Chauvet cannot adequately account for our liturgical participation in the infinite. See Geldhof, "Thought and the Eucharist: Philosophical Models and Their Theological Appropriation," *Ephemerides Theologicae Lovanienses* 86 (2010): 97–98.

209. Karl-Heinz zur Mühlen, "Luther II: Theologie," in *Theologische Realenzyklopädie*, vol. 21, ed. Gerhard L. Müller (Berlin: Walter de Gruyter, 1991), 554.

so that Christ truly gives himself to us in the Eucharistic gifts.[210] Luther focused his exposition of the liturgy on the Augustinian notion of the sacrifice of praise. The assembly's prayers and hymns are an acceptable offering to God.[211] The faithful respond to Christ's sacrifice on the Cross and his offer of forgiveness. Luther sharply distinguished between the prayers offered and the power of the Word active in the liturgy.[212]

As noted at the beginning of this chapter, Luther's stance is closely tied to his insistence that we are justified by faith alone. In other words, his rejection of any sacrificial *work* goes to the heart of his entire theological project: we are dealing with much more than a misunderstanding between Luther and his contemporaries. His refusal of merit in Christian good works is also closely linked with his view of the priesthood. Luther inherited some basic philosophical presuppositions from his Catholic teachers and their medieval predecessors. That is, Luther's theology is rooted in a univocal approach to causality: He presumes that if God acts, we receive, and thus we do not act. But if we act, then God does not act.[213] In this approach, our good works would take away from God's glory and obscure the truth that salvation is a gift. Luther rejects any application of the model of principal and instrumental causality to the sacramental realm. Thus, he says that Christ is the only priest at Mass.[214] Charles Morerod has shown that Luther's sacramental theology partly depends on the philosophical assumptions (1) that an action has one cause and (2) that instruments are not real causes. We find similar presuppositions in the writings of John Calvin.[215]

For Luther, the key to understanding the Eucharistic liturgy is the juridical category of a testament. A testament involves a promise and an inheritance that a dying person leaves us. Jesus has left us a promise that we will receive forgiveness of sins through the Cross. This forgiveness is our inheritance, and we obtain it by faith. The Last Supper is thus essen-

210. Joachim Staedtke, "Abendmahl III/3: Reformationszeit," in *Theologische Realenzyklopädie*, vol. 1, ed. Gerhard Kraus and Gerhard L. Müller (Berlin: Walter de Gruyter, 1977), 111.

211. Gillian R Evans, "Opfer V: Mittelalter bis Neuzeit," in *Theologische Realenzyklopädie*, vol. 25, ed. Gerhard L. Müller (Berlin: Walter de Gruyter, 1995), 281.

212. Martin Luther, *The Babylonian Captivity*, 49–53.

213. Charles Morerod, *Ecumenism and Philosophy: Philosophical Questions for a Renewal of Dialogue* (Ann Arbor, Mich.: Sapientia Press, 2006), 83–93.

214. Evans, "Opfer V," 281.

215. Morerod, *Ecumenism and Philosophy*, 93–103.

tially a Word event, a promise signified by the prayers of the Last Supper celebration and through material things, namely, bread and wine. Luther interprets memorial through the confession that the Church makes of Christ's promise.[216] Since the Eucharistic liturgy is effective by the faith that it elicits in its participants, it does not benefit those who are absent. It is not offered for others, for faith is a personal act made in response to Christ's last testament, the promise that is remembered by those who participate in the liturgy.[217]

Luther thus separates the Last Supper from the paschal meal. He does not reduce memorial to a mere act of calling to mind past saving events, yet he refocuses the entire Eucharistic doctrine on the power of God's word, on God's promise pronounced by the minister in the words of institution, a word active today as it addresses the sinner directly.[218] The slain lamb has a place only insofar as the signs point to the true Lamb. Luther considers the Last Supper as a testament in abstraction from Christ's corporeal presence. Finally, Luther's vision of the Last Supper places it in opposition to the Old Testament. He wants to go beyond the law, with its ineffective works, and have only the Gospel, with its promise of salvation by faith.[219] This is crucial: Luther separates the Last Supper from its Jewish roots.

Two final comments on Luther are in order. First, Luther realized that he was opposing an ancient theological tradition of Eucharistic sacrifice. Indeed, earlier in this chapter, we saw how the doctrine that the Church offers Christ as victim to the Father is firmly planted in the anaphora of various liturgical families. Luther's stance implies that many Church Fathers and our most ancient Eucharistic prayers transmit a grave doctrinal error. Second, his refusal of instrumental causality goes beyond a rejection of the ministerial priesthood, for it also touches upon the entire Catholic vision of the Church's and the sacraments' role in salvation.[220]

216. Oswald Bayer, *Promissio: Geschichte der reformatorischen Wende in Luthers Theologie*, Forschungen zur Kirchen- und Dogmengeschichte 24 (Göttingen, Germany: Vandenhoeck & Ruprecht, 1971), 251.

217. Urfels, *La Pâque du Messie*, 304–7.

218. Bayer, *Promissio*, 252

219. Urfels, *La Pâque du Messie*, 312–17.

220. The German ecumenical working group overlooks the contradictions between Luther and widespread early Christian liturgical belief in Eucharistic sacrifice. See Leppin and Sattler, *Together at the Lord's Table*, 105–14. It implicitly accepts a rupture in the *lex orandi*.

The previous remarks should not obscure the fact that some contemporary Protestant leaders and theologians have reconsidered the question of Eucharistic sacrifice. For example, George Hunsinger proposes that the following formulations would be acceptable from a Reformed (Calvinist) Protestant perspective. First, Christ expiated for our sins once and for all, yet the fruits of this saving work are made available to us daily, apparently also in the Eucharist.[221] Second, Hunsinger is not at ease with the language of Christians offering sacrifice, but he can accept a *representation* of a sacrifice. He seeks to avoid the idea of a repetition of Christ's sacrificial act. The meaning of the term "representation" becomes crucial. Hunsinger's description of the Eucharist as a re-actualization of the Cross holds promise, while also needing more precision.[222] Third, Hunsinger recognizes the link between the Last Supper and the Passover: we commune in the Paschal Lamb.[223] His proposal deserves further reflection, especially on the link between sacrifice, Christ's corporeal presence, and the identity of the Eucharistic celebrant.

Finally, while contemporary theological discussions across the confessional divide hold much promise, it is important to recognize that Luther's rejection of Eucharistic sacrifice as understood by the Catholic tradition gained immediate acceptance among all the leading Protestant Reformers (such as John Calvin), and continues to be part of the basic Protestant confessional stance.[224]

221. Hunsinger, *The Eucharist and Ecumenism*, 136–39.

222. Hunsinger, *The Eucharist and Ecumenism*, 138–39, 144–45, 171–72.

223. Hunsinger, *The Eucharist and Ecumenism*, 142–45.

224. Hunsinger, *The Eucharist and Ecumenism*, 109–10. This rejection of Eucharistic sacrifice also includes communities with a relatively high sacramental theology, such as the Anglicans. See the Pontifical Council for Promoting Christian Unity, "The Official Roman Catholic Response to the Final Report of ARCIC (1991)," in *Anglicans and Roman Catholic Catholics: The Search for Unity*, ed. Christopher Hill and E. J. Yarnold (London: SPCK/CTS, 1994), 162.

CHAPTER 6

THE SUBSTANTIAL PRESENCE OF CHRIST IN THE EUCHARIST

In our study of John 6 and the Last Supper, we found good reasons to hold that these texts teach a strong Eucharistic realism. The raw language of Jesus about eating his flesh and blood shocked his interlocutors. Christ's words at the Last Supper, understood within its Passover setting, point in the same direction. This exegesis finds confirmation in patristic doctrine and ancient Eucharistic practice. From Ignatius of Antioch forward, the Fathers consistently affirmed that the Eucharistic food and drink simply are Christ's body and blood. This teaching was perceived to be part of the apostolic heritage.[1]

The last few decades have seen a wide-ranging debate on the nature of Christ's presence in the Eucharistic gifts. Before Vatican II, we already

1. Bruce Marshall, "The Eucharistic Presence of Christ," in *What Does It Mean to "Do This"? Supper, Mass, Eucharist*, ed. Michael Root and James J. Buckley, The Pro Ecclesia Series (Eugene, Ore.: Cascade Books, 2014), 55–56.

find the beginning of a quest for a theology less bound to Aristotelian and scholastic categories, a quest that has the aim of rendering the doctrine intelligible to contemporary man. Starting in the mid-twentieth century, some theologians proposed that the greatest transformation in the gifts involves a change of purpose (trans-finalization) or meaning (trans-signification). Edward Schillebeeckx made a change of meaning central to his vision of this sacrament, though without denying a deeper, metaphysical modification of the gifts.[2] Louis-Marie Chauvet appropriated the tools of the philosophy of language and phenomenology to offer a Eucharistic theology radically centered on symbolic efficacy, in an effort to go beyond any notion of substantial presence.[3] Leading liturgical scholars have sought to develop a doctrine of Christ's "dynamic presence," in contrast to the "static presence" of a mere substance. Cesare Giraudo posits the presence of Christ's body and blood in the *event* of his Passion, with appeal to the category of an efficacious memorial.[4] Among Protestant theologians, the wide divergence, which began among Martin Luther, Huldrych Zwingli, and John Calvin, on the nature of Christ's presence in the Eucharist continues. In the latter group, one finds everything from a corporal, quasi-substantial presence (Luther) to a mere symbol of Christ (Zwingli), with various options in between (including Calvin).

Vatican II said little on Christ's presence in the Eucharistic gifts, yet affirmed the doctrine of Trent.[5] In his 1965 encyclical *Mysterium Fidei*, Paul VI called for firm adherence to the doctrine of transubstantiation. But, in general, Catholic preaching and catechesis since Vatican II rarely offer much instruction on the nature of Christ's presence in the Eucharist, or on how the gifts on the altar change.

The heart of this chapter lays out a Thomistic account of Christ's presence in the gifts. Since the biblical treatment of this theme has already been undertaken, I begin with a survey of the Fathers' teaching, followed by a brief journey to fourteenth-century Byzantium. I then turn to the

2. Edward Schillebeeckx, *The Eucharist* (London: Sheed & Ward, 1968), 130–50.

3. Louis-Marie Chauvet, *Symbol and Sacrament: A Sacramental Reinterpretation of Christian Existence*, trans. Patrick Madigan and Madeleine Beaumont (Collegeville, Minn.: Liturgical Press, 1995), 382–408.

4. Cesare Giraudo, *In unum corpus: Traité mystagogique sur l'eucharistie*, trans. Éric Iborra and Pierre-Marie Hombert (Paris: Cerf, 2014), 532–34 (discussed above).

5. *Sacrosanctum Concilium*, no. 7.

controversy surrounding Berengar of Tours, which triggered significant medieval developments in Eucharistic doctrine. The systematic section includes a brief philosophical exposition of the basic notions of substance and accident, which advanced readers may choose to skip. I then focus on Aquinas's influential theology of transubstantiation (or the change of the gifts) and Christ's abiding presence in the gifts (the result of transubstantiation). I will analyze his doctrine and argue for its coherence in the face of alternatives. I also seek to make this complex and subtle teaching more accessible by setting forth two analogies: the soul's presence within the body and the Incarnation. The chapter continues with a survey of Luther and other leaders of the Protestant Reformation, along with the teaching of the Council of Trent that partly responds to them. Luther and Trent are best understood in light of medieval scholastic theology, and so I analyze their teachings after the study of Aquinas. I conclude with a short analysis of key objections to a classical, scholastic account of Eucharistic presence, especially those of Schillebeeckx and Chauvet, by pondering their work in light of Pope Paul VI's encyclical *Mysterium Fidei*.

The Theology of Christ's Corporeal Presence in History

Patristic Theologies of Eucharistic Presence

Eucharistic realism is strikingly ancient. Writing to the Smyrnaeans (in Asia Minor) in the early second century, Ignatius of Antioch warns against those who abstain from the Eucharist: "they do not confess that the Eucharist is the flesh of our Savior Jesus Christ, which suffered for our sins, and which the Father in his loving-kindness raised from the dead."[6] Ignatius polemicizes against the Docetists, who deny the reality of Christ's humanity. On the contrary, the Eucharist is the body of the glorified Christ. Ignatius posits a continuity of identity between Christ's historical, risen, and Eucharistic body.[7]

6. Ignatius of Antioch, "Letter to the Smyrnaeans," no. 7, in *The Epistles of St. Clement of Rome and St. Ignatius of Antioch*, ed. James A. Kleist, Ancient Christian Writers 1 (New York: Paulist Press, 1978), 92.

7. Moll, *Die Lehre von der Eucharistie als Opfer* (Cologne: Peter Hanstein, 1975), 96.

Writing around the year 150, Justin Martyr's *First Apology*, chapter 66, states:

For we do not receive these things as common bread and common drink; but in like manner as Jesus Christ our Savior, having been made incarnate by the God's logos, took both flesh and blood for our salvation, so also have we been taught that the food eucharistized through the word of prayer that is from Him, from which our blood and flesh are nourished by transformation, is the flesh and blood of that Jesus who became incarnate.[8]

Both the Incarnation and the conversion of the Eucharistic gifts come about by the initiative of the Logos. The Word of God (the Son) acts so as to become incarnate, and he acts to make of bread and wine his flesh and blood. The Logos descends from heaven to become man in the womb of the Blessed Virgin Mary. The Logos made flesh descends again in the Eucharistic gifts. The analogy between the Logos's incarnate presence in history and in the sacrament constitutes a veritable key for Greek patristic Eucharistic theology.[9] The analogy centers on the way in which the Son is present to us. Justin affirms continuity from the Incarnation to the Eucharist: in each, we find the same flesh and blood, that of the Savior.

Irenaeus of Lyon insists that the Eucharist is Christ's own blood and his own flesh: "[Jesus] has acknowledged the cup (which is a part of the creation) as His own blood, from which He bedews our blood; and the bread (also a part of the creation) He has established as His own body, from which He gives increase to our bodies."[10] Irenaeus's realism also emerges when he argues that our flesh is saved because it is fed with Christ's flesh and blood.[11] The means of salvation corresponds to the reality being saved: Christ's real and immortal body taken into ourselves causes our bodily resurrection.[12] Irenaeus adds that the Eucharist is con-

8. Justin Martyr, *First Apology*, chapter 66, in *First and Second Apologies*, ed. and trans. Leslie William Barnard, Ancient Christian Writers 56 (New York: Paulist Press, 1997).

9. Johannes Betz, *Eucharistie in der Schrift und Patristik*, Handbuch der Dogmengeschichte 4.4a (Freiburg im Breisgau: Herder, 1979), 34; also Betz, *Die Eucharistie in der Zeit der griechischen Väter*, vol. 1.1: *Die Aktualpräsenz der Person und des Heilswerkes Jesu im Abendmahl nach der vorephesinischen griechischen Patristik* (Freiburg im Breisgau: Herder, 1955),271.

10. Irenaeus of Lyon, *Treatise Against Heresies*, bk. 5, chap. 2, no. 2, in Irenaeus of Lyon, *Contre les hérésies, livre V*, ed. Adelin Rousseau, Sources chrétiennes 125 (Paris: Cerf, 1969).

11. Irenaeus of Lyon, *Treatise Against Heresies*, bk. 5, chap. 18, no. 5.

12. Betz, *Eucharistie in der Schrift und Patristik*, 36.

stituted of a heavenly and an earthly element. This phrase likely refers to the source or origin of the gift, namely, the Logos and the bread. It may also refer to the act of invoking the Logos onto the earthly gifts, so that when the prayer of consecration calls upon Jesus the Logos to descend, he comes into the Eucharistic elements.[13]

John Chrysostom stands as the leading representative of the "Antiochene school," which emphasized the presence of Christ's humanity in the Eucharist. By representing (in ritual form) the Passion and Resurrection of Christ, the mystery (the saving historical deed) becomes present in the "type."[14] Chrysostom refuses to separate the sign from the reality signified. His conviction in the corporeal presence of Christ emerges in several ways. First, the oblation offered today is the same that was offered at the Last Supper.[15] Second, Christ's words transform (*metaruthmizei*) the gifts. Indeed, the power of his words at the Last Supper spans across time to all Eucharistic celebrations.[16] Third, the body that we receive is the same that was crucified for us.[17] Fourth, Chrysostom employs provocative language to point to the mystical encounter available in sacramental eating: we eat Christ, we place our teeth on his flesh, so as to be joined with him and to fulfill our desires.[18]

In general, the Greek Fathers emphasize the transforming power of God's Word that is evoked in the prayer of the epiclesis. They hold that the prayer of consecration reaches all the way to the being (*ousia*) of the Eucharist, and not just its purpose or meaning. Yet the same Fathers spend little time reflecting on how this change occurs.[19] Some Greek Fa-

13. Betz, *Eucharistie in der Schrift und Patristik*, 37; also Betz, *Die Eucharistie in der Zeit der griechischen Väter*, 1.1:301–2; Antonio Orbe, *Introduction à la théologie des IIe et IIIe siècles*, trans. Joseph M. López de Castro, Agnès Bastit, and Jean-Michel Roessli, Patrimoines: Christianisme (Paris: Cerf, 2012), vol. 1, 736; Moll, *Die Lehre von der Eucharistie als Opfer*, 174.

14. Ángel García Ibáñez, *L'eucaristia, dono e mistero: Trattato storico-dogmatico sul mistero eucaristico*, Sussidi di teologia (Rome: EDUSC, 2006), 156n122.

15. John Chrysostom, "Homily on 2 Timothy," 2.4 (PG 62:612), cited in García Ibáñez, *L'eucaristia, dono e mistero*, 157.

16. García Ibáñez, *L'eucaristia, dono e mistero*, 157n123.

17. John Chrysostom, "Homily on 1 Corinthians," 24.4 (PG 61:203–4), cited in García Ibáñez, *L'eucaristia, dono e mistero*, 159.

18. See Roch A. Kereszty, *Wedding Feast of the Lamb: Eucharistic Theology from a Biblical, Historical and Systematic Perspective* (Chicago: Hillenbrand Books, 2007), 107.

19. Jean-Marie Roger Tillard, "Théologie, voix catholique: La communion à la Pâque du Seigneur," in *Eucharistia: Encyclopédie de l'eucharistie*, ed. Maurice Brouard (Paris: Cerf, 2002), 406.

thers prefer to speak of the Eucharist as a "pneumatic" or "spiritual body." The key background text is 1 Corinthians 15: Christ's risen body overflows with the Holy Spirit and his gifts.[20] In this context, the term "pneumatic" or "spiritual" is not opposed to the term "corporeal."

Ambrose of Milan marked the Eucharistic doctrine of the west as few other Fathers of the Church did. He also transmitted and developed the teaching of the Greek Fathers. Some key characteristics of his catecheses deserve brief mention. In Ambrose, we frequently find the language of the "conversion" of the gifts, or the use of verbs such as "to change" and "to transfigure."[21] This involves a supernatural effect on the very nature of the thing seen and received.[22] Ambrose unfolds his teaching by comparing the Eucharistic change to nature miracles in the Old Testament.[23] The sacramental change is made possible by the divine word that can create out of nothing, a power that can thus also change creatures in extraordinary ways. Ambrose's favorite analogy for Eucharistic transformation is the Incarnation:

> Let us use his own examples, and by the mysteries of the Incarnation let us establish the truth of the mysteries. Did the process of nature precede when the Lord Jesus was born of Mary? If we seek the usual course, a woman after mingling with a man usually conceives. It is clear that the Virgin conceived contrary to the course of nature. And this body which we make is from the Virgin. Why do you seek here the course of nature in the body of Christ, when the Lord Jesus himself was born of the Virgin contrary to nature? Surely it is the true flesh of Christ, which was crucified, which was buried; therefore it is truly the sacrament of that flesh.[24]

Neither the change in Mary's womb nor that on the altar can be explained by nature. Ambrose seems to detect a consistent pattern in God's saving works, from Old Testament miracles to the Annunciation and the liturgy.

20. Jean-Marie Roger Tillard, *L'Eucharistie: Pâque de l'Église*, Unam sanctam 4 (Paris: Cerf, 1964), 28–29. For an English translation, see *The Eucharist: Pasch of God's People* (Staten Island, N.Y.: Alba House, 1967).

21. Raymond Johanny, *L'eucharistie centre de l'histoire du salut chez saint Ambroise de Milan*, Théologie historique 9 (Paris: Beauchesne, 1969), 89–112.

22. García Ibáñez, *L'eucaristia, dono e mistero*, 166–67.

23. Ambrose of Milan, *The Mysteries*, 9.50–54, in *Theological and Dogmatic Works*, trans. Roy Deferrari, The Fathers of the Church 44 (Washington, D.C.: The Catholic University of America Press, 1963).

24. Ambrose, *The Mysteries*, 9.53, in *Theological and Dogmatic Works*, 25–26.

Faith in the Virginal conception becomes a pedagogical step to grasp the mystery of the Eucharist. Christ's true flesh was in Mary's womb, was on the Cross, rose from the dead and is now on the altar. We now have the same flesh, for it is "from the Virgin." Ambrose also posits an identity between Christ's historical, glorified, and Eucharistic body. At the same time, Christ's mode of Eucharistic presence is distinct, such that he is not consumed in a material mode, that is, not in the way of normal food.[25]

Augustine continues Ambrose's Eucharistic realism while accentuating his doctrine in a different way. The Bishop of Hippo gives no explanation of Eucharistic conversion, yet he acknowledges the reality.[26] In Sermon 229, he instructs the neophytes: "What you can see here, dearly beloved, on the table of the Lord, is bread and wine; but this bread and wine, when the word is applied to it, becomes the body and blood of the Word."[27] Here and in Sermon 272, we find a clear refusal to separate the Eucharistic sign from the glorified body of the Lord: "So what you can see then, is bread and a cup; that's what even your eyes tell you; but as for what your faith asks to be instructed about, the bread is the body of Christ, the cup the blood of Christ."[28] This mysterious, qualified identity of the signs or external elements with Christ's body and blood help to account for the following, striking exhortation: "Not only do we commit no sin in worshipping it [the Eucharist], we would sin if we did not."[29] Such an act of worship makes sense only if there is a hidden, metaphysical change of the gifts.[30]

But the focus of Augustine's Eucharistic sermons lies elsewhere, namely, on the Eucharist as spiritual nourishment and the ecclesial effects thereof. In his *Tractates on the Gospel of John*, Augustine emphasizes believers' spiritual union with Christ in the sacrament, which comes by

25. García Ibáñez, *L'eucaristia, dono e mistero*, 168–69.

26. J. L. van der Lof, "L'eucharistie et présence réelle selon saint Augustin," *Revue des études augustiniennes* 10 (1964): 295–304.

27. Augustine, "Sermon 229," no. 1, in *Sermons (184–229Z) on the Liturgical Seasons*, trans. Edmund Hill, The Works of St. Augustine 3.6 (Hyde Park, N.Y.: New City Press, 1993), 265.

28. Augustine, "Sermon 272," in *Sermons (230–272B) on the Liturgical Seasons*, trans. Edmund Hill, The Works of St. Augustine 3.7 (Hyde Park, N.Y.: New City Press, 1994), 300.

29. Augustine, *Expositions of the Psalms* 98.9, in *Expositions of the Psalms 73–98*, trans. Maria Boulding, The Works of St. Augustine 3.18 (Hyde Park, N.Y.: New City Press, 2002), 475.

30. I follow Kereszty's reading of Augustine, and his critique of Johannes Betz's interpretation (Kereszty, *Wedding Feast of the Lamb*, 122–23, 128n24).

eating the glorified, Spirit-filled body, a body seen with the eyes of faith. Here, the distinction between the *res* (the hidden reality, especially the body and blood), the *virtus* (the spiritual, nourishing power of his body and blood), and the visible sign is key.[31]

The Fathers' witness to Christ's corporeal presence in the Eucharist is clear, when they refer to the result or outcome of Eucharistic conversion. Yet their teaching also remains discrete: we have neither a clear affirmation of transubstantiation nor a contradiction thereof.[32] That is, they say little about the action by which Christ's body and blood come upon the altar, although they employ the language of creation or transfiguration. Finally, I have only given a brief sample of patristic theologies of Christ's presence in the gifts. We will encounter still more witnesses in subsequent chapters, when we consider patristic approaches to the consecration and to communion.

Medieval Byzantine Theologies of Eucharistic Presence

The doctrine of Christ's corporeal presence in the Eucharist also finds firm adherents in the Byzantine tradition. Here, a key figure is the fourteenth-century theologian Nicholas Cabasilas, who synthesized the Greek Fathers and offered a doctrine that became highly influential in many eastern Orthodox Churches. Nicholas follows the language and teaching of various Greek Fathers in speaking of the transformation or *metabolē* of the Eucharistic gifts. He holds that, with the offertory, the gifts of bread and wine have been removed from the profane sphere so as to become an offering to God. Then comes the ultimate change of the gifts, which Cabasilas locates at the epiclesis that follows the words of institution. Here we find a standard eastern medieval reading of the Greek Fathers through the lens of John Damascene, an issue to be taken up later. The gifts transformed into Christ' body and blood are infinitely holy. The body on the altar is the body that was truly tortured and crucified, the blood on the altar is the very blood shed on the Cross. Cabasilas holds that one should remain

31. Augustine, tractate 26, no. 11, in *Tractates on the Gospel of John, 11–27*, trans. John W. Rettig, The Fathers of the Church 79 (Washington, D.C.: The Catholic University of America Press, 1988); also Augustine *Expositions of the Psalms* 98, no. 9; García Ibáñez, *L'eucaristia, dono e mistero*, 175–76.

32. Betz, *Die Eucharistie in der Zeit der griechischen Väter*, 1.1:318.

silent on the manner of the gifts' conversion. He knows of but refuses to adopt the doctrine of transubstantiation.[33]

However, the Church was silent neither about Christ's two natures, nor about his two wills. Why, then, should she remain silent on the change of the gifts on the altar? Heresy also calls for a response. The east did not experience great controversy about Eucharistic presence as the west did, so the east has never had to surmount the difficulty. Theology advances in the face of heresy, when it is compelled to give new answers to new problems.

The Berengar Controversy and Its Aftermath

There were no major Eucharistic controversies in the early Church. Indeed, it was accepted doctrine that the gifts on the altar underwent a metaphysical change, so that Christ's very body and blood became present therein. Only some heretical sects like the Gnostics doubted this teaching. The first great debate on Eucharistic presence occurred in the ninth century, and the first doctrinal crisis came only in the eleventh century.

In this time period, a dominant older sacramental vision, which easily saw the signs or figures as participating in the realities that they signify, began to fade. The sacramental language of Augustine was still used, but some medieval readers could no longer grasp its full meaning. One important example is Berengar of Tours, who employed a more dialectical, rational type of theology, in which he applied the philosophical categories of form and matter to the Eucharist. In Berengar's thought, the form is part of a thing's constitutive principles, but it also includes all of its sensible properties. His notion of form resembles a combination of Aristotle's accidents and substantial form. Berengar used the term "matter" to refer to the subject that has these properties, a usage that again differs from that of Aristotle. Since the sensible properties of the Eucharistic gifts do not change at Mass, Berengar refused the notion that the form of bread and wine changes, and since the form does not change, neither does the substance, as the substance includes the form. Berengar had an

33. Nicholas Cabasilas, *Commentary on the Divine Liturgy*, trans. J. M. Hussey and P. A. McNulty, 5th ed. (Crestwood, N.Y.: St. Vladimir's Seminary Press, 2002), chap. 17; Job Ihor W. Getcha, "La théologie sacramentaire byzantine: La synthèse de Nicolas Cabasilas et Syméon de Thessalonique" (Habilitation Thesis, University of Lorraine, Department of Theology, 2012), 187–89.

underdeveloped philosophy of substance: he maintained that substance is wholly accessible to the senses. As a result, the sacrament and the hidden reality of Christ's body and blood become separated, for the symbol is no longer filled with what it symbolizes.[34] Berengar also ridiculed the idea that Christ's body could simultaneously be present in heaven and on multiple altars.[35]

In the year 1059, a Roman Synod compelled Berengar to retract and to sign a confession. The latter apparently reflects the hyperrealism of some of his contemporaries: Christ's body and blood are said to be present "sensibly [*sensualiter*] not only in sacrament," so that his body is broken by our hands and teeth.[36] Still, the main purpose of the synod's declaration was to exclude the reduction of the Eucharist to a sign of an absent reality, a worthy aim that was clouded by problematic language and concepts. Berengar soon retracted this confession. He later signed a second confession composed at yet another Roman Synod held in 1079 and presided over by Pope Gregory VII. Here, we find more nuanced phrasing, and the language of substantial change is used for the first time in a magisterial text.[37] Such language refers to a real change of the gifts, while avoiding the problematic terms and possible confusion present in the 1059 confession. It would take the next two centuries to work out in greater detail the meaning of transubstantiation.

A good analogy for this process of doctrinal clarification is the Creed of Nicaea: at the first ecumenical Council, the Fathers employed new terminology and essentially proposed a new metaphysical category so as to explain what philosophy alone cannot grasp. Nicaea also went beyond the language and concepts of Scripture, for heresy made this necessary to explain a biblical doctrine, namely, the doctrine of the full divinity of Christ. It took decades after the Council of Nicaea to clear up the meaning of *homoousios*: in some ways, that issue was not resolved until the First Council of Constantinople (381).

Numerous eleventh- and twelfth-century theologians helped to clari-

34. Hans Jorissen, *Die Entfaltung der Transsubstantionslehre bis zum Beginn der Hochscholastik*, Münsterische Beiträge zur Theologie 28.1 (Münster, Germany: Aschendorff, 1965), 6–7.

35. Lawrence Feingold, *The Eucharist: Mystery of Presence, Sacrifice and Communion* (Steubenville, Ohio: Emmaus Academic, 2018), 239.

36. DH 690.

37. DH 700.

fy the nature of the change of the Eucharistic gifts and Christ's corporeal presence therein, which prepared the way for later magisterial teaching and the master synthesis worked out by Aquinas. I will summarize these theologians' key insights, following the work of Lawrence Feingold. First, they developed a clear distinction between substance and accidents. Second, this distinction allowed them to posit a change of bread substance into body substance and wine substance into blood substance, while holding that the accidents remain the same. Third, they identified this change as a unique miracle: reason cannot explain it simply by recourse to natural causes. Fourth, to sidestep the excessive realism of Berengar's opponents, they insisted on the presence of the whole Christ in each part of the gifts: Christ's bones and teeth are not broken when the faithful consume his body. Fifth, the theology of concomitance began to emerge: Christ's body is present with the blood, and vice versa, while his soul and divinity are also present in each. Sixth, Hugh of St. Victor and Peter Lombard developed the triple distinction of *sacramentum tantum*, *res et sacramentum*, and *res tantum*. The species of bread and wine are the *sacramentum tantum*, which signify the body and blood (*res et sacramentum*) contained therein, that is, the substance of the body and blood. The body and blood abide with the sign, are invisible, and point to another reality, which is the grace (*res tantum*) that they impart.[38]

Transubstantiation was first taught dogmatically in 1215 by Pope Innocent III and Lateran Council IV. Responding to the Cathar movement, which denied the corporeal presence of Christ at Mass, the Council defined in its constitution *On the Catholic Faith* that Christ's "Body and blood are truly contained in the sacrament of the altar under the appearances (*speciebus*) of bread and wine, the bread being transubstantiated (*transubstantiatis*) into the body by the divine power and ... wine into the blood."[39] The following decades witnessed growing precision and depth to this doctrine.

38. Feingold, *The Eucharist*, 243–57.

39. Lateran Council IV, *On the Catholic Faith*, DH 802.

A Systematic Theology of Eucharistic Conversion and Presence

Unlike in the previous chapter, I will treat Protestant objections and the Tridentine response to them after my systematic treatment of the present Eucharistic theme. I do this for two reasons. First, the controversies around Eucharistic presence that began in the sixteenth century remain too obscure without a good grasp of scholastic Eucharistic doctrines on this theme. Second, Trent and the subsequent magisterium owe much to the scholastic developments that inform my speculative approach to the topic. For the sake of clarity, I will also treat major twentieth- and twenty-first-century objections to transubstantiation at the end of this chapter.

Lateran IV recalls that transubstantiation is first a mystery of faith, one that we seek to explain as much as is possible, yet without exhausting the mystery. The theme of mystery will form the preface of this section. I then briefly consider the reasons for Christ's corporeal presence in the Eucharist and explore the link between presence and substance. I also include a philosophical excursus on substance and accidents, which may benefit some readers. Thence I proceed to an analysis of transubstantiation and Christ's substantial presence in the gifts, in that order. The former stands at the service of the latter, for the doctrine of transubstantiation helps (1) to specify how bread and wine become Christ's body and blood, and (2) to exclude theories that ultimately do not posit the conversion of bread and wine into the body and blood. The doctrine of Christ's substantial presence excludes reductive interpretations (e.g., the reduction of the gifts to a mere sign) as well as sacramental hyperrealism. It serves to protect the perpetual practice of adoring the Eucharistic gifts (during and after the liturgy) and our faith that communion grants the most intimate contact with Christ's own body and blood.

A Mystery of Faith

The doctrine of Christ's corporeal presence in the Eucharist cannot be proven by reason, when reason simply relies on the senses: "That the true body and blood of Christ are in this sacrament cannot be grasped by the senses, but only by faith, which relies on the authority of God himself."[40] We believe God's word when he tells us that he gives his flesh and blood as food and drink. The doctrine of his substantial presence serves to uphold the mystery as a mystery, that is, without exhausting its meaning. Transubstantiation accounts for how Christ's body and blood come to be present on the altar, yet it does so in a way that does not fully satisfy the mind. Hence, natural science will never help us to know whether Christ is present in the Eucharist, body and blood, soul and divinity. Our senses of vision and touch tell us that bread and wine accidents are on the altar, which would normally lead the mind to judge that bread and wine substance are present. Only faith guided by our hearing of Christ's words at the Last Supper knows that the gifts on the altar have a deeper identity that escapes our sense experience.

Here, too, an analogy with the mystery of the Incarnation seems useful. No medical or scientific exam undertaken on Christ's body during his lifetime would have detected his divinity and Messianic identity. The apostles' senses and reason allowed them to recognize Jesus' true humanity, yet their hearing of his words and seeing of his miracles led them to the judgment of faith, that he was (and is) truly the Son of God.

This Eucharistic faith, expressed by Lateran IV, Trent, and Vatican II, rests on a series of pillars or witnesses.[41] The first is the Eucharistic realism of John 6, which we have already explored. The second is a long exegetical tradition of the Last Supper. For example, John Damascene states:

> The bread and wine are not a figure of the body and blood of Christ—God forbid!—but the actual deified body of the Lord, because the Lord himself said: "This is my body"; not "a figure of my body" but "my body" and not "a figure of my blood" but "my blood."[42]

One could cite many other ancient authors. In short, the symbolic reading of the words of institution (which we noted is possible from a purely exegetical, literary perspective) is excluded by tradition. A third pillar of the conciliar teaching is the adoration we offer to the Eucharist on the

40. Thomas Aquinas, *Summa theologiae* III, q. 75, a. 1.

41. DH 802, 1651, and 4007, respectively.

42. John Damascene, *On the Orthodox Faith*, bk. 4, chap. 13, trans. Frederic H. Chase, The Fathers of the Church 37 (New York: Fathers of the Church, 1958), 360.

altar. We can recall Augustine's phrase: "Not only do we commit no sin in worshipping it [the Eucharist], we would sin if we did not."[43] The Church's ancient and continuing practice of worshipping the Eucharist makes sense only if Christ is substantially present in the gifts.

Why Christ's Corporeal Presence?

For every mystery of salvation, we can pose the question, "Why has God chosen to do this?" On the foundation of faith, we look for the divine motives, specifically, in the pattern of his saving design. Why was God born of a virgin? Why did Jesus die on the Cross? Why does he give us his body and blood to adore and consume?

A first reason for Christ's corporeal presence is that it gives us a victim that we can offer in sacrifice to God. Only in this way will our sacrifice be one with the Cross, where the same body and blood were given over for our salvation.[44] Now the various Eucharistic prayers from antiquity forward consistently refer to the celebration as a sacrifice (including the offering of a victim). Yet the Spirit would not allow all the liturgical families to go astray for two millennia, for in that case, he would have been wholly absent from the Church, leaving her in a profound error. Therefore, the Eucharist is a sacrifice, and it must be one sacrifice with the Cross. And so, Christ must be present as victim, which entails a bodily presence.

A second reason to insist on Christ's corporeal presence is that it accounts for the primacy of the Eucharist among the sacraments, one that we can see consistently expressed throughout the history of the Church's liturgical practice. Now Christ is present as high priest and acting in each of the sacraments: he baptizes through the priest or deacon, he confirms through the bishop, and so forth. If the Eucharist were another ritual of this kind of efficacy, then we would not be able to explain its place at the summit of the sacramental order.[45]

A third reason for the corporeal presence is that Jesus thereby responds to our natural human longing to touch him as friend and spouse of the soul. Now Christ has ascended to heaven body and soul, yet he refuses to leave us orphans. Instead, he consoles us with his bodily pres-

43. Augustine, *Expositions of the Psalms* 98, no. 9.

44. Marshall, "The Eucharistic Presence of Christ," 58.

45. Thomas Aquinas, *Summa theologiae* III, q. 75, a. 1.

ence as the most powerful means to friendship with him. In the words of Aquinas:

in our pilgrimage, he does not deprive us of his bodily presence, but unites us to himself in this sacrament through the truth of his body and blood. Therefore, he says in John 6:57: "He who eats my flesh and drinks my blood abides in me and I in him." Therefore, this sacrament is the sign of the greatest charity, and lifts up our hope, on account of such a familiar union of Christ with us.[46]

Jesus' disciples can love him in a properly human way, knowing him by faith and touching him with love. As Bruce Marshall explains, "The Eucharist is Christ's answer, prepared in advance, to the plea that marks the whole of our earthly journey: 'Stay with us Lord, for evening draws near, the day is now far spent' (Lk 24:29)."[47] The disciples at Emmaus speak for us. His response is to break bread, to make himself known by celebrating the Eucharist.

From Corporeal Presence to Substance

Christ is truly, corporeally present on the altar. From this statement of faith, Aquinas and a long line of medieval and later scholastic theologians will draw an immediate consequence: he is therefore substantially present on the altar. This move from corporeal presence to substantial presence may appear to be questionable. Yet in Aquinas, the underlying logic is straightforward: if we want Christ, who is friend and the mystical bridegroom, to be present, not just a sign or reminder of him, and not just his power, but his very flesh and blood, then the consecrated gifts on the altar must be the substance of his human, bodily existence. Take the picture of your mother that hangs on the wall of your bedroom. Your mother is not substantially present in your room, if all you have of her is that picture. It is a sign or image of her, but it is not her in the fullest sense of the term "is." When she visits and enters your room, then she will be corporeally, indeed *substantially* there. This also applies to Christ on the altar, though with some key qualifications.

Aquinas along with Trent and a venerable theological tradition insist on approaching the Eucharistic gift through the category of substance.

46. Thomas Aquinas, *Summa theologiae* III, q. 75, a. 1.
47. Marshall, "The Eucharistic Presence of Christ," 59.

Now this is not simply a model or theory that helps us to think about reality. Rather, Thomas's claim is that this category authentically expresses reality, both creaturely and divine reality. He insists that all of reality is either substance or accident.

A metaphysical approach to the mysteries of the faith is not new. The three divine persons are consubstantial (Nicene-Constantinople Creed), Christ is one person with two natures (Councils of Ephesus and Chalcedon), and he has a human substance, which includes body and blood substance. The notions of person, nature, and substance apply to both human and divine realities. They are part of metaphysics, and metaphysics seeks the basic principles of everything. Only because we can grasp these categories, and only because they apply also to God, can we make intelligible, reliable statements about him, such as: "God is one in nature."

An objector might fear that we project merely human ideas onto the Eucharist when we speak of the substance of Christ's body and blood. But the answer to such objections is that these categories are essential if we are to say anything meaningful and reliable about God and his saving work, while also avoiding contradictions. In fact, these categories do not reduce the mystery to a human idea. For example, we speak of human personhood, but no creature has yet discovered all the richness contained in this very reality of human personhood. We speak of the natures of things, but Aquinas was convinced that it mostly remains a mystery to us, even the nature of a fly! Thus, when we speak of the substance of Christ's body and blood, we do not exhaust a mystery or wrap our minds around it. Rather, we arrive at a better yet still partial understanding of that mystery. Theology proceeds on the basis of what Christ has instituted, on his words at the Last Supper, in which he indicates the presence of a substance (body and blood). We also protect the mystery in such a way that our adoration of the Eucharist does not become absurd or an act of blindly following tradition. We adore the host because the body, blood, soul, and divinity of Christ are substantially present therein.[48]

48. Thomas Aquinas, *Summa theologiae* III, q. 75, a. 1.

Excursus: The Metaphysics of Substance and Accidents

Evidently, a basic understanding of Thomas's Aristotelian theory of substance and accidents is essential if we are to grasp his teaching on transubstantiation. The following introduces that topic for the non-specialist with limited background in Aristotelian or scholastic philosophy. After treating some basics of substance and accident, I will consider substantial and accidental change. Transubstantiation is an extraordinary type of substantial change.

We take a first look at substance and accident from three perspectives. First, the notion of substance is in some ways inscribed into our way of speaking. We say: "Robert has a great tan after his vacation on the beach," or "Mary has lost weight recently." Skin color, body weight, and all sorts of properties that our senses identify are attributed to things, to individuals. Aristotle and Aquinas hold that language manifests something of reality, that language is a generally reliable indicator of how things really are. Robert is a substance, the verb "has" connotes that some property *actually* belongs to him (being in act), and "a tan" denotes an accidental modification of his substance. Loosely speaking, accidents are among the properties of things, and substance is that which has various properties.

Second, all living beings that we encounter by our senses are a collection of complex parts and properties, and these parts interact. We might think of the human digestive process. The operations of the various parts of things are so harmonious and complementary that they point to a deeper unity. In scholastic terms, action manifests being, and operational unity cannot be accounted for by appealing to a felicitous instance of an accidental unity of parts. Rather, it points to a unity that holds the parts together at a level that is deeper than their operation.[49] Substance ultimately accounts for the operational unity of things.

Third, in our experience, we find that things have a continuity of identity, despite many changes that they undergo. Take the lifespan of a human being. Most or all of her body cells are replaced during her lifetime. Her weight, skin color, and all sorts of physical properties change, and

49. Leo J. Elders, *La métaphysique de saint Thomas d'Aquin dans une perspective historique*, Bibliothèque d'histoire de la philosophie (Paris: Vrin, 1994), 282.

yet, a single person endures through all these changes. Some underlying reality remains the same, from the womb until death.

Note that a person's soul is not the only thing that remains permanent. I have the same body that I had many years ago, yet it is different. There is a real identity between my body as it existed in my mother's womb, my body at childhood, and my body right now. Everything that has changed about my body since my conception pertains to accidents: my brain power, the skills that I have developed, my physical strength, and so on. Each human being is a substance, and everything that can change about a person during his or her lifetime is an accident. Substance accounts for the identity of each person's body.

This brings us to a standard Aristotelian definition of substance and accident: a substance is that which exists by itself (*per se*), and an accident is a property or aspect of a thing that exists in another.[50] In view of transubstantiation, Thomas will modify these two definitions in the following way: substance is a quiddity or essence to which it belongs not to be in another, and accident is a quiddity to which it belongs to exist in another. Aquinas argues philosophically that being cannot be part of a metaphysical definition, because being is not a genus (hence, his theology does not simply impose a new definition of substance and accident onto philosophy). His argument helps to account for the following situation: after the consecration, the accidents of bread and wine do not exist in a created substance, but abide simply by a miraculous, direct divine intervention.[51] Strictly speaking, they do not exist in another (except in God's power). Thomas here employs his distinction between being and essence: the essence of a substance is apt or tends to have *esse* by itself, while the essence of an accident is apt to have *esse* in another.[52]

In our day, some would object that the metaphysics of substance cannot be reconciled with the natural sciences. However, the methods of modern and contemporary science are adequate in order to study that aspect of reality that can be quantified. But substance is precisely at a level of being that cannot be quantified. I am either fully human or not. The

50. Elders, *La métaphysique de saint Thomas d'Aquin*, 285, 290.

51. Thomas Aquinas, *Summa theologiae* III, q. 77, a. 1.

52. Édouard-Henri Wéber, "L'incidence du traité de l'eucharistie sur la métaphysique de s. Thomas d'Aquin," *Revue des sciences philosophiques et théologiques* 77 (1993): 195–218.

study of substance belongs to philosophy and theology, whose work complements that of natural science, as long as each discipline recognizes the proper limits of its methods.

We might also recall that claims against common sense or classical philosophy that appeal to today's natural science often carry with them a whole series of unspoken philosophical presuppositions. For example, the objection mentioned above may presuppose that only that aspect of the universe that natural science can study is real. Yet natural science cannot prove such a claim. There is no scientific proof that only the things that science observes by its chosen methods exist. This is simply a materialistic dogma.

I proceed to the second main part of this excursus, where I treat substantial and accidental change. These are the basic kinds of changes that occur in creatures. In substantial change, a thing ceases to be what it is and becomes a different kind of thing. When the wood burns, it is no longer wood. When the dog dies, it is no longer a dog. Whenever something dies, it undergoes substantial change. This type of change always involves either (1) generation (the coming into being of some new substance or substances) or (2) corruption or decomposition (the ceasing to be of the original substance or substances). In accidental change, a thing retains its identity and is modified in some incidental way. Any change that a substance undergoes after its generation or coming to be and before its death or corruption is an accidental change.

All change involves a *terminus a quo*, a *terminus ad quem*, and an agent of change. In simple terms, all change has a point of origin, an outcome, and a cause of the change. That is, every change comes from somewhere and ends up somewhere. We can take the example of human conception. Here, the actual fruitfulness of mother and father are the beginning term of the change. The act of procreating causes a substantial change, and the end result is the embryo. The mother's egg that became fructified was simply an egg in act before procreation, but now it is no longer an egg in act. The father's sperm was a sperm in act, but no longer is a sperm in act. Both egg and sperm have taken on a new actuality through the fusion and pairing of their genetic material, in the embryo (an embryo in act, which was in potency). Before conception, sperm and egg were both potentially embryo, but not actually an embryo. Sperm and egg have been transformed into an embryo: a substantial change. Sperm and egg matter have taken on a new form, a form of a distinct human being. Without sperm and egg, we can never arrive at the embryo. Both sperm and egg had to change, losing one actuality and taking on another actuality, so that substantial change could happen. Here we have a natural substantial change. Transubstantiation will be both like and unlike natural substantial change. This account of substantial change will be important for Thomas's treatment of consubstantiation.[53]

Aquinas and Transubstantiation

The thirteenth century was the most fruitful period of reflection on transubstantiation. In the early Church, Arius and Nestorius had provoked new Christological answers. In the Middle Ages, Berengar showed the need for new explanations in Eucharistic theology.

Berengar posed a series of challenges. When we eat the Eucharist, does our stomach digest Jesus? If we consume Jesus at Mass, does he have to keep creating new matter in heaven in order to feed all of us?[54] At the fraction rite during Mass, do we inflict injury or pain on Jesus?[55] Berengar thought that he could conquer his hyperrealist opponents by showing the absurd consequences of their position. Aquinas developed what is arguably the most coherent and profound theology of transubstantiation. This theology allowed him to maintain a rigorous Eucharistic realism while avoiding Berengar's traps.

Aquinas developed his doctrine of transubstantiation within a framework of principles.[56] First, the accidents of bread and wine are on the altar

53. For further reading on substance and accident, I recommend Leo Elders, *The Metaphysics of Being of St. Thomas Aquinas in a Historical Perspective* (Leiden, Netherlands: Brill, 1993), chapters 17–18; Edward Feser, *Scholastic Metaphysics: A Contemporary Introduction* (Heusenstamm, Germany: Editiones Scholasticae, 2014), chapter 3; and parts of two works by Henri-Dominique Gardeil, *Introduction to the Philosophy of St. Thomas Aquinas*, vol. 2, *Cosmology*, trans. John A. Otto (Eugene, Ore.: Wipf & Stock, 2009), chap. 1; *Introduction to the Philosophy of St. Thomas Aquinas*, vol. 4, *Metaphysics*, trans. John A. Otto (Eugene, Ore.: Wipf & Stock, 2009), chap. 4.

54. Gary Macy, *The Theologies of the Eucharist in the Early Scholastic Period* (Oxford: Clarendon Press, 1984), 59; Marcia L. Colish, *Peter Lombard*, vol. 2, Brill's Studies in Intellectual History 41.2 (Leiden, Netherlands: E. J. Brill, 1994), 552–53.

55. Colish, *Peter Lombard*, 2:553.

56. Here I follow Marilyn McCord Adams, *Some Later Medieval Theories of the Eucharist: Thomas Aquinas, Giles of Rome, Duns Scotus and William Ockham* (Oxford: Oxford University Press, 2010), 85–87.

before and after the consecration. The host and contents of the chalice retain the flavor, feel, texture, nourishing, and quenching properties of bread and wine. They have the quality, quantity, and other accidents of bread and wine, but not the substance of bread and wine. The accidents are real, that is, they are not a deception or just appearances. Second, Christ's body and blood come upon the altar by the consecration, yet his glorified body remains in heaven. That is, the glorified body remains unchanged in heaven, without any new perfection or modification added to it. Third, a single body cannot be extended in two places at once. For example, the miracle of bilocation involves a saint's bodily presence in one place and the appearance of that saint's body in a second place, but not the same body's physical presence in both places, meaning, a person's bodily presence in both places with its accidents. Here, the question is: how can Christ's body be both in heaven and on the altar? To the eyes of reason, this seems impossible. The theology of transubstantiation seeks to show that Christ's corporeal presence on the altar is not irrational. Aquinas and other medievals worked out their theologies while seeking to retain these three principles.

In *Summa theologiae* III, question 75, article 1, Thomas first establishes on the basis of Scripture and tradition that Christ is truly, corporeally, substantially present in the gifts. Then, in article 2, he shifts to the theme of how the substance comes to be on the altar. Here, he considers a number of theories that seek to explain the change of gifts on the altar. Thomas's method is as follows: he excludes various possibilities as theologically impossible, which will leave him with only one real possibility to explain the change. He takes as a given our faith in Christ's corporeal presence. Then, by eliminating the alternatives, he proceeds to show that transubstantiation alone accounts for that presence. This is also called the *via negativa* (the way of negation), and it is exactly how Aquinas proceeds in his doctrine of God. For the Eucharist, Thomas will demonstrate the mode of change, specify its result, or end-term, with technical concepts, and recognize what remains unknown. He offers not just a theory but the best possible description of a change that is *sui generis* in creation.

Thomas takes up two alternative explanations on how Christ's body and blood come to be substantially present on the altar: (1) consubstantiation or impanation, and (2) annihilation (which is close to substitution).[57] Thomas's own approach (the third explanation) will be transubstantiation, which he will also refer to as conversion.

The first theory (consubstantiation) has similarities with Martin Luther's ideas and those of the twentieth-century Russian Orthodox theologian Sergius Bulgakov.[58] In consubstantiation, the key claim is that the substances of bread and wine, body and blood exist together in the Eucharistic gifts. We thus have a matter of addition. This theory has an advantage, as it more easily accounts for how the accidents of bread and wine continue to exist after the consecration, because they still exist in bread and wine substance. Within this theory, we find two possible approaches. The first says that bread and wine substance exist side-by-side with body and blood substance, but without being metaphysically linked.[59] This would be "con-substantiation" in the strict sense. A more adventuresome version of the first theory goes back to the twelfth-century theologian Rupert von Deutz and some disciples of Berengar: it is called impanation. This theory proposes the union of Christ's body to bread substance, somewhat like the two natures being joined in Christ. Rupert apparently thought that the hidden, invisible bodily substance of Christ takes on the substance of bread and wine, somewhat like the Son of God taking on a human nature in Mary's womb.[60] Rupert drew a meaning from an analogy between the Incarnation and the Eucharist that the Greek Fathers had employed for a different purpose, yet the German monk did not intend to teach heresy.

The second theory emerged before Aquinas but gained new complexity after his lifetime. Aquinas challenged the notion that God destroys bread and wine substance so as to replace them with body and blood substance (which is called "annihilation theory"). A similar theory was developed later in the writings of John Duns Scotus and William of Ockham. Both Franciscans held that Lateran Council IV taught that bread

57. Thomas Aquinas, *Summa theologiae* III, q. 75, aa. 2–3.

58. Sergius Bulgakov, *The Holy Grail and the Eucharist*, trans. Boris Jakim (Hudson, N.Y.: Lindisfarne Books, 1997), 115–16. For Luther on consubstantiation, see the section below.

59. Aymon-Marie Roguet, notes to Thomas Aquinas, *Somme théologique, L'eucharistie*, vol. 1, *3a, Questions 73–78* (Paris: Desclée et Cie, 1960), 305.

60. P. Séjourné, "Rupert de Deutz," in *Dictionnaire de théologie catholique*, ed. É. Amann, vol. 14 (Paris: L. Letouzey et Âne, 1920), col. 197.

and wine become body and blood, which is Thomas's position.[61] However, Scotus and Ockham argue that this is simply what God chose to do, and we know that he made this choice because the Council said so. Yet in his absolute power, God could have (in another universe or economy of salvation) chosen to change the gifts on the altar by substituting body substance for bread substance and blood substance for wine substance. In this hypothesis (never realized), bread and wine substance simply cease to be, while body and blood substance take their place. This is called "substitution theory." Here, we have a succession of substances, without a causal link between them.[62] Aquinas will argue against various annihilation theories, but similar arguments of his would apply to a critique of substitution theory.[63]

In the face of these alternative theories, Aquinas argues that God mysteriously changes bread and wine substance into body and blood substance. Here, bread and wine *become* body and blood. As he explains this teaching, Aquinas prefers the Latin term *conversio* over *mutatio* or change to describe the conversion of the gifts. The term *conversion* is more specific than the word *change* (the latter could apply to the first two theories as well). Latin Fathers such as Ambrose used similar terms, but with a less precise, non-Aristotelian meaning. We also find similar language in the Greek Fathers. Cyril of Jerusalem interprets the change of the gifts on the altar as a conversion of one thing into another (*metabolōn*).[64] Gregory of Nyssa speaks of a trans-elementation (*metastoixeiosis*) of bread into body and wine into blood.[65]

Aquinas's opening argument targets the first theory (consubstantiation), and it is simple: Christ cannot move down from heaven onto the altar in the sense of changing place.[66] That is, he cannot move into the host and settle there alongside bread and wine substance, in the sense of

61. Marshall, "The Eucharistic Presence of Christ," 70–71.

62. David Burr, "Scotus and Transubstantiation," *Medieval Studies* 34 (1972): 340–58; Adams, *Some Later Medieval Theories*, 151.

63. Thomas Aquinas, *Summa theologiae* III, q. 75, a. 3.

64. Cyril of Jerusalem, "Mystagogical Lecture 4," nos. 1–2, 6–9, in *Catéchèses mystagogiques*, ed. Auguste Piédagnel, trans. Pierre Paris, Sources chrétiennes 126 bis (Paris: Cerf, 1966).

65. Gregory of Nyssa, *Great Catechetical Oration*, 37, no. 10; cited in García Ibáñez, *L'eucaristia, dono e mistero*, 590–91.

66. Thomas Aquinas, *Summa theologiae* III, q. 75, a. 2.

leaving heaven. A sound biblical Christology demands this stance. Following the Letter to the Hebrews, faith holds that the glorified Christ permanently dwells in heaven, where he does not cease to intercede for us. Also, Christ's bodily existence is incorruptible and perfect: were each Mass to effect a metaphysical change in Christ's glorious body, then he would either be gaining or losing some perfection in his glorified state, which contradicts the biblical notion that he abides perpetually in a consummated state. This first argument excludes one possible account on behalf of consubstantiation.

Thomas's second argument is also straightforward: revelation tells us what gift Christ has imparted to us in the Eucharist. The center of that revelation is found at the Last Supper, especially as consistently interpreted by tradition. Now Jesus said neither "This bread is my body," nor "This wine is my blood." The words of institution themselves indicate the presence of one reality, not two: they say nothing about bread and wine. Nor does he say "Here is my body," as if his body were here, somewhere in the bread.[67] Consubstantiation cannot adequately account for Jesus' words at the Last Supper.

To this, Luther would object that 1 Corinthians and other biblical texts still speak of *bread* in reference to the Eucharist (1 Cor 10:16 reads: "The bread that we break, is it not a participation in the body of Christ?").[68] If it is no longer bread, then why call it that? The classic answer would be that the term *bread* recalls that Christ is the true bread who gives us his very body as food for the life of the world (Jn 6). As a further response to Luther, we can say that God cannot make one thing to be two realities (i.e., both body and bread).[69] This logical and metaphysical claim is crucial: the Eucharist has one substantial identity, not two. In the words of Bruce Marshall: "This is the Eucharistic counterpart to our denial, in the doctrine of the Trinity, that the Son is identical with the Father, and to our denial, in the doctrine of the Incarnation, that humanity is identical with divinity."[70] Thus, Father and Son are one nature,

67. Thomas Aquinas, *Summa theologiae* III, q. 75, a. 2.

68. George Hunsinger, *The Eucharist and Ecumenism: Let Us Keep the Feast*, Current Issues in Theology (Cambridge: Cambridge University Press, 2008), 29.

69. Herbert McCabe, *God Still Matters*, ed. Brian Davies (London: Continuum, 2002), 117.

70. Marshall, "The Eucharistic Presence of Christ," 70.

but distinct as persons. Christ is one person, but exists in two modes, two natures. Christ is not two things. The Eucharist is one substance, but it abides under distinct accidents, and so the gifts cannot be both body and bread. Luther's appeal to Scripture ignores a contradiction of reason. But Scripture and reason cannot contradict, hence, Luther has misread Scripture.

Aquinas's third argument against consubstantiation is complex yet crucial. An appeal to Christ's body substance being added to an abiding bread substance fails to explain a change in the Eucharist. Consubstantiation *posits* a change, but it fails to *explain* why Christ's body begins to be present here in this host. Since the glorified Christ dwells in heaven, without alteration, we cannot posit a change in him in order to explain why he begins to be present on the altar as well (by analogy, the Incarnation involves no change in the Son's divinity, but a change in creation, namely, the union of his humanity to his divine person). Consubstantiation refuses a change in the bread. This means that there is no candidate left to be the starting point, or *terminus a quo*, of change in the gifts. Consubstantiation claims that the body and blood arrive on the altar, but it fails account for how this can occur, since neither bread nor wine change. By analogy, without a doctrine of Trinitarian processions and relations, we have no way of accounting for the distinction of persons in the Trinity, leaving us with blind faith in a mystery, a teaching that remains completely dark to our minds.

Aquinas takes this argument further as he refutes annihilation theory. Here, the opponent argues that bread and wine substance cease to be present, and denies that they are converted into body and blood. This solution appears to be simpler than that of Aquinas. But he rejects this answer for failing to explain how body and blood substance come to be on the altar.[71] Thomas and his interlocutors agree that the accidents of bread and wine do not change. They also agree that Christ's glorified body and blood substance do not change. But where does the presence of Christ's body and blood substance *on this altar* come from (*terminus a quo*)? It comes from bread and wine substance, which lose their bread and wine actuality and become (by a miraculous divine deed) body and blood

71. Thomas Aquinas, *Summa theologiae* III, q. 75, a. 3; Adams, *Some Later Medieval Theories*, 89.

substance. Body and blood substance are here ("under" the accidents) only because the bread and wine substance that were here (under the accidents) have become body and blood substance. Without a *terminus a quo*, a beginning term of the change, there is no change at all. Hence, both consubstantiation and annihilation theory fail.

Let us note that an appeal to a divine creative act to save annihilation theory will not do. For creation is not a change, just a coming to be of what was not before. The human being's immortal soul was not changed when God infused it into the body, for it did not exist before that moment. The immortal soul was created *ex nihilo* by God. Here, we have a divine cause and a *terminus ad quem* or end term (your soul exists!), but no *terminus a quo*. Creation out of nothing cannot explain how Christ's body and blood come to be on the altar, because his body and blood preexist the Mass. Christ's body and blood already existing in glory also come to be on the altar. Thus, this new presence of Christ cannot be the result of an act of creation. Now because it is not creation, the change of the gifts involves some term from which it comes: it is a change, not creation. Consequently, a *terminus a quo* which is in act 1 must lose that actuality. But since the whole of bread and wine substance cease to be, we cannot say that *something* takes on a new actuality, somewhat as the mother's egg (in act 1) *takes on* the new actuality of the embryo (act 2). In Eucharistic conversion, there is no common subject between act 1 (bread and wine) and act 2 (body and blood). Rather, one thing is converted into something else: the most radical change possible in all of creation.

If bread and wine substance are converted into body and blood, then nothing of bread and wine substance remains. Thus, only one substance is present under the accidents, and consubstantiation is wrong. Now annihilation or substitution theory agrees that bread and wine substance are no longer there after the consecration. But this theory denies the causal link between bread substance and body substance as opposite terms of the divine deed. The theory says that bread and wine substance cease to be, while body and blood substance begin to be here. For Thomas, it is possible for God to withdraw existence from bread and wine substance. But annihilation or substitution theory has no way to account for why body and blood substance begin to be here, where they were not before. This theory seems to imply the creation of body and blood substance, which is unacceptable. The theory speaks of a change that is impossible, for again, there is no *terminus a quo* for the change of the gifts.

Thus, the coming to be of Christ's body on the altar depends on a previously existing substance being changed. Why is Christ's body present here, in this host? Because the whole of the bread substance (not just part of it) that was on the altar has been converted into body substance. Nothing of bread substance is left, but instead of simply ceasing to be, it has been miraculously turned into a body substance. Through his power, God is the cause effecting the presence of the body on the altar (by the consecration), which turns bread substance (*terminus a quo*) into body substance (*terminus ad quem*). Thomas insists that the change in the gifts on the altar involves a wholly supernatural metaphysical process, mostly mysterious but not absurd. We are looking at a miracle that is partly intelligible.

We can also take a step beyond Aquinas and note something odd about annihilation or substitution theory: it implicitly treats natural creation as accidental or superfluous for our salvation. Annihilation theory makes earthly creation nothing but the occasion of our being blessed by the Eucharist. Here, God has to perform a miracle in order to remove our gifts. The Church's contribution seems to become an obstacle to salvation. In substitution theory, our gifts of bread and wine must cease to exist, so that God alone can take over. He does not elevate our gifts, but simply replaces them. With transubstantiation, God makes creation and the Church participate in man's salvation. The Eucharist involves an elevation of the cosmos and manifests the dignity of man's act of bringing gifts before God.

In *Summa theologiae* III, question 75, article 4, Thomas notes that transubstantiation has no equivalent among natural types of change. It is absolutely supernatural. Aquinas signals that his theology goes beyond anything that Greek metaphysics ever imagined. For Aristotle, transubstantiation would have seemed unimaginable. Aristotle did not even hold for creation out of nothing, so how could he imagine that God would change the entire substance of a thing without changing the accidents of bread and wine? In other words, transubstantiation hardly reduces the Eucharistic mystery to Greek metaphysical categories. Rather, it takes metaphysics to its limits, as it describes a *sui generis* situation.

In *Summa theologiae* III, question 75, article 5, Aquinas mentions objections that refer to transubstantiation as a mode of deception. The senses point the mind to the presence of a substance very different from that of Christ's body. Thomas responds that the senses are not deceived, since they are made to know accidents, and thus they correctly perceive bread and wine accidents in the Eucharist. But the mind is made to know being and substance, and here, faith in Christ's words at the Last Supper tells us the identity of the substance.

Aquinas has been talking about whole being conversion, that is, the whole of bread and wine substance being changed into the substance of Christ's body and blood. Now a corporeal substance consists not only of matter, but also of form (its intrinsic, non-quantifiable organizing principle). Yet the form of a human body is an immaterial soul. However, this does not mean that bread becomes Christ's human spirit. At *Summa theologiae* III, question 75, article 6, Aquinas answers an objection in this way: "the form of the bread is converted into the form of the body of Christ insofar as the latter gives corporeal existence, not insofar as it gives existence animated by such a soul."[72] Christ's human soul has multiple functions: it gives life to the body and organizes its functions, and it also enables purely spiritual acts such as knowing and loving. The former, lower functions of the human soul are not immaterial, for they are found also in other animals. Indeed, any body is matter organized by a substantial form. Hence, since bread substance becomes a body, it becomes matter that is informed, that is, a living, animated body. Furthermore, as a living human body, it is joined to his *whole* human soul, and not just to its lower functions. Thus, Christ's immaterial soul is also present in the Eucharist, as it comes with the presence of his body (by concomitance, to be discussed soon). Yet bread does not become Christ's immaterial soul. We thereby avoid positing a metaphysical absurdity: God can miraculously change one body into another, one corporeal being into another, but he cannot change bread substance into pure spirit (the immaterial soul), and even less can he change wine substance into his divinity. Nothing ever becomes fully divine (properly speaking), nor does anything become a soul.

72. Thomas Aquinas, *Summa theologiae* III, q. 75, a. 6, ad 2.

Rather, a soul begins to exist in a body. The conversion of bread and wine substance is extraordinary, but not absurd.[73]

At *Summa theologiae* III, question 75, article 7, we learn that transubstantiation occurs in an instant. That is, when the signification of the words of consecration over the host is complete, the substance of Christ's body is present. Similarly, when the consecration over the cup is complete, the substance of Christ's blood is present. The words of consecration are not a magical formula in which each word has a supernatural effect. Rather, the words *taken as a whole* signify a substantial change. The key is signification—more precisely, the signification of a conversion applied to material gifts, so that the sign is not just informative but primarily performative. The words have an instrumental power to change the gifts insofar as they signify, and by God's power, they realize what they signify. At the end of the consecration pronounced over the host, the signification that the gifts have become the gift of Christ's body has been perfected.[74] At the end of the consecration pronounced over the cup, the signification that the gift in the cup has become Christ's blood has been perfected. The utterance of the words has a temporal succession, for it takes several seconds to pronounce them, but the complete signification is attained when the sentence is finished.

We might wonder why the change of gifts is instantaneous. First, the teaching has patristic precedence, for example, in Gregory of Nyssa.[75] Second, the analogy with the Incarnation would seem to call for it: at a particular moment, Mary in fact became the Mother of God (right at the Annunciation, it would seem).

Aquinas on Christ's Substantial Presence

I now turn to Christ's abiding, substantial presence in the gifts. Here, I take up the following sub-themes: (1) how the accidents mediate access to Christ's body and blood; (2) the presence of the whole Christ in the sacrament; (3) the presence of Christ in each part of the gifts; (4) how

73. Stephen L. Brock, "St. Thomas and the Eucharistic Conversion," *The Thomist* 65 (2001): 550–52.

74. Thomas Aquinas, *Summa theologiae* III, q. 75, a. 7, ad 1 & 3; Aymon-Marie Roguet, notes to Thomas Aquinas, *Somme théologique, L'eucharistie*, 1:402.

75. Betz, *Die Eucharistie in der Zeit der griechischen Väter*, 1.1:305.

Christ's body and blood continue to remain in the gifts; and (5) how the bread and wine accidents abide after transubstantiation.

After the consecration, the only substance present is that of Christ's body and blood. The sacrament is said to contain the body and blood of Christ. We need to explore the precise sense that the verb "to contain" has in this context. Here, the sacramentality of the Eucharist is key. This sacrament is at once sign and presence, consisting of accidents and substance.

The accidents make up the visible element of the sacrament. Now a sacramental sign mediates what it signifies: the consecration effects what it signifies (this is "the power of the sacrament"), so that the abiding signs of bread and wine contain what they symbolize. At *Summa theologiae* III, question 76, article 1, we read: "From the power of the sacrament is present under the species of this sacrament that into which the substance of preexisting bread and wine is directly converted, as is signified by the words of the form, which [words] are effective in this sacrament just as in other sacraments."[76] Later in the same *Summa* article, Thomas speaks of Christ's body "being contained" in this sacrament.[77] In the above citation, the term "species" refers to the bread and wine accidents, especially insofar as they are signs. Thanks to the consecration, the species of bread and wine can mediate what they signify, namely, spiritual food and drink. In the Eucharist, the accidents mediate as signs. In the other sacraments, a saving power is signified and thus contained, but in this sacrament, the sign contains something greater than a saving power, for the very substance of Christ's body and blood is in this sacrament. The conversion of the substance makes possible an extraordinary form of sacramental mediation. Christ's body and blood come to us through the accidents, because the latter signify the former (as nourishment), and because the consecration is an efficacious sign, one that signifies transubstantiation.[78]

In classical Eucharistic theology, the word "contain" has a metaphysical-sacramental meaning: it signals that the accidents (as signs) really mediate access to Christ. The term does not have a spatial meaning, as

76. Thomas Aquinas, *Summa theologiae* III, q. 76, a. 1, corpus.

77. Thomas Aquinas, *Summa theologiae* III, q. 76, a. 1, ad 2.

78. Charles Journet, *The Mass: The Presence of the Sacrifice of the Cross*, trans. Victor Szczurek (South Bend, Ind.: St. Augustine's Press, 2008), 160.

if Christ's body and blood were circumscribed and limited to this place. We can contrast the manner in which the signs contain Christ's body and blood to the way in which the body contains the soul: my soul is currently limited to a particular time and place, but that limitation does not apply to Christ's glorified humanity.[79] Now we rightly adore the host and the cup, for the Eucharistic accidents, as signs, mediate a human corporeal substance that is joined to the divine substance. We adore Christ, whose divine substance comes with the body and blood substance signified, as the reality signified is present where the Eucharistic sign is found.[80]

The issue of containing has already led us to the question whether Christ's body and blood are in a place (in the technical sense of the term). In *Summa theologiae* III, question 76, article 5, Thomas discusses how the dimensions or quantity of bread and wine mediate the presence of Christ's body and blood substance to a place (e.g., the altar on which the host lies). Aquinas holds that the accidents or species are in a place (thanks to quantity), but that Christ is not "in that place," in the sense that his corporeal substance is not limited to this altar (for then it could not be on other altars). Thomas also firmly maintains that the bread and wine accidents grant access to Christ's body and blood substance in a way that no other part of creation does. This is why we rightly adore the gifts on the altar.

Aymon-Marie Roguet offers the following analogy: a soul is not in and of itself in a place, because it is pure spirit, and place pertains to physical realities. But a soul is in a place accidentally (we might say, indirectly), insofar as it is united to a body. Through the body that is in a place (with its body accidents), the soul is in a place.[81] If you wish to reach my mind and heart, then you need to communicate with my soul through my body. Where is my soul? It is in my body, and it is *here* because or insofar as my body is *here* (I return to this analogy below).

The question of how bread and wine accidents contain or are linked

79. We can also contrast the relation between the Eucharistic accidents or signs to the body and blood with the relation of Christ's two natures. For in the Eucharist, Christ does not actually take on bread quantity, texture, or appearances, nor does he take on the nature of bread or wine substance (no consubstantiation). But in the Incarnation, a human nature is joined to the very person of Christ.

80. Here, I partly anticipate the discussion of concomitance below.

81. Roguet, notes to Thomas Aquinas, *Somme théologique, L'eucharistie*, 1:317.

to Christ's body and blood substance can mostly be answered through the *via negativa*. In the Eucharist, bread accidents and body substance (or wine accidents and blood substance) are not wholly separate, for if they were, I would not obtain spiritual contact with Christ's body and blood, and his invitation to eat his body and to drink his blood would be a lie (hence, revelation excludes that option). Yet bread accidents and body substance are clearly not hypostatically joined. In the Eucharist, bread accidents and body substance are linked not exactly as my accidents are linked to my body. However, they are linked in such a way that Jesus' body substance touches my body and soul when I touch those accidents, and I obtain contact with his corporeal substance in a way that the spiritual power flowing from his body penetrates my body and soul during communion. Still, we lack any satisfying positive description of the relation between Christ's corporeal substance and the Eucharistic accidents. This should not surprise us, for Trinitarian theology and other aspects of theology function very similarly.

I should add one last point to the question of this link. Normally, accidents and substance stand in a relation of mutual dependence. The substance gives existence to the accidents, but the substance of my body needs the accidents to function in a particular mode in order for it to continue to exist. This is because the accidents are real modifications of creaturely substances. But Christ's body and blood substance do not take on this relation of mutual dependence with bread and wine accidents, for the latter are not modifications of his body and blood substance. In other words, when a host is consumed, the substance of Christ is not consumed. Rather, bread accidents are consumed. However, Christ's body substance acts upon the person communing in the host, and his body acts through the bread accidents. This is analogous to the Incarnation, where Christ speaks, touches, and heals those who come to him with faith and a desire for healing, while his divine substance remains immutable, all the while being contained in his body and soul.

I turn to the second theme concerning Christ's substantial presence in the Eucharist. The Church has consistently believed held that the whole Christ is present in the gifts: his body and blood, soul and divinity. This faith is manifested in the longstanding practice of adoring the consecrated gifts. It also has a good biblical foundation, namely, in John 6, especially as interpreted by Cyril of Alexandria and Thomas Aquinas: Christ's flesh and blood are vivifying because they are joined to his divinity.[82]

Theology is faith seeking understanding, and we can better see the intelligibility of Eucharistic faith with the help of the notion of concomitance. In the sacraments, the spiritual gift signified (by word and gesture) in the sacramental materials or act is made present by the very act of signification. The words of institution directly signify the presence of Christ's body and blood. His body and blood substance are therefore present by "the power of the sacrament" or the fruitfulness of signification enacted *in persona Christi*. Now the words of consecration do not directly signify the presence of Christ's divinity. More specifically, by the consecration, bread substance becomes body substance, and wine substance becomes blood substance.[83] The doctrine of concomitance says that whatever is now really united to Christ's body is also present in the Eucharist. The glorified Christ's body is truly joined to his immaterial soul and to his divinity. Thus, when bread substance is converted into Christ's risen body at the consecration, his soul also becomes present in the host. The same holds for his divinity: It is present in the host because the body is present. Indeed, his body and blood are united, and so the blood is present in the host. Finally, when the wine is converted into the blood, his body, soul, and divinity are also present in the cup.

Here, the claim is not that bread substance becomes Christ's soul or divinity. As we saw earlier, God converts one material substance into another, but he does not convert any creaturely reality into the divinity, nor any material reality into an immaterial soul (this would be a metaphysical absurdity). Hence, we say that Christ's soul and divinity become present with the body and the blood. Substantial conversion pertains to the latter, not the former.

The doctrine of concomitance has important pastoral implications. The faithful who receive only the host still receive the whole Christ. The layman who is very intolerant of gluten and drinks only from the cup thereby receives the whole Christ. In each case, the sign of communion is imperfect, yet spiritual contact with Christ's body and blood is obtained.

Since the whole Christ is present in the gifts, the accidents of his body

82. Thomas Aquinas, *Commentary on the Gospel of John*, chap. 6, lectio 6, no. 959.

83. Thomas Aquinas, *Summa theologiae* III, q. 76, a. 2.

and blood are also present therein, but by mode of substance, not by mode of accident.[84] His accidents are present because of concomitance, meaning, they cannot be separated from his body and blood substance. His accidents such as quantity are present in the gifts, but they do not extend in space. His body and blood have a particular dimension in heaven, where his accidents function in their proper, glorified mode. His accidents are in the Eucharistic gifts, but as they are present by mode of substance, they do not function in this sacrament as accidents. This accounts for the fact that his body and blood substance are not made available to our sense of vision and touch.

This may be the strangest aspect of the doctrine of Christ's substantial presence in the Eucharist, yet we rightly affirm it. First, the accidents of Christ's body are really united to his glorified body: we cannot separate them (for his risen body would not be truly human without them). Second, the accidents cannot be present by their proper mode, since this would entail (a) Christ leaving heaven and (b) a sensible change in the gifts on the altar. Third, the only way we can posit the presence of Christ's body accidents in the Eucharist is by the only other mode of presence that remains, namely, by mode of substance. Again, we employ the *via negativa*: no other explanation is possible, and while our positive mental grasp of this claim is minimal, it remains coherent. We cannot *imagine* this presence, just as we cannot imagine substance, yet we can *conceive* it.

Christ's body accidents are present in the gifts, but they do not operate as accidents. Here, we can draw a comparison with a scene from the Book of Daniel, chapter 3, in which three young Israelites are thrown into a great furnace. The fire is present, it shines but it does not burn: the three are miraculously preserved from death. The substance and accidents of the fire are present, but much of its operation or activity is miraculously impeded.[85] Similarly, the accidents of Christ's glorified body are present in the Eucharist, but without limiting his body to this or that altar, and without giving his body extension in space here and now.

The consequence for Eucharistic piety is that a body substance that

84. Thomas Aquinas, *Summa theologiae* III, q. 76, a. 4.

85. Joseph Pohle, *Lehrbuch der Dogmatik in sieben Büchern*, 7th ed., vol. 3, Wissenschaftliche Bibliothek, Series 1: Theologische Lehrbücher 22 (Paderborn, Germany: Ferdinand Schöningh, 1922), 230–31.

is not extended in space by its own accidents cannot be harmed or diminished. In other words, this is the metaphysical explanation for why we cannot crush Jesus' bones or teeth by eating the Eucharist, precisely because his whole body is present by mode of substance in the host, and so is present in an impassible way.[86]

The previous paragraphs already touch on the third theme of this section: the whole of Christ's body and blood substance are present in each part of the gifts, each small part of the host, each drop contained in the cup. Of course, his soul and divinity are also in those parts.

Let us note that liturgical practice implies this doctrine. The amount of bread and wine species consumed has never been linked with a greater or lesser spiritual fruitfulness of communion. Furthermore, over the centuries, the sacred species have been treated with the greatest reverence, even when only some smaller fragments of hosts remain on a paten or a few drops remain in the chalice. This practice would border on idolatry if Christ himself were not present in these species.

Interestingly, the doctrine of substance illumines both liturgical practices just mentioned, for, in and of itself, substance is not quantifiable. A substance is present in act or not, whereas accidents can be greater or less. In the Eucharist, Christ's body is present only in a substantial mode, which means that it must be equally present in each part of the gifts, within each host (large or small), and also within each part of the host. Likewise, his blood is present only in a substantial mode, and so it is equally present in each drop contained in the cup. Indeed, all of Christ is present only by mode of substance. The question: "How much Christ is there?" is somewhat like asking, "How much of you is present in your body?"

Lawrence Feingold notes how the medieval theologian Guitmund of Aversa (d. 1090/1095) uses in an illuminative way the analogy between the soul's presence in the body and the presence of Christ's body and blood substance in this sacrament. The human soul is fully present and operative in every part of the body to which it belongs. By its nature, the soul cannot be divided, for it does not have separable parts. Similarly, Christ's body and blood substance cannot be divided.[87] Hence, Christ

86. Thomas Aquinas, *Summa theologiae* III, q. 77, a. 7.

87. Feingold, *The Eucharist*, 251–52, 280. Guitmund of Aversa, *On the Truth of the Body and Blood of Christ in the Eucharist*, trans. Mark G. Vaillancourt, The Fathers of the Church, Mediaeval

is never harmed when the priest breaks the hosts to prepare for communion. Rather, we divide the sign, so that we do not affect Christ's substance. We modify the quantity of the sign, and quantity is an accident.

This aspect of the doctrine of substance helps us to enter into our fourth theme, namely, how long Jesus' presence in the gifts perdures. Christ remains in the gifts as long as the accidents of bread and wine continue to exist and to signify a substance (his body and blood as spiritual nourishment).[88] The doctrine of enduring substance linked to the perduring accidents reinforces the fact that Christ's substantial presence is an objective reality, one that does not depend on our faith for its actuality. Nor does he cease to be corporeally present when the liturgy ends, that is, as long as the accidents of the host (in the tabernacle) abide.

We can understand this notion by going back to the sign function of accidents: the Eucharist is a sacrament, and sacraments are signs of a sanctifying reality. This is the primary definition of the sacraments. The species are signs by which Christ is present (the Eucharist) and his grace is given (as a sacrament of the New Covenant). The Eucharist is a sign insofar as it is visible and sensible. The accidents function as signs of the body and blood of Jesus given as food and drink (via the consecration and the liturgical setting). When the accidents decompose, when the host no longer tastes like bread and the content of the cup no longer tastes like wine, then the sign of spiritual food and drink ceases to be. As the sign ceases, the sacrament comes to an end, and so, the substance of Christ's body is no longer there, for Christ is present in the Eucharist in a *sacramental* mode. The Eucharistic body is given in the mode of a sign of spiritual nourishment, of the Passover lamb. Once this sign ceases to be (as a sign), the body and blood present through that sign are no longer present.

Note that we are dealing with the objective capacity of the host to signify, and not whether a person sees the host so that it can actually signify to someone right now (e.g., the hosts in a closed tabernacle). We are not concerned with the fact that the host is perceived as a sign, but with the fact that it is a sign and has the capacity to signify.

The accidents help us to discern the presence of Christ in the host and

---

Continuation 10 (Washington, D.C.: The Catholic University of America Press, 2009), bk. 1, chap. 19, p. 107.

88. Thomas Aquinas, *Summa theologiae* III, q. 76, a. 6; q. 77, a. 4.

in the cup, for through the liturgical setting and the words of consecration, they have become signs of Christ's presence. A consecrated putrefied host is no longer the body, while a *putrefying* host is no longer the Eucharist at some point in the process of corruption. A significant change in taste, solidity, color, or size causes the substance of the body to cease. We thus have borderline cases, and these lead us to exercise prudence. We place a putrefying host into a glass of water, and we treat the small fragments in patens and on corporals or altar cloths as the body of Christ, for we do not presume to have metaphysical certitude about the identity of the underlying substance when no such certitude can be attained. By comparison, a crumb of bread is still bread, but when its quantity is radically reduced, bread substance ceases to be.

At this point, one might wonder whether Eucharistic miracles (in which the accidents change), can be harmonized with this doctrine. Aquinas holds that, in the case of an enduring miracle (as when human flesh is seen or a host becomes bloody and remains in this way), the key to Christ's substantial presence is the perdurance of the most basic accident, namely, the quantity of the bread (or wine) species. If the latter remains stable, then some of the accidents abide, and so do Christ's body and blood. The changes in the other accidents only strengthen the sign-value, for "it becomes the figure of the truth itself, namely, to show by the miraculous apparition that in the sacrament there is truly Christ's body and blood."[89]

Thomas's highly metaphysical theology of how Christ's presence perdures in the Eucharist provides a theological account of two venerable practices. First, it shows the reasonableness of an ancient ecclesial practice, namely, bringing the Eucharist to the home-bound and the sick after Mass (as witnessed by Justin Martyr and Cyprian).[90] Already in the second and third centuries, this was an uncontroversial practice. Also, in fourth-century Egypt, during the Church's persecution, the laity could take communion home and consume it during the week.[91] Second,

89. Thomas Aquinas, *Summa theologiae* III, q. 76, a. 8.

90. Justin Martyr, *First Apology*, chap. 67; Cyprian of Carthage, *Ceux qui sont tombés (De lapsis)*, trans. Michel Poirier, notes by Graeme Clark, Sources chrétiennes 547 (Paris: Cerf, 2012), no. 26. See also Pohle, *Lehrbuch der Dogmatik*, 3:212.

91. Basil the Great, "Epistle 93," in *Letters 1–185*, trans. Agnes Claire Way, notes by Roy J. Deferrari, The Fathers of the Church 13 (Washington, D.C.: The Catholic University of America Press, 1951).

Aquinas's doctrine explains the reverence given to the consecrated gifts reserved in a special place ever since the eleventh and twelfth centuries.[92] This practice involves a harmonious development of the primitive ecclesial traditions just mentioned: in both cases, we find a pastoral expression of the firm conviction that the presence of Christ abides in the consecrated host beyond the time of the Eucharistic liturgy. Eucharistic theology needs to manifest the reasonableness of longstanding liturgical and pastoral practices.

Up to this point, I have focused on the miraculous change of bread and wine substance and the abiding, supernatural presence of Christ's body and blood substance, a single miracle that continues to have its effect as long as the bread and wine accidents do not corrupt. I now turn to the second miracle involved in every consecration: the abiding presence of bread and wine accidents. This is our fifth and last theme within the broader topic of Christ's substantial Eucharistic presence.

For Aquinas, it is important to emphasize the reality of these accidents. First, bread and wine accidents are essential for the Eucharist's sacramental nature: it involves a spiritual gift imparted via visible signs. The accidents allow for the signification of spiritual food and drink. If we are to eat Christ's body and drink his blood, then we need to eat and drink sensibly and sacramentally. Second, our senses are not deceived, for indeed, they are made to know accidents, so the sensing of bread and wine is exactly what should occur at Mass.[93] Third, the senses fall short, because sacraments belong to the mystery of faith. Normally, the accidents manifest to us the nature of the substance that underlies them, for example, as the use of language (an action, which is an accident) manifests the presence of a rational, human substance. As noted, it belongs to the intellect to know substance, and the liturgy communicates this truth about the substance of the gifts on the altar by the words of consecration, other prayers, and various gestures. Fourth, the reality of the accidents enables Christ's simultaneous substantial presence on multiple altars and in multiple tabernacles. A body substance is always present with some accidents functioning in their proper mode. But Christ's own body accidents can

92. Pohle, *Lehrbuch der Dogmatik*, 3:215.

93. Thomas Aquinas, *Summa theologiae* III, q. 75, a. 5, ad 2.

function in their proper mode only in heaven. Hence, he is present in the liturgy through accidents that are not his.

Bread and wine accidents continue to exist and to operate after transubstantiation: the host nourishes, the cup can inebriate. How can this be? Here, theology's task is to show that the Eucharist does not involve an absurdity, and to manifest the intelligibility of the faith without exhausting its richness.

With the consecration, the bread and wine accidents lose their metaphysical subject whence they derived their existence (bread and wine substance). At *Summa theologiae* III, question 77, article 1, Aquinas's answer follows from his previous arguments that eliminate the possibility of consubstantiation. The latter theory can easily account for the existence of bread and wine accidents after the consecration, while the doctrine of transubstantiation does so with greater difficulty. In this text, Thomas also refutes various alternative accounts that seek new subjects or underlying substances that might hold bread and wine accidents in being: the glorified body of Christ, the surrounding air, etc. The only possibility left is for God to intervene directly and to preserve the accidents in existence.[94] Here, divine power does what substance normally does for its accidents. The notion of a divine intervention allowing subject-less accidents to exist was commonly held from Peter Lombard forward.[95] Thomas gives it more nuance via a metaphysical principle partly derived from Neoplatonism:[96]

> Since an effect depends more on the first cause than the second cause, God, who is the first cause of substance and accident, can through his own infinite power conserve an accident in being, [even] with the substance having been taken away, the substance through which an accident was conserved in being as through its proper cause; just as God can also produce other effects of natural causes without the natural causes, as when he formed a human body in the womb of the Virgin with a male seed.[97]

94. Thomas Aquinas, *Summa theologiae* III, q. 77, a. 1; Jörgen Vijgen, *The Status of Eucharistic Accidents 'sine subiecto'*, Quellen und Forschungen zur Geschichte des Dominikanerordens, Neue Folge 20 (Berlin: Akademie Verlag, 2013), 247.

95. Wéber, "L'incidence du traité," 207.

96. Vijgen, *The Status of Eucharistic Accidents*, 249.

97. Thomas Aquinas, *Summa theologiae* III, q. 77, a. 1.

All creatures are secondary causes, whose ability to be causes depends on God as the first cause of existence. Their being, nature, and operative power depend on God's operative power. In every instance of actualization (or efficient causality), a created cause transmits actuality derived from the first cause.[98] Bread and wine substance normally transmit *esse* to bread and wine accidents. The Creator is intimately involved in every creatures' exercise of efficient causality (one being acting on another) as well as the causal efficacy of substances upon their accidents. Now what secondary causes can do, the primary or divine cause can also do independently of them, as long as it does not contradict reason. Thus, the accidents of bread and wine continue to have the being that they possessed before the consecration. This is illustrated by Mary's virginal conception, where divine power substitutes for the male seed, and the normal two secondary causes of pro-creation are reduced to one.

On this point, Thomas's theology benefits considerably from his original metaphysics, namely, the real distinction between essence and existence. One might object that Aquinas contradicts sound metaphysics by making an accident exist "by itself," which essentially turns it into a substance. But Thomas responds that "to exist by itself" cannot be part of a proper definition of accidents, since definitions should not include being, as being is not a genre. Instead, Thomas modifies Aristotle's definition of accidents in the following way: to be an accident is to have "a quiddity to which it belongs to have being in another."[99] Here, the focus is on essence or quiddity. An accident is not a thing, but a form, and that form includes a real distinction of quiddity or essence and existence. It normally belongs to accidents to have being or existence from their substance. But in the case of the Eucharist, the accidents have being directly from the primary cause, without the normal mediation of a substance.

Aquinas is well-known in the history of theology for proposing that quantity is the most basic accident of corporeal beings. Quantity mediates being to the other accidents, namely, both the being received from

98. For a good overview of Aquinas's doctrine of primary and secondary causality, see Michael J. Dodds, *Unlocking Divine Action: Contemporary Science and Thomas Aquinas* (Washington, D.C.: The Catholic University of America Press, 2012), 190–99.

99. Thomas Aquinas, *Summa theologiae* III, q. 77, a. 1, ad 2; Wéber, "L'incidence du traité," 211–17.

the substance before Eucharistic conversion and the being upheld directly by God's power after the conversion of the gifts. All other accidents presuppose quantity, and it becomes their "quasi-subject" after the consecration. This subtle teaching need not retain us here.[100] However, we can note that this stance allows Thomas to economize on the number of miracles: God does not directly uphold each accident in being, but rather does so through a single act of giving *esse* to quantity. The same divine act enables the accidents to continue to operate in their normal mode (such as the operation of nourishing bodies).[101] Action follows upon being and depends on it. Again, Thomas keeps the number of miracles to the minimum necessary to account for Eucharistic faith.

We can look back to the twin doctrines of transubstantiation and Christ's substantial presence in the gifts, and see how they resolve various thorny problems. Both doctrines help to explain the abiding accidents that our senses perceive. They account for the possibility of multiple Masses being celebrated simultaneously in the world, where Christ becomes corporeally present on many altars at once, without affecting his glorified existence in heaven. Both doctrines avoid the crude realism of the first confession that was demanded of Berengar. We do not crunch Jesus' bones, for we do no violence to the substance of his body when we consume the host and drink from the cup. Christ's body can be broken only in its proper species, that is, in its proper accidents. This happened during his Passion, while the resurrected and ascended Lord has become utterly impassible.

Two Analogies for the Eucharist: The Soul in the Body and the Incarnation

We have seen that some Greek Fathers compare Christ's presence in the Eucharistic gifts to the Incarnation. I also pointed to Guitmund of Aversa's analogy between the soul's presence in the body and the presence of Christ's whole body and blood in each part of the host and cup. I wish to pursue both analogies further. The doctrines of transubstantiation and Christ's substantial presence always will be difficult to communicate to

100. See Thomas Aquinas, *Summa theologiae* III, q. 77, a. 2; Vijgen, *The Status of Eucharistic Accidents*, 252–57.

101. Thomas Aquinas, *Summa theologiae* III, q. 77, a. 3.

those with little philosophical formation. When used within proper limits, these two analogies can render the doctrines more accessible. I begin with the analogy between the soul's presence in the body and the presence of Christ's body and blood in the Eucharistic gifts.[102] My aim in using this analogy is not to argue for a purely spiritual presence of Christ on the altar. Each analogy has its limits.

The first point of comparison is more of a contrast, as it helps to keep before our eyes the distance between a sacrament's unity (between the sign and the reality signified) and the unity of the human being (of soul and body, or form and matter, a unity of substance). The human soul is intimately joined to the body, yet soul and body are distinct. Christ's body and blood are really distinct from the accidents of bread and wine: they are united only insofar as the reality signified (the substance) is in the sign. Here, substance and accidents are distinct in their nature and existence. Now your soul is an immaterial reality, unlike your body. That is why it is possible for your soul to be separated from your body at death. Christ's body and blood substance can and do exist separately from the accidents of bread and wine, somewhat as the soul can be separated from the body: Christ exists in heaven, even if no Mass is celebrated. By contrast, the body cannot exist without the soul, but bread and wine accidents can exist without the body and blood substance.

Second, your body mediates access to your soul and your whole person. The way to communicate with you and your soul is through your body. By bodily communication, I gain some access to your mind and your heart. Christ's body and blood are present to us through the accidents, somewhat as your soul is present to me through your body. Christ's body and blood are accessed through the accidents of bread and of wine, insofar as they are signs of his body and blood.

Third, following Guitmund's analogy, your soul is present in your whole body. Your soul is present in the body in a non-quantifiable way, as principle of operation, as giving life. The soul is not divided, as if fifty percent were present in the brain, and fifty percent in the other parts of the body. The soul is indivisible, so that it is wholly present in each part of the body. Yet if some part of the body were lost, the soul would not di-

102. Pohle, *Lehrbuch der Dogmatik*, 3:228.

minish. By its nature, the soul cannot be quantified, for it is an immaterial reality. Rather, it is joined to a quantifiable body, without itself becoming quantifiable. The question, "How much soul do you have?" is absurd. All of Christ's body substance is present in the consecrated host, and if the host is divided, the whole Christ will still be in each part, as the signified is in the sign. Like an immaterial soul, a substance is neither more nor less, though corporeal substance in general is linked with an accident of quantity (while remaining distinct from the accidents). A substance either exists wholly in act or exists only in potency. Thus, before your parents conceived you, you were only in potency, your existence was a possibility but not actual. After your conception in your mother's womb, you existed in act. As the human body ages, it can diminish, while the soul remains wholly present until death. In the Eucharist, the quantity of bread and wine can diminish, but Christ's body and blood substance remain present, until the accidents corrupt. In and of themselves, Christ's body and blood do not depend on the accidents for anything, in contrast to the soul-body relation.

Fourth, both the soul and Christ's substance are invisible to our eyes, yet they are real. The soul is largely inaccessible to the methods of natural science, for it is not a physical reality that our measuring instruments can detect, nor can it be quantified. We know about the soul as a result of philosophy's reasoning from visible effects to the cause needed to account for those effects (e.g., the kind of intelligence needed to explain the existence of language, the proper subject for abstract thought, etc.). Likewise, in the natural realm, substance is detected by the intellect, not by the senses. Also, the fact that you are a single substance cannot be discovered by scientific investigation: rather, it is a philosophical claim. We discover substance because we seek to account for the operative unity of things, their stable identity that goes beyond a simple sum of quantifiable parts like body cells, organs, and systems. Philosophy tells us about the soul and substance, but science does not. For similar reasons, we would not expect our sense observation or scientific investigation into the chemical constitution of consecrated hosts to gain insight about the presence or absence of Christ's body and blood substance, yet the latter is very real, just as the soul and my own substance are real. Reason can discover the existence of soul and substance in natural things, and similarly, faith accepts the existence of Christ's body and blood substance in this Eucharist, by belief in his words at the Last Supper.

The analogy between the soul's presence in the body and Christ's substantial presence in the Eucharistic gifts is helpful, but it can also lead us astray. For example, the soul is immaterial, while the substance of Christ's body and blood are a corporeal reality. There is no perfect analogy for the Eucharist.

I now turn to the second analogy: the Incarnation and Christ's substantial presence in the Eucharist. This analogy must be applied with great care. The key is to focus on the Eucharist as the continuation of the Incarnation in sacramental form, which is to say that the Eucharist is not a new Incarnation. The Eucharist allows the friends of Christ to encounter him in a way similar to his first disciples' experience during his earthly life.

First, in the Incarnation, the Logos becomes present in the flesh. The Son of God himself abides among us. He does not simply act in a new way, but his very divine substance becomes accessible in a concrete, visible form. There are different kinds of divine presence: God abides in the Jerusalem temple, he dwells in his saints and prophets, is present in his Word whereby he speaks to us, and he is present as acting in all the sacraments. But nothing matches the divine presence in the body and soul of Jesus of Nazareth. Likewise, Eucharistic presence surpasses God's other modes of presence, his presence in creatures, in human beings, in holy persons, in the Scriptures, and so on. Now clearly, *presence* is an analogous term. By the Incarnation, the Son of God comes to a particular time and place. Similarly, by transubstantiation, the glorified body of Christ (joined to his divinity) become substantially present on the altar, and this surpasses his operative presence in our hearts by grace. In baptism and any other sacrament, we have Christ's operative presence, but in the Eucharist, we have that and more.

Second, the Incarnation of the Son of God in the womb of Mary goes beyond the laws of nature. The change is miraculous, for a true human nature is joined hypostatically to the eternal Son. Likewise, Christ's substantial presence in the sacrament surpasses nature's laws.

Third, Christ's humanity is real, it is not an illusion. The bread and wine accidents are real as well. God's saving action therefore respects the integrity of creation.

Fourth, the Son's being and action were not limited to one place by the Incarnation. His divine substance did not depart from heaven, as kenosis is not a literal emptying of the Son's divinity. Nor was the saving action of the Son limited to those immediately present to the body of Jesus. Similarly, Christ's glorified body can be on many altars at once, all the while remaining in heaven. Furthermore, the spiritual power of Christ's Spirit-filled body can transform many believers at the same time. However, this analogy is limited for, *contra* Luther, Christ's body is not omnipresent as is Christ's divinity.

Fifth, when Christ suffered on Calvary, his divinity was neither wounded nor diminished, for he suffered only in his humanity. His body was crushed, but not his divine nature. We crush bread accidents when we digest a host, yet we do not harm or diminish Christ's glorified body, for that body remains immutable.

Sixth, by touching Christ's humanity, we enter into spiritual contact with the Logos and are saved. Similarly, when we touch the Eucharistic signs, we eat Christ's body and are saved. The metaphysical change of the gifts enables a mediation, one that divinizes, just as the Incarnation offers a new mediation of God's nature that divinizes us. Yet in neither case are we dealing with magic, for faith makes this touch spiritually life-giving.

Seventh, to extend the last point, in Jesus, we have a presence that is at once stable and dynamic: Christ touches the sick and heals them, he tells sinners that they are forgiven and makes it to be so. This is possible because the divine nature dwells in bodily form. In the Eucharist, we also have a stable and a dynamic presence, for Jesus substantially abides on the altar, and his body is brimming over with divine power and charity. Neither in Christ nor in the Eucharist should we oppose stable and dynamic presence. Rather, the latter follows from the former. Christology should inform our Eucharistic theology. In other words, contemporary critiques of a "static" Eucharistic presence are a theological cul-de-sac.

Eighth, in Jesus, the apostles saw a man and confessed the presence of the Son of God. In the Eucharist, we see bread and wine but confess the presence of Christ's body and blood, as well as his soul and divinity. The apostles adored and worshipped Christ, while we adore and worship him in the host and cup. We and the apostles worship the Word incarnate.

Protestant Objections and Conciliar Responses

Martin Luther on Eucharistic Presence

The great medieval scholastic theologians worked out somewhat diverse accounts of transubstantiation. In the thirteenth century, some philosophers suggested that the doctrine contradicted reason. In the fourteenth century, the Oxford theologian John Wycliffe expressed the same critique. He considered substance to be inseparable from physical extension, so he could accept neither transubstantiation nor consubstantiation.[103] Wycliffe had some followers, yet the most influential critique of transubstantiation was formulated by Martin Luther. Let us note that his stance emerged against the background of late medieval nominalist philosophy that had already attacked transubstantiation as irrational.

Throughout his life, Luther affirmed a corporeal presence of Christ in the Eucharist: he believed that the faithful eat Christ's flesh and drink his blood. For Luther, the words of institution need to be taken literally.[104] Luther thinks that the words of institution are God's word that effect the presence of Christ's body and blood on the altar.[105] However, he rejects any scholastic notion of the priest's instrumental power as a means whereby God effects the change of the gifts on the altar.

Luther sees transubstantiation as a vain philosophical attempt to explain a mystery.[106] He holds for what can be called "con-substantiation," for he maintains that the bread and wine wholly abide, while the body and blood become present to us in and through the bread and wine. Luther justified this in two ways. First, he appeals to Paul's language in 1 Corinthians 11:26: "As often as you eat this bread and drink the cup, you proclaim the Lord's death until he comes." Here, Luther takes Paul to

103. Ian Christopher Levy, "The Eucharist in the Fourteenth and Fifteenth Centuries," in *The Oxford Handbook of Sacramental Theology*, ed. Hans Boersma and Matthew Levering (Oxford: Oxford University Press, 2015), 238–43.

104. Frank Ewerszumrode, *Mysterium Christi spiritualis praesentiae: Die Abendmahlslehre des Genfer Reformators Johannes Calvin aus römisch-katholischer Perspektive*, Reformed Historical Theology 19 (Göttingen, Germany: Vandenhoek & Ruprecht, 2012), 44–47.

105. Joachim Staedtke, "Abendmahl III/3: Reformationszeit," in *Theologische Realenzyklopädie*, vol. 1, ed. Gerhard Kraus and Gerhard L. Müller (Berlin: Walter de Gruyter, 1977), 113.

106. Mickey L. Mattox, "Sacraments in the Lutheran Reformation," in Boersma and Levering, *The Oxford Handbook of Sacramental Theology*, 276.

speak literally. Second, he argues by analogy with the Incarnation. Luther appeals to Cyril of Alexandria as he argues that, as the divinity is joined to the humanity and the latter becomes life-giving, so bread and wine become life-giving by their conjunction with the body and blood.[107] But Luther also refused to explain how they are joined.[108]

Generally, Luther scholars reject the label of *consubstantiation* and argue that the German Reformer never affirmed any theology of substance. However, this misses a crucial distinction. Trent appeals to a notion of substance that transcends the limits of Aristotelian philosophy (see below). In this sense, the kind of consubstantiation theory that Trent rejects also includes Luther's theory, and the use of the term "substance" is appropriate to describe Luther's theology: he held that the deep-down being or core reality of bread and wine remained, and that is partly what Trent means by substance. For the word primarily refers to the essential being of the thing, that aspect of things which is beyond the appearances.

To explain how Christ can be really present on many altars in the world, Luther proposes the omnipresence or ubiquity of Christ's resurrected body. Just as God is present everywhere by his divine nature, so the Son of God is everywhere in his human nature.[109] Luther appeals to the hypostatic union: the one person of Christ is inseparable from his divine and human nature. Luther goes well beyond saying that Christ's humanity operates everywhere: he thinks Christ is personally present in his two natures throughout the universe. Luther posits the closest relation between the two natures, at the risk of mingling them.[110] He attributes divine properties to Christ's human nature, in order to account for how Christ's body and blood can be simultaneously present on the altar and in heaven. No Catholic theology of transubstantiation makes such a move.

Finally, Luther does not think that Christ's Presence depends on the faith of the recipient of communion. Rather, Christ's flesh and blood are received even by sinners and unbelievers. Luther holds for an objective

107. Ian Christopher Levy, "Affirming Real Presence from a Historical Perspective," *Lexington Theological Quarterly* 38 (2003): 33.

108. Gordon A. Jensen, "Luther on the Lord's Supper," in *The Oxford Handbook of Martin Luther's Theology*, ed. Robert Kolb, Irene Dingel, and L'Ubomir Batka (Oxford: Oxford University Press, 2014), 328.

109. Mattox, "Sacraments in the Lutheran Reformation," 279.

110. Ewerszumrode, *Mysterium Christi*, 48–50.

presence of Christ's flesh and blood, one that comes via the celebration of the Last Supper, and not the individual subject's spiritual disposition.[111]

Huldrych Zwingli's Eucharistic Theology

One of the most influential early Protestant Eucharistic doctrines was developed by the Swiss theologian Huldrych Zwingli. It finds echoes among contemporary Pentecostals and various nondenominational Protestants. Zwingli sees both the Eucharist and baptism as mere symbols. He rejects any corporeal change in the gifts on the altar, and even criticizes Luther on this point.[112] As we saw in our first chapter, Zwingli holds that a corporeal presence of Christ would lead to cannibalism. Zwingli argues that, at the Last Supper, the words of institution really mean, "This signifies my body," and "This signifies my blood." He tends to separate the spiritual and corporeal realms (perhaps under the influence of Platonism). He cannot see how bread and wine can be more than physical indications or representations of God's invisible work. For Zwingli, the sacraments operate parallel to and at the same time as God's invisible work, but God does not work through the sacraments in order to give us grace. Zwingli argues that Christ's body and blood cannot be present in the Eucharist because they are in heaven, as they have been ever since the Ascension. He holds that the Eucharist is only a memorial. Zwingli maintains that believers are transformed into Christ's (mystical) body, but that the gifts on the altar are not changed. God's saving power is present at believers' celebration of the Last Supper, but God works directly in us. As a mere sign, the Eucharist manifests or makes known God's saving work.[113] Zwingli ultimately clashes with John 6 and the whole of the ancient doctrinal and liturgical tradition.

John Calvin's Eucharistic Theology

Calvin's Eucharistic theology stands between that of Zwingli and Luther. He rejects the notion that the Eucharist is a mere sign, but he also refuses

111. Ewerszumrode, *Mysterium Christi*, 51, 58; Jensen, "Luther and the Lord's Supper," 329.

112. Bernard Sesboüé, "La doctrine sacramentaire du concile de Trente II: L'Eucharistie et le sacrifice de la Messe," in *Les signes du salut*, ed. Henri Bourgeois, Bernard Sesboüé, and Paul Tihon, Histoire des dogmes 3 (Paris: Desclée, 1995), 160.

113. Ewerszumrode, *Mysterium Christi*, 41–44.

Luther's affirmation of Christ's corporeal presence in the Eucharist. He partly reacts to problematic late medieval Catholic Eucharistic theologies (like that of William of Ockham) which seemed to underestimate the metaphysical depth of the bread and wine accidents.[114] He rightly insists on keeping the Eucharist in the sacramental order of signs, but thinks that this excludes the Catholic position.

Calvin fails to see how Christ's glorified body can simultaneously be in heaven and on many altars. The Geneva reformer's motive was to uphold the reality of Christ's humanity.[115] He therefore rejects a presence of Christ's body and blood in the gifts on the altar, which is illustrated by his firm opposition to any adoration of the gifts.[116]

However, Calvin intends to posit a real communion of believers with Christ's flesh and blood. Calvin thinks that when the believer partakes of bread and wine in the celebration of the Lord's Supper, he is joined to Christ's own body and blood. What does this mean? First, Christ's presence is spiritual, meaning it is founded on faith and nourishes faith. Second, Calvin employs the image of believers being drawn into heaven to commune in Jesus' body and blood, so that his life-giving power may flow into their hearts.[117] However, they do not consume his body. Third, the Holy Spirit constitutes the link between Christ and the faithful.[118] There are striking similarities between Calvin's description of the effect of Eucharistic communion and Aquinas's theology of how the other sacraments impart grace and spiritual contact with Christ.

Calvin insists that the substance of bread and wine continue to be present on the altar during the Eucharistic celebration and also during communion. In his critique of Catholic doctrine, he responds to annihilation theories. He also seems to conflate Catholic belief with Berengar's first confession. Calvin's critique of transubstantiation seems to target some Catholic theologies, but not that of Aquinas.[119] Calvin's teaching

114. Ewerszumrode, *Mysterium Christi*, 247–48.

115. Brian Gerrish, *Grace and Gratitude: The Eucharistic Theology of John Calvin* (Eugene, Ore.: Wipf & Stock, 2002), 176.

116. John Calvin, *Institutes of the Christian Religion*, trans. Henry Beveridge (Peabody, Mass.: 2008), bk. 4, chap. 17, no. 35.

117. Gerrish, *Grace and Gratitude*, 174–79.

118. Ewerszumrode, *Mysterium Christi*, 160–62.

119. Ewerszumrode, *Mysterium Christi*, 167–68, 238, 249.

has been widely accepted in the Reformed and Anglican communities.[120] As with Zwingli, Calvin's Eucharistic theology clashes with John 6 and the faith of the early Church.[121]

Trent on Transubstantiation and Christ's Substantial Presence in the Gifts

The Council of Trent set out to counter a number of Protestant claims about the Eucharist. Its *Decree on the Sacrament of the Eucharist* (completed in 1555) includes chapters that give a positive teaching of the faith, and canons that express the ecclesial doctrine that must be confessed. The canons are formulated negatively, that is, they forbid certain teachings that are either against the faith or erroneous, depending on the canon.[122]

According to the first canon, one cannot deny that in the Eucharist, Christ's body and blood, soul and divinity are "truly, really, and substantially contained."[123] Chapter 2 of the decree shows this doctrine's foundation: Christ's words at the Last Supper, the constant teaching of the saints, and the constant faith of the Church.[124] Chapter 3 distinguishes Christ's presence in his natural mode of existence in heaven from his sacramental presence in the Eucharist. Properly speaking, Christ is in one place (in heaven), yet he is substantially present in the Eucharistic host and cup at each Mass.[125] Chapter 3 discusses concomitance: Christ's blood is also in the host and his body is present in the cup. Trent appeals to the hypostatic union to ground this teaching.[126] Chapter 4 goes on to teach that the substance of bread is converted into Christ's body, and the substance of wine into his blood. The Council calls this the constant teaching of the Church.[127] This excludes Luther's consubstantiation. The second canon states that the conversion of the substance is fittingly called transubstan-

120. Staedtke, "Abendmahl III/3: Reformationszeit," 118.

121. For a more in-depth study of the sixteenth-century Reformers' theologies of Eucharistic presence, see also Brett Salkeld, *Transubstantiation: Theology, History and Christian Unity* (Grand Rapids, Mich.: Baker Academic, 2019).

122. Hubert Jedin, *Geschichte des Konzils von Trient*, vol. 3 (Freiburg im Breisgau: Herder, 1970), 284–85.

123. Council of Trent, *Decree on the Sacrament of the Eucharist*, DH 1651.

124. Council of Trent, *Decree on the Sacrament of the Eucharist*, DH 1637.

125. Council of Trent, *Decree on the Sacrament of the Eucharist*, DH 1636.

126. Council of Trent, *Decree on the Sacrament of the Eucharist*, DH 1640; also canon 3.

127. Council of Trent, *Decree on the Sacrament of the Eucharist*, DH 1642.

tiation.[128] The argument given is biblical: Christ identified the food in his hands at the Last Supper as his body. He said: "This is my body," not "here is my body." The second phrase would have opened the door for the presence of another substance such as bread substance. Trent does not take up Aquinas's metaphysical argument against consubstantiation, partly because there was disagreement about this among the Catholic theologians. Canon 4 rejects the idea that Christ is present only during the sacrament's use or celebration, or the notion that he is no longer present when the Eucharist is reserved in the tabernacle, which is against Luther. Canon 8, in contradiction to Calvin, excludes the doctrine that Christ is eaten only spiritually, not sacramentally and really.[129]

Let us now analyze some key elements of Trent's *Decree on the Sacrament of the Eucharist*. There was no extensive debate on transubstantiation and the Real Presence. There was a minor debate on the use of the term "transubstantiation." Some Council Fathers considered it too new (it was only 450 years old!) and preferred to limit themselves to patristic terms such as "conversion." But even these critics thought that the word "transubstantiation" expressed the constant Eucharistic faith of the Church.[130] The commission of bishops and theologians responsible for the draft engaged in a brief discussion on the precise language of substance, accidents, and species.

The conciliar text is very careful in its language. It refers to "species," not "accidents." It freely uses the term "substantially present," and notes that the change that occurs at the consecration is "fittingly and properly called transubstantiation." Trent seeks to prevent the canonization of a specific school of theology. By not employing the term "accidents," the Council avoids giving the impression of canonizing Aristotelian philosophy. The language of "substance" could be found in conciliar texts since Lateran IV, and such terminology was used in the twelfth century by various theologians whose categories were not primarily Aristotelian.[131] The

128. Council of Trent, *Decree on the Sacrament of the Eucharist*, DH 1652.

129. Council of Trent, *Decree on the Sacrament of the Eucharist*, DH 1654; 1658.

130. Jedin, *Geschichte*, 3:38–47, 270–76; C. Gutierrez, *Trento: Un concilio para la unión (1550–1552)*, vol. 3, *Estudio*, Corpus tridentinum hispanicum 4 (Madrid: Instituto Enrique Florez, 1981), 114.

131. Hans Jorissen, *Der Beitrag Alberts des Großen zur theologischen Rezeption des Aristoteles am Beispiel der Transsubstantiationslehre*, Lectio Albertina 5 (Münster, Germany: Aschendorff, 2002), 2–4.

language of the conversion of the gifts is ancient—for example, it is found in Ambrose. It is also a way to translate into Latin the Greek Fathers' teaching, who use terms such as *metabolē*, as we saw above.[132] The acts of the council debates clearly state the intention to avoid medieval theological disputes and to ground all doctrine in Scripture, tradition, the Fathers, councils, popes, and the consensus of the Church.[133] The language of species is more directly related to the economy of signs than is the language of accidents. The fact that half the drafting committee considered the terms "accident" and "species" synonymous is irrelevant, because this may not represent the majority of the bishops.[134] Trent does not define its terms, though its way of using "substance" or "species" gives us strong indications of their meaning. Substance refers to the concrete being of Christ's body, while species refers to what appears to our senses (without being reduced to appearances).[135] Trent certainly takes "substance to mean a thing of a definitive kind that exists independently."[136]

The prudence and reticence of Trent on the theme of transubstantiation has another motive: the Council needed to respond to Luther and the Protestant theologians. Trent appeals to the consensus of the Fathers and the medievals. The language of conversion has a broad enough sense to include Church Fathers like Ambrose who never pondered precisely how God converts the gifts on the altar.

Trent's qualified way of employing the term "transubstantiation" signals that its main objective was not the imposition of a particular language about the Eucharistic change, but a key conviction that such language expresses, namely, that a *radical, corporeal, and metaphysical change* takes place in the host and cup during the consecration. The language of transubstantiation should be used insofar as it is the most adequate linguistic means to communicate this conviction about the metaphysics of the Eucharist. The Council specifically wants to say that Jesus really gives

132. Sesboüé, "La doctrine sacramentaire du concile de Trente II," 160.

133. García Ibáñez, *L'eucaristia, dono e mistero*, 299.

134. Edward Yarnold, "Transubstantiation," in *The Eucharist in Theology and Philosophy: Issues of Doctrinal History in East and West from the Patristic Age to the Reformation*, ed. Istvan Perczel, Réka Forrai, and György Geréby, Ancient and Medieval Philosophy, Series 1, vol. 35 (Leuven: Leuven University Press, 2005), 387.

135. García Ibáñez, *L'eucaristia, dono e mistero*, 297, 301.

136. Marshall, "The Eucharistic Presence of Christ," 68.

his body and blood for adoration and consumption, and not just signs of his body and blood. Its use of the terms "truly, really, substantially" clearly excludes a merely figurative reading of Christ's words at the Last Supper. The same language shows that the conversion of the gifts ends (or "terminates") in the very substance of Christ's body and blood.

Evaluating Recent Objections to Eucharistic Substance

As noted at the start of this chapter, among Catholic theologians the most influential alternatives to a scholastic, Tridentine vision of Eucharistic presence have been motivated by developments in modern philosophy and the natural sciences. The alternate theories especially invoke trans-signification (Schillebeeckx) or, in a more postmodern vein, employ a phenomenological (or partly Heideggerian) vision of symbolic efficacy (Chauvet).

Edward Schillebeeckx on Transignification

I have argued that transubstantiation remains intelligible, and that it is best compared to other kinds of metaphysical changes and realities. The past few decades have witnessed a theological tendency to strive for a post-metaphysical doctrine of Eucharistic presence, especially the notion of transignification. While I shall focus on the theory of Edward Schillebeeckx, I should note that twentieth-century transignification theories include notable differences.

Schillebeeckx develops his theological proposal on the basis of his reading of the Council of Trent. He interprets the dogma of transubstantiation as the inevitable result of a worldview shaped by Aristotle and scholastic philosophy. That is, the Fathers of Trent could not help but think of presence in terms of substance and accident.[137] Schillebeeckx seeks to adapt Eucharistic doctrine to the categories of modern philosophy, especially phenomenology. He accepts the notion of transignification, a change of meaning in the Eucharistic gifts, a new meaning that is established by God, yet without reducing transubstantiation to

137. Schillebeeckx, *The Eucharist*, 53–59, 74–75.

trans-signification. In the liturgical setting, bread and wine obtain a new signification. Here, Christ gives himself, so that the offerings on the altar bring Christ's self-gift to us. The sign of his presence changes us, and when we respond to his gift, his presence is completely realized. We do not make Christ present by our faith, for our response presupposes his presence, yet reciprocity (our welcoming his gift by faith) somehow heightens his presence. Schillebeeckx insists that we leave Aristotelian substance behind as inadequate. He concludes that some metaphysical change of the gifts must be posited, yet he does not elaborate on the nature of this change. His own positive explanation remains at the level of a change in sign and meaning.[138]

Schillebeeckx's proposal falls short primarily because of what it excludes. Phenomenological analysis on the meaning of liturgical signs seems wholly compatible with a classical theology of Eucharistic presence. But Schillebeeckx's historical reading of Trent risks placing all of the councils and dogmatic statements of the popes into isolated intellectual ghettos. That is, universal philosophical and theological truth claims seem to become impossible. Consequently, notions such as "nature" or "persons" are categorized as time-bound categories that express something about the Trinity or Christ, but that can always potentially be replaced by new categories. If no lasting definition of the meaning of presence (such as "actuality," "substance") is possible, then how can we ever identify doctrinal continuity between older and newer theologies of Eucharistic presence? How can we confidently posit a shared doctrine of faith with our spiritual ancestors? The Church has continually affirmed a Eucharistic realism on the foundation of Christ's words at the Last Supper, and to protect this realism, no better doctrine has been found than the affirmation of a substantial presence of the body and blood.

Three other difficulties in Schillebeeckx's stance should be noted. First, Christ gives himself in every sacrament. What is unique about the Eucharist is the gift of his own body and blood: here, his humanity is present in a way that is different from his humanity's presence in baptism. Schillebeeckx does not seem to account for this difference. Second, Kereszty rightly points out that the notion of a "completion" of Christ's

138. Schillebeeckx, *The Eucharist*, 131–34, 141, 149–51.

Eucharistic presence by our faith response takes away from the primacy of grace in the Eucharist: Christ simply makes his body and blood present, even if our response is lacking.[139] Third, while the Flemish theologian posits a metaphysical presence of Christ that goes beyond a change of meaning, he gives no explanation of what this ontology entails. He thus fails to make the case that his approach is theologically and pastorally more fruitful than the Tridentine teaching. Indeed, the regions of Europe where Schillebeeckx's thought was most influential have seen a sharp decline in Eucharistic faith.

Louis-Marie Chauvet's Post-metaphysical Theology of Eucharistic Presence

Phenomenology also strongly influenced Chauvet's notion of Eucharistic presence, as did Heidegger's critique of classical metaphysics. The French theologian's starting point is Trent's description of transubstantiation as being "most aptly" suited to describe the change of the gifts. On this basis, he seeks to completely redefine Eucharistic presence.[140] Chauvet especially worries that Aquinas's insistence on the complete presence of Christ's being via the consecration (and so before communion) expels the Church from the Eucharistic mystery. Instead, Christ comes into the gifts not from heaven, but from the assembly, for his is a presence "for us." The Eucharistic bread and wine only have being as a being-for-us, to be offered, poured out, eaten and shared.[141] The symbolism of bread demands this. The Eucharist is also Christ's communication of himself. Onto-theologians such as Aquinas mistakenly seek to define some being underneath the signs, but we should always remain focused on the mediations, on language. The Eucharist is the most essential bread, it is what nourishes. The central Eucharistic sign is the breaking of the bread, for it best manifests Christ's gift of his life and the Eucharist as communion. Chauvet deliberately limits all of his reflections to the level of the sign and, more specifically, to the conventional sign, that is, the sign not in relation to the reality signified but

139. Kereszty, *Wedding Feast of the Lamb*, 220.

140. Chauvet, *Symbol and Sacrament*, 383. For an overview, see Conor Sweeney, *Sacramental Presence after Heidegger: Onto-theology, Sacraments and the Moral Life* (Eugene, Ore.: Cascade Books, 2015), chap. 2.

141. Chauvet, *Symbol and Sacrament*, 387–91.

simply in its capacity to bring meaning to those who perceive it. Finally, he explicitly grounds his notion of presence on Heidegger's philosophy, for whom presence and absence are simultaneous.[142]

Chauvet's meditation on bread and wine seems open to appropriation for a scholastic theology of Eucharistic signs. Chauvet's primary weakness appears to be his insistence on replacing metaphysical theology with a purely symbol-driven approach. His proposal falls short for several reasons. First, there is no clear theology of creation in his work. That is, he tells us that creation is a gift, but he has no account of what God *does* in creating.[143] Nor is it clear how phenomenology can provide an answer here: Heidegger certainly cannot, given his refusal to say anything about God in philosophy. Chauvet seems to have no theology of divine action, and thus, he cannot give any account of how God changes the gifts (beyond the realm of symbol). Second, Chauvet explicitly rejects scholastic theologies of Eucharistic presence, but, in fact, he also implicitly refuses any patristic account of the change of the being of the Eucharistic gifts. Chauvet's acceptance of Heidegger's critique of classical metaphysics entails a refusal of patristic sacramental theologies. Third, as a consequence, Chauvet has no evident account for why we should adore the gifts on the altar, as he has no explanation of how these gifts change, except at the level of symbol. Fourth, again as a consequence, the analogy of the Incarnation dear to the Fathers and their theologies of the epiclesis no longer makes sense. For Chauvet gives no account of how the very flesh and blood of Christ have come into our midst. His focus is on what the signs of bread and wine mean for us. Thus, Chauvet conflicts with the perennial *lex orandi*. Fifth, for Chauvet, the gesture of breaking bread takes theological priority over other elements of the Last Supper, including the words of institution. Perhaps this is because he cannot integrate a literal reading of those words into his theology. His appeal to Christ's self-communication in the Eucharist is welcome, yet it remains without elucidation. Overall, he essentially unfolds a theory of the *sacramentum tantum*.[144] But this cannot suffice.

142. Chauvet, *Symbol and Sacrament*, 398–407.

143. Chauvet, *Symbol and Sacrament*, 548–51.

144. For a brilliant critique of Chauvet's reductive reading of John 6, see Emmanuel Perrier,

Paul VI's *Mysterium Fidei* and Its Consequences for Catholic Theology

I conclude this chapter by arguing that, with the help of Pope Paul VI, we can grant that neither Schillebeeckx nor Chauvet provide us with adequate substitutes for transubstantiation and the theology of Christ's substantial, corporeal presence. Their proposals can serve a complementary role via the positive contributions that they offer.

In the year that Vatican II reached completion, Paul VI issued an urgent message in his encyclical *Mysterium Fidei*. The Council had in fact built on Trent's teaching concerning Christ's substantial presence, though its focus lay elsewhere. Paul VI found that some Catholic theologians were ignoring Trent altogether. The pope firmly refused the reduction or radical reinterpretation of transubstantiation to trans-signification or trans-finalization (a change of purpose). Rather, it was crucial to affirm also the extraordinary change of the whole substance of bread and wine into the body and blood.[145] Christ's presence is corporeal, not just spiritual, which requires a supernatural change in the gifts.[146] The constant practice of worshipping the consecrated gifts confirms this teaching.[147] Thus, trans-signification could complement transubstantiation, but could not do more. We can say the same of Chauvet's theology, applying the principles set forth by Paul VI.

Inspired by Pius XII, Paul VI maintains that the Church's appeal to substance in her Eucharistic teaching is not simply the appropriation of a time-bound concept. Nor is it simply the adoption of Aristotelian metaphysics.

> These formulas—like the others that the Church used to propose the dogmas of faith—express concepts that are not tied to a certain specific form of human culture, or to a certain level of scientific progress, or to one or another theological school. Instead they set forth what the human mind grasps of reality through

"Le Pain de Vie chez Louis-Marie Chauvet et saint Thomas d'Aquin: Représentation de l'inconnaissable ou terme de l'union spirituelle?" *Revue Thomiste* 113 (2013): 195–234.

145. Paul VI, *Mysterium Fidei*, Encyclical Letter, September 3, 1965, no. 11.

146. Paul VI, *Mysterium Fidei*, no. 46.

147. Paul VI, *Mysterium Fidei*, nos. 55–56.

necessary and universal experience and what it expresses in apt and exact words, whether it be in ordinary or more refined language.[148]

Like Pius XII in his encyclical *Humani Generis*, and like the later encyclical *Fides et Ratio* by John Paul II, Paul VI holds that ecclesial dogmatic definitions that employ metaphysical categories (such as "consubstantial with the Father") can be intelligible to the common person. The various theological schools can strive to give those categories greater technical precision, which can further illumine the mystery and help to prevent theological error.[149]

A commonsense notion of substance is present in our general perception of other human beings as centers of abiding identity. For example, the human being remains the same substance from his mother's womb until death, despite the radical physical changes that occur. Or again, a change of substance in the Eucharist will have some similarities with someone's being generated, so that a being is now present among us that was not with us before. These examples can help us to grasp Paul VI's doctrinal intention.

However, one should also note that a general classical and medieval consensus in both philosophy and culture on the nature of substance has been lost, which requires great care in appealing to commonsense notions of substance today. For example, a Cartesian theory of substance as an extended thing in space conflicts with transubstantiation. Contemporary philosophical ideas of substance (especially in analytic philosophy) are widely diverse and often incompatible with transubstantiation. Thus, appeals to the "really real" aspect of the Eucharist cannot suffice to communicate this teaching, since the sense of "real" remains too vague. Also, the accidents of bread and wine are real. Nor is it enough to speak of substance as a substrate, in distinction from its properties (for substance also has properties, based on its nature). Rather, we should also speak of something that exists on its own, has a stable identity, stable features (e.g., the rationality of a human substance) and an intrinsic unity (the person is a

148. Paul VI, *Mysterium Fidei*, no. 24. For the Latin, see *Acta Apostolicae Sedis* 57 (1965), 758.

149. See Guy Mansini, "The Historicity of Dogma and Common Sense: Ambroise Gardeil, Reginald Garrigou-Lagrange, Yves Congar, and the Modern Magisterium," *Nova et Vetera* (English Edition) 18 (2020): 111–38. See also my essay "Implicit Philosophy and Hermeneutics: Metaphysics and the Historicity of Thought in Light of *Fides et Ratio*," *Angelicum* 95 (2018): 201–18.

single substance).[150] The theological and catechetical challenge of making metaphysically formulated dogma accessible to the faithful confronts us not just in Eucharistic doctrine, but in Trinitarian and Christological teaching, as well as in anthropology and ethics.

150. Here, I draw inspiration from Joshua P. Hochschild, "Substance Made Manifest: Metaphysical and Semantic Implications of the Doctrine of Transubstantiation," paper presented at the Metaphysics Colloquium of the Institute for Saint Anselm Studies, Saint Anselm College, Manchester, N.H., June 5–6, 2013; available online at https://philarchive.org/archive/HOCSMM-2.

CHAPTER 7

THE CONSECRATION, THE EPICLESIS, AND THE WORDS OF INSTITUTION

Now that we have studied the mode of Christ's presence in the gifts, we can ponder how (liturgically) he comes to be present in the gifts. According to the typical eastern Orthodox position in our day, the epiclesis is the efficacious means to change the gifts on the altar, precisely when it follows the words of institution. In the west, the Council of Florence and a longstanding theological consensus hold that the change of the gifts happens with the words of the institution. Today, theologians such as Herbert Vorgrimler see the whole Eucharistic prayer as consecratory, a stance that seems to find support in the Fathers.[1] Meanwhile, Cesare Giraudo appeals to both the words of institution and the epiclesis as consecrato-

1. Herbert Vorgrimler, *Sacramental Theology*, trans. Linda M. Maloney (Collegeville, Minn.: The Liturgical Press, 1992), 150.

ry, without fixing a precise moment in which the gifts change. Giraudo speaks of a non-physical, sacramental time inscribed within the liturgy.[2]

The present chapter begins with a historical survey. With the Fathers, the liturgy, and magisterial teaching as foundation, I take up a series of systematic questions. First, which part of the Eucharistic prayer brings about the change of the gifts, and why? Second, what is the spiritual power of prayers such as the epiclesis, and what do they manifest about God's saving work in the liturgy? That is, if the epiclesis is not consecratory, does it bring another spiritual fruit? Third, are the positions of east and west necessarily contradictory? Fourth, must we speak of a specific moment in which the gifts change, or should we leave this question unanswered? These questions are hardly secondary. When can we begin to adore or worship the gifts on the altar? Also, the centrality of the epiclesis for much of the east brings with it a difference in emphasis in ecclesiology and the theology of the priesthood, as does the western emphasis on the words of institution. This theme also deserves reflection.

In chapter 3, the study the history of the liturgy showed the widespread and perhaps universal use of the institution narrative in the ancient liturgies. However, the simple presence of that narrative in the various anaphora does not automatically indicate that it bears an essential (or exclusive) consecratory function. The present chapter ponders the Fathers and the ancient liturgies from a different angle, one that strives to uncover what (if any) consecratory function was attributed to the words of institution, the epiclesis, or the anaphora as a whole. As I proceed, I will employ the term "consecration" to refer to the prayer that in fact is the means whereby Christ's body and blood come unto the altar.

A Historical Study of the Consecration of the Gifts

The Consecration in the Ancient Church

As we consider the witness of the Fathers, we should recall that they often were not concerned with the question of which precise prayer was essential for the consecration. Also, the exact moment of consecration was

2. Cesare Giraudo, *In unum corpus: Traité mystagogique sur l'eucharistie*, trans. Éric Iborra and Pierre-Marie Hombert (Paris: Cerf, 2014), 545, 557–65.

usually not a question that they posed. Such silence does not indicate a denial, yet it should be taken into account.

In pre-Nicene liturgical practice, we find the Greek terms *epikalein*, *epikaleisthai* and *epiklēsis*, which mean "to name" and "to apply the name" or "to call upon in prayer." One calls upon God, the divine Logos, or the Holy Spirit to sanctify or change the bread.[3] The earliest epiclesis calls upon the Logos. Beginning in the third century, and especially starting in the mid-fourth century, we find a Spirit epiclesis, a prayer calling upon the Spirit to accomplish a saving act. The primitive Eucharistic prayers generally have one or two epicleses. The first epiclesis of the Roman canon, which begins with the words "Bless and approve this offering" addresses God the Father. This text is already mentioned by Ambrose in the fourth century, and it may go back to the third century.[4] An epiclesis can precede or follow the words of institution. The second and third Eucharistic prayers of the new Roman rite have epicleses both before and after the words of institution. Numerous ancient eastern Eucharistic prayers have an epiclesis after those words. In sum, an epiclesis asks the Father, the Logos, or the Spirit to bless the gifts, to change them, to make the gifts fruitful in the Church, to make the sacrifice acceptable, and so on.

The Fathers clearly saw the Eucharistic prayer as fruitful. Earlier, we encountered a Logos epiclesis in Justin Martyr, a prayer that likely refers to the institution narrative. For Irenaeus, the words pronounced over the Eucharistic gifts are efficacious, but only because the Word himself has power over creation. Irenaeus thus signals the divinity of the Logos who is invoked over the gifts.[5] Irenaeus too has a Logos epiclesis. He might suggest that the whole Eucharistic prayer is consecratory.[6] Origen refers to the Eucharistic bread as that "over which the Name of God and

3. Michael Zheltov, "The Moment of Eucharistic Consecration in Byzantine Thought," in *Issues in Eucharistic Praying*, ed. Maxwell Johnson (Collegeville, Minn.: The Liturgical Press, 2010), 263–64.

4. Louis Bouyer, *Eucharist: Theology and Spirituality of the Eucharistic Prayer*, trans. Charles Underhill Quinn (Notre Dame, Ind.: University of Notre Dame Press, 1968), 237–38, 243.

5. Irenaeus of Lyon, *Treatise Against Heresies*, bk. 4, chap. 18, no. 5; Antonio Orbe, *Teología de San Ireneo IV: Traducción y comentario del libro IV del "Adversus haereses"* (Madrid: Biblioteca de Autores Cristianos, 1986), 254.

6. Irenaeus of Lyon, *Treatise Against Heresies* bk. 1, chap. 13, no. 2; Edward Schillebeeckx, *L'économie sacramentelle du salut*, trans. Yvon van der Have, Studia Friburgensia 95 (Fribourg, Switzerland: Academic Press, 2004), 277.

of Christ and of the Holy Spirit has been invoked."[7] Origen evokes a fully Trinitarian epiclesis. In the background stands the biblical notion that naming something has a unique spiritual efficacy, namely, that the Lord, being invoked, takes possession of something and sanctifies it. Also, in Scripture, to name God is to reveal or manifest him.[8] Athanasius has a striking passage in a homily to the newly baptized, in which he exclaims that the Logos descends onto the bread and cup via long and miraculous prayers. He sometimes employs the terms Logos (Word) and Pneuma (Spirit) interchangeably.[9] Athanasius may be designating the entire Eucharistic prayer as an epiclesis, for he speaks of long prayers as consecratory. Gregory the Great describes the "sacrificial prayer" (or the Roman canon) as consecratory.[10] Neither these nor other Fathers explicitly teach that the entire Eucharistic prayer and only the whole prayer consecrates. Nor do they deny that the gifts are changed at a precise moment during that prayer. But they transmit to us a deep sense of mystery and reverence for the whole Eucharistic prayer. It is full of spiritual power, as it brings us heavenly gifts and lifts our souls up to God by evoking his saving deeds.

The *Apostolic Tradition* of Hippolytus (a third-century liturgical text) has perhaps the earliest liturgical reference to the Spirit. After the words of institution, the celebrant asks God to send the Spirit upon the offering, so that those who partake of it might be filled with the Spirit, be gathered in unity and strengthened in faith.[11] Hippolytus does not say if the Spirit does anything to the gifts themselves: his focus is on the recipients.[12] Also, it is not clear whether Hippolytus posited a clear distinction between the Logos and the Spirit.

The *Apostolic Constitutions* reflects the western Syrian liturgy in the

7. Origen, commenting on 1 Corinthians 7:5, cited by Zheltov, "The Moment of Eucharistic Consecration in Byzantine Thought," 264. For the Greek text, see Claude Jenkins, "Origen on 1 Corinthians, part 3," *Journal of Theological Studies* 9 (1908): 502.

8. Zheltov, "The Moment of Eucharistic Consecration in Byzantine Thought," 266–67.

9. Athanasius, *Fragmenta* VII (PG 26:1325CD), cited by Johannes Betz, *Eucharistie in der Schrift und Patristik*, Handbuch der Dogmengeschichte 4.4a (Freiburg im Breisgau: Herder, 1979), 89.

10. Schillebeeckx, *L'économie sacramentelle du salut*, 277–78.

11. See the edition of the *Apostolic Tradition* in *Prex Eucharistica: Textus e variis liturgiis antiquioribus selecti*, ed. Anton Hänggi and Irmgard Pahl, Spicilegium Friburgense 12 (Fribourg, Switzerland: Éditions universitaires Fribourg, 1968), 81.

12. John H. McKenna, *The Eucharistic Epiclesis: A Detailed History from the Patristic Era to the Modern Era*, 2nd ed. (Chicago, Illinois: Hildenbrand Books, 2009), 8–9

middle or end of the fourth century and has affinities with the Liturgy of St. Mark. Without a preceding epiclesis, the presiding bishop recalls Christ's suffering and then proceeds to the institution narrative.[13] Then, the celebrant asks God (the Father) to send the Holy Spirit upon the sacrifice, so that he may "show" or "declare" (*apophainō*) the bread to be the body and the cup to be the blood.[14] The meaning of "showing" remains in dispute. In ancient profane use, it meant "to operate, to effect or to cause."[15]

Eucharistic epicleses that mention the Holy Spirit mostly developed in the east during the fourth century, especially in the context of the raging doctrinal disputes surrounding the Holy Spirit's divinity. The attribution to the Spirit of some type of change in the Eucharistic gifts (and the faithful through the gifts) reinforced belief in the Spirit's distinct identity and his divinity.[16]

Cyril of Jerusalem mentions a prayer to the Holy Spirit, an epiclesis that asks that the gifts be changed. The priest calls upon God (the Father) to send the Holy Spirit upon the gifts, that he may make (*poiēsē*) the bread the body of Christ and the wine the blood of Christ. He adds that whatever the Spirit has touched has been sanctified and converted (*metabeblēsai*).[17] He may also be using the term "epiclesis" in reference to the whole Eucharistic prayer.[18]

A key fourth-century witness is the Liturgy of St. Basil. After the words of institution, the priest asks the Spirit to bless and sanctify the gifts on the altar, and to show or present (*anadeixai*) to us in the bread the body of Christ. The last verb ("to show") does not have the sense of

13. See the edition of the *Apostolic Constitutions* in Hänggi and Pahl, *Prex Eucharistica*, 90–93; Edward J. Yarnold, "The Liturgy of the Faithful in the Fourth and Early Fifth Centuries," in *The Study of the Liturgy*, rev. ed., ed. Cheslyn Jones, Geoffrey Wainwright, Edward Yarnold, and Paul Bradshaw (Oxford: Oxford University Press, 1992), 234–36.

14. McKenna, *The Eucharistic Epiclesis*, 12–13.

15. Schillebeeckx, *L'économie sacramentelle du salut*, 257.

16. Congar, *Je crois en l'Esprit Saint* (Paris: Cerf, 2002), vol. 3, 300–301.

17. Cyril of Jerusalem, "Mystagogical Lecture 5," no. 7. There are historical and theological arguments that Cyril's liturgy included the institution narrative. That is, we lack a firm basis to maintain that Cyril attributes the change of gifts to a Spirit epiclesis without an institution narrative. See Edward J. Yarnold, "Anaphoras without Institution Narratives?," *Studia Patristica* 30 (1997): 401–6.

18. Schillebeeckx, *L'économie sacramentelle du salut*, 276.

making or changing the gifts, but of making something known.[19] A later edition of this liturgical text includes an attribution of the change of gifts to the Spirit, but the earlier editions do not.[20] The same epiclesis asks that those who partake in the gifts may be united with one another, and also that they might find mercy and not condemnation.[21] The earliest Liturgy of St. Basil therefore links the epiclesis with the transformation of those who receive the gifts, while a later version also connects the epiclesis with the change of the gifts.

The epiclesis in the Liturgy of St. John Chrysostom calls upon God to send the Holy Spirit onto the gifts, to make (*poiēson*) the bread Christ's body and to convert (*metabalōn*) the content of the cup into Christ's blood. The epiclesis also mentions the purpose of this change, namely, the unity of the faithful with one another and their communion with the Spirit.[22] The institution narrative precedes this epiclesis. The change of the gifts is attributed to the Spirit. Note the close link between the change of the gifts and the transformation of the recipients.

Interestingly, Chrysostom's own teaching on the consecration is somewhat ambiguous. In a sermon on the treason of Judas, he explains: "The priest is the representative when he pronounces those words, but the power and the grace are those of the Lord. 'This is My Body,' he says. This word changes the things that lie before us."[23] The text posits a link between the institution narrative and the change of the gifts. John also attributes the efficacy of the words to Christ, not to the priest, though this need not exclude the priest's instrumental action. Since God's power acts in or through these words, Christ's body becomes present. But in another work, Chrysostom explains that the priest calls upon the Spirit to come and touch the gifts:

> the priest stands before the altar, raising his hands to heaven, calling the Holy Spirit to come and touch the [gifts] set forth.... And when the Spirit gives the

19. Zheltov, "The Moment of Eucharistic Consecration in Byzantine Thought," 267–69; Hänggi and Pahl, *Prex Eucharistica*, 236.

20. Congar, *Je crois en l'Esprit Saint*, 3:302.

21. Hänggi and Pahl, *Prex Eucharistica*, 236–39.

22. Zheltov, "The Moment of Eucharistic Consecration in Byzantine Thought," 270.

23. John Chrysostom, *De Proditione Judae*, Homilies 1–2 (PG 49:380). The English translation is from McKenna, *The Eucharistic Epiclesis*, 54.

grace, when He descends, when He touches the gifts which are set forth ... then you see the Lamb, already slain.[24]

Here, the Spirit working at the moment of the epiclesis seems to make the Lamb present in the gifts on the altar. John's overall teaching thus remains unclear.[25] However, inspired by Nicholas Cabasilas, some theologians read Chrysostom as holding the following position: Christ's words retain their power once and for all, but need to be applied to the gifts at the Eucharistic celebration via the epiclesis.[26]

Gregory of Nyssa has a complex, ambiguous teaching on the power of the epiclesis. He states: "the bread, as says the apostle, 'is sanctified by the Word of God and prayer' ... it is at once changed into the Body by means of the Word, as the Word itself said, 'This is my Body.'"[27] He holds that the change of the gifts happens in an instant. Gregory seems to identify "the Word" that changes the gifts with the institution narrative. But elsewhere, he explains:

bread ... is at first common bread, but when the sacramental action consecrates it, it is called, and becomes, the Body of Christ. So with the sacramental oil; so with the wine: though before the benediction they are of little value, each of them, after the sanctification bestowed by the Spirit, has its several operation.[28]

The gifts' sanctification by the Spirit could refer to the epiclesis. Here too, we seem to be dealing with a single moment in time, with an instantaneous change. But even if Gregory refers to the epiclesis, we are left with an unresolved tension between two of his texts on the function of the institution narrative and epiclesis within the Eucharistic liturgy.[29]

Ambrose refers to the change of the Eucharistic gifts in three different works. Ambrose's most important text on the consecration comes from

24. John Chrysostom, *De coemet. et de cruc.* 3 (PG 49:398). The English translation is by Zheltov, "The Moment of Eucharistic Consecration in Byzantine Thought," 283.

25. Zheltov, "The Moment of Eucharistic Consecration in Byzantine Thought," 283.

26. McKenna, *The Eucharistic Epiclesis*, 56.

27. Gregory of Nyssa, "Catechetical Oration 37," nos. 105–7, cited by Zheltov, "The Moment of Eucharistic Consecration in Byzantine Thought," 282. For the Greek text, see James Herbert Srawley, *The Catechetical Oration of Gregory of Nyssa* (Cambridge: Cambridge University Press, 1903), 149–51.

28. Gregory of Nyssa, "Oration on the Baptism of Christ," cited by Zheltov, "The Moment of Eucharistic Consecration in Byzantine Thought," 282.

29. Zheltov, "The Moment of Eucharistic Consecration in Byzantine Thought," 282.

book 4 of his *On the Sacraments*. This work also provides the most ancient witness to the Roman canon.[30] Ambrose mentions no Spirit epiclesis, either before or after the words of institution. His teaching on the consecration is valuable. First, Ambrose refers to a precise moment of consecration: "that bread is bread before the words of the sacraments."[31] He also specifies: "there was no body of Christ before the consecration."[32] The words of consecration are those of Jesus. This is so because of the doctrine of the creative Word of God.[33] Ambrose distinguishes between the praise of God in the liturgical prayer and the expression of Christ himself that the priest uses: the latter has a unique power.[34] Ambrose then explains which words are those of Christ. Ambrose recites an account of the Last Supper, with the words of institution at the heart of the narrative. He also carefully distinguishes between the evangelist's own words and the words of Jesus. Ambrose explains that before the phrase, "take and drink," the evangelist speaks his words. But then, we have Christ's words: "Take and drink of this, all of you; for this is my blood"[35] Before these words, the chalice contains wine and water, "but when Christ's words have been added, then blood is effected."[36] The same distinction holds for the blessing of the bread. First comes the evangelist's introduction of the setting: "On the day before he suffered." Ambrose continues: "Before it is consecrated, it is bread; but when Christ's words have been added, it is the body of Christ."[37]

The canon mentioned by Ambrose in the same context supports an interpretation that locates the change of the gifts at the words of institution.[38] As the historian of theology Pierre-Marie Gy points out, just before the institution narrative, the canon asks God to accept the Church's gifts and sacrifices (plural), while after the institution narrative, the canon

30. Schillebeeckx, *L'économie sacramentelle du salut*, 265.

31. Ambrose, *The Sacraments*, in *Theological and Dogmatic Works*, trans. Roy Deferrari, The Fathers of the Church 44 (Washington, D.C.: The Catholic University of America Press, 1963), bk. 4, chap. 4, no. 14.

32. Ambrose, *The Sacraments*, bk. 4, chap. 4, no. 16.

33. Ambrose, *The Sacraments*, bk. 4, chap. 4, no. 15.

34. Ambrose, *The Sacraments*, bk. 4, chap. 4, no. 14.

35. Ambrose, *The Sacraments*, bk. 4, chap. 5, no. 22.

36. Ambrose, *The Sacraments*, bk. 4, chap. 5, no. 23.

37. Ambrose, *The Sacraments*, bk. 4, chap. 5, no. 23.

38. Ambrose, *The Sacraments*, bk. 4, chap. 5, no. 21; chapter 6, no. 27.

employs the singular: "an immaculate victim, a spiritual [*rationabilem*] victim, an un-bloody victim" (this is still in our Roman canon). The shift thus focuses to a single offering, that of Christ's body and blood. Also, in Ambrose's canon, before the words of institution, the priest asks God to make the offering "spiritual" (*rationabilis*), but after the words of institution, the gift is simply called "spiritual." The progression of the anaphora supports a close link between the change of the gifts and the words of institution.[39]

The ancient Roman canon that we know has two epicleses, neither of which mentions the Spirit, though a later evolution of the canon does ask the Spirit to come upon the gifts.[40] Before the words of institution, the canon asks God (the Father) to be pleased with the offering, to bless, approve, and perfect it, so that it may become Christ's body and blood. Here, the epiclesis looks forward to the conversion of the gifts. Later comes another epiclesis, in which God is asked to send his angel to carry the gifts to the heavenly altar, so that those who receive the gifts may be filled with grace and blessing.[41] Here, the epiclesis focuses on the fruitfulness of the gifts, not the change of the gifts themselves.

Among the Syrian theologians of antiquity, many held that the gifts are converted through the words of institution. Thus, Severus of Antioch (early sixth century) writes:

> The priest . . . pronounces his words as in the person of Christ . . . "This is my Body which is given for you: do this in remembrance of me;" while over the cup again he pronounces the words, "This cup is the New Covenant in my Blood, which is shed for you." Accordingly, it is Christ who still even now offers, and the power of His divine words perfects the things that are provided so that they may become His Body and Blood.[42]

39. Pierre-Marie Gy, "Doctrine eucharistique de la liturgie romaine dans le haut moyen âge," in *La liturgie dans l'histoire* (Paris: Cerf, 1990), 197. Gy's insight is one reason that I doubt the historical reinterpretation of Ambrose's theology of the consecration set forth by Christiaan Kappes, *The Epiclesis Debate at the Council of Florence* (Notre Dame, Ind.: University of Notre Dame Press, 2019), 78–92.

40. Giraudo, *In unum corpus*, 387–89.

41. McKenna, *The Eucharistic Epiclesis*, 34.

42. Severus of Antioch, "Letter 3," no. 3. The English translation is from Ernest Walter Brooks, *The Sixth Book of the Select Letters of Severus, Patriarch of Antioch, in the Syria Version of Athanasius of Nisibis*, vol. 2 (London: Williams & Norgate, 1904), 238.

Other writings by Severus confirm this teaching, yet he also states that the change of the gifts comes about by the power of the Holy Spirit. He sees no contradiction here, but his focus remains on the words of institution. Also, Syrian theologians such as James of Edessa (eighth century) and John of Dara (ninth century) hold the same position. In short, attributing the change of the gifts to the institution narrative is hardly an exclusively Latin position.[43] However, Theodore of Mopsuestia attributes the conversion of the gifts to the epiclesis.[44]

The eastern Orthodox often cite John Damascene, and suppose him to teach that the change of the gifts comes about precisely with and at the epiclesis. John's texts are hard to interpret. In one key passage, he writes:

> if by his will God the Word Himself became man and without seed caused the pure and undefiled blood of the blessed Ever-Virgin to form a body for Himself; if all this, then can He not make the bread His body and the wine and water His blood? In the beginning He said: "Let the earth bring forth the green herb," and even until now, when the rain falls, the earth brings forth its own shoots under the influence and power of the divine command. God said, "This is My body," and, "This is My blood," and "This do in commemoration of me," and by His almighty command it is done, until He shall come: for what He said was "until He come." And through the invocation [*epiclēseos*] the overshadowing power of the Holy Ghost becomes a rainfall for this new cultivation.... And now you ask how the bread becomes the body of Christ and the wine and water the blood of Christ. And I tell you that the Holy Ghost comes down and works these things which are beyond description and understanding.[45]

It is not clear what Damascene means by the term *epiclesis*. Later authors such as Nicholas Cabasilas will read it in a limited, technical sense. But Damascene may simply be referring to an invocation of God's name or even the Eucharistic prayer as a whole.[46]

Zheltov indicates that Damascene becomes even harder to interpret

43. Zheltov, "The Moment of Eucharistic Consecration in Byzantine Thought," 284–85.

44. Theodore of Mopsuestia, "Homily 15," no. 10, in *Katechetische Homilien*, vol. 1, trans. Peter Bruns, Fontes Christiani 17.1 (Freiburg im Breisgau: Herder, 1994).

45. John Damascene, *On the Orthodox Faith*, bk. 4, chap. 13, trans. Frederic H. Chase, The Fathers of the Church 37 (New York: Fathers of the Church, 1958), 356–57. For the Greek text, see *Die Schriften des Johannes von Damaskos*, ed. Bonifatius Kotter, Patristische Texte und Studien 12 (Berlin: Walter de Gruyter, 1972), 193–94.

46. Zheltov, "The Moment of Eucharistic Consecration in Byzantine Thought," 285–86.

when he turns to the question of how to use the term "antitype." This was a standard early patristic term for the Eucharist. In the face of the Nestorian and Iconoclast controversies, the seventh-century author Anastasius Sinaita rejected its use for the changed gifts on the altar, for fear of separating the gifts on the altar from the presence of Christ, much as the Iconoclasts separated the holy images from the Person of Christ. Damascene was faced with the problem of how to reconcile the use of the term "antitype" in the Liturgy of St. Basil with Anastasius's teaching. He chose the following solution: he restricted its legitimate liturgical use to the moment before the change of the gifts. Now everyone knew that the Liturgy of St. Basil uses the word "antitype" after the institution narrative. But Damascene's readers had apparently forgotten that the liturgy of Basil comes from an ecclesial culture were the term "antitype" can apply to the changed gifts. Damascene's explanation of the liturgy of Basil is problematic, for it now seems that the term "antitype" refers to unchanged gifts on the altar, precisely after the words of institution.[47] Damascene tries to squeeze Anastasius and the liturgy of Basil into a theology in which "antitype" means the same thing, when in fact it does not. Thus, Damascene left us with a confusing text that was often misread as having taught that the words of institution have no direct relation to the conversion of the gifts on the altar.

The ancient liturgical and patristic witnesses on the epiclesis manifest the following patterns. First, starting in the fourth century, most epicleses call upon the Spirit. Second, some epicleses after the institution narrative ask for a change of the gifts. Third, many epicleses that follow the words of institution ask for the sanctification of the gifts or of the faithful. Fourth, there is no clear, consistent patristic testimony about the precise moment of consecration. On the one hand, Ambrose and a few Syrian theologians link this moment with the words of institution. On the other hand, many Fathers remain ambiguous: they might relate the change of the gifts to the institution narrative and the epiclesis, or perhaps to the whole Eucharistic prayer, without giving precision. Overall, the exact moment of the conversion was not an issue, even though some Fathers hold for an instantaneous change.

47. Zheltov, "The Moment of Eucharistic Consecration in Byzantine Thought," 285–89.

Medieval Byzantine Doctrines of the Epiclesis

The first Greek author who clearly identified the moment of the conversion of the gifts was Nicephorus, patriarch of Constantinople (d. 828). He states that this change happens at the epiclesis. Nicephorus strives to follow John Damascene.[48]

This brings us to the influential fourteenth-century Greek theologian Nicholas Cabasilas. In his *Commentary on the Divine Liturgy*, he explains what happens before the epiclesis:

> The priest recites the story of that august Last Supper ... repeating those words [of Christ], the celebrant prostrates himself and prays, while applying to the offerings these words of the Only-Begotten, our Savior, that they may, after having received his most Holy and all-powerful Spirit, be transformed (*metablēthēnai*)—the bread into His holy Body, the wine into his precious and sacred Blood.[49]

For Cabasilas, the gifts cannot be transformed without the institution narrative and the epiclesis together. The epiclesis applies to the gifts that are on the altar today the power of the words of institution that Jesus himself recited two thousand years ago.[50] Now Cabasilas was also an ecumenist who wanted to show that the Latin and Greek liturgies agree on this point. He identifies a prayer in the Roman canon as the consecratory epiclesis, which begins with the words "Humbly, we beseech you O Lord," in Latin, *Supplices te rogamus*. This phrase follows the institution narrative. Here, the Latin priest asks God to send his angel to take the sacrifice from the altar on earth to the altar in heaven. This heavenly transport transforms the gifts.

Cabasilas's theology was adopted widely in the Christian east, yet not by all. For example, George Scholarios, a fifteenth-century patriarch of Constantinople, held the Latin position. We find that the east is not homogenous. Since the seventeenth century, it is eastern Orthodox doctrine that the epiclesis (after the words of institution) effects the transformation of the gifts, but that the institution narrative should also be recited.[51]

48. Zheltov, "The Moment of Eucharistic Consecration in Byzantine Thought," 272–73.

49. Nicholas Cabasilas, *Commentary on the Divine Liturgy*, trans. J. M. Hussey and P. A. McNulty, 5th ed. (Crestwood, N.Y.: St. Vladimir's Seminary Press, 2002), 69–70; Zheltov, "The Moment of Eucharistic Consecration in Byzantine Thought," 276.

50. Congar, *Je crois en l'Esprit Saint*, 3:304.

51. Zheltov, "The Moment of Eucharistic Consecration in Byzantine Thought," 276–81;

The Roman Magisterium on the Consecration

In the middle of the fifteenth century, the Council of Florence was convened to seek the reunion of east and west. The pope and western theologians sought to define for both east and west that the words of institution change bread and wine into Christ's body and blood. The eastern representatives objected that such a declaration would make union more difficult. On one side, the Greek bishops were not prepared for the debate. On the other side, the western bishops and theologians presented arguments drawn from the Fathers and the western liturgies, but failed to ponder the structures of the eastern anaphora on their own terms (including those in the liturgies of St. John Chrysostom and St. Basil).[52] We can see that Florence was in no position to offer a dogmatic teaching that applies to the Byzantine rites.[53]

Nevertheless, the consecration did become an object of conciliar definition, and we will see shortly for whom it was intended. In its *Decree for the Armenians*, Florence declared that the form of the Eucharist consists of the words of institution.[54] The text draws extensively from Aquinas's teaching.[55] The same decree refused any condemnation of the Greeks. In the *Decree for the Jacobites* (*Cantate Domino*, addressed to the Ethiopians and the Copts), Florence cites the words of consecration for the host ("For this is my body") and the chalice (all the way up to the phrase "for the forgiveness of sins").[56] The Council adds that one should not doubt that after the priest has completed these words, the gifts on the altar have become Christ's body and blood.

McKenna, *The Eucharistic Epiclesis*, 85–87. The key text is the Greek version of Peter Moghila's *The Orthodox Confession of the Catholic and Apostolic Eastern Church*, from the year 1640. For the English version, see *Sources of Christian Theology I: Sacraments and Worship*, ed. P. Palmer (London, 1957), esp. 261.

52. Joseph Gill, *The Council of Florence* (Cambridge: Cambridge University Press, 1959), 272–75, 280–81. Gill points out how the pope's theological adviser John of Torquemada refused to acknowledge that the epiclesis in the Liturgy of St. Basil is directed to the Eucharistic gifts, as he restricted the meaning of the epiclesis to the Spirit's work in the mystical body.

53. For a fascinating look at this history, see Kappes, *The Epiclesis Debate at the Council of Florence*.

54. Council of Florence, *Decree for the Armenians*, DH 1321.

55. To be specific, Florence uses Thomas's popular work, *On the Articles of Faith and the Sacraments of the Church*.

56. Council of Florence, *Decree for the Jacobites*, DH 1352.

Trent reaffirmed that, with the consecration (or the words of institution, as the context shows), Christ's body and blood are on the altar.[57] Trent responded to Protestant Reformers who refuse transubstantiation and limit Christ's presence to the moment of communion.[58] The Tridentine Fathers did not seek to revisit the Florentine controversy.

We need to identify the precise doctrinal intention of both councils. Such an ecclesial body can teach without defining something as a truth of faith (as Vatican II frequently did). On this question, the young Edward Schillebeeckx makes two key claims. First, the consecratory power of the words of institution is a teaching of faith. Second, the doctrine that these words alone consecrate (without the epiclesis) is not a teaching of faith. The reason for this twofold claim is that Florence refused to condemn the more common Greek position (that of Cabasilas), while Trent's canon does not take up the question of the epiclesis. Schillebeeckx also mentions the case of the sixteenth-century Dominican Ambrosius Catharinus, who held that, *in the oriental rites*, the words of institution and the epiclesis together consecrate the gifts.[59] Catharinus's work was placed on the index of forbidden books for a time, but later removed.[60] In short, Florence or another council can determine the form of the Eucharist for the Latin Church (and the Armenians) without teaching a dogma.[61]

The teaching of Florence has at least two sources. Starting in the late twelfth century, the we find a common Latin practice of elevating the host for adoration immediately after the words of institution. This liturgical devotion quickly took root among the people.[62] Second, Florence relies on Aquinas's theology of sacramental form. For Thomas, since the words of institution clearly signify the conversion of the gifts into Christ's body and blood, then, following his general principle that Christian sacraments effect what they signify, the utterance of these words over bread

57. Council of Trent, *Decree on the Sacrament of the Eucharist*, chap. 4, DH 1642; canon 4, DH 1654.

58. McKenna, *The Eucharistic Epiclesis*, 84; Lawrence Feingold, *The Eucharist: Mystery of Presence, Sacrifice and Communion* (Steubenville, Ohio: Emmaus Academic, 2018), 310.

59. Schillebeeckx, *L'économie sacramentelle du salut*, 272–74.

60. Congar, *Je crois en l'Esprit Saint*, 3:313n55.

61. My interpretation of Florence and Trent differs from that of Philippe-Marie Margelidon, *Le sacrement de l'eucharistie: Corpus Domini Jesu Christi*, Bibliothèque de la Revue Thomiste (Paris: Parole et Silence, 2019), 198–202.

62. Schillebeeckx, *L'économie sacramentelle du salut*, 280.

and wine by the minister who can speak in Christ's person and who has the intention of consecrating is effective.

A Systematic Theology of the Consecration

The Councils of Florence and Trent have defined for the Latin Church that the gifts on the altar become Christ's body and blood through the words of institution. To better grasp the significance of this teaching and its relation to eastern Orthodox claims, I will return to an issue already raised in chapter 3, namely, the distinction between the essence of a sacrament and its sign or concrete expression. Without this distinction, any solution to this debate will likely elude us. I will then consider theological reasons that support the teaching of Florence. Next, I will take up the significance of the epiclesis beyond its consecratory function: What does it manifest and what does it effect? We also need to take up the charge that Florence leads to a fragmentation of the Eucharistic prayer. Then, using Congar's approach, I will ask whether an agreement is possible between east and west on this issue. Finally, I will evaluate the alternative proposals set forth by Vorgrimler, Giraudo, and John McKenna.

The Church's Eucharistic teaching and any theological account thereof especially stand at the service of her longstanding liturgical practice. Ecclesial and theological teaching generally seek to make sense of established liturgical practice that has endured over time and been accepted by the Church, to show the harmony of the practice with Scripture and various established doctrines.[63] For example, faith tells us that Christ instituted the sacraments. We also see a certain diversity of liturgical practice, and somewhat diverse teachings among the saints about the efficacy of this or that part of the liturgy. Church teaching and theological reflection can point to harmony among these elements, while at times also proposing modifications on the grounds of Scripture, dogma, or sound theological reasoning.[64]

63. Schillebeeckx, *L'économie sacramentelle du salut*, 320.

64. The liturgy is not a transmission of revelation on par with Scripture, since not all of the liturgy transmits revelation. One of many examples would be the new Eucharistic prayers in the Roman rite. Consider also that the Church can modify many elements of the liturgy in light of other sources. For example, some fourth century Fathers modified the epiclesis in order to reinforce belief in the Spirit's divinity.

To bring out this harmony, modern theologians have developed a distinction between (1) the essence or signification of the sacrament and (2) the exterior rite. This distinction became explicit in the work of seventeenth-century scholastic John of Saint Thomas. We can find traces of it before that time, and the Church's teaching on the sacraments essentially assumes it. The distinction will help us to understand the function of the epiclesis and the words of institution in the liturgy as practiced through the centuries.[65]

As I proceed, another distinction is in order. The sacrament of the Eucharist is the substantial presence of Christ's body and blood under the signs of bread and wine. In this way, the Eucharist is different from other sacraments, which are the word and gesture themselves (such as pouring water with the Trinitarian formula). Yet the distinction between the essence of the sacrament and its exterior rite can be applied to the form of the Eucharist. The other six sacraments essentially consist of acts that signify a sanctifying reality, where a signification is concretized through particular words and gestures. These sacraments (and the Eucharistic form) are faith expressions of a signification or an intention. Some gestures (the priest taking of bread and wine) are apt to express an intention (the presence of body and blood), and the gestures are given precision by the ritual utterance of words (a prayer) that are also apt to express a more specific intention (the presence of Christ's body and blood).[66] Neither the gesture alone nor the words taken by themselves bring about the sacrament, but the fusion of the two is a symbolic act, the concretization of a sacred signification. Now the signification includes a word of faith (a prayer) and a liturgical gesture apt to express a particular gift of grace, yet that signification could be concretized by various prayers and gestures. The words and gestures used in the liturgy incarnate or particularize this signification.[67]

Christ has instituted the essence (or substance) of the sacraments (including the essence of Eucharistic form and matter), which also means that he has determined their signification. He established that his body

65. Schillebeeckx, *L'économie sacramentelle du salut*, 321–22. Schillebeeckx prefers to speak of the substance of the sacrament rather than its essence.

66. Schillebeeckx, *L'économie sacramentelle du salut*, 330–35.

67. Schillebeeckx, *L'économie sacramentelle du salut*, 346–47; McKenna, *The Eucharistic Epiclesis*, 211.

and blood would be given to us as spiritual food and drink and as the perfect sacrifice, to be offered by the Church through her priests, using prayers and gestures that are fitting to express this gift and this sacrifice. Yet he need not have instituted the precise form or prayer by which this signification is realized. Now as we saw in chapter 3, in the history of the Eucharistic liturgy, we find the Church's continual insistence that wheat bread and wine of the grape be used for the Eucharist. This unbroken practice reflects Christ's intention, namely, to determine the matter of the sacrament, or the precise gesture that would concretize the essence of the sacrament.[68] As for the sacramental form of the Eucharist, the history of the liturgy and its interpretation by the saints and theologians is more ambiguous. Also, the widespread or even universal use of the words of institution in the various anaphora is not an automatic proof that it was believed to be the means to change the gifts. The issue could not be treated in an exhaustive manner by medieval Latin scholastics, partly because these theologians enjoyed only limited knowledge of ancient and eastern liturgies.[69]

The Church has been given the ministry of determining and safeguarding the sacramental rituals, including their form and matter. That is, she preserves the essence or signification of Eucharistic form and matter (and of the other sacraments), and she ensures that this essence is expressed and celebrated in a fitting manner, one that also respects liturgical tradition. Thus, as Pius XII could determine that the matter of the sacrament of priestly ordination consists in the laying on of hands, so five centuries earlier, the Council of Florence could determine that the matter of the same sacrament consists of the handing over of chalice and paten.[70] The Council of Florence established that, for the Latin and Armenian Churches, the words of institution bring about the change of the gifts, but without condemning competing doctrines emanating from the Greeks.[71]

I now offer two arguments to show the liturgical, doctrinal coherence of the Florentine teaching, to show why it is reasonable for the Church

68. Schillebeeckx, *L'économie sacramentelle du salut*, 349.
69. Schillebeeckx, *L'économie sacramentelle du salut*, 339–42.
70. Schillebeeckx, *L'économie sacramentelle du salut*, 351.
71. Schillebeeckx, *L'économie sacramentelle du salut*, 272–73.

to teach in this way. In addition, the west needs to give an account of the liturgical function of the epiclesis.

First, the moment of consecration is important, for it allows us to answer a very legitimate question of the faithful, namely when we may begin to adore the gifts. Some scholars of liturgy risk going against eight centuries of western practice of adoring the host and cup after the words of institution. On what basis do we exclude this practice (which continues today) from the *lex orandi*, a practice supported by the very language of the Roman canon? Also, historically, the east displays striking diversity on the matter, which renders an eastern appeal to the *lex orandi* more complex. As Michael Zheltov points out, Pseudo-Germanus of Constantinople's *Historia Ecclesiastica* may witness to a medieval eastern practice of adoring the gifts after the words of institution.[72] This would match the testimony of Basil Bessarion and other Greek bishops, given at the Council of Florence.[73] Zheltov further notes that some early medieval Byzantine lives of the saints associate the change of the gifts with the call to communion (at the words: "holy things to the holy"), meaning, not at all with the anaphora. This doctrine was sidelined by Cabasilas. Overall, the east tends to emphasize the spiritual efficacy of manual acts or gestures, for example, the elevation of the gifts, or placing a consecrated host into wine.[74] The common Latin practice of adoring the gifts after the praying of the words of institution therefore has some support in the Greek tradition. Overall, the eastern Orthodox claim that the epiclesis is the moment of consecration seems tentative.

Second, following Benoît-Dominique de la Soujeole, we can propose a Christological argument that it is fitting for the Eucharistic gifts to be changed at the words of institution. As we saw in an earlier chapter, for Aquinas, Christ's humanity is the conjoined instrument of his divine nature. Christ's salutary divine action is not parallel to his human actions;[75] rather, Jesus' saving divine acts pass through his holy humanity, so that his human words, acts, and gestures share in that activity. Also, his humanity is an instrument whereby the Holy Spirit is given, for the Spirit

72. Zheltov, "The Moment of Eucharistic Consecration in Byzantine Thought," 289–90.

73. Gill, *The Council of Florence*, 271–72.

74. Zheltov, "The Moment of Eucharistic Consecration in Byzantine Thought," 291–301, 305.

75. Thomas Aquinas, *Summa theologiae* III, q. 19, a. 1.

comes in any outpouring of sanctifying grace.[76] This doctrine is rooted in the *Filioque*: The Father and the Son together eternally spirate the Spirit. This order of the divine persons continues in the saving economy: The Incarnate Word gives the Spirit. The Spirit does not come to us without being given by the Son. Thomas insists that the Spirit's mission extends his eternal procession from the Father and the Son. The Trinity's action in the economy is marked by the eternal Triune life and manifests it. There is no separation between God in himself and God among us.[77] At the Last Supper, Jesus' words and gestures were the efficacious means whereby he breathed the Spirit who converted the gifts of bread and wine. Jesus *in his humanity* institutes the Eucharist and the other sacraments because he is the instrument by which the Spirit operates in all the sacraments. The mediating work of Christ's humanity should stand at the center in this, the greatest sacrament. The epiclesis before the words of institution found in some rites points forward to the Spirit's coming, to be realized by Christ's saving theandric (or divine-human) deed. In some eastern rites, the subsequent epiclesis explicitly acknowledges this work of the Spirit. It completes the signification begun in the institution narrative, which manifests the Incarnate Word remaking creation by his creative word animated by the Spirit, who operates in each of Jesus' saving words and deeds. In short, the Eucharistic teaching of Aquinas and Florence supports a Chalcedonian Christology without necessarily obscuring the role of the Spirit.[78]

The preceding point already leads us to ponder the meaning of the epiclesis, including the type of epiclesis (typical in the west) that does not directly signify the change of gifts. Here, three further considerations are in order, namely, the so-called principle of distension, the need to highlight the Spirit's consecratory role and the ecclesial fruits of the Eucharist.

First, I turn to the classical liturgical "principle of distension." Various elements of the Mass articulate by word and gesture that which will occur or has already occurred. Thus, in the rite of presbyteral ordination,

76. Thomas Aquinas, *Summa theologiae* III, q. 8, a. 1, ad 1.

77. Thomas Aquinas, *Summa theologiae* III, q. 43, aa. 2–3, 6; Gilles Emery, *The Trinitarian Theology of St. Thomas Aquinas*, trans. Francesca Aran Murphy (Oxford: Oxford University Press, 2007), chapter 15.

78. Benoît-Dominique de la Soujeole, "La forme de l'eucharistie," *Revue Thomiste* 103 (2003): 95–101.

the newly ordained receives the chalice and paten from the bishop as a sign that he receives the power to celebrate the Eucharist. Yet the bishops' laying on of hands and prayer of ordination occurred several minutes before. When the priest receives the paten and chalice as a sign of his new spiritual power to celebrate the Mass, he has already received that power in the prayer of ordination. Something analogous can be found in the Eucharistic liturgy. Due to the limitations of human words, the Mass cannot express in a single moment the richness of the gift being realized at a particular moment.[79] The same phenomenon can be explained from the perspective of the needs of the faithful. The liturgy's downward mediation of transmitting divine gifts such as Jesus' body and blood must be complemented by its upward mediation of guiding the faithful in right and devout prayer to God, in worship, sacrifice, and praise. Apparently repetitious prayers teach and inspire the priest and all the faithful to ask God's blessing in various forms, even though that blessing might be received previously or subsequently.[80]

Second, the epiclesis makes clear that the transformative power of Christ's words over the gifts is inseparable from the Spirit's action upon the bread and wine. Christ's action in the priest is possible by the power of the Spirit that dwells in his humanity and thus also passes through the priest. The epiclesis heightens the expression of the priest's and the Church's dependence on the Spirit for every blessing obtained in the Eucharistic liturgy.

Third, in many Eucharistic prayers, the epiclesis asks that the Eucharistic gifts may sanctify and unite those who partake of them. The Church thus begs the Spirit to act in the hearts of those present, so that communion may lead to the deeper integration of the members of Christ's body with their head and with one another (that is, with the whole Church).[81] Bouyer has signaled the ancient Jewish origins of this prayer, which looks

79. Congar, *Je crois en l'Esprit Saint*, 3:311–12; S. Salaville, "Épiclèse eucharistique," in *Dictionnaire de théologie catholique*, ed. E. Mangenot, vol. 5 (Paris: Librairie Letouzey et Âne, 1913), col. 294.

80. Michon M. Matthiesen, *Sacrifice as Gift: Eucharist, Grace and Contemplative Prayer in Maurice de la Taille* (Washington, D.C.: The Catholic University of America Press, 2013), 108.

81. McKenna, *The Eucharistic Epiclesis*, 136–37; Joseph Pohle, *Lehrbuch der Dogmatik in sieben Büchern*, 7th ed., vol. 3, Wissenschaftliche Bibliothek, Series 1: Theologische Lehrbücher 22 (Paderborn, Germany: Ferdinand Schöningh, 1922), 254.

forward to Israel's eschatological unity.[82] In the language of Henri de Lubac: the Eucharist makes the Church.[83]

I have argued that the teaching of Florence on the form of the Eucharist has a sound liturgical and theological basis. Still, some worry that western theologies of this type risk fragmenting the Eucharistic prayer.[84] Aquinas provides a striking example. He holds that a priest can consecrate bread and wine while skipping all the other parts of Mass, even though this is gravely sinful.[85] Here, we should keep in mind Thomas's broader theological project. His approach to the words of institution allows him to account for the presence of true Eucharistic celebrations outside the visible bounds of the Catholic Church, for instance, by validly ordained schismatic priests, whose prayers in the name of the people (*offerimus*) are false, since they are not in communion with the Church.[86] Still, Aquinas's argument almost exclusively focuses on the priestly character (the metaphysical seal) and the efficacy of the words of institution uttered with the intention of consecrating.

It is noteworthy that many theologians of Aquinas's era did not accept his position.[87] In addition, de la Soujeole appeals to none other than Thomas to argue that it is essential for the priest to follow the Church's intention, which is to celebrate a sacrament. Consequently, the minister consecrates by intending to celebrate the Church's ritual, in which the sign of the consecration is bound up with the signs of the other prayers.[88] We might also add the following argument: the priest should intend not just to convert bread and wine into Christ's body and blood, but also to celebrate a sacrifice (or at a minimum, not to refuse this act). If the lat-

82. Bouyer, *The Eucharist*, 311.

83. This phrase expresses the driving theme of Henri de Lubac's classic study, *Corpus Mysticum: L'Eucharistie et l'Église au Moyen Âge, étude historique* (Paris: Aubier, 1949). English translation: *Corpus Mysticum: The Eucharist and the Church in the Middle Ages*, trans. Gemma Simmonds and Richard Price (London: SCM Press, 2006).

84. Congar, *Je crois en l'Esprit Saint*, 3:294–99, 306.

85. Thomas Aquinas, *Summa theologiae* III, q. 78, a. 1, ad 4. We should distinguish Thomas's position from the idea of later theologians that a wicked priest could consecrate all the bread in a bakery.

86. Thomas Aquinas, *Summa theologiae* III, q. 78, a. 7.

87. Pierre-Marie Gy, "Prière eucharistique et paroles de la consécration," in *La liturgie dans l'histoire* (Paris, Cerf, 1990), 217.

88. De la Soujeole, "La forme de l'eucharistie," 102. He appeals to *Summa theologiae* III, q. 64, a. 8, ad 2–3.

ter is essential to intending a consecratory act *in persona Christi*, then it seems that a cultic setting is necessary for the words of institution to be fruitful.[89] The Eucharist is essentially both sacrament and sacrifice.

This solution has at least three advantages. First, it makes sense of the traditional discipline that, if the priest happens to discover after the consecration that the host placed on the altar was in fact not bread, he can begin the consecration again without repeating the prayers that precede the words of institution.[90] The priest remains within the liturgical setting that gives the consecration its full, sacrificial, and ecclesial signification, while the consecration itself is the prayer that effects the change of gifts. Second, this approach gives a theological account of the priest who suffers imprisonment for the sake of the Gospel, obtains bread and wine and secretly celebrates the Mass as best he can, with the words of institution included. Third, this solution reunites the consecration with the rest of the Eucharistic prayer, yet without sacrificing the *lex orandi* of the Roman rite.

Latin theology can therefore respect both the integrity of the Eucharistic prayer and longstanding liturgical practices proper to its rite. Indeed, as the west continues its dialogue with eastern Orthodoxy, attentiveness to the logic of each liturgy will be crucial. As Congar points out, different ecclesial cultures stand behind this controversy. The sacramental culture of the west is more Christo-centric, that of the east, marked as is it by fourth-century controversies, is more oriented toward the Trinity as a whole. The west places greater emphasis on the priest's instrumental action and insists that he operates *in persona Christi*, as a sacramental reality who represents Christ. Thus, the Latin sacramental formulas use fewer prayers asking for God's intervention and more indicative formulas, such as "I baptize you," and "I absolve you from your sins." The Byzantine tradition, without denying that the priest prays *in persona Christi*, focuses more on the minister's prayer on behalf of the Church, using words such as, "He is baptized," and, "May God forgive you." The Eucharistic epiclesis is said in the plural form (east and west). Thus, the west highlights the action of the priest, while the east highlights the action of the

89. Bernard Leeming, in his *Principles of Sacramental Theology*, (London: Longmans, 1956), 484–85, makes a similar point.

90. Schillebeeckx, *L'économie sacramentelle du salut*, 281.

whole Church. In the Eucharistic liturgy, especially since the twelfth century, the west has placed greater emphasis on Christ's substantial presence, while the east, without denying or minimizing this truth, tends to emphasize more the Spirit's sanctifying work through the sacred gifts on the altar. Finally, the west highlights the sacraments' historical continuity with Christ, while the east highlights the present descent of the heavenly Jerusalem by the power of the Spirit.[91] Each liturgical culture possesses a particular and irreplaceable richness. The east might risk minimizing the words of institution, while the west may risk minimizing the epiclesis. The Roman liturgy itself strongly suggests that the words of institution are the moment of consecration, while the eastern liturgies lean toward the epiclesis. Eucharistic theology needs to take this into account.

In light of all this, how might the Latin and Byzantine traditions reach agreement? Congar offers the following proposal. The priest should intend to celebrate according to his proper rite, which may affect how the gifts change. We might nuance this point and say: in celebrating a rite, the priest accepts the structure and meaning of that rite, and his intention is shaped by it. Hence, the Latin priest's intention is to pronounce the words of institution not as a narrative but in applying them to the gifts on the altar. The Byzantine priest's intention to consecrate focuses on the epiclesis, to celebrate the mystery by asking the Spirit to make the words of institution fruitful. Now this need not mean that, in the oriental rites, the gifts actually change only when the epiclesis has been pronounced.[92] Perhaps the west can remain apophatic about what occurs in eastern Orthodox liturgies, somewhat as the eastern liturgical traditions have themselves been diverse in their answers over the centuries.

Of course, there is one eastern Eucharistic prayer that (at least in its contemporary use) has no explicit institution narrative, namely, Addai and Mari. What do we make of this anaphora? Our historical study above noted that its ancient form remains uncertain. The current use has the words of institution present in a dispersed way. Now the Chaldean rite of the Catholic Church has prayed the Addai and Mari with the words of institution since at least the sixteenth century, if not before, with gen-

91. Congar, *Je crois en l'Esprit Saint*, 3:314–15.
92. Congar, *Je crois en l'Esprit Saint*, 3:313.

uflections following each consecration.[93] Rather than seeing this as an unfortunate western imposition (if it was imposed), we might note that the practice has taken root. In addition, the ancient anaphora closest to Addai and Mari (Theodore, Nestorius, and Sharar) all use the institution narrative. It therefore seems to constitute no violation of Addai and Mari's theological and liturgical culture to propose that an explicit institution narrative be inserted into the anaphora of the Assyrian Church of the East.

To conclude, we can return to the alternative theories indicated at the beginning of this chapter and ask: Why not posit the whole Eucharistic prayer as consecratory? First, I have already given a partial response above, on the importance of the liturgical context for the words of institution. Second, the proponents of the notion that entire Eucharistic prayer is what changes the gifts tend to appeal to the Fathers, yet only some Fathers seem to suggest this, always with a note of ambiguity, and without a direct answer to the question posed. Third, it is hard to see how this notion can be reconciled with the adoration shown to the Eucharistic gifts after the words of institution throughout the west over the past eight hundred years. Nor is it clear how the proposal can respect the teachings of Florence and Trent.

Vorgrimler and other theologians prefer to avoid any talk of a single moment of consecration. For example, John McKenna thinks that the insistence on a precise moment of consecration brings with it an excessive focus on the substantial presence of Christ and risks obscuring his personal presence. While he seeks to affirm a bodily presence of Christ in the Eucharist, McKenna (drawing on Schillebeeckx) holds that "this is no more real than the mutual presence of Christ and his faithful in the life of grace."[94] McKenna's notion of presence is too univocal: the encounter with Christ dwelling in our hearts is authentic, yet not simply the same as encountering him in the sacraments. Nor is it clear why Christ's presence to us is somehow diminished by a theology of transubstantiation. For just as the hypostatic union enables a deeper encounter with the Son of God, so transubstantiation makes possible a spousal encounter with the same

93. *Missel chaldéen: L'ordre des mystères avec les trois anaphores, selon le rite de la sainte Eglise de l'Orient*, ed. Francis Alichoran and P. Perrier (Paris: Eglise chaldéenne, 1982), 16, 82–83.

94. McKenna, *The Eucharistic Epiclesis*, 198.

Son in his very flesh and blood. McKenna seems to fear a substantial, non-personal presence of Christ's body and blood; but what would such a presence even be?

Finally, Giraudo proposes that the words of institution perfect the epiclesis and vice versa, so that each is fully consecratory. This claim involves no contradiction, says Giraudo, since the change of the gifts happens in "sacramental time." We should leave behind our natural notion of chronological time and accept a vision of time that is analogous to Trent's doctrine of Christ's Eucharistic body not being in a "place." Just as natural place (as an accident) cannot explain Christ's corporeal presence, so natural time cannot explain when or how the gifts are changed.[95] Yet Giraudo gives little explanation of what sacramental time is. Nor is it clear that the analogy with sacramental place works. Scholastic theologians worked out highly complex theories of Eucharistic accidents, in reliance on a long philosophical tradition of reflection on substance and accident. For example, philosophy allowed them to posit substance and place as distinct yet also linked: Christ is "in heaven" as in a place, and he is "on the altar" insofar as his body and blood become accessible through the accidents that are properly in that place. Giraudo posits a category of sacramental time that has no clear philosophical or theological foundation. Indeed, for him, sacramental and chronological time appear to be parallel or separated, unlike the substance of Christ (his body and blood) and the place of the bread and wine accidents. That is, we do in fact access Christ's body and blood through a particular place. Giraudo's exclusion of chronological time risks disincarnating the sacrament.

Conclusion

Sacraments effect what they signify, in the context of a minister's intention and the faith of the Church. The Church can know how she is to celebrate various sacraments in order to ensure their fruitfulness, as when we use the Trinitarian formula and water in baptism. Her conviction is rooted in longstanding liturgical practice. Marked differences therein can justify distinct doctrines in east and west. The more apophatic style of the

95. Giraudo, *In unum corpus*, 559–60.

east can be respected, even as the west follows its own tradition rooted in Ambrose, the language of the Roman canon, and centuries-old patterns of liturgical worship. Here, a distinction between temporary practices and an established *lex orandi* is crucial: Latin theology cannot simply set aside its own liturgical heritage. The Florentine doctrine on the form of the Eucharist harmonizes beautifully with faith in the *Filioque* and with a Christology that closely links the coming of the Spirit to the action of Christ's humanity. None of this entails a marginalization of the epiclesis: its signification of the Spirit's work in the liturgy is crucial, and the prayer brings a new grace to the assembly and to the whole Church. Also, the Florentine teaching on the consecration need not separate the words of institution from their liturgical context. The words of institution do indeed effect a change of the gifts, when the minister celebrates the sacrament of the Eucharist as a sacramental sacrifice. In the New Passover, Christ's presence is at once corporeal (the Lamb) and personal (the Messiah), without tension or competition, as in the Incarnation. This celebration is a grace that takes root in the Church's time, which is the time of pilgrims, a time linked with transcendence. Hence, we can indeed say "when" the victorious lamb is in our midst.

CHAPTER 8

THE MINISTER OF THE EUCHARIST

The study of the consecration naturally leads us to ponder the identity and role of the minister of the Eucharist, the one who celebrates this sacrament with and for the Church. Previous chapters already began to touch on this theme. In the chapter on the institution of the Eucharist, we saw the significance of Christ's command at the Last Supper to "do this" in his memory. The chapter on sacrifice placed much emphasis on the representation of Christ as offering his body and blood. I now take up other fundamental aspects of the minister of the Eucharist. The following does not entail a synthesis of the theology of the priesthood. Rather, I will focus on the bishop and priest as celebrant of the Eucharistic sacrifice. This specification calls for clarification: the present aim is not to remain strictly within the limits of a Tridentine doctrine of the priesthood as essentially ordered to the Eucharistic sacrifice. Instead, I will place this valuable teaching within the broader perspective of Vatican II, that is, in relation to the priest's overall mission, his relation to the bishop, and the priest's role of praying in the name of the whole Church.

The present chapter circles around the following questions: First, who can celebrate the Eucharist, and why? Second, what is the minister's relation to Christ? (Both of these questions are of great concern to our Protestant brethren.) Third, what is the priest's relation to the Church? Fourth, what is the significance of the minister's gender? Fifth, what matters must be considered regarding concelebration? I take up these questions via a survey of biblical, liturgical, and patristic witnesses, and then answer them through a systematic treatment.

The Minister of the Eucharist in Scripture, the Early Church, and the Magisterium

The New Testament offers only a few clues about the identity of the presider at Eucharist. For example, the Acts of the Apostles mentions the breaking of the bread on several occasions, which likely is a Eucharistic reference. Luke usually does not specify who leads this ritual. However, in the most important reference (Acts 2:42–46), Luke probably means that the apostles presided.[1] Other passages either explicitly or perhaps implicitly show Paul presiding (esp. Acts 20:7–8).[2] In Jerusalem, the breaking of the bread took place in the homes of Christians (Acts 2:42–46). Some authors argue that the head of the household would have presided, regardless of any sacramental ordination.[3] This claim lacks a textual foundation. Also, the early Christian liturgy's structure was heavily marked by Jewish ritual, including prayers at Jewish meals. In the Jewish culture, the identity and function of the presider for such prayers was strictly regulated. This means that, from a strictly historical perspective, it is highly unlikely that early Christian practice would include few regulations or instructions on who presides at the Eucharist.[4]

1. Jean-Pierre Torrell, *A Priestly People: Baptismal Priesthood and the Priestly Ministry*, trans. Peter Heinegg (New York: Paulist Press, 2013), 103–5.

2. Xavier Léon-Dufour, *Le partage du pain eucharistique selon le Nouveau Testament* (Paris: Seuil, 1982), 31–32. Paul also breaks bread at Acts 27:35, but this may or may not be a Eucharistic setting. See Darrell L. Bock, *Acts*, Baker Exegetical Commentary on the New Testament (Grand Rapids, Mich.: Baker Academic Press, 2007), 710.

3. Edward Schillebeeckx, *Ministry: A Case for Change* (London: SCM Press, 1981), 30.

4. Hervé-Marie Legrand, "La présidence de l'Eucharistie selon la tradition ancienne," *Spiritus* 69 (1977), 410–11. Legrand also thinks it possible that Acts 13:1–2 shows that the "prophets and

The most valuable biblical evidence for our argument is found in the Gospel accounts of the Last Supper. First, we saw in chapter 3 that Jesus instituted a new sacrifice in the Upper Room. In ancient Judaism, it would have been unthinkable not to specify who is the minister of the sacrifice. Second, we have noted the Passover setting of the Last Supper. In Jewish Passover custom, the identity of the presider is crucial. Third, at the Last Supper, Jesus is gathered with "the twelve" (Mk 14:17, Mt 26:20) or "with the apostles" (Lk 22:14). There is no evidence that others were present in the room. In chapter 3, we noted the possible cultic sense of "do this." In any case, it is clear that Jesus commands the memorial celebration of his Last Supper, and does so while addressing a very specific group of disciples.[5] The implication is that those (or at least some of those) who share in the apostles' mission will also preside at the Eucharist.

But who would have led the celebration in the first and second centuries? Was it just apostles, bishops, and priests, or perhaps also other leaders, such as prophets, as some historians argue? In the early Church, "prophets" may have held an ecclesial office linked with a charismatic gift. They may also have presided at Eucharist.[6] In chapter 10, verse 6, of the *Didache*, we find a thanksgiving prayer that may be part of a weekday Eucharistic liturgy, a prayer that can be recited by a prophet (an itinerant, missionary figure who does not belong to the local church). The text later calls the prophets "your high priests." They are said to render a sacerdotal service.[7] This description could signal that the prophets in question may be presbyters.[8] But this point remains disputed.[9] A clear reference to the Eucharist is found later, in chapters 14–15, where the bishops and deacons exercise a leading though unspecified role.[10] Overall, the *Didache*

teachers," holders of ecclesial offices, presided at liturgy. For the reference to prophets, see the discussion of the *Didache* below.

5. Torrell, *A Priestly People*, 103.

6. Legrand, "La présidence de l'Eucharistie," 411.

7. *Didache*, chap. 13, verse 1.

8. Albert-Marie de Monléon, *Charismes et ministères dans l'Écriture, et l'expérience de l'Église*, Chemins ouverts (Paris: Desclée de Brouwer, 1995), 104.

9. Thomas O'Loughlin, "Are 'the Bishops ... the "High Priests" Who Preside at the Eucharist'?: A Note on the Sources of the Text of *Sensus Fidei*," *New Blackfriars* 98 (March 2017): 236.

10. Michel-Yves Perrin, "Pratiques et discours eucharistiques dans les premiers siècles (des origines jusqu'à la fin du IVe siècle): Considérations introductives," in *Eucharistia: Encyclopédie de l'eucharistie*, ed. Maurice Brouard (Paris: Cerf, 2002), 110; Niederwimmer, *The Didache: A*

hardly allows us to draw firm conclusions about the minister of the Eucharist. It does not clearly show laymen presiding at Eucharist. Yet if these interpretations hold, then the text confirms three things: (1) there is some regulation over who presides, (2) the one who celebrates also preaches the word, and (3) the one who celebrates also (but not always) shares in the work of governing the community.

Ignatius of Antioch is the first explicit witness to a threefold division of hierarchical ministers, namely, bishops, presbyters, and deacons. This historical fact does not exclude the possibility that this threefold structure existed before Ignatius. However, in the first century, the terminology used for the Church's official ministers was somewhat fluid. In his *Letter to the Smyrnians*, Ignatius reserves the presiding function at Eucharist to the bishop and to those commissioned by the bishop. He explains that every local church has one bishop, assisted by several presbyters and by deacons, who gather around him for the Eucharist, which is the sacrament of unity, the sign and celebration of the members' communion with their bishop, and thus with Christ.[11]

In his *First Apology*, Justin Martyr states that the one who presides over or governs the Church also presides at Eucharist. He does not use specific terms such as *bishop* or *presbyter* to describe this minister.[12] But Eusebius of Caesarea's *Ecclesiastical History* mentions a letter by Irenaeus of Lyon that refers to the Roman Easter liturgy in the year 154, at which the bishop presides.[13] Nothing in Justin's writings about the Sunday Eucharist contradicts Irenaeus's witness.

Writing in the late second century, Tertullian mentions that the presider of the Eucharist presides also over the Church. He speaks of presbyters and ordained persons.[14] After leaving the Church for the Montanist movement, Tertullian composed *The Exhortation to Chastity*, where he

---

Commentary, trans. Linda M. Maloney, Hermeneia: A Critical and Historical Commentary on the Bible (Philadelphia: Fortress Press, 1998), 243–44. See also chapter 13 of the *Didache*.

11. Ignatius of Antioch, "Letter to the Smyrneans," no. 8; Legrand, "La présidence de l'Eucharistie," 413–14.

12. Justin Martyr, *First Apology*, chaps. 65, 67.

13. Eusebius of Caesarea, *Ecclesiastical History*, bk. 5, chap. 24, no. 17, as mentioned in Legrand, "La présidence de l'Eucharistie," 416. See Eusebius of Caesarea, *Ecclesiastical History, Books 1–5*, trans. Roy J. Deferrari (Washington, D.C.: The Catholic University of America Press, 2005).

14. See Tertullian, *De Corona*, chap. 3, no. 3, in Tertullian, *Opera Montanistica*, vol. 2, ed. Aem. Kroymann, CCSL 2 (Turnhout, Belgium: Brepols, 1954), 1043.

states that where ordained ministers are absent, two or three laypersons can gather and celebrate the Eucharist.[15] In early Church history, Tertullian stands isolated on this point. The only known supporting case is found in the practice of some fourth-century lay missionaries to Ethiopia, who apparently celebrated the Eucharist.[16] However, the ancient tradition consistently follows another path.

Hippolytus of Rome's *Apostolic Tradition* gives a fairly detailed description of the Eucharistic celebrant in the episcopal ordination rite. The celebrant is the one who presides over the church, has been elected by the people, and has been ordained and received an apostolic charism. He is compared to the high priest of the Old Testament. Hippolytus is the first Christian writer to use classic sacerdotal language in an explicit way when referring to the Eucharistic presider.[17] For Hippolytus, it is also evident that presbyters can celebrate the Eucharist, for example, when they concelebrate with the bishop immediately after their own ordination. The new Roman Rite for presbyteral ordination has largely integrated this third century prayer of ordination. Here, the charge of shepherding the flock through the Holy Spirit's power is mentioned first, and then comes the task of offering the Church's Eucharistic gifts.[18] Hippolytus's text had considerable influence on other ancient liturgical traditions.[19]

Cyprian of Carthage maintains that only a bishop or presbyter celebrates the Eucharist. This is because the Last Supper serves as the essential model for the Eucharist. Christians are to imitate Christ's celebration of the Last Supper. Thus, just as Christ had a unique role as presider at the Last Supper, so does the priest or bishop at the liturgy. The priest can celebrate the Eucharist because he participates in Christ in a special way. He

15. Tertullian, *De Exhortatione Castitatis*, chap. 7, no. 3, in *Opera Montanistica*, 2:1024–1025.

16. Legrand, "La présidence de l'Eucharistie," 418–19; Legrand refers to Theodoret of Cyrus's *Ecclesiastical History*, bk. 1, chap. 23, no. 5. See Theodoret of Cyrus, *Histoire ecclésiastique*, trans. Pierre Canivet, Sources chrétiennes 501 (Paris: Cerf, 2006).

17. Hippolytus of Rome, *Apostolic Tradition*, nos. 3, 34, as mentioned in Legrand, "La présidence de l'Eucharistie," 416–17. For the text of Hippolytus, see the edition by Paul F. Bradshaw, Maxwell E. Johnson, and L. Edward Phillips, eds., *The Apostolic Tradition: A Commentary*, Hermeneia: A Critical and Historical Commentary on the Bible (Philadelphia: Fortress Press, 2002).

18. Legrand, "La présidence de l'Eucharistie," 422–23.

19. Bernard Botte, "Holy Orders in the Ordination Prayers," in *The Sacrament of Holy Orders: Some Papers and Discussions concerning Holy Orders at a Session of the Centre de Pastorale Liturgique, 1955* (London: Aquin Press, 1957), 19.

is a type or vicar of Christ.[20] Enrico Mazza points out that, for Cyprian, the priest can imitate Christ's role at the Last Supper, for he has received a special outpouring of the Holy Spirit. Hence, the priest's actions become the very actions of Christ. This ensures the identity of the Mass with the Last Supper.[21]

The liturgical scholar Bernard Botte signals that the early rites of priestly ordination tend to make greater reference to the presbyters' cooperation with the bishop in the governance of the local church than to their Eucharistic function. However, the latter function is part of the former, as we will see shortly. Finally, Botte notes that the ancient Byzantine rite of priestly ordination indicates the presbyter's task of offering sacrifice, while one version of the ancient Roman rite of ordination (found in the Gelasian Sacramentary) speaks of the presbyters changing the offering of the people into Christ's body and blood.[22]

Let us consider one major reason for the patristic insistence that a priest or bishop preside at Eucharist. For Ignatius, Tertullian, Hippolytus, and Cyprian, the bishop is the normal presider at the Eucharist because he presides also over the local ecclesial community. Why this link between Eucharistic presiding and shepherding the flock? First and above all, the local Eucharistic assembly was the local Church in act. Thus, the Eucharist was called *synaxis*, which means assembly or gathering. We can see this, for example, in the fourth-century moral and liturgical compilation, the *Apostolic Constitutions*.[23] To attend the Eucharist was to be a member of the Church, and vice versa. To receive the Eucharist was to be in a state of communion with the Church. The sign of being in mortal sin or without the true faith was to be excluded from communion. Receiving the body of Christ meant being in communion with his mystical body, as mediated through the local church. The bishop was responsible for keeping vigil that only those with right faith and Christian morals receive communion. Second, the Eucharistic prayer must reflect the true faith. Before the fourth century, this prayer was usually pronounced without a set text but

20. Cyprian of Carthage, "Letter 63," nos. 2, 10, 14, 17–19.

21. Enrico Mazza, *The Celebration of the Eucharist: The Origin of the Rite and the Development of Its Interpretation*, trans. Matthew J. O'Connell (Collegeville, Minn.: Liturgical Press, 1998), 125–28.

22. Botte, "Holy Orders in the Ordination Prayers," 7–11, 16.

23. *Apostolic Constitutions*, bk. 2, chap. 39, nos. 1–2.

according to a fixed structure.[24] In the fourth and fifth centuries, Eucharistic prayers became the site of theological battles regarding the raging Christological controversies.[25] Only one whose faith has been approved as in harmony with the faith of the bishops can preside. The presider's faith must be the bishop's faith, and the faith of his brother bishops.

I briefly return to Botte's study of ancient rituals for episcopal and presbyteral ordinations. Based on his survey of Hippolytus' *Apostolic Tradition*, the Egyptian ordination ritual Serapion, and the Byzantine and Roman rites, he notes the following theological pattern in these liturgical texts: First, the hierarchy appears as a reality willed by God. Second, the Eucharist is a collective act, not the solitary sacramental deed of one minister (though Botte does not deny a unique role to the minister). Third, the bishops and priests are not delegates of the community, even if the faithful elect them. Fourth, the bishops are successors of the apostles, and thus they can mediate divine gifts. By implication, the presbyters have a share in that succession and privilege of mediation. Fifth, episcopal or presbyteral consecration imparts spiritual gifts, whereby the recipients may build up the Church.[26] Overall, Botte shows that, following the *lex orandi* of these ordination prayers, the ability to celebrate the Eucharist is not delegated by the people, but comes from above. This neatly matches a similar pattern in the New Testament. As Albert Vanhoye has noted, in the New Testament, the Church's ministers are not delegates of the assembly but instruments of Christ.[27]

By the third century, a clear pattern emerges: bishops and presbyters, and no one else, celebrate the Eucharist. First- and second-century evidence does not offer any evident contradiction of this rule (the schismatic Tertullian does not count). The pattern finds explicit confirmation in the regional Council of Arles (314), canon 15, and the Council of Nicaea (325), canon 18.[28] The great fourth-century Fathers confirm this practice.

24. Louis Bouyer, *Eucharist: Theology and Spirituality of the Eucharistic Prayer*, trans. Charles Underhill Quinn (Notre Dame, Ind.: University of Notre Dame Press, 1968), 136.

25. Hervé-Marie Legrand, "Communion ecclésiale et Eucharistie aux premiers siècles," *L'année canonique* 25 (1981): 129–35.

26. Botte, "Holy Orders in the Ordination Prayers," 20–27.

27. Albert Vanhoye, *Prêtres anciens, prêtre nouveau selon le Nouveau Testament* (Paris: Éditions du Seuil, 1980), 316.

28. Ángel García Ibáñez, *L'eucaristia, dono e mistero: Trattato storico-dogmatico sul mistero eucaristico*, Sussidi di teologia (Rome: EDUSC, 2006), 468–69.

Ambrose mentions that the Eucharistic sacrifice is realized by an ordained minister.[29] In the midst of the Donatist controversy, Augustine argues that the minister of the Eucharist is an ordained bishop or priest, regardless of his personal holiness: Christ still acts through him as through his servants.[30]

The last theme shows the close link between Christ's priestly presence at the Eucharist and the presiding function of the bishop or priest. For the Fathers were convinced that Christ himself is the chief celebrant of every Eucharist: he is the host of the sacrificial meal, the heavenly high priest offering a single sacrifice already completed on the Cross in the presence of his Father, the high priest who acts through human instruments here below. Thus, Origen's *Commentary on Matthew* describes the Last Supper as both a past and a present reality. Jesus continues to give food and drink, but now we are his guests or companions at table. Christ even drinks the cup with us, says Origen.[31] In a Holy Thursday homily from the year 400, falsely attributed to Cyril of Alexandria, Theophilus of Alexandria also expounds on the Last Supper as a present reality: the Incarnate Logos invites us to the banquet to feed on his flesh and blood, and there Christ himself hosts and serves us. He is at once the priest and the offering.[32] In his *Mystagogical Catecheses*, Cyril of Jerusalem follows Origen's lead as he refers to Christ's action at the Last Supper as a present, liturgical reality: As Christ once transformed water into wine at the Wedding at Cana, so now he transforms wine into blood. For this reason, we can partake of his flesh and blood with full confidence.[33] The implication is that Christ himself changes the gifts today.[34]

29. Ambrose, *Explanatio Psalmorum* XII, ed. M. Petschenig, Corpus Scriptorum Ecclesiasticorum Latinorum 64 (Vindobonae: Verlag der Österreichischen Akademie der Wissenschaften, 1999), no. 38.25–26, pp. 203–4.

30. Bruce Marshall, "What Is the Eucharist? A Dogmatic Outline," in *The Oxford Handbook of Sacramental Theology*, ed. Hans Boersma and Matthew Levering (Oxford: Oxford University Press, 2015), 506.

31. Origen, *In Matth. Comm.*, sermon 86, quoted in Betz *Die Eucharistie in der Zeit der griechischen Väter*, 1.1:94.

32. Pseudo-Cyril of Alexandria, *Hom. 10 in coenam myst.* (PG 77, 1017CD), quoted in Betz, *Die Eucharistie in der Zeit der griechischen Väter*, 1.1:97.

33. Cyril of Jerusalem, "Mystagogical Lecture 4," [illegible]

34. Johannes Betz, *Die Eucharistie in der Zeit der griechischen Väter*, vol. 1.1: *Die Aktualpräsenz der Person und des Heilswerkes Jesu im Abendmahl nach der vorephesinischen griechischen Patristik* (Freiburg im Breisgau: Herder, 1955), 101–2.

In medieval times, we find important magisterial interventions on the question of who presides at Eucharist. In the face of new popular religious movements, Pope Innocent III and Lateran Council IV (in 1215) taught that only a priest (or bishop) can celebrate Mass.[35] Trent faced Protestant objections to the legitimacy of the sacramental priesthood. In response, the Tridentine *Decree on the Sacrament of Holy Orders* affirmed that Christ transmitted a priestly power to the apostles at the Last Supper, in order that that they (and their successors) could consecrate bread and wine, so that these gifts become Christ's body and blood.[36] Here, the existence of the ministerial priesthood and its origin in Christ was at issue. These doctrines are taken up in the teachings of Vatican II, which I will consider in the next section.[37]

A Systematic Theology of the Eucharistic Celebrant

Our historical survey has shown the consistent practice of having a bishop or a priest celebrate the Eucharist. I noted the patristic doctrine of Christ's priestly presence at Mass. In chapter 3, we saw the traditional teaching that, at the Last Supper, Jesus commissioned the apostles and their successors to celebrate the Eucharist, to "do this in memory of me," a classical reading supported by recent biblical exegesis. Christ imparts to the twelve a commission and a spiritual gift, a call and a spiritual power. This commission and gift continue in the ministry of bishops and priests. Exactly what is this gift and how is it exercised? That question will run through this section.

The present study will proceed in five steps. First, I look to the liturgical prayers for indications on the function of the minister. Second, I will discuss the minister's instrumental, metaphysical causality. Third, I will take up the theme of representation, as I expand on the treatment of this topic from the study of Eucharistic sacrifice. This includes a study of how the priest represents the Church, a much-debated issue. Fourth, I extend the last point by pondering the celebrant's relation to the people, in light

35. Lateran Council IV, *De fide Catholica*, DH 802.

36. Council of Trent, DH 1771; García Ibáñez, *L'eucaristia, dono e mistero*, 470–71.

37. See, for example, *Lumen Gentium*, nos. 10–11, 21, 28; *Presbyterorum Ordinis*, no. 2.

of Vatican II. Finally, I will offer a brief treatment of disputed questions surrounding concelebration.

Lex orandi and the Celebrant of the Eucharist

The Eucharistic prayers manifest a twofold pattern for the celebrant's action. I will base my argument on the Roman rite, but the same pattern can easily be found in other liturgical families. I will then consider the significance of this pattern in light of other theological doctrines, especially Christology and general principles of sacramental theology. The liturgy is a source of theology, yet we should note that, just as we read Scripture with the lens of the creeds and the metaphysical theologies that support them, so we interpret the liturgy.

In the epiclesis, the presider begs God the Father to send his Holy Spirit upon the gifts so that they may become Christ's body and blood. The priest makes a request, one that will surely be accepted by God. The prayer expresses the priest's utter subordination to God. The epiclesis is said in the plural form, for the priest acts on behalf of the entire Church. In the name of the Church, he asks that the Spirit come onto the gifts. The liturgy shows the priest to be a servant of the Church in the very act of presiding at the Eucharist.

At the words of institution, the celebrant does not say "This is Christ's body," but "This is my body." The priest's prayer is unique, for nowhere else does he seem to be as fused with Christ himself. The closest instance would be the Roman rite's formula of absolution in sacramental reconciliation, where the priest says: "I absolve you from your sins."

Finally, throughout the Eucharistic prayer (in the various liturgical families of east and west), the presider consistently speaks in the first-person plural. As he utters prayers of praise, petition and thanksgiving, he addresses the Father with formula such as "We offer to you …" or "Almighty God, we pray …." Here too, the priest speaks for the whole Church.

We have two types of liturgical formulas that point to the priest's unique role. First, at the epiclesis, the priest expresses his and the Church's complete dependence on the Spirit. In the prayers that precede and follow the consecration, he speaks to God the Father in the name of the whole Church. Here, we have the priest and the Church praying to God.

Second, at the consecration, the priest manifests his radical identity with Christ.[38]

The Instrumental Causality of the Priest: Acting *in persona Christi*

The celebrant's action at Mass involves an extension of Christ's priestly ministry. Few have shown this as well as Aquinas. For Thomas, the mode of Christ's action in the priest at Mass follows (analogously) from the manner in which Christ's divine power worked through his sacred humanity during his ministry on earth. Earlier, we studied the instrumental activity of Christ's humanity: grace or a share in divine life are poured out through his human words and deeds, by the actions of his human mind and heart, soul and body. That is, Christ's two natures do not operate in parallel fashion. This metaphysical Christology, with its roots in the Greek Fathers and great Christological councils (from Ephesus to Constantinople III) sheds light on how we are saved through Christ's humanity. The same metaphysical Christology illumines the celebrant's mediating work at Mass.

Aquinas grounds the Church's cultic acts in Christ's priesthood.[39] This ensures that her sacrifice is in fact none other than Christ's. One way we share in his priestly work is by an extension of his instrumental activity to the liturgy itself. That is, ritual words and deeds share in the instrumental power of Christ's human words and deeds. The most powerful instance of this participation is found in the priest's consecration of the Eucharistic gifts.[40]

Thomas refuses the stance of Bonaventure and perhaps others who separate the consecration into two parallel acts, the transforming, invisible work of the uncreated Word and the words of the priest.[41] Aquinas

38. Cesare Giraudo disagrees with this approach and argues that the Church speaks by the priest throughout the Eucharistic prayer, including the words of institution (so that the first type of prayer mentioned above includes the second). Below, I will show why this position cannot hold. See Giraudo, "'In persona Christi' 'In persona Ecclesiae': Formule eucaristiche alla luce della 'lex orandi,'" *Rassegna Teologia* 51 (2010): 189–95.

39. Thomas Aquinas, *Summa theologiae* III, q. 22, a. 4.

40. Thomas Aquinas, *Summa theologiae* III, q. 78, a. 1, ad 1.

41. Bonaventure, *On the Eucharist: Commentary on the Sentences, Book IV, Dist. 8–13*, trans. Junius Johnson, Dallas Medieval Texts and Translations 23 (Leuven, Belgium: Peeters, 2017), d. 10, part 2, a. 1, q. 3.

holds that God does not work alongside the liturgical rite but through it. Speaking of the words of institution, Thomas says:

> there is in the words of the formulae of this sacrament a created power which causes the change to be wrought in it: an instrumental power, however, as in the other sacraments, as was stated above [question 62, articles 3–4]. For since these words are uttered from the person of Christ, it is from His command that they receive their instrumental power from Christ, just as his other deeds and sayings have their salutary power instrumentally, as noted above [question 48, article 6; question 56, article 1].[42]

Christ's command at the Last Supper to "do this" in his memory includes a promise that his power will be active in the Eucharistic liturgy. Ambrose explained the change of the Eucharistic gifts by appealing to the creative power of Christ's words. At the beginning of the quotation above, Thomas seems to extend Ambrose's insight. The words of consecration participate in the re-creative power of God's word. The same power that was active in Jesus' human words and gestures at the Last Supper remains active today.[43]

Aquinas later locates this power in the signification. Evidently, the latter is actualized through particular ritual words and deeds, but the words themselves have no magical force.[44] Rather, they are powerful only insofar as they signify. The signification is fruitful because Christ (and the minister who acts in his person) signifies by the power of his divine nature. The liturgical words are the means to signify Christ's saving deed. The Lord's creative word primarily acts in the communication of meaning, not via physical sounds floating in the air.

When Aquinas directly treats the question of the minister of this sacrament, he begins with the consecration. That is, the priest's action in the liturgy manifests his being.

> this sacrament [of the Eucharist] is of such dignity that it is confected only in the person of Christ. Now whoever does something in the person of another, must have a power conceded from the other ... when the priest is ordained, a power is conferred to him to consecrate this sacrament in the person of Christ; for in this

42. Thomas Aquinas, *Summa theologiae* III, q. 78, a. 4.
43. Thomas Aquinas, *Summa theologiae* III, q. 78, a. 1, ad 1.
44. Thomas Aquinas, *Summa theologiae* III, q. 78, a. 4, ad 3.

way is he placed in the position of those to whom it was said by the Lord: "Do this in memory of me."[45]

To confect means to consecrate. Within the sacramental order, where words and gestures share instrumentally in Christ's sanctifying power, the phrases "This is my body ... this is my blood," bear a spiritual power. But how can one utter these words in the first-person singular? How can one speak in Christ's voice and spiritually effect his body and blood? It is only if one has received authority and the instrumental power to speak as Christ does. The term "power" refers to the priest's unique relation, as minister and instrument, to Christ. We need to understand "power" in the biblical and philosophical sense (as in Jesus' power to heal), and not the usual political sense that the word has today. The priest has been changed so as to render a new service to the mystical body. Unlike baptism, where the words and gestures alone bear an instrumental spiritual power, the consecration comes about by (1) the spiritual power of words and deeds (the means of signification), and by (2) an instrumental power given to the minister.[46] The last element follows from the unique form of the consecratory words: the presider who says "This is my body" and thereby brings Christ's body unto the altar must be united to Jesus in a unique way. Thus, in the consecration, we have two instruments: the power to act in the name of Christ (which the priest received at ordination), and the power of the Lord's words (joined to the priest's intention). We have a stable power and a passing power. Christ acts through both instruments, one joined to the other. Now because of its instrumental status, the priest's power is actualized by Christ and stands in complete dependence on Christ.[47] That is, because Christ is intensely active as principal cause, the priest's act of consecrating can and does instrumentally effect the change of the gifts on the altar. Christ and his minister act together to produce a single effect: bread and wine substance are converted into the body and blood. The effect comes wholly from Christ and wholly from the minister. Each retains his own operation: the voice is the min-

45. Thomas Aquinas, *Summa theologiae* III, q. 82, a. 1.

46. Thomas Aquinas, *Summa theologiae* III, q. 82, a. 1, ad 1.

47. Bruce D. Marshall, "The Whole Mystery of Our Salvation: Saint Thomas Aquinas on the Eucharist as Sacrifice," in *Rediscovering Aquinas and the Sacraments: Studies in Sacramental Theology*, ed. Michael Dauphinais and Matthew Levering (Chicago: Hillenbrand Books, 2009), 59–62.

ister's, the gesture and the intention he formulates to celebrate Mass are his, while the principal (and thus sufficient) power to change the gifts is Christ's.

We have just linked the mystery of the Incarnation with the mystery of the priest as Eucharistic celebrant. We now look to another connection, that of the priest and the mystery of the Church. This helps us to contemplate anew another aspect of the saving economy.

The Instrumentality of the Priest: Acting *in persona Ecclesiae*

In the consecration, we ponder Christ's and the priest's downward mediation whereby the gifts of Jesus' body and blood are brought to us. Here, a sacrament is completed, in which the Father brings his Son and a share in divine life to his people, two gifts that enable us in turn to make an offering to him and to give him right worship. In the rest of the Eucharistic prayer, we especially ponder Christ's and the priest's upward mediation, as they offer the people's praise and thanksgiving, adoration and intercession to the Father, together with the body and blood of the victim. In the consecration, the priest acts in the person of Christ, but elsewhere in the Eucharistic prayer, he acts in the person of the Church.[48] By his ordination, the priest has been conformed to Christ the head. When he abides in communion with the Church through faith and in unity with the pope and bishops, the priest can act with her, such that his liturgical acts are simultaneously the Church's acts. Unity with the pope and bishops involves the concrete realization of ecclesial communion. The Eucharistic prayers mention communion with the pope and bishops, for this is one condition for offering sacrifice in the name of the Church. There is a deputation, but not so as to act *in place of* Christ or the Church. Rather, the priest celebrates in Christ the head and with Jesus' members. Behind this vision stands a patristic and medieval notion of representation.[49] Christ and the Church act through the minister in unique ways: (1) Jesus as a metaphysical cause directly moves the priest to realize the sacrament, and (2) the Church as a moral cause, and as Christ's mystical body, offers to the

48. Bernard Dominique Marliangeas, *Clés pour une théologie du ministère: In persona Christi, in persona Ecclesiae*, Théologie historique 51 (Paris: Beauchesne, 1978), 131.

49. Marliangeas, *Clés pour une théologie du ministère*, 128, 138.

Father the sacrifice of her head.[50] The petitions offered to God in the Eucharistic prayer are accepted by him as coming from the whole Church.[51] She supplies what is lacking in the minister's faith and holiness.[52] This theological principle explains (1) how the Mass of a schismatic priest can have the substantial presence of Christ's body and blood, though it cannot constitute an offering pleasing to the Father, and (2) how the liturgical prayers of a weak priest can be as fruitful as the liturgical prayers of a holy priest. As Thomas explains:

> The prayer said at Mass can be considered in two ways. In one way, inasmuch as it has efficacy from the devotion of the priest who is praying. And thus, there is no doubt that the Mass of a better priest is more fruitful [than the Mass of a sinful priest]. In another way, the prayer said at Mass [can be considered] inasmuch as it is offered by the priest in the person of the whole Church, whose minister the priest is. This ministry also remains in sinners, as was said above about Christ's ministry [being active in sinful priests when they consecrate the Eucharist]. Hence, also in this way, not only is the prayer of the sinful priest said at Mass fruitful, but also all of his prayers which he does in the ecclesiastical offices are fruitful, in which he bears the person of the Church. Although his private prayers are not fruitful, according to Proverbs 28:9: "He who has turned away his ears from hearing the law, his prayers will be an abomination."[53]

Jean-Pierre Torrell shows how Vatican II integrates and develops Aquinas's vision of the priest acting in the person of the Church. First, the priest does not act in his own name. Rather, "He is just the representative, and, in reality, it is the One he represents who acts through him, with the qualities, the rights, and the efficaciousness that are all his own ... it is the entire body that is acting through him."[54] Second, there is a deep unity between the priest's action in the person of Christ and in the person of the Church, so that the latter is part of the former. Third, it follows from the previous two points that the Church is the true subject of the liturgical act.[55] The liturgy is "an action of Christ the priest and of his body."[56]

50. Christ is an efficient cause of transubstantiation, and the Church's moral causality is a kind of final causality.

51. Thomas Aquinas, *Summa theologiae* III, q. 82, a. 7, ad 3.

52. Thomas Aquinas, *Summa theologiae* III, q. 64, a. 9, ad 1.

53. Thomas Aquinas, *Summa theologiae* III, q. 82, a. 6.

54. Torrell, *A Priestly People*, 148.

55. Torrell, *A Priestly People*, 148–49.

56. *Sacrosanctum Concilium*, no. 7.

Here, the notion of representation is key: we need to explore it further, especially with regard to the question of the priest's gender.

Representing Christ and the Church

In the liturgy, *to act* in the person of another is also *to represent* him. The former notion highlights a metaphysical link with another, while the latter theme highlights a relation by signification: the two are, in fact, inseparable. The Eucharistic celebrant represents Christ and the Church. The minister primarily represents Christ at the consecration (where the sacrament is realized, as God's gift to us), and he primarily represents the Church during the rest of the Eucharistic prayer (where the consecrated gift is given back to the Father in sacrifice, our gift to him). This claim is disputed, so we need to see why this is the case. Among other things, it pertains directly to the issue of the male priesthood.

First, at the consecration, the priest does not simply quote Christ, for he is more than an ambassador who speaks in the place of another. In the liturgical readings, we also quote Christ, so the minister's act of speaking at the consecration must involve more than an act of quotation.[57] In addition, the priest needs to apply these words to the gifts on the altar. For as a quote, Christ's words pertain only to the gifts in his hands at the Last Supper two thousand years ago. But the priest prays the words as pertaining to the gifts in his hands today. Aquinas calls this "praying by mode of signification" and not just by mode of recitation.[58] Also, the priest's function is not simply to repeat someone else's words, but to speak as a free, rational individual, with the intention of celebrating according to the Church's intention, in imitation of Jesus at the Last Supper. The priest images Christ himself in a way that befits our dignity as beings created in God's image, with reason and freedom.

Second, at the consecration, the priest utters words that belong to Christ, and not to the Church. For if the Church were the primary subject speaking at the consecration, then in saying "This is my body," the

57. Sara Butler, "*In Persona Christi*: A Response to Dennis M. Ferrara," *Theological Studies* 56 (1995): 69–76.

58. Thomas Aquinas, *Commentary on the Sentences*, bk. 4, d. 8, q. 2, a. 1, quaestiuncula 4, ad 4, in *Commentary on the Sentences, Book IV, Distinctions 1–13*, trans. Beth Mortensen, Latin/English Edition of the Works of St. Thomas Aquinas 7 (Green Bay, Wisc.: Aquinas Institute, 2017); *Summa theologiae* III, q. 78, a. 5; Butler, "*In Persona Christi*: A Response," 71–72.

minister's words would no longer be true, since the Church's body and blood are not on the altar, except by mode of sign.[59] The Church has a corporeal body insofar as her members have bodies, and our bodies enlivened by grace are not on the altar, they are in the pews or next to the altar. It is true that the consecrated hosts and cup signify the Church, but the gifts identified at the consecration are not the corporeal presence of the Church. Rather, the gifts on the altar signify and substantially contain Christ's body, while the same gifts signify the Church and her unity, through the many grains joined in one host, and many grapes joined in one cup.

Third, during the consecration, the priest represents Christ at the Last Supper speaking to the apostles, who represent the twelve tribes of Israel. So, in a way, the priest represents Christ speaking to the whole Church. Thus, when the celebrant says "This is my body," he represents Christ speaking to the Church *as distinct from him*. It is not Christ and the Church who together say, "This is my body." Rather, by these words, Christ addresses the Church (represented at the Last Supper by the apostles). Now if the priest represents Christ speaking to the Church, then he represents Christ the head speaking to the mystical body, the ecclesial body, which is represented by all those present at Mass. Indeed, Vatican II's *Presbyterorum Ordinis* states that, by his priestly ordination, the priest acts in the person of Christ the head. But this implies that he acts as distinct from the mystical body.[60]

This doctrine leads directly to another: at Mass, the priest represents Christ the bridegroom. The images of head and bridegroom are closely linked, as we see in St. Paul's Letter to the Ephesians:

> For the husband is the head of the wife as Christ is head of the Church, his body.... Husbands love your wives, as Christ loved the church and gave himself up for her ... no man ever hates his own flesh, but nourishes and cherishes it, as Christ does the church, because we are members of his body (Eph 5:23, 25, 29–30).

Christian marriage involves a relation of love to another as to one's own flesh, because of the charity by which Christ the head loves his own

59. Guy Mansini, "Representation and Agency in the Eucharist," in *The Word Has Dwelt among Us: Explorations in Theology* (Naples, Fla.: Sapientia Press, 2008), 148.

60. *Presbyterorum Ordinis*, no. 2.

mystical body. In the case of Jesus, this relation leads to his complete self-offering for his spouse, even unto death. On the Cross, Christ gave himself up for the Church, offering up his body for her. More than anywhere else, this self-offering is symbolized in the consecration, where Christ's body and blood are separated in sign, thus making the sacrifice of the Cross present. Here, at Mass, the speaker is Christ in his act of self-giving at the Last Supper, which in turn signifies the gift of his life on the Cross. At the Last Supper, Jesus spoke to the Church, saying: "This is my body, which will be given up for *you*." The priest symbolizes this act. Also, the Eucharist and all the sacraments ensure the spiritual fruitfulness of the Church, which is the finality of Christ's mystical marriage to his ecclesial bride. Hence, the Eucharist as the greatest sacrament is celebrated by one who represents Christ as bridegroom, the one who fructifies the Church.[61] The Mass is filled with spousal imagery. At the Cross, Christ the Bridegroom offered his body for his mystical Bride. Albertus Magnus gives us a marvelous image of Jesus at the Last Supper: "For he held himself in his hands, and he fed his intimate friends with himself and so, as if inebriated by their sweetness and charity, has nothing of himself in which his most beloved will not share."[62] At Mass, the Cross is made present, and the Bridegroom offers to the Church his very own body to eat, thus renewing their corporeal union, the consummation of their mystical marriage, the union of their very bodies.

The images of spousal union and the fruitfulness of Christ's sacrifice for his bride come together in the eschatological aspect of the Mass: Christ's mystical marriage is an invisible reality that is signified in the Mass, so that the Eucharistic liturgy is a participation in the wedding feast

61. Alejandro Blas Miquel Ciarrochi, "Sponsus Ecclesiae, sicut Christus: Sobre il simbolismo nupcial del sacerdote dese Hugo de San Víctor hasta Santo Tomás de Aquino" (Dissertation, John Paul II Pontifical Institute for the Study of Marriage and Family, Pontifical Lateran University, 2015), 310, 320.

62. Albertus Magnus, *On the Body of the Lord*, trans. Albert Marie Surmanski, The Fathers of the Church: Mediaeval Continuation 17 (Washington, D.C.: The Catholic University of America Press, 2017), d. 1, chap. 3, 51. In his biblical commentaries, Albert presents the figures of the apostles, as well as every person's friendship with Christ, through the lens of bridal mysticism. For his treatment of the apostles, see Albert's comments on Matthew 4:20 in his *Super Matthaeum, Capitula I-XIV*, ed. Bernhard Schmidt, Cologne Edition 21.1 (Münster, Germany: Aschendorff Verlag, 1987), chap. 4, p. 97b. On friendship with Christ, see Albert's exposition of John 21:7–9 in his *Enarrationes in Joannem*, Borgnet Edition 24 (Paris, 1899), 704b–706a.

of the Lamb, the celestial liturgy that has already begun.[63] To signify this marriage, the priest represents Christ to the Church as a living sign. Here, the importance of the Son of God choosing to become man and not woman emerges. We thus also see the importance of the male priesthood.[64] One might be tempted to say: "But it is only a sign." Indeed, it is a sign, and therefore, everything depends on it! Thus, we need a man to represent Christ as bridegroom: we need a male priesthood. Without it, we would have Christ as Bride speaking to the Bride, which simply destroys the spousal imagery. The doctrine of the male priesthood and marriage as a union of man and woman go together. By consummating her mystical marriage again with Christ in corporeal, Eucharistic union, the Church becomes fruitful, bringing to life new children, adopted sons and daughters of the Heavenly Father. A Church with female priests would be unable to signify its dependence on Christ her head. In the realm of grace, what is not signified is lost. This logic transcends the question of egalitarianism, for in the sacramental order, equality does not entail identical functions, as we also see in marriage and family life.

It turns out that nuptiality and headship are interchangeable. The priest shares in Christ's nuptial relation to the Church: representation follows upon the priest's metaphysical conformity to Christ the High Priest, to Christ as Bridegroom, which occurs at priestly ordination. The bishop shares in the spousal relation to the Church even more than does the priest: this is signified by his Episcopal ring, a sign of mystical espousal.[65]

The Celebrant's Relation to the People

The previous considerations remain incomplete, for they risk giving the impression that the Eucharistic celebrant's main function is simply to do something on behalf of the people, as if he acted without them. But Vatican II's teaching on the liturgy and priesthood recovered a broader patristic vision of Eucharistic celebration that integrates more clearly the actions of priest and people. This vision complements well our study of

63. *Sacrosanctum Concilium*, no. 8.

64. Guy Mansini and Lawrence Welch, "The Durable Synthesis of *Presbyterorum Ordinis*," 241–45, in *The Word Has Dwelt among Us: Explorations in Theology*, by Guy Mansini (Naples, Fla.: Sapientia Press, 2008), 213–56.

65. Thomas Aquinas, *Commentary on the Sentences*, bk. 4, d. 24, q. 3, a. 2, quaestincula 1, ad 3; q. 3, a. 3c; *Summa theologiae* III, q. 8, a. 6, ad 3; Miquel Ciarrochi, *Sponsus Ecclesiae*, 310–11, 327, 334.

Eucharistic sacrifice and the essential role for the Church's offering of love to receive the fruits of the Cross.

The priestly ministry is intimately related to the common priesthood of believers. In Vatican II's *Decree on the Ministry and Life of Priests*, we read:

> Since they share in the function of the apostles in their own degree, priests are given the grace by God to be the ministers of Jesus Christ among the nations, fulfilling the sacred task of the Gospel, that the oblation of the gentiles may be acceptable and sanctified in the Holy Spirit. For it is by the apostolic herald of the Gospel that the People of God is called together and gathered so that all who belong to this people, sanctified as they are by the Holy Spirit, may offer themselves "a living sacrifice, holy and acceptable to God" (Romans 12:1). Through the ministry of priests the spiritual sacrifice of the faithful is completed in union with the sacrifice of Christ the only mediator, which in the Eucharist is offered through the priests' hands in the name of the whole Church in an un-bloody and sacramental manner.... For their ministration, which begins with the announcement of the Gospel, draws its force and power from the sacrifice of Christ and tends to this.[66]

The preaching and teaching of the bishops and priests guide believers to order their lives, so as to progress in the imitation of Christ, that is, in the whole life of virtue, especially charity. All virtuous acts done in grace already please God (including the good deeds of those who have implicit faith, and dwell beyond the bounds of the visible Church), but these acts become part of the perfect sacrifice when believers intentionally join their daily good deeds and sufferings to the offering of Christ on the altar. The priest is far more than a person ordained to say Mass, for he is also sent to assist the bishop in his prophetic and royal office of shepherding, whose finality is to lead the pilgrim people of God toward greater holiness.[67]

Paragraph 10 of *Lumen Gentium* teaches that the ministerial and common priesthood of believers are ordered to one another. That is, the

66. *Presbyterorum Ordinis*, no. 2.

67. Damien Logue helpfully reads *Presbyterorum Ordinis* (nos. 4 and 13) to teach that the priest's first role (in the order of generation) is preaching, but its purpose is the perfect spiritual sacrifice of believers, so that the priest's primary role (in the metaphysical order) is the celebration of the Eucharist. See Logue, "Le premier et le principal du sacrement de l'ordre," in *Questions disputées autour du sacrement de l'ordre*, ed. Philippe-Marie Margelidon, Sed Contra (Perpignan, France: Artège Lethielleux 2018), 111.

minister's identity is to serve the people, whom he leads and forms to offer pleasing sacrifice, while the people exercise their royal priesthood in their whole life, as they bring the Gospel to the world and join in the Eucharistic sacrifice, by offering themselves and Christ's body and blood to the Father with and through the priest. *Lumen Gentium* adds that their mode of offering is distinct from the priest's.[68] There are two ways of participating in Christ's priesthood; such a distinction is not a question of higher or lower, but of diverse modes of sharing in Christ's priestly activity.[69]

Vatican II's teaching on the active, conscious participation of the faithful at Mass finds a direct link with the union of their spiritual sacrifices and the offering of Christ's body and blood. That is, the faithful are not passive recipients of an offering made by the priest alone. Rather, they offer themselves and their secular activities, join their minds and hearts to the priest's prayer, and manifest their participation in the sacrifice by making the responses, which also signify their participation in the sacrifice.[70] In the Old Testament, the whole people offer sacrifice to God by the minister. We might also recall Augustine's vision of the Eucharist, where the head is not offered without the members.[71] This joint offering is signified by the presence and participation of the people. Hence a "private Mass" without an acolyte remains an exception, for while it is a true offering (as the priest acts in the person of Christ and of the Church), the people are not adequately represented. We might also note that a Mass with only a priest and acolyte enjoys a venerable tradition in the West. The presence of other members of the community is not essential for representation, since the acolyte represents the Church, and not a local community. The Mass is the sacrifice of the whole Church, and not one group within the Church.

Presbyterorum Ordinis, number 2, teaches that bishops and priests enact their entire ministry in the person of Christ the head. That is, while such action finds its preeminent form in the sacraments, it is not limited to that realm. This doctrinal development of Vatican II, taken together

68. *Lumen Gentium*, no. 11.

69. Torrell, *A Priestly People*, 140–41. For a fuller (and excellent) study of the common priesthood of the faithful and their sacrificial acts, see Lawrence Feingold, *The Eucharist: Mystery of Presence, Sacrifice and Communion* (Steubenville, Ohio: Emmaus Academic, 2018), chap. 11.

70. *Sacrosanctum Concilium*, no. 14; *Lumen Gentium*, no. 34; *Presbyterorum Ordinis*, no. 5.

71. Augustine, *City of God*, bk. 10, chap. 6; Feingold, *The Eucharist*, 411, 415.

with our previous considerations on the relation of priest and people, leads to the following insight: the idea that a priest would leave the decision of a person's worthiness or proper disposition for communion *solely* to the discretion of the individual's conscience (and so withhold the application of the Church's established moral tradition and sacramental discipline) ultimately turns Vatican II's teaching on the presbyterate upside down.[72] For it essentially nullifies the priest's ministry of prophet and shepherd in the person of Christ the head, so that a member of the body acts alone on a matter directly pertaining to his or her manner of sharing in the Church's worship. This approach reduces the priest to a sacramental minister, thus creating the very division in the priest's ministerial life that Vatican II sought to avoid. It also negates the ancient tradition that the presider at Eucharist governs (or shares in the governance of) the assembly. Furthermore, a bishop who decides to leave such decisions solely to the individual's conscience does not act as shepherd but abdicates part of his own exercise of the royal office. Here, the stakes are high.

Concelebration

Many questions surround the contemporary practice of concelebration. What is its spiritual value? Should individual Masses be preferred? If many priests are present, is it best for one to celebrate while other priests simply attend Mass and not celebrate that day? What did Vatican II call for?

The practice of Eucharistic concelebration can be found in various witnesses of the ancient Church, starting with Ignatius of Antioch and Hippolytus of Rome (third century). Among the ancient testimonies, we consistently find a reference to priests celebrating with their bishop, so that the entire local Church gathered in a single liturgical act. This act expresses and actualizes the collegial nature of the priesthood, and the priests' union with their bishop. There are many gaps in the historical data.[73] However, we find no clear evidence of a widespread ancient practice

72. The Church's sacramental discipline has never been primarily guided by the individual's conscience, since this privatizes the sacraments, which are by their nature public acts, acts that manifest the Church's faith and moral convictions about the essential aspects of the following of Christ. Here, Paul's pastoral instructions in 1 Corinthians are an essential guide.

73. P. Tihon, "De la concélébration eucharistique," *Nouvelle revue théologique* 86 (1964): 580–89.

of frequent concelebration of priests without their bishop. Also, the ancient Church did not reflect extensively on the fruits of the Eucharistic sacrifice, which is ultimately crucial for the doctrine and practice of concelebration. The east never ceased the practice of concelebration, a practice that must be respected.

The majority of theologians and liturgists agree that a concelebrated Mass remains a single sacrifice, regardless of the number of concelebrants. It is not many Masses. For the ancient east, this doctrine follows from the purpose of concelebration: one altar, one sacrifice, one shared act of celebrating to manifest the unity of the celebrants. Leading twentieth-century scholars of liturgy such as Lambert Beauduin and Bernard Botte maintain that this doctrine still holds.[74] Leading theologians who promote the frequent use of concelebration (e.g., Karl Rahner) as well as theologians who critique the newer practice (e.g., Joseph de Sainte-Marie) agree with this judgment.[75] It is also the judgment of the Sacred Congregation of Rites in its 1965 decree *Ecclesiae semper*, which speaks of the concelebrants making the offering by one sacramental act.[76] No magisterial text published since then contradicts this position. Nor has any convincing theological argument been made that there are as many sacrifices as there are concelebrants.

Ecclesiae semper presupposes the teaching of Pius XII, who in turn summarized a longstanding theological consensus. The basic principle articulated by Pius XII is as follows: each Mass is a distinct sacramental representation of the Cross, and thus a distinct application, here and now, of the fruits of the Cross to the Church. In a 1954 discourse, Pius XII noted that in each Mass, Christ acts anew by the celebrating priest (a doctrine rooted in the practice of saying several Masses for a single intention, a custom followed by Gregory the Great and countless priest saints after

74. Lambert Beauduin, "La concélébration," *La maison de Dieu* 7, no. 3 (1946): 7–26; Bernard Botte, "Note historique sur la concélébration dans l'église ancienne," *La maison de Dieu* 35, no. 3 (1953): 13.

75. Karl Rahner, *Die vielen Messen und das eine Opfer: Versionen 1949/1951 & 1966*, Sämtliche Werke 18: Leiblichkeit der Gnade, Schriften zur Sakramentenlehre (Freiburg im Breisgau: Herder, 2003); Joseph de Sainte-Marie, *The Holy Eucharist, The World's Salvation: Studies on the Holy Sacrifice of the Mass, Its Celebration and Its Concelebration*, (Leominster, England: Gracewing, 2015), chaps. 1–3.

76. Sacred Congregation of Rites, *Ecclesiae semper*, March 7, 1965, *AAS* 57 (1965), 410–12.

him).[77] That is, Christ's act of self-offering becomes present now. Hence, this act has a different value from a priest's devout attendance at Mass (contrary to a theory promoted by Rahner).[78] In a 1956 discourse, Pius XII explains that, in a concelebrated Mass, Christ simply acts through many ministers, who act as one.[79] This implies that the number of sacrifices is not multiplied, for in a single Eucharistic liturgy, Christ acts as one through many instruments. Given this implication, it follows that the concelebrants truly consecrate and offer the sacrifice, but they accomplish one sacramental sacrifice, not many. Distinct Masses multiply the presence *to us* of Christ's sacrificial act. But in a single Mass, only one such act is made present, either via one minister or via several. *Ecclesia semper* and subsequent magisterial texts are wholly in line with this reading of Pius XII's 1956 address.[80]

The notion of Christ's performing a single act through the concelebrants is explicitly sustained by Aquinas. Like Innocent III, he held that the concelebrants consecrate the host together, in opposition to the idea that only the principal celebrant consecrates.[81] In other words, there is a single act of making the victim present on the altar (by the separate consecration of bread and wine into the body and blood). After the consecration of the cup is completed, a single perfect offering is made by all the concelebrants (and by the people through them). The concelebrants then commune in the same sacramental victim. We see that the act of consecrating is one, the act of offering is one, and the act of the priests uniting themselves with the victim on behalf of the Church remains one, for they

77. Pius XII, "Allocutio, November 2, 1954," *AAS* 46 (1954), 669.

78. Rudolf Michael Schmitz, "La concelebrazione eucaristica," in *Il mistero eucaristico*, ed. Antonio Piolanti, Pontificia Accademia Teologica Romana (Vatican City: Libreria Editrice Vaticana, 1983), 502.

79. Pius XII, "Address, September 22, 1956," *AAS* 48 (1956), 717–18.

80. Joseph de Sainte-Marie, *The Holy Eucharist, The World's Salvation*, 6–12, 16–20. Paul Tirot argues that Pius XII and *Ecclesia semper* imply a virtual multiplicity of sacrificial offerings within the single sacramental offering of the concelebrants, an implication that is not clearly in the texts. Also, the standard reading of Aquinas sees one sacrifice that is wholly offered by each concelebrant, just as each concelebrant instrumentally operates the whole consecration, without multiplying sacrifices. That reading may well stand behind Pius XII's address. See Paul Tirot, "La concélébration et la tradition de l'Église," *Ephemerides liturgicae* 101 (1987): 50–52.

81. Thomas Aquinas, *Summa theologiae* III, q. 82, a. 2. The issue was debated in the thirteenth century. For example, Albert the Great took the opposite position in his *On the Body of the Lord*, d. 6, tractate 4, chap. 2.

partake in the victim jointly made present and jointly offered. In other words, there is no sufficient element in the ritual to multiply sacrificial acts. Francisco Suárez and his disciples sought to find such an element by appealing to the priest's intention, but this argument falls short, since a sacramental act is both interior and exterior.[82]

At Mass, Christ celebrates through the priest, and this impedes us from placing neat limits on the fruitfulness of any one Mass. Yet the Church does not receive infinite fruits from a single Mass, since we always bring particular intentions to Mass, and those fruits are poured out according to the fervor of devotion present in the Church militant (the receptivity of the Church's heart). Jesus' sacrifice was completed on the Cross, and he has saved the world, yet the spiritual effects of the Passion are applied or realized in particular circumstances by our participation therein. At Mass, our exterior, sacramental sacrificial act is the instrument whereby Christ acts, and the interior offering of love the means by which we receive his action. The fruits of the Passion are also distributed in the world by countless other instruments, from fasting and corporal acts of mercy to holy hours. As the instruments multiply, so do the fruits.[83]

Now because the received fruits of a single Mass cannot be clearly limited and are abundant, the Church remains free to allow concelebrants to accept a stipend and a particular intention for their sacerdotal participation in the Mass. We cannot precisely measure grace. And yet, we know that grace has degrees of abundance: a fervent *Our Father* brings fewer blessings than a whole vespers service celebrated with the same fervor. Thus, we can say that two Masses bring greater fruit than one Mass, without knowing precisely how much greater.[84] At the same time, we need to remember the different ecclesiology of the east, which has supported the continued practice of concelebration, and thus not rush to identify a medieval and modern Latin liturgical practice as inherently superior to that of the east.

Vatican II honors the ancient practice of concelebration as a sign of

82. Joseph de Sainte-Marie, *The Holy Eucharist, The World's Salvation*, 46–47.

83. Here, it is good to recall the Calvary is not a potential sacrifice that is then actualized by the Mass, but rather a sacrifice whose power is always actual in the world via many instruments and intermediaries.

84. For the canonical aspects of concelebration and Mass stipends, see Guillaume Derville, *Eucharistic Concelebration: From Symbol to Reality* (Montreal, Canada: Wilson & Lafleur, 2011).

the unity of the priesthood and called for its reintroduction. *Sacrosanctum Concilium* mentions a few particular circumstances in which concelebration is desirable (such as the Chrism Mass and Holy Thursday Mass) and leaves other applications to the judgment of the ordinary.[85] The same text notes that each priest retains the right to celebrate Mass individually. The decree *Ecclesiae semper* was issued to implement *Sacrosanctum Concilium*. The decree notes that two characteristics—(1) the unity of the priesthood and (2) the Mass as the action of the whole people of God—are better manifested in concelebrated Masses than in Masses celebrated by a single priest. The document favors a greater use of concelebration, without precision.

No conciliar or post-conciliar magisterial document proposes an alternative to the theology of the fruits of the Mass summarized above. In fact, the main alternative was offered by Karl Rahner in his influential work, *The Many Masses and the One Sacrifice*, first published in 1949 and revised with Rahner's approval by his disciple Angelus Häussling in 1966. The earlier editions of the work render the relation of Christ's sacrificial act to the priest's act ambiguous. The book's second edition reduces the priest's ritual act to a mere sign. That is, for Rahner, each Mass is only a symbol of Christ's sacrifice, and the priest's act constitutes no new application or making present of that sacrifice. The only element that determines the reception of the fruits of Calvary today is the devotion elicited by the Mass. Rahner seems to focus or even limit that devotion to those physically present at Mass. He thus makes two radical claims: (1) he separates Christ's sacrificial act from the priest's ritual act, and (2) he makes the number of Masses celebrated irrelevant, except insofar as they elevate devotion (apparently, of those attending).[86] The first claim is hard to reconcile with Trent and contradicts Pius XII. The second claim renders the common western medieval and modern practice of saying many Masses for one intention superfluous. Here, we have a rupture with the *lex orandi*, a way of praying that goes back at least to Gregory the Great.

Let us specify what devotion does not mean: it is not a feeling of fervor or experience of dedication to God. Devotion is a disposition or

85. *Sacrosanctum Concilium*, no. 57.

86. Rahner, *Die vielen Messen und das eine Opfer*, 115, 129, 137–41 (1966 edition); Schmitz, "La concelebrazione eucaristica," 514–15.

act of the will, and, like charity, it is hard to measure. Its intensity can be glimpsed indirectly, with probability, over time, in the context of a rich sacramental life. Rahner recommends that a priest attend another's Mass instead of celebrating an individual Mass, if this helps his devotion. But how can the priest easily determine his progress in devotion?

The challenge today is to honor the place of concelebration in the Church, for it is a venerable ancient tradition, as well as the *lex orandi* proper to the west. The principle of *lex orandi* does not simply apply to eastern liturgies, or only to ancient liturgies and post-Vatican II western liturgies, but to the whole of the tradition. In other words, we should strive to maximize both the rite's representative function and the fruits of the sacrifice. That is, in some contexts, concelebration is most appropriate, yet daily concelebration (especially without one's bishop) seems hard to justify.[87] Other factors need to be kept in mind in the quest for the right liturgical practice. On the one hand, the decision not to concelebrate usually means celebrating an individual Mass, with or without a server. When no server is present, the character of the Mass as the paschal banquet is not signified as well. On the other hand, daily concelebration may well diminish the priest's awareness of his sacrificial role, as his ritual prayer and gestures are minimized. The priest should be attentive to how concelebration or individual Masses foster his reverence for the body and blood and his sense of awe before the sacred ritual. Other questions should be asked. Do concelebrants say their vesting prayers and make other acts of spiritual preparation before Mass? Does the priest rush through his "private Mass"? Does the concelebrated Mass have greater solemnity (such as singing), which fosters reverence? The practice of concelebration deserves greater theological reflection.

87. The case of religious communities seems more complex, especially Sunday Masses and special community feasts or vows celebrations, where the shared Eucharistic offering by all the members of the community becomes a most fitting sign.

CHAPTER 9

EUCHARISTIC COMMUNION

The finality of Christ's substantial presence in the Eucharist is our communion with him. He gives himself so that we may be united with him, our body and soul to his humanity and divinity. The Eucharist is our share in the heavenly wedding banquet, a participation in the saints' perfect worship of the victorious Lamb and spousal union with the Bridegroom.

Communion has been at the center of several intense ecclesial debates in recent years. To enter into these questions fruitfully, we need not only the biblical data and witness of tradition, but a clear sense of how to employ these sources. For this reason, I begin with some hermeneutical tools for a theology of Eucharistic communion. Thence, I move to a study of Scripture and the witness of the early Church. The systematic section that follows will have Aquinas as guide, for he integrates in a clear and thorough way the riches of biblical and patristic teaching on communion.[1] Finally, I turn to a more direct treatment of today's disputed questions.

1. Jean-Marie Roger Tillard, *L'Eucharistie: Pâque de l'Église*, Unam sanctam 4 (Paris: Cerf, 1964), 155–56.

Hermeneutical Principles for a Theology of Communion

Some of the dividing lines in the contemporary debate on Eucharistic communion derive from very different uses of Scripture and tradition in theological arguments. Unless we have a clear and well-grounded hermeneutic, the rest of our theology will remain shaky.

First, the more explicitly Eucharistic biblical texts have priority in theological and pastoral considerations and should guide our reading of the less explicitly Eucharistic texts. For example, at the Last Supper, Jesus gives to his apostles his body to eat and his blood to drink. That is, the Eucharist is for his disciples, meaning, those who confess Jesus. The image of Jesus' table fellowship with sinners who have not yet confessed their faith in Christ need not signify that the Eucharist is for non-believers or sinners, for in the Gospel stories about Jesus eating with sinners, the Eucharistic reference is less clear. As Ådna Jostein states: "The Last Supper is not a continuation of the table fellowship with 'tax collectors' and 'sinners', but a meal with a completely different focus."[2]

This leads us to a second principle of interpretation: prophecies or figures of the Eucharist remain partial in their pedagogical value. Take the manna, which all the Israelites in the desert ate each day. This miracle is a figure of the Eucharist. Yet this does not mean that all Christians must eat the Eucharist each day. Rather, the manna signifies that the Eucharist is essential food for the pilgrimage through life and should be received frequently.

Third, whatever theology of communion we derive from Scripture, it must account for all of Scripture, and not contradict any part thereof. The doctrine of biblical inspiration prevents us from playing one "biblical theology" off against another in dialectical fashion.

Fourth, we read Scripture through the lens of the Church Fathers and

2. Ådna Jostein, "Jesus' Meals and Table Companions," in *The Eucharist: Its Origins and Contexts: Sacred Meal, Communal Meal Table Fellowship in Late Antiquity, Early Judaism, and Early Christianity*, vol. 1, *Old Testament, Early Judaism, New Testament*, ed. David Hellholm and Dieter Sänger, Wissenschaftliche Untersuchungen zum Neuen Testament 376 (Tübingen: Mohr Siebeck, 2017), 352.

the liturgical tradition. For the latter, I refer to (a) the liturgical prayers, and (b) the signification of liturgical acts and gestures, like eating and drinking, (c) the symbolism of the Eucharistic elements of bread and wine, and (d) constant liturgical practice and discipline, such as the treatment of public sinners.

Scripture and the Fathers on Eucharistic Communion

Sacramental Communion in the Bible

The theme of Eucharistic food already emerges with the image of the manna. It is celestial food, supernatural food that no human being can offer. The manna fell only in the desert: the miracle stopped once the Israelites entered the Promised Land. The Eucharist, like other sacraments, is for pilgrims. There is no Eucharistic communion in heaven, but simply the contemplation of the Trinity and the Lamb. The manna was essential sustenance to reach the Promised Land. Likewise, the Eucharist is essential to survive on the path. This strongly suggests that infrequent communion was not intended by Christ.

The perfect manna was revealed in John 6, and the same text fittingly indicates several fruits of Eucharistic communion. Christ's flesh and blood bring the spiritual life that he wins on the Cross, and life for the body at the Resurrection. It is like the seed of eternal life (6:51–54). John 6 also teaches that, when we eat his flesh and blood, Christ dwells in us and we in him (6:56). This points to the intimate friendship with Christ that the Eucharist brings about. Eucharistic communion intensifies a communion of love, a communion that is an imitation of the Father dwelling in the Son and the Son dwelling in the Father. Hence, at the Last Supper, Jesus says to his disciples that they are no longer servants but friends (15:15).

The Last Supper was a Passover meal, and Christ's celebration in the Upper Room fulfills this central ritual of the Old Covenant. The Passover ritual, including the eating of the lamb, protects God's people from spiritual death. It enables the Exodus from slavery to the Promised Land, a path from the life of slavery to a life of true worship. Hence, the Eucharist helps to bring about one's gradual liberation from sin or habits of sin, strengthening us to resist temptation, as one gains distance from spiritual Egypt. It offers protection from evil.

The body and blood were given to the apostles, who represent the twelve tribes of Israel. The members of God's people eat the New Passover Lamb. At the Last Supper, Jesus celebrated and instituted a new sacrifice to perfect the Passover sacrifice. Like the Old Passover, the New Passover is a sacrificial meal. Hence, those who are willing to make a sacrifice with the Church and to partake of the sacrificial victim are called to communion.

St. Paul's Eucharistic teaching has a strong emphasis on the unity of the Church: "Because there is one bread, we who are many are one body, for we all partake of the one bread" (1 Cor 10:17). This is why serious sins against one's brothers in Christ are incompatible with a fruitful sharing in the Eucharistic body. Sins against unity impede fruitful communion (hence Paul's moral exhortations), while communion intensifies the mutual unity of the body's members.

At 1 Corinthians 11:27–32, Paul exhorts his listeners to discern the body of Christ. The one who eats Christ unworthily must answer for this sin. Indeed, some at Corinth have fallen sick and even died because they ate the Eucharist unworthily! Paul is likely thinking of the practice of some rich Corinthians who excluded poorer Christians from their part of the *agape* meal when the community gathered. The principle he articulates is that a believer who commits a grave sin and refuses to repent commits sacrilege by receiving the Eucharist.[3]

Eucharistic Communion in the Early Church

Ignatius of Antioch draws together Eucharistic communion, charity, and ecclesial unity, especially unity with the bishop. In his "Letter to the Smyrnaeans," he notes that the Docetists fail to practice love of neighbor, divide the Church by their disputes, and refuse to confess that the Eucharist is Christ's flesh.[4] The virtues opposed to each of these vices are essential. The similarities with 1 Corinthians are evident. For Ignatius, the

3. George T. Montague, *First Corinthians*, Catholic Commentary on Sacred Scripture (Grand Rapids, Mich.: Baker Academic, 2011), 198–200. See also Hans Bernhard Meyer, *Eucharistie: Geschichte, Theologie, Pastoral*, Gottesdienst der Kirche 4 (Regensburg: Friedrich Pustet, 1989), 79.

4. Ignatius of Antioch, "Letter to the Smyrnaeans," no. 7.

Eucharist can be celebrated fruitfully only in communion with the bishop. Ignatius offers a teaching that will be dear to Augustine: Communion strengthens the Church's unity and charity, and it can be effective only if it is received within an existing bond of ecclesial unity and charity.[5]

Justin Martyr is clear on the necessary disposition for communion.

> And this food is called among us *Eucharist,* of which no one is allowed to partake except one who believes that the things which we teach are true, and has received the washing that is for the remission of sins and for rebirth, and who so lives as Christ has handed down. For we do not receive these things as common bread nor common drink.[6]

The Eucharist is for the baptized, those who have been formally or publicly incorporated into the Church. It calls for a common faith, not just in the person of Christ and the Eucharist, but acceptance of the Church's one faith ("the things which we teach"). Finally, communion presupposes the following of Christ, or fidelity to the moral life taught by him. The Eucharistic teachings of Ignatius and Justin find a consistent echo throughout the writings of the subsequent Church Fathers and ancient liturgical practices.[7]

Ignatius also began a beautiful tradition of describing the Eucharist as spiritual medicine, a source of immortality. Many Fathers, especially in the east, will take up this theme. Cyril of Alexandria sees the medicinal power of the Eucharist as inseparable from its capacity to divinize. Sins are spiritual illnesses of which we are healed. Christ already began to teach this lesson in the Gospel, when he cured the sick via physical contact: his body transmits the divine, life-giving power to the sick, which shows that our spiritual illnesses are healed by touching his Eucharistic body.[8] In the west, Ambrose of Milan presents the Eucharist as a spiritual remedy for our daily sins.[9]

The ancient liturgical texts and patristic writings abound with refer-

5. Tillard, *L'Eucharistie: Pâque de l'Église*, 120. I return to Augustine in the systematic section below.

6. Justin Martyr, *First Apology*, chap. 66, in *First and Second Apologies*, ed. and trans. Leslie William Barnard, Ancient Christian Writers 56 (New York: Paulist Press, 1997), 70.

7. For a good overview, see Tillard, *L'Eucharistie: Pâque de l'Église*, chap. 3.

8. Cyril of Alexandria, *Commentary on Luke*, chap. 4, no. 38 (PG 72, 552A-C), cited in Tillard, *L'Eucharistie: Pâque de l'Église*, 123–24.

9. Ambrose, *The Sacraments*, bk. 4, chap. 5, nos. 23–26.

ences to communion as a means to forgiveness of daily sins. The same tradition draws a consistent distinction between sins that communion takes away and those that impede healing by contact with the Eucharist. Let us take two examples. John Chrysostom calls for a purification of conscience before communion. He warns that he will refuse to commune those whose unworthiness is known to him. For the unrepentant sinner, Eucharistic food becomes like the food that a very sick stomach expels, which renders his spiritual condition even worse.[10] Chrysostom echoes 1 Corinthians. In his *Tractates on John*, Augustine draws a clear distinction between grave sins and lesser sins. We are to bring our innocence to the altar, which does not exclude bearing some sins, as long as they are not mortal.[11] Grave sins are like a virulent illnesses that must first be healed by public reconciliation with the Church.[12]

We find this distinction between two types of sins operative from the earliest post-biblical witnesses forward (and implied in 1 Corinthians and 1 John). Both the *First Letter of Clement* as well as the *Didache* call for contrite confession and prayer for "indeliberate" sins, while greater sins demand not just confession but penance and satisfaction before readmission to the Eucharist.[13] This doctrine and practice can be found all through the ancient Church. For example, Theodore of Mopsuestia encourages frequent communion for healing from our daily sins. But graver sins call for a different medicine. In "Catechetical Homily 16," he exhorts grave sinners not to rely on their own judgment, but to turn to the experts (the shepherds) to obtain healing. Theodore gives examples of such sins simply by quoting 1 Corinthians 5:11–12: "adultery, greed, idolatry, drunkenness, an insulter, a thief." Whoever refuses the priests' remedies for these sins ruptures with the Church.[14]

Theodore of Mopsuestia also places great emphasis on the eschatological effects of Eucharistic communion. This doctrine, firmly rooted

10. John Chrysostom, *On the Baptism of Christ and Epiphany*, nos. 3.4–5 (PG 62, 28–30); John Chrysostom, *De Proditione Judae*, Homily 1.6 (PG 49, 380–81), both cited in Tillard, *L'Eucharistie: Pâque de l'Église*, 131.

11. Augustine, *Tractates on the Gospel of John*, tractate 26, no. 11.

12. Augustine, "Letter 54," cited in Tillard, *L'Eucharistie: Pâque de l'Église*, 150.

13. *1 Clement*, 2.3; *Didache*, 4.14, 14.1; Bernhard Poschmann, *Penance and the Anointing of the Sick*, trans. Francis Courtney (New York: Herder & Herder, 1964), 24, 87–88.

14. Theodore of Mopsuestia, "Homily 16," nos. 39, 43, in *Katechetische Homilien*, vol. 1, trans. Peter Bruns. Fontes Christiani 17.1 (Freiburg im Breisgau: Herder, 1994).

in John 6, enjoyed prominence from the second century forward. Ignatius of Antioch unfolds this theme as he speaks of the Eucharist as "the medicine of immortality."[15] He grounds this doctrine on the gift received in communion: the glorified flesh of Christ. Our bodies are conformed to Christ's risen body. For Ignatius, the Eucharist as medicine heals our spiritual wounds, precisely to prepare us for lasting union with Christ.[16] Later in the second century, Irenaeus links the Eucharist's eschatological fruit with the hope of resurrection that it grants. He also compares the Eucharist to a seed that grows into a plant. Eucharistic nourishment will raise up our bodies, restoring us to full communion with God, body and soul.[17] Cyril of Alexandria picks up on the image of the seed, and emphasizes that incorruptibility is the natural outcome of Christ's flesh dwelling in us.[18] Cyril insists that intimate, corporeal union with Christ leads to resurrection.[19] In the epiclesis of Addai and Mari, the Spirit's sanctification is sought so that the gifts may bring hope of resurrection and life in the heavenly kingdom. The Eucharist's eschatological fruits emerge often in various anaphora, both eastern and western.

A Systematic Theology of Eucharistic Communion

With the help of the biblical and patristic survey just undertaken, I now turn to a theme-centered study of the particular fruits, or spiritual effects, of communion. Aquinas has a rich doctrine of Eucharistic communion. He will help us to ponder the deeper meaning of Scripture and the liturgy, and to consider several burning pastoral issues.

Aquinas's first explanation of the effects of the Eucharist employs a simple analogy:

15. Ignatius of Antioch, "Letter to the Ephesians," no. 20, in *The Epistles of St. Clement of Rome and St. Ignatius of Antioch*, ed. James A. Kleist, Ancient Christian Writers 1 (New York: Paulist Press, 1978), 68.

16. Tillard, *L'Eucharistie: Pâque de l'Église*, 188–89.

17. Irenaeus, *Treatise Against Heresies*, bk. 4, chap. 18, no. 5; bk. 5, chap. 2, no. 3.

18. Cyril of Alexandria, *Commentary on the Gospel of John*, bk. 4, chap. 2 (commenting on John 6:54; PG 73, 581), trans. David R. Maxwell, ed. Joel C. Elowksy, Ancient Christian Texts (Downers Grove, Ill.: IVP Academic, 2013), 238.

19. Tillard, *L'Eucharistie: Pâque de l'Église*, 195.

The effect of this sacrament ought to be considered first and indeed principally from the perspective of that which is contained in this sacrament, which is Christ. Just as he who came into this world visibly conferred the life of grace onto the world, according to John 1:17: "Grace and truth were made through Jesus Christ," so also by coming sacramentally into man causes the life of grace, according to John 6:58 [v. 57]: "He who eats me lives forever because of me." Hence also Cyril says: "The vivifying Word of God, uniting himself to his own flesh, made it vivifying.... Therefore, it was fitting that he would unite himself to our bodies through his own sacred flesh and precious blood, which we receive by a vivifying benediction, in the bread and wine."[20]

The starting point of a theology of communion is not a phenomenological analysis of eating, but a teaching of faith, the confession of Christ's hidden, corporeal presence in the Eucharist. Our *Summa* passage presumes that confession, as it employs the analogy with the Incarnation. The Incarnation is part of the Son's visible mission: God comes to us in the flesh. The Logos became man and thus brought a share in divine life to the world, to all those who believe. After the Ascension, the Logos enters the world again in bodily form, through the Eucharistic gifts. Now the most basic effect of grace is to grant a participation in eternal life. That Christ's Eucharistic body has this effect is itself revealed in John 6. In each case, the divinity joined to Christ's humanity makes his coming life-giving (his visible and his sacramental coming). Aquinas then cites Cyril of Alexandria's *Commentary on Luke*, which echoes Cyril's teaching on John 6. Since divine life is mediated by Christ's body in the economy as a whole, the union of our bodies with his Eucharistic flesh and blood becomes a most fitting means to receive a share in this life. We thus find a solid foundation to ponder the fruits of communion, a foundation grounded on three points: (1) the ecclesial confession of Christ's Eucharistic presence, as supported by the liturgical and patristic tradition, (2) the Johannine teaching on the power of Christ's flesh, and (3) a Christology rooted in the Council of Ephesus (Christ is one person or hypostasis), whose dogma helps us to avoid misreading John's bread of life discourse. Let us note that Aquinas's own exposition of John 6 also makes the Spirit's presence in Christ's humanity essential for that sacred human-

20. Thomas Aquinas, *Summa theologiae* III, q. 79, a. 1.

ity's life-giving power. Pneumatology has not gone missing in Thomas's theology of communion.[21]

Clearly, all of the sacraments give grace, but the Eucharist gives it in abundance, for "what is common to all the sacraments is attributed most of all to the Eucharist by reason of its excellence."[22] Aquinas seeks to honor the immense spiritual power of the Eucharist, as it contains not just Christ's saving power but the very author of grace. In another passage, he says that, when we simply ponder the gift contained, but in abstraction from the recipient, "this sacrament has the power to remit any sins by the Passion of Christ, which is the fount and cause of the remission of sins."[23] Christ's body and blood and the power of his Passion contain the power to forgive any sin, and yet, not all sins can be forgiven by communion. Now Thomas has no intention of placing limits on grace. Rather, when he insists that some benefits are not received through communion, it is out of (1) obedience to Scripture, such as Paul's warning about eating unworthily, and (2) attentiveness to the liturgical signs. In other words, communion brings boundless blessings, but as manifested by Scripture and the signification of the sacrament. There is no generic grace that binds up any and every spiritual wound. The graces attained via communion can be discovered by contemplating (1) the gift received, (2) the mode of receiving it, and (3) the spiritual state of the recipient. Having just pondered the first of these elements, I now take up the second and third.

Aquinas considers the mode of receiving the sacrament of the Eucharist in a text that follows shortly after the passage quoted above on the Incarnation:

> the effect of this sacrament is considered from the mode by which this sacrament is passed on, which is by way of food and drink. And so, every effect which material food and drink brings about in corporeal life, namely that it sustains, augments, repairs and delights, all this the sacrament does for spiritual life ... Hence

21. Thomas Aquinas, *Commentary on the Gospel of John*, chap. 6, lectio 8, no. 993. See the following edition: Thomas Aquinas, *Commentary on the Gospel of John, Chapters 1–8*, ed. the Aquinas Institute, trans. F. R. Larcher, Latin/English Edition of the Works of St. Thomas Aquinas 35 (Lander, Wyo.: The Aquinas Institute for the Study of Sacred Doctrine, 2013).

22. Thomas Aquinas, *Summa theologiae* III, q. 73, a. 4, ad 2.

23. Thomas Aquinas, *Summa theologiae* III, q. 79, a. 3.

the Lord says: in John 6:56 [v. 55]: "My flesh is true food, and my blood is true drink."[24]

This dense passage integrates several of Thomas's central convictions in his sacramental theology. First, the analogy between natural human life and sacramental life is Aquinas's preferred way of seeing the sacramental order as a whole. Thus, baptism is spiritual birth, confirmation growth into adulthood, Eucharist is eating and drinking, extreme unction is for a good death, and so on.[25] Basic aspects of human life such as birth and death provide the ideal entryway for God's pedagogy. Second, part of this overall analogy is revealed: baptism truly is a new birth (Jn 3) and the Eucharist is truly food and drink (Jn 6). These aspects of the analogy are not theological constructs or theories. Third, Aquinas insists on taking the analogy as far as possible. If Christ chose to bring us the greatest sacrament in the form of food and drink, then virtually every aspect of these natural gifts becomes revelatory: *every* effect that natural food and drink have for us, spiritual food and drink also have. Natural food and drink sustain, augment, restore, and delight. The Eucharist sustains and augments the life of grace begun by the sacrament of baptism, or begun anew by sacramental penance. The Eucharist restores the strength of virtue, lost through sin and vice, especially by augmenting charity. The sacrament also incites us to acts of charity, and these acts take away venial sins, thus bringing spiritual healing.[26] The Eucharist delights the soul, like sweet manna and wine that inebriates.

Aquinas's exposition of Eucharistic food and drink focuses on the individual's act of eating and drinking. That is, he generally does not use this image to speak of a shared banquet. However, the communal dimension emerges when he expounds on another aspect of the Eucharistic sign, namely, the many grains united in one host and many grapes contained in one cup. Again, the liturgical sign manifests the spiritual benefit that it brings. Aquinas adopts the teaching of 1 Corinthians 11 and St. Augustine.[27] As Gilles Emery points out, for Thomas, this unity of many grains

24. Thomas Aquinas, *Summa theologiae* III, q. 79, a. 1.

25. Thomas Aquinas, *Summa theologiae* III, q. 65, a. 1.

26. Thomas Aquinas, *Summa theologiae* III, q. 79, a. 4. For more on penance and forgiveness, see especially q. 87, aa. 1–2.

27. Thomas Aquinas, *Summa theologiae* III, q. 79, a. 1.

and grapes, "is not inconsequential, since the sacrament effects that which is represented or signified, that is, the true Body of Christ and the mystical Body. Thus, in Thomas, the ecclesial signification serves to manifest that the sacrament effectively produces this grace."[28] Thus, the members who partake of this sign simultaneously become more fully united with their head and with one another. There simply is no tension between vertical and horizontal communion, between our relation with Christ and our relation with the Church. Emery also notes that the ecclesial fruit of communion is not parallel to other spiritual benefits imparted to us. That is, it is not as if our personal union with Christ or our new share in God's holiness are given in addition to our deeper incorporation into the Church. Rather, Eucharistic communion sanctifies us precisely by joining us more closely to Christ, the head, and to his mystical body, the Church.[29] Numerous aspects of the liturgy reinforce the importance of this theme of unity. As we saw previously, many Eucharistic prayers include an epiclesis that asks God to make the gifts of Christ's body and blood a means of unity for those who partake therein. More than the other sacraments, the Eucharist fortifies the unity of the Church.

The Eucharist brings this spiritual fruit especially because it pours forth an abundance of charity. Thomas makes this link by returning to the image of spiritual food and drink and by appropriating Augustine's theology of love. As Emery explains, in communion,

> the food is not transformed into the one who eats, but rather, the one eating is changed (*convertetur*) into the food that he eats. This understanding is clearly a development of Augustine's thought. The effect proper to the Eucharist, as Thomas expresses it, is the transformation (*transformatio*) of man into Christ by love ... our *conversio* into Christ, a union or *adunatio* into Christ: in other words, incorporation into Christ.[30]

Christ instituted the Eucharist as the most powerful signification of corporeal and spiritual union with him. Eating implies assimilation, but the analogy must be modified when it comes to spiritual union with the Incarnate Word and the consumption of Christ's incorruptible, glorified

28. Gilles Emery, "The Ecclesial Fruit of the Eucharist in St. Thomas," in *Trinity, the Church and the Human Person: Thomistic Essays* (Naples, Fla.: Sapientia Press, 2007), 157.

29. Emery, "The Ecclesial Fruit," 161.

30. Emery, "The Ecclesial Fruit," 159.

body and blood. He does not become like us or part of us, hence, we must become like him and be conformed to him ever more closely. But such intense union can come about only through charity. In the Eucharist, we partake in the ultimate sign of charity, his bodily life given up for us. We become like the gift received.

With Augustine, Thomas holds that the ecclesial bond of unity and the bond of charity are closely intertwined. That is, charity is the ultimate measure of the degree to which we are united to the Church. Now charity presupposes faith, since love presupposes knowledge, and charity needs the knowledge of faith (implicit or explicit) in order to love Christ, for we cannot love what we do not know. The Eucharist brings about "incorporation into the mystical body by the union of faith and charity."[31] All who are saved partake of the effects of the Eucharist, at least by anticipation (including baptized babies and those justified by implicit faith), so that they "spiritually" (but not always sacramentally) eat and drink Christ: "in spiritually eating the flesh of Christ and in spiritually drinking his blood we become participators in the Church's unity which is caused by charity."[32] This theology is related to yet distinct from the practice of "making a spiritual communion" (treated below).

The Eucharist imparts charity, while also presupposing an existing bond of faith and charity. Through baptism (at least as desired, but especially by receiving it sacramentally), we become members of the Church and are united to her. Sacramental reconciliation restores the ruptured bond of unity and charity. In this way, we can account for the constant ecclesial practices of (1) reserving the reception of the Eucharist to believers, and (2) refusing the sacrament to those in grave sin, on the basis of 1 Corinthians 11.

This charity comes by the Holy Spirit. Commenting on John 6:63, Thomas explains:

> the flesh of Christ, considered in itself, profits nothing.... But if it is united to the Spirit and his divinity, it profits many, because it makes those who receive it

31. Thomas Aquinas, *Commentary on the Gospel of John*, chap. 6, lectio 7, no. 976.

32. Thomas Aquinas, *Commentary on the Gospel of John*, chap. 6, lectio 7, no. 969. For spiritual eating without sacramental reception, see *Summa theologiae* III, q. 79, a. 1, ad 1. Aquinas here explains a means of contact with the spiritual reality (*res*) or spiritual gift of the sacrament by those who cannot access it.

abide in Christ, for man abides in God through the Spirit of love: "We know that we abide in God and God in us, because he has given us his Spirit" (1 Jn 4:13).[33]

The body of Christ overflows with the Spirit, he who is eternally the gift of love between Father and Son, and this same Spirit does in us what he does in the Trinity, namely he binds persons together in charity. The Spirit leads us to Christ, who in turn brings us to the Father.

All of this implies a Trinitarian mystical theology. Aquinas holds that, with each gift of habitual charity, we also enjoy a new coming of the Holy Spirit into our hearts, and this grace involves a simultaneous visitation of the eternal Logos with his light or wisdom.[34] Gilles Emery writes:

> the *Summa* [*theologiae*] acknowledges the presence of the new [invisible] missions [of Son and Spirit] not only in exceptional spiritual experiences, but also in a progress in the virtues or in the growth in grace, and whenever the indwelling of the divine persons seems to have brought some "new thing" to bear, that is, when progress toward union with God encounters a new state of grace or inspires new acts, which could be voluntary poverty or the acceptance of martyrdom, but also the reception of the sacraments.[35]

The Eucharist transforms us into Christ by charity. This theme helps to account for the teaching of John 6, that eating Christ's flesh and drinking his blood bring about a mutual indwelling: Christ in us and we in him. It is an *abiding* communion, and so, this involves a new outpouring of habitual charity (as an abiding spiritual disposition of the will to love God above all things). Now every sacrament grants some share in habitual grace. By the Eucharist, Christ refashions our hearts in the image of his heart: he makes us love the things he loves, and as he loves them, in a selfless, life-giving way. In this way, we are also conformed to the Spirit, who is rightly called personal Love in the eternal life of the Trinity.[36]

We call the Eucharist the sacrament of friendship, for it provokes an intensification of the charity received in baptism, allowing us to share

33. Thomas Aquinas, *Commentary on the Gospel of John*, chap. 6, lectio 8, no. 993.

34. Thomas Aquinas, *Summa theologiae* I, q. 43, aa. 5–6; Bernhard Blankenhorn, *The Mystery of Union with God: Dionysian Mysticism in Albert the Great and Thomas Aquinas*, Thomistic Ressourcement 4 (Washington, D.C.: The Catholic University of America Press, 2015), 249–59.

35. Gilles Emery, *The Trinitarian Theology of St. Thomas Aquinas*, trans. Francesca Aran Murphy (Oxford: Oxford University Press, 2007), 386.

36. Thomas Aquinas, *Summa theologiae* I, q, 43, a. 3, ad 1–2; Emery, *The Trinitarian Theology of St. Thomas Aquinas*, 260, 376–78.

more fully in the exchange of hearts that is the mark of friendship. The Son took on a nature like ours, so that our hearts may become like his, through contact with his flesh and blood. Once we see the Eucharist as the sacrament of friendship, many other Eucharistic doctrines fall into place (e.g., the Eucharist presupposes faith, by which alone we can know Christ as our true friend). Roch Kereszty rightly notes that the Eucharist brings a fully effective spiritual communion only when Christ's gift of himself is in turn met by our self-giving.[37] That is, we welcome his gift by love of him. We must be willing to let Christ guide our lives if communion is to have an effect in us. And so, communion presumes a life of charity in the recipient, the existing reciprocity of friends.

Thomas sees a link between the gift of Christ's charity offered in the Eucharist and the experience of delight and spiritual joy in communion. He notes that two kinds of charity are made available in communion: habitual and actual. The virtue of charity inclines the believer to selfless acts of love. But actual charity is the very act of love that the Spirit incites in us, if we are receptive. Thomas partly grounds this doctrine on John Damascene's comparison of the Eucharist to a burning coal on fire with the divinity, and by appeal to 2 Corinthians 5:14: "The love of Christ urges us on."[38] Communion should normally elicit an act of love for Christ the bridegroom, in the moment and thereafter. Also, the Eucharist disposes the recipient to better love his or her neighbor as well.

Aquinas connects the actual charity that the Eucharist pours into the well-disposed, attentive recipient with an experience of spiritual delight, sweetness, and refreshment. Thomas references the Song of Songs (5:1): "Eat, friends, and drink, and be inebriated, my dearly beloved."[39] The Eucharist delights the soul by provoking an act of charity, and love naturally produces joy in the beloved. Spiritual wine inebriates and brings about joy, much as the consumption of natural wine brings joy to the heart and

37. Roch A. Kereszty, *Wedding Feast of the Lamb: Eucharistic Theology from a Biblical, Historical and Systematic Perspective* (Chicago: Hillenbrand Books, 2007), 194. This is not to say that we must make a conscious, undistracted act of love and self-giving in the moment of Communion in order to receive its spiritual benefits. Rather, this primarily concerns the best spiritual disposition for such an act.

38. Thomas Aquinas, *Summa theologiae* III, q. 79, a. 1, ad 2.

39. Thomas Aquinas, *Summa theologiae* III, q. 79, a. 1, ad 2 & a. 8. For Aquinas's bridal mysticism, see Serge-Thomas Bonino, *Saint Thomas d'Aquin, lecteur du Cantique des cantiques* (Paris: Cerf, 2019).

pleasure to the body. A similar reading of Song of Songs 5:1 can be found in Albertus Magnus:

> For since it is characteristic of loved ones that they mutually dwell in each other through desire, he would not say, "Eat, friends, and drink," unless he sought to enter into them through his body and blood and soul and divinity. Nor would he say, "Be inebriated, my loved ones," unless he desired that they, likewise forgetful of themselves, also desire to enter into God through incorporation.[40]

Albert evokes a mystical experience available to any believer. Such experience is hardly limited to the moment of communion, yet it is rightly concentrated therein, so that Christ may teach us about his wondrous, substantial, and dynamic presence. Why should believers not expect such an experience to occur most of all in the moment when they can touch the body of the divine bridegroom? Albert insists: "For fire penetrating into the marrow teaches the power of this love by which Christ pours himself into us and draws us into himself; nor can anyone know this power other than by intimate love."[41] The lives of many saints confirm that the Eucharist is the place *par excellence* to experience divine sweetness.

Aquinas continues the patristic teaching that communion causes the forgiveness of venial sins. He traces this gift back to the signification of the Eucharist as food. Just as natural food restores lost physical energy and strength, so spiritual food restores spiritual strength. We grow weak through venial sin, and strong when sin is taken away. Aquinas means that the Eucharist takes away the fault of venial sin or the guilt incurred. He shows how this occurs by speaking of the *res sacramenti*, the invisible reality imparted by the sacrament. The term *res sacramenti* refers to charity, but now considered as a means to forgiveness. An elevated habitual charity and new acts of charity elicited by the power of the Eucharist lead to forgiveness.[42] Here, 1 Peter 4:8 surely stands in the background: "love covers a multitude of sins." Thomas does not say that communion always takes away the guilt incurred for *any* venial sins committed since the last confession or the last fruitful communion. He does not present

40. Albertus Magnus, *On the Body of the Lord*, d. 1, chap. 3, trans. Albert Marie Surmanski, The Fathers of the Church: Mediaeval Continuation 17 (Washington, D.C.: The Catholic University of America Press, 2017), 51.

41. Albertus Magnus, *On the Body of the Lord*, d. 1, chap. 2, pp. 47–48.

42. Thomas Aquinas, *Summa theologiae* III, q. 79, a. 4.

a complete substitute for the sacramental confession of venial sins. Rather, communion brings forgiveness of some and potentially all venial sins. Communion may do this indirectly by habitual charity, enabling more frequent acts of love that cover our sins. A new gift of actual charity directly causes forgiveness.[43] This doctrine emphasizes man's active cooperation in the life of grace.

Thomas is convinced that Christ's institution of the Eucharist in the form of food and drink is a powerful revelation. Sacramental food and drink strengthen and delight, restore lost energy and bring joy. By contrast, in baptism, we are buried with Christ, we die to sin and rise to new life with him (Rom 6). Aquinas likes to point out that food and drink are for the living, not the dead. Spiritual regeneration comes through baptism, spiritual resurrection through penance, but spiritual food and drink are for those who are already spiritually alive.[44] Aquinas insists that the Eucharistic signs are part of God's grand pedagogy. His reading of the signs also makes sense in light of 1 Corinthians 11 and constant liturgical practice. We can appropriate well the patristic image of the Eucharist as spiritual medicine only if we read it together with the Fathers' other teachings and the biblical doctrine that they presume. Aquinas develops his doctrine on the foundation of St. Paul's stark warnings in 1 Corinthians 6 and 11 not to eat the body of the Lord unworthily: such an act involves both a profanation of the most sacred gift and a weakening of the body that is the Church.

Yet Aquinas also holds that communion can forgive mortal sins, when received by a person who is neither conscious of the mortal sin nor attached to it.[45] He presents the case of a person not sufficiently contrite for his or her sins, but who approaches the Eucharist with devotion, thereby obtaining full contrition.[46] Here, Aquinas probably thinks of someone who previously confessed a grave sin, but in whom the fruit of the

43. Réginald Garrigou-Lagrange, *De eucharistia, accedunt de paenitentia: Questiones dogmaticae, Commentarius in Summam theologicam S. Thomae* (Paris: Desclée de Brouwer, 1943), 201–2.

44. Thomas Aquinas, *Summa theologiae* III, q. 79, a. 3.

45. The following paragraphs on mortal sin and the Eucharist integrate material from the following essay: Bernhard Blankenhorn, "L'eucaristia nella vita matrimoniale: Medicina dei peccatori o sacramento dei vivi?" in *Eucaristia e Matrimonio: Due sacramenti, un'alleanza*, ed. José Granados and Stefano Salucci (Siena, Italy: Cantagalli, 2015), 127–49.

46. Thomas Aquinas, *Summa theologiae* III, q. 79, a. 3.

sacrament of penance did not fully take root, due to a lack of openness to the sacrament's effect of contrition. Thomas also suggests that when one lacks awareness of an unconfessed mortal sin, communion brings pardon.[47] Overall, Aquinas proposes that two elements need to be present: (1) the person is not aware of being guilty of a mortal sin, and (2) he is not attached to that sin.

Aquinas holds that sufficient contrition for sins often precedes sacramental confession.[48] In the examples given in the *Summa theologiae*, the Eucharist brings sufficient contrition for three kinds of mortal sin: (1) sins already confessed, but where contrition remains too weak; (2) forgotten sins; and (3) sins committed without awareness of their gravity. Elsewhere, Thomas mentions the situation when confessors are not available. In a case of necessity, when there is awareness of mortal sins, sacramental confession is not bypassed but delayed (until the first opportunity) and its fruit anticipated. The Eucharist can heighten the contrition of the penitent in question.[49]

Aquinas's argumentation respects the sign character of the sacraments. First, the person's sin is not public, that is, his state of life is not in evident contradiction of Christ's moral teaching. The sin is hidden to everyone, and in most of the scenarios described by Thomas, the sin is hidden even to the one who committed it. Second, the person in question does not intend to contradict the sacramental sign. He does not receive spiritual food in order to be forgiven a grave fault, because he sees no grave fault. He does not treat Eucharist as a replacement of sacramental confession of grave sins. Third, the communicant must lack the intention to commit these or other grave sins in the future, and he would be sorrowful for the hidden sins if he became aware of them. Thus, the communicant in ques-

47. Thomas Aquinas, *Summa theologiae* III, q. 79, a. 3; Aymon-Marie Roguet, notes to Thomas Aquinas, *Somme théologique, L'eucharistie*, vol. 1, *3a, Questions 73–78* (Paris: Desclée et Cie, 1960), 294.

48. Gilles Emery, "Reconciliation with the Church and Interior Penance: The Contribution of Thomas Aquinas on the *Res et Sacramentum* of Penance," in *Trinity, the Church and the Human Person: Thomistic Essays* (Naples, Fla.: Sapientia Press, 2007), 187.

49. Thomas Aquinas, *Commentary on First Corinthians*, chap. 11, lectio 7, no. 690. See the following edition: Thomas Aquinas, *Commentary on the Letters of Saint Paul to the Corinthians*, ed. B. Mortensen and E. Alarcón, trans. F. R. Larcher, B. Mortensen, and D. Keating, Latin/English Edition of the Works of St. Thomas Aquinas 38 (Lander, Wyo.: The Aquinas Institute for the Study of Sacred Doctrine, 2013).

tion fully intends to respect the moral law and to submit himself to the Church's power of the keys exercised in the sacrament of penance.

We have seen that the forgiveness of sins is an effect of communion, via the charity it imparts. Here too, we find an eschatological fruit: Eucharistic charity brings us closer to our heavenly destiny. Finally, hope should increase whenever we receive communion with a proper understanding of the gift imparted, namely, that it is the glorified Christ who gives himself to us, in a foretaste of the heavenly banquet.[50] This hope should be accompanied by a holy desire. The Eucharistic hymn *Adoro te devote*, likely composed by Aquinas, ends thus: "Jesus whom I now gaze at veiled, when shall that which I so desire come to pass? So that seeing you, your face revealed, I may be blessed with the vision of your glory."[51] Communion in Christ's hidden body and the gift of charity that it brings cannot but intensify the longing to see that hidden Christ without the sacramental veils.

I should come back to the patristic theme of the Eucharistic body as a cause of our future bodily resurrection. It is evident that the Eucharist does not operate a visible, physical change in its recipient's bodies. The gift of incorruptibility is essentially a delayed effect of communion, yet it is caused precisely by the indwelling of Christ, which grows with every fruitful communion. We can also posit the beginning of a share in bodily glorification in this way: the wounds of sin in our passions are gradually healed through Eucharistic communion.[52] Christ's irascible and concupiscible appetites were and are perfect, as will ours be in our resurrected bodies. By conformity to his risen body, we can begin to share in the restoration of that part of our soul that stands on the border between the immaterial and material, which is the passions. If this claim is sound, then we can look to the Eucharist to diminish our anger, increase our fortitude, weaken lust or other disordered longings, and to gradually shape in us wholesome desires for bodily goods.

50. Lawrence Feingold, *The Eucharist: Mystery of Presence, Sacrifice and Communion* (Steubenville, Ohio: Emmaus Academic, 2018), 525.

51. Translation by Paul Murray, *Aquinas at Prayer: The Bible, Mysticism and Poetry* (London: Bloomsbury, 2013), 244. For the authenticity of the prayer, see Jean-Pierre Torrell, *Initiation à saint Thomas d'Aquin: Sa personne et son œuvre*, 2nd ed. (Paris: Cerf, 2015), 178.

52. Kereszty, *Wedding Feast of the Lamb*, 196.

Excursus: Spiritual Communion

The outbreak of the Coronavirus (Covid-19) in early 2020, a veritable modern plague, has heightened the relevance of the theology and practice of spiritual communion. In times of Eucharistic famine, what hidden spiritual treasures might the Church rediscover?[53]

Augustine helped to lay the foundation for a solid theological account of how the grace of the Eucharist can be obtained by anticipation. In his Tractates on John, the Latin Father explains Jesus' bread of life discourse. The Israelites in the desert ate manna but still died, for they lacked faith in the hidden reality signified by the miraculous bread. But Moses, Aaron, and other devout Israelites understood and believed well, so that they desired and tasted both the visible and the spiritual manna. We find different figures in the Old and New Covenants (the manna in the desert, the visible sign on the Church's altar), while the spiritual reality (or *res*) given therein is the same. Augustine applies this lesson to his flock: the visible sign is one thing, while its power is something else. He exhorts his listeners to bring their innocence to the altar, so as to eat the Eucharist not just sacramentally but also spiritually, and so to obtain eternal life.[54] The hidden reality signified, offered, and received is the unity of the Church, which is caused by the Spirit's gift of charity.[55]

Eight centuries later, Aquinas picked up on Augustine's pastoral exegesis. In his *Commentary on the Gospel of John*, Thomas asks why young children (in the Latin Church) do not receive communion, for apparently, Christ himself made it necessary for salvation, as when he solemnly proclaims: "Unless you eat the flesh of the Son of Man, and drink his blood, you have no life in you" (Jn 6:53). Thomas answers with an appeal to the notion of attaining a sacrament by desire.[56] He also notes that, just as the catechumen who dies before the Easter Vigil can be saved through his desire for baptism, so the baptized believer still lacking access to the

53. This section presents a modified version of an article published April 8, 2020, in the online periodical, *Church Life Journal*, entitled, "A Short History and Theology of Spiritual Communion." I am grateful to the journal's editor, Artur Sebastian Rosman, at the McGrath Institute for Church Life of the University of Notre Dame for allowing this portion to be republished.

54. Augustine, *Tractates on the Gospel of John*, tractate 26, nos. 11–12.

55. Augustine, *Tractates on the Gospel of John*, tractate 26, nos. 13, 15; tractate 27, no 6.

56. Thomas Aquinas, *Commentary on the Gospel of John*, chap. 6, lectio 7, no. 969.

Eucharist can obtain its spiritual fruit, and this, even by an implicit desire (as in the case of children who have not reached the age of reason).[57] In his *Summa theologiae*, Aquinas pursues this analogy with baptism by desire further. One can eat the Eucharist "spiritually" before eating it sacramentally in two ways: (1) in the Old Covenant, where the faithful Israelite ate the physical manna and the spiritual food provided therein, as well as (2) in the New Covenant, by a desire to receive the sacrament of the Eucharist. Thomas adds a precision to Augustine's exegesis: sacramental eating should not be seen as superfluous, for actual reception of the visible sign induces a richer spiritual effect than does spiritual eating alone.[58]

Augustine, Thomas, and other saints laid the doctrinal foundation for a practice that gained popularity starting in late medieval times, namely, that of making a "spiritual communion." Spiritual masters like St. Teresa of Ávila and St. Alphonsus Liguori have given this practice particular attention, as have the Council of Trent and Pius XII.[59]

Alphonsus and other spiritual masters set forth a basic structure for the practice of spiritual communion. First, the practice presupposes that one be in a state of grace. If this is not the case, then an act of sincere contrition should come first.[60] Next, while an act of spiritual communion can be done anywhere, a Church with a tabernacle is the ideal place (even if the Blessed Sacrament is not exposed for adoration). When possible, it should coincide with the celebration of Mass in another place (to which the believer can deliberately join himself). Alphonsus begins each day's meditation with a Scripture passage that has a Eucharistic theme. Fittingly, the first response to Scripture (and the Blessed Sacrament) should be an act of faith, especially in Christ and his Eucharistic presence. Here, particular attention to his Passion (and other mysteries of Christ) would be laudable. Then follows a deliberate act of charity, an expression of love for God and neighbor. Francis de Sales sees spiritual communion's essence

57. Thomas Aquinas, *Summa theologiae* III, q. 68, a. 2; q. 73, a. 3.

58. Thomas Aquinas, *Summa theologiae* III, q. 80, a. 1, ad 3.

59. Council of Trent, *Decree on the Sacrament of the Eucharist*, chap. 8; Pius XII, *Mediator Dei*, no. 117; William of Saint-Thierry, *Lettre aux frères du Mont-Dieu (Lettre d'or)*, ed. Jean Déchanet, Sources chrétiennes 223 (Paris: Cerf, 1975), nos. 115–19; Teresa of Avila, *Way of Perfection*, chapter 37, in *Collected Works of St. Teresa of Avila*, trans. Kieran Kavanaugh and Otilio Rodriguez, vol. 2 (Washington, D.C.: Institute of Carmelite Studies, 1980).

60. Louis de Bazelaire, "Communion spirituelle," in *Dictionnaire de théologie catholique*, ed. E. Mangenot, vol. 3 (Paris: Librairie Letouzey et Âne, 1908), 1297, 1299.

in the soul's desire for the Eucharistic Christ, that is, the heart's expression of loving desire.[61] Here one speaks to Christ about one's hunger and thirst for the spiritual food and drink that are perfectly contained in his Eucharistic body and blood, and thereby simultaneously incites a greater interior hunger and thirst. Alphonsus also sees the importance of a petition for lasting union with Christ, or an explicit invitation for him to come into one's soul.[62] Such language evokes the classic doctrine of the invisible missions of Son and Spirit, namely, the coming of Son and Spirit into our minds and hearts with gifts of habitual wisdom and charity.

This contemplative act brings many graces, though usually not gifts equal to the spiritual fruits obtained by sacramental eating.[63] Aquinas's theological principle is sound: the sacrament's institution by Christ implies that a merely spiritual communion does not suffice as a permanent practice, for otherwise, the Old Testament figures would have been enough for the economy of salvation.

Recent Controversies on Communion

Communion for Non-Catholic Christians?

Eucharistic communion presupposes a unity of faith. Paul, in 1 Corinthians 11:26, posits an explicit link between communion and a shared Christological faith. Yet Paul also assumes a common faith on all essential matters of doctrine among those coming to the Eucharist, essentially, the reception of apostolic teaching. Or consider the warning in 2 John not even to greet schismatics. Thus, in the Christian tradition, a lack of shared doctrine on any essential matter of faith has consistently been considered an impediment to communion.

At the Last Supper, we see Jesus giving the flesh and blood of the New Passover Lamb to his disciples. The liturgical tradition and all the doctors of the Church agree that we are given Christ's very own body and blood, and Christ as a victim. At communion, we say "Amen," which is a

61. Francis de Sales, *Introduction to the Devout Life*, trans. Allan Ross (Westminster, Md.: Newman Press, 1953), part 2, chap. 21.

62. Alphonsus Liguori, *Visits to the Most Holy Sacrament and to the Holy Virgin for Every Day in the Month* (London: T. Jones, 1849), xiv–xvii.

63. Bazelaire, "Communion spirituelle," 1299.

confession of faith in the gift received. We adore the Passover Lamb, and we also say "Amen" to the act of offering the Lamb to God the Father, the Lamb now consumed in a sacrificial banquet. During communion, the "Amen" is authentic only if we accept the truth of the gift being offered. This implies that non-Christians should not receive communion.[64] But what about Protestant believers who long to share the Eucharist with us?

In the spring of 2018, the German Bishops Conference published a guide (*Mit Christus Gehen: Der Einheit auf der Spur*) on how to discern when the Protestant spouse of a Catholic person can receive communion.[65] The document encourages such couples to reach their own decision in their conscience, after a dialogue with a pastor or lay pastoral assistant.[66] It sees the inaccessibility of communion for the Protestant spouse as possibly a spiritual risk for the marriage, and thus sometimes a case of "grave necessity."[67] Protestant spouses who hunger for the Eucharist and decide in favor of communion are asked to affirm Catholic faith in the Eucharist.[68] The conference's text bases itself on post-conciliar magisterial documents, as well as canon 844.3–4 of the 1983 Code of Canon Law, which describe situations in which Eucharistic communion and some other sacraments may be given to non-Catholic Christians. In these documents, we find a consistent reference to communion in cases of grave necessity and the need for the recipient to manifest Catholic faith in the sacrament received.[69]

64. Some theologians argue that the Eucharist is essentially a shared meal of believers who together offer a prayer of thanksgiving to God. From this perspective, refusing Communion to our separated brethren attending the liturgy would be unthinkable. See Thomas O'Loughlin, "Theologies of Intercommunion: Responding to a Recent Papal Request," *New Blackfriars* 97 (May 2016), 372–87. O'Loughlin's approach is univocal: he analyzes the Eucharist exclusively from the perspective of a sacred meal. He refuses to posit the question of which Eucharistic presence is confessed by those who commune. He also seems to imply that Protestants present at Mass could refuse assent to the Church's offering of Christ the victim, a doctrine clearly expressed in the Eucharistic prayers from antiquity to our day, yet still receive Communion. In this scenario, the Eucharistic prayer would no longer manifest the shared faith of those who eat and drink the sacrificial body and blood of Christ. O'Loughlin thus separates the Church's *lex orandi* from the significance of Communion.

65. The guide can be found online at https://www.dbk.de/fileadmin/redaktion/diverse_downloads/dossiers_2018/08-Orientierungshilfe-Kommunion.pdf. Accessed June 30, 2018.

66. *Mit Christus Gehen*, nos. 9, 21, 57.

67. *Mit Christus Gehen*, no. 18.

68. *Mit Christus Gehen*, no. 56.

69. See the encyclicals of John Paul II, *Ecclesia de Eucharistia*, no. 45, in *Encyclicals* (Trivandrum,

The German Bishops Conference's document emphasizes the shared Christological and Eucharistic faith of Catholics and Protestants. It gives little attention to the consistent Protestant rejection of Eucharistic sacrifice (perhaps with some Anglicans being excepted) and the general refusal of the doctrine of Christ's corporeal and substantial presence in the Eucharist (with the exception of classical Lutherans who hold for consubstantiation).[70] Nor does it mention the universal Protestant refusal of a sacramental priesthood. The text therefore obscures the fact that the Protestant spouse who comes to accept Catholic Eucharistic faith has already ceased to be Protestant, yet without clearly and intentionally becoming Catholic. This document seems to describe a person on the path to conversion. The same logic of discernment and possible exceptions would apply to catechumens and candidates who are preparing to enter the Church and are married to a practicing Catholic: given their faith in the Eucharist, if some experience of pain or exclusion were caused by their inability to receive together with their spouse, then they seemingly could discern that it is appropriate to receive, even regularly, well before being formally received into the Church. Yet such a pastoral practice would have been unthinkable in the tradition. It would turn the entire process of Christian initiation upside down. Or again, the same principle should allow a person who refuses to enter RCIA due to opposition to the Church's moral teaching to still receive communion, if they come to a Catholic faith in the Eucharist. This too would have been unthinkable to the Church Fathers and saints.

The German Bishops Conference document does not consider that the shared Eucharistic faith also needs to be public. This is implied in Paul's teaching, and consistently treated as essential in liturgical practice over the centuries. A good example can be found in Justin Martyr, who witnesses to the practice that the presider of the Eucharist shepherds the people to ensure right faith and morals. A discreet dialogue between a pas-

Kerala, India: Carmel International Publishing House 2005); John Paul II, *Ut Unum Sint*, April 17, 2003, no. 46, in *The Encyclicals of John Paul II*, ed. J. Michael Miller (Our Sunday Visitor, 1996).

70. The German Lutheran-Catholic ecumenical study group largely sidesteps these issues of sacrifice and substantial presence in its proposal for intercommunion: Volker Leppin and Dorothea Sattler, eds., *Together at the Lord's Table: A Votum of the Ecumenical Working Group of Lutheran and Catholic Theologians* (Freiburg im Breisgau: Herder, 2020), 133–37. Oddly, this ecumenical document ignores the heavy consequences that its proposals bear for Catholic-Orthodox relations.

tor and a couple of mixed confessional belonging does not render a common Eucharistic faith public, and it ignores the abiding divisions of faith (especially on ecclesiology and perhaps morals). From Ignatius of Antioch forward, Eucharistic communion has been seen as the manifestation of the Church's unity, of the members' unity in faith and love with the presider and the bishop. Such an ecclesiology, deliberately reemphasized at Vatican II, can hardly be integrated with the guide published by the German Bishops Conference, a text whose pastoral concern is comprehensible. The pastoral consequences of the proposal are easy to predict: the Eucharist will be seen as the sacrament of hospitality, where all are welcome, as long as they accept some part of Catholic belief in practice. Here, we have the privatization of the sacraments, of the Church's most public act.

The magisterial and canonical texts cited by *Mit Christus Gehen* point in a different direction. Canon 844 sets out the conditions under which a Protestant person may seek out Eucharist, penance, and anointing of the sick from a Catholic minister. It says that there must be the danger of death or another grave necessity. This language implies rarity. A good example would be a dying person who manifests Catholic faith in the sacraments, who has sought and continues to bear a strong inclination to enter the Catholic Church, yet who lacks the time and opportunity to pursue this path in a formal way. I use this example because the presence of a *coherent* Catholic Eucharistic faith implies faith in a sacramental priesthood (to offer one sacrifice with Christ), the acceptance of tradition (with liturgy as its first vehicle), the importance of unity with the bishop named in the Eucharist, and all the rest of Catholic teaching on the Eucharist. Here, it would be crucial to have some signs of the person's disposition to accept a coherent Catholic faith, and thus of visible unity with the Church, all the while recognizing the person's limitations in the reception of adequate instruction and spiritual guidance to render that faith fully explicit. Hence, as he comments on canon 844, John Paul II notes that "the denial of one or more truths of the faith regarding these sacraments and, among these, the truth regarding the need of the ministerial priesthood for their validity, renders the person asking improperly disposed to legitimately receiving them."[71]

71. John Paul II, *Ecclesia de Eucharistia*, no. 46, in *Encyclicals*, 34.

Eucharistic communion manifests, presumes, and reinforces the visible and spiritual unity of those partaking therein, and it offers supernatural nourishment on the path to heaven. Both ends of communion must be fostered. The Eucharist is not a means to visible unity, but a means to deeper spiritual communion on the foundation of a visible communion of faith and life. Now visible unity is not simply a matter of all or nothing. Thus, we share a partial visible unity with the eastern Orthodox, for we profess the same Creed and celebrate the same sacraments, with the same sacramental faith. We lack perfect visible unity, essentially with regards to the role of Peter's successor in the Church. We have a partial though lesser unity with the Protestant communities. The key text on this topic is paragraph 8 of *Lumen Gentium*: The Church of Christ subsists in the Catholic Church, but is present to a lesser degree elsewhere.

Since Vatican II, the magisterium has called for a balanced pursuit of the two ends mentioned above. That is, in some extraordinary cases, eastern Orthodox believers may seek out Catholic sacraments of anointing, penance, and Eucharist. Here, it is a question of urgent spiritual need, that is, a lack of access to their own ministers and their own sacraments. The aim is thus not to foster visible unity via the Eucharist (hence, we do not concelebrate the Eucharist with eastern Orthodox bishops or priests, although we pray together). The eastern Orthodox have retained a fully Catholic and coherent faith in the sacraments, (e.g., faith in a sacramental priesthood). Hence, they can receive the sacraments fruitfully, since the rites have no positive effect without faith in the saving reality being offered. Eastern Orthodox believers should not be presumed to bear the personal guilt of schism, just as we do not presume this for today's Protestant believers: schism is not an inherited sin. An eastern Orthodox believer shares the Catholic moral teaching rooted in the Gospel. Canon 844 mentions the necessity of the person's proper disposition, in other words, the living out of Christian morals (and thus the presence of charity). Here, the magisterium judges the person's spiritual need of the sacraments to bear greater weight than the presence of perfect visible unity.[72]

72. Vatican Council II, *Decree on the Oriental Churches* (*Orientalium Ecclesiarum*), nos. 26–27; Pontifical Council for the Promotion of the Unity of Christians, *Ecumenical Directory* (March, 1993), nos. 123–25.

It is not clear whether such sacramental reception can be regular or frequent.

Communion for the Divorced and Civilly Remarried?

Popes John Paul II, Benedict XVI, and Francis have spoken of the need to better integrate into the Church's life those couples who have experienced the pain of civil divorce, and, while their marriage has not been canonically declared null, have entered into a new civil marriage.[73] They are called to holiness and to share in many aspects of ecclesial life.

In *Amoris Laetitia*, Pope Francis calls for a greater recognition of cultural and subjective influences in moral decision making: "Because of forms of conditioning and mitigating factors, it is possible that in an objective situation of sin—which may not be subjectively culpable, or fully such—a person can be living in God's grace, can love and can also grow in the life of grace and charity, while receiving the Church's help to this end."[74] In other words, sometimes a person committing what is objectively speaking an act that is intrinsically sinful, such as premarital or extramarital intercourse, may not incur the guilt of a mortal sin, as a result of inadequate moral deliberation, which comes from poor catechesis, the influence of the surrounding culture, and other impediments to the formation of a Christian conscience.[75] Such obstacles have grown in recent decades in Western culture.

This historical development in turn calls for a more positive tone, of invitation rather than condemnation. Pope Francis desires careful discernment, so that pastors who accompany persons in complex and morally problematic situations encourage them to progress in the moral life by taking small steps forward.[76] This pastoral approach should also be animated by a deep respect for each person's conscience, as they seek to apply

73. John Paul II, *Familiaris Consortio*, nos. 83–84, in *The Post-Synodal Apostolic Exhortations of John Paul II*, ed. J. Michael Miller (Huntington, Ind.: Our Sunday Visitor, 1998); Benedict XVI, *Sacramentum Caritatis*, no. 29; Francis, *Amoris Laetitia, The Joy of Love: Post-Synodal Apostolic Exhortation* (Vatican City: Libreria Editrice Vaticana, 2016), chap. 8.

74. Francis, *Amoris Laetitia*, no. 305.

75. Francis, *Amoris Laetitia*, no. 301. See the helpful commentary by Basile Valuet, "*Amoris Laetitia*: Le chapitre VIII est-il une révolution?" *Revue Thomiste* 116 (2016): 585–618.

76. Francis, *Amoris Laetitia*, no. 305.

the law of Christ in their lives.[77] At the same time, the wise and merciful shepherd will heed St. Paul's urgent warning to the Corinthians to discern the body of the Lord (1 Cor 11). Pastoral accompaniment should not obscure how sin weakens the life of the whole community.

The synod of bishops on the family and the post-synodal apostolic exhortation *Amoris Laetitia* have generated much controversy. Various bishops and episcopal conferences have subsequently issued pastoral guidelines that show various points of perplexity and great difficulty (even outright contradiction between some episcopal documents) on the admission the divorced and civilly remarried to communion. This situation cannot last, given the immense confusion created among the faithful in some parts of the Church. Also, the pastoral consequences of theological and pastoral principles accepted for these cases must be seen for other cases: young Catholics who engage in premarital sex, persons who act upon a same-sex attraction, and other situations. Here, revolutionary pastoral practices or radical ambiguity on Gospel morals will only intensify catechetical confusion and the malformation of consciences.

In this situation, it is crucial to hold firm on sacramental as well as moral *principles* of Scripture and constant tradition. Also, Thomas, along with a venerable theological tradition, calls for nuance in the *application* of those principles to complex moral situations.[78] The International Theological Commission's 2009 document on natural law states:

> It is impossible to remain at the level of generality, which is that of the first principles of the natural law. In fact, moral reflection must descend into the concreteness of action to throw its light on it. But the more it faces concrete and contin-

77. Francis, *Amoris Laetitia*, nos. 300–302.

78. Thomas Aquinas, *Summa theologiae* I-II, q. 94, a. 4, corpus: "For since speculative reason deals principally with necessary things, which are such that it is impossible for them to be otherwise, truth is found without exception in the particular conclusions.... By contrast, practical reason deals with contingent things, which include human actions, and so even if there is some sort of necessity in the universal principles, nonetheless, the further down one descends to particulars, the more exceptions there are ... in practical matters, there is the same practical truth or correctness for everyone only with respect to the universal principles and not with respect to the particulars" (trans. Alfred Freddoso, https://www3.nd.edu/~afreddos/summa-translation/TOC.htm). Serge-Thomas Bonino notes that, in addition to this distinction, for Thomas, the positive norms of the natural moral law do not always oblige, unlike the negative norms, such as, "You shall not commit adultery." See Bonino, "Saint Thomas Aquinas in the Apostolic Exhortation *Amoris Laetitia*," *The Thomist* 80 (2016): 513–16.

gent situations, the more its conclusions are affected by a note of variability and uncertainty.[79]

Lawrence Feingold draws upon the work of Rocco Buttiglione as he proposes one scenario in which a divorced and civilly remarried person might receive communion. In confession, the penitent's status as divorced and civilly remarried (without abstinence) becomes manifest to the confessor, with signs of what Feingold calls inculpable ignorance. The confessor might ask whether the penitent understands the contradiction between his or her behavior and God's will. If the penitent says "no," then the confessor could ask: "But if you became convinced that this behavior is a serious contradiction of God's will, would you change it?" If the answer is "yes," then, says Feingold, perhaps footnote 351 of *Amoris Laetitia* would open the door to the reception of communion. Feingold notes that all of this should be done in a way that avoids scandal.[80]

Is this scenario acceptable? At the very least, I would add a double nuance. First, it should not be said that such persons lack the moral strength to change, as this would contradict the Council of Trent, which condemns the idea that God's grace may not suffice to carry out his commandments.[81] Rather, in some cases, a malformed moral conscience constitutes a major difficulty. Post-Christian western culture has produced a new kind of doctrinal and moral ignorance among some of the faithful. During sacramental confession, this can manifest itself not so much as inculpable ignorance as a perplexity of the penitent's conscience, especially when they struggle to judge well between contradictory doctrinal proposals offered by various bishops, priests, theologians, or catechists. Second, to further nuance Feingold's approach, the persons in question should already be in the habit of receiving communion, with the sincere conviction that this pleases God. I propose that the confessor should not encourage them to *begin* going to communion. Rather, he should look for a path whereby they come either to see that they should not receive the sacrament, or to change their action (so as to return to Eucharistic com-

79. International Theological Commission, *In Search of a Universal Ethic: A New Look at the Natural Law* (London: Catholic Truth Society, 2012), no. 53.

80. Feingold, *The Eucharist*, 553–54; Rocco Buttiglione, "*Amoris Laetitia: Risposte ai critici*," *Lateranum* 83 (2017): 191–240.

81. Council of Trent, *Decree on Justification*, DH 1536.

munion). The confessor should ask himself: how can I bring this person to the fullness of salvation, without relativizing Jesus' teaching?

The focus of pastoral care for persons in irregular situations should be on catechesis, spiritual accompaniment, the regular attendance of Mass, participation in prayer groups and other types of Christian fellowship, and the practice of the corporal works of mercy. Also, no one should presume that a particular couple's situation must, by itself, put them in a state of mortal sin. Let us recall that lack of access to communion is not a sign of condemnation.

Why do I propose to read *Amoris Laetitia* in this way? The reasons are moral and sacramental. First, Christ's teaching on marriage and adultery is strikingly clear (Mt 5). Indeed, it shocked his contemporaries, who had accepted divorce and remarriage for Jewish men. The practice of the early Christians shows that this teaching was not interpreted as an ideal for which they could aim, but a life-giving precept to be applied. It is crucial to hold firm to this principle: relativizing the value of clear Gospel teaching does great pastoral harm.

Second, the notion of intrinsically immoral acts is one of the great accomplishments of the Christian moral tradition. That is, however circumstances or ignorance might diminish moral culpability, some kinds of moral acts always remain objectively disordered, an obstacle to spiritual flourishing.[82] John Paul II's encyclical *Veritatis Splendor* taught the negative precepts of the natural law always oblige. He adds that the Church has always taught that one may never choose the kinds of acts that Christ forbids (including adultery, referencing Mt 19).[83] The proposal of some that sexual relations outside of the marriage setting can be life-giving contradicts this doctrine and puts the indissolubility of marriage in question.[84] The denial of *Veritatis Splendor*'s importance harms the moral and spiritual authority of the Church's current teaching, and risks reducing

82. John Finnis, *Moral Absolutes: Tradition, Revision, and Truth* (Washington, D.C.: The Catholic University of America Press, 1991).

83. John Paul II, *Veritatis Splendor*, Encyclical Letter, August 6, 1993, no. 52. See *The Encyclicals of John Paul II*, ed. Miller.

84. Mats Wahlberg, "The Two Faces of *Amoris Laetitia*," *First Things*, April 4 (2017), https://www.firstthings.com/web-exclusives/2017/04/the-two-faces-of-amoris-laetitia, accessed April 15, 2017.

all magisterial pronouncements to prudential judgments adapted to the culture. The Church thus loses her prophetic voice.

Third, from St. Paul through the whole of tradition, Eucharistic communion has been linked with moral practice in harmony with the words and example of Christ. In the constant liturgical and penitential tradition, the shepherd of the flock has an essential role in deciding who can commune, so that the decision does not belong to the recipient alone. The case, in 1 Corinthians 5, of Paul's disciplining the man who sleeps with his stepmother is a good example. The sacraments are the Church's public acts, her public manifestation of the kind of faith and moral life necessary to follow Christ consistently. As public acts, the sacraments are part of God's pedagogy, teaching the faithful which pattern of life leads to Christ and which does not. Admitting persons to communion who are known to live in an extramarital relation may signal to the community's members the moral acceptability of such a choice (regardless of the individual's conscience or moral culpability). As communal acts, the sacraments cannot be administered solely according to the moral discernment of the recipient, since this privatizes the Church's public rites. Furthermore, the pastor's decision primarily applies objective moral standards that judge visible or outward actions. He cannot discern whether a person in an irregular situation abides in a state of grace.[85] Rather, he might identify signs of diminished moral culpability or probable signs of the working of grace in a person's path of conversion. The pastor can recognize that the circumstances in some hard cases may render the person's (subjective) moral standing before God ambiguous (which is distinct from the false claim that objectively disordered moral acts can become life-giving). The individual's standing before God often remains a mystery open to God alone.

In all difficult cases, the pastor should offer a pastoral presence centered on God's mercy, a mercy that calls each person to conversion. The priest needs to walk with persons, with the ultimate aim of bringing them to participate in Eucharistic communion. And in fidelity to St. Paul, he

85. José Granados, Stephan Kampowski, and Juan José Pérez-Soba, *Amoris Laetitia: Accompagnare, discernere, integrare: Vademecum per una nuova pastorale familiare* (Siena, Italy: Cantagalli, 2016), 126.

needs to safeguard the common spiritual good of the Church by protecting the holiness of the sacraments, including that of the marriage bond.

Conclusion

The Eucharist is not the sacrament of the perfect. Rather, it is spiritual food and drink for those whose lips and heart say "Amen" to the gift received and to all that this entails, saying "Amen" to the Church who offers the gift and making a commitment to follow Christ's way, with a decision to leave behind whatever contradicts discipleship, so as to limp along the way of the Cross.

Communion with Christ entails communion with the Church: the vertical and horizontal dimensions go together. Communion is neither the individual's solitary encounter with God nor merely a sign of communal belonging. Rather, intimate contact with the Bridegroom in his very flesh and blood entails an ever-deeper participation in the covenant community that is the Church. One of the motives for protecting Eucharistic realism at all cost is to maximize the personal, spousal aspect of communion. Eucharistic realism in turn entails ecclesial realism. With Henri de Lubac, we can say that the effect of the Eucharist that is the Church must be adequate to its cause, which is Christ's Eucharistic body.[86] We confess more firmly that the Church is Christ's body when we discern his body on the altar.

The firm link between the Eucharist and the Church was recognized and lived by countless saints, among whom St. Catherine of Siena stands out. One day, before the liturgy, Catherine was illumined by God on the Church's tribulation. She then prayed thus before Mass, where "in Communion the soul most sweet tightens the bonds between it and God and knows its truth better. It is in God and God is in it, as a fish in the sea and the sea in the fish."[87] She then asked God for the reform of the Church. If we follow her example, communion received with fervor should elicit a

86. De Lubac, *Corpus Mysticum: L'Eucharistie et l'Église au Moyen Âge, étude historique* (Paris: Aubier, 1949), 289–90.

87. Catherine of Siena, *Book of Divine Teaching*, chaps. 1–2, quoted in Journet, *The Mass: The Presence of the Sacrifice of the Cross*, trans. Victor Szczurek (South Bend, Ind.: St. Augustine's Press, 2008), 194.

deep confidence that God will purify the Church's members and lead her to a safe harbor.

The Eucharist stands at the heart of the spiritual life, guiding each person along a unique path, as Journet explains:

> The effects of the Eucharistic Communion are multiple: They have the liberty and unpredictability of an entry of God into the soul. They can by turns console and distress the soul, illuminate and submerge it by eddies coming from the night of our Savior's agony. They can confound it by the sight of its own weakness and needs. They can reveal to it the passion of the Church, crucified on five continents and in humanity's distresses. Nevertheless, all multiplicity of its effects tends toward one end: the consummation of the spiritual life.[88]

The Eucharist stands at the center of the life of a persecuted Church, and thus of everyone committed to the way of the Cross. But the Cross leads to the fullness of life, which the Bread of Life gives.

88. Journet, *The Mass*, 196.

BIBLIOGRAPHY

General Studies and Works

Albertus Magnus. *On the Body of the Lord.* Translated by Albert Marie Surmanski. The Fathers of the Church: Mediaeval Continuation 17. Washington, D.C.: The Catholic University of America Press, 2017.

Auer, Johann. *A General Doctrine of the Sacraments and the Mystery of the Eucharist.* Washington, D.C.: The Catholic University of America Press, 1996.

Bauerschmidt, Frederick Christian. "The Eucharist." In *The Oxford Handbook of Catholic Theology*, edited by Lewis Ayres and Medi Ann Volpe, 277–93. Oxford: Oxford University Press, 2019.

Bonaventure. *On the Eucharist: Commentary on the Sentences, Book IV, Dist. 8–13.* Translated by Junius Johnson. Dallas Medieval Texts and Translations 23. Leuven: Peeters, 2017.

Boersma, Hans, and Matthew Levering, eds. *The Oxford Handbook of Sacramental Theology.* Oxford: Oxford University Press, 2015.

Bourgeois, Henri, Bernard Sesboüé, and Paul Tihon, eds. *Les signes du salut.* Histoire des dogmes 3. Paris: Desclée, 1995.

Bouyer, Louis. *Eucharist: Theology and Spirituality of the Eucharistic Prayer.* Translated by Charles Underhill Quinn. Notre Dame, Ind.: University of Notre Dame Press, 1968.

Bulgakov, Sergius. *The Holy Grail and the Eucharist.* Translated by Boris Jakim. Hudson, N.Y.: Lindisfarne Books, 1997.

Chauvet, Louis-Marie. *Symbol and Sacrament: A Sacramental Reinterpretation of Christian Existence.* Translated by Patrick Madigan and Madeleine Beaumont. Collegeville, Minn.: Liturgical Press, 1995.

Fagerberg, David W. *Theologica Prima: What Is Liturgical Theology?* 2nd ed. Chicago: Hillenbrand Books, 2004.

Feingold, Lawrence. *The Eucharist: Mystery of Presence, Sacrifice and Communion.* Steubenville, Ohio: Emmaus Academic, 2018.

García Ibáñez, Ángel. *L'eucaristia, dono e mistero: Trattato storico-dogmatico sul mistero eucaristico.* Sussidi di teologia. Rome: EDUSC, 2006.

Geldhof, Joris. "Liturgy as Theological Norm: Getting Acquainted with 'Liturgical Theology.'" *Neue Zeitschrift für Systematische Theologie und Religionsphilosophie* 52 (2010): 155–76.

———. "Thought and the Eucharist: Philosophical Models and Their Theological Appropriation." *Ephemerides Theologicae Lovanienses* 86 (2010): 83–106.

Giraudo, Cesare. *In unum corpus: Traité mystagogique sur l'eucharistie*. Translated by Éric Iborra and Pierre-Marie Hombert. Paris: Cerf, 2014.

Granados Garcia, José. *Tratado general de los sacramentos*. Sapientia fidei. Madrid: Biblioteca de Autores Cristianos, 2017.

Guitmund of Aversa. *On the Truth of the Body and Blood of Christ in the Eucharist*. Translated by Mark G. Vaillancourt. The Fathers of the Church, Mediaeval Continuation 10. Washington, D.C.: The Catholic University of America Press, 2009.

Hoping, Helmut. *Mein Leib für euch gegeben: Geschichte und Theologie der Eucharistie*. Freiburg im Breisgau: Herder, 2011.

Innocent III / Lothar of Segni. *Il Sacrosanto Mistero dell'Altare (De sacro Altaris Mysterio)*. Edited by Stanislao Fioramonti. Monumenta studia instrumenta liturgica 15. Vatican City: Libreria Editrice Vaticana, 2001.

Irwin, Kevin W. *Models of the Eucharist*. New York: Paulist Press, 2005.

Kereszty, Roch A., ed. *Rediscovering the Eucharist: Ecumenical Conversations*. New York: Paulist Press, 2003.

———. *Wedding Feast of the Lamb: Eucharistic Theology from a Biblical, Historical and Systematic Perspective*. Chicago: Hillenbrand Books, 2007.

Kilmartin, Edward J. *The Eucharist in the West: History and Theology*. Edited by Robert J. Daly. Collegeville, Minn.: Liturgical Press, 1998.

Leeming, Bernard. *Principles of Sacramental Theology*. London: Longmans, 1956.

Levering, Matthew. *Sacrifice and Community: Jewish Offering and Christian Eucharist*. Illuminations: Theory and Religion. Oxford: Blackwell, 2005.

Margelidon, Philippe-Marie. *Le sacrement de l'eucharistie: Corpus Domini Jesu Christi*. Bibliothèque de la Revue Thomiste. Paris: Parole et Silence, 2019.

Marshall, Bruce. "What Is the Eucharist? A Dogmatic Outline." In Boersma and Levering, *The Oxford Handbook of Sacramental Theology*, 500–516.

Mazza, Enrico. *The Celebration of the Eucharist: The Origin of the Rite and the Development of Its Interpretation*. Translated by Matthew J. O'Connell. Collegeville, Minn.: Liturgical Press, 1998.

McKenna, John H. *Become What You Receive: A Systematic Study of the Eucharist*. Chicago: Hildenbrand Books, 2012.

McPartlan, Paul. *The Eucharist Makes the Church: Henri de Lubac and John Zizioulas in Dialogue*. Edinburgh: T&T Clark, 1993.

———. *Sacrament of Salvation: An Introduction to Eucharistic Ecclesiology*. Edinburgh: T&T Clark, 1995.

Meyer, Hans Bernhard. *Eucharistie: Geschichte, Theologie, Pastoral*. Gottesdienst der Kirche 4. Regensburg: Friedrich Pustet, 1989.

Michel, Albert. "La messe chez les théologiens postérieurs au Concile de Trente: Essence et efficacité." In *Dictionnaire de théologie catholique*, edited by É. Amann, vol. 10.1, cols. 1143–1316. Paris: L. Letouzey et Âne, 1928.

Mudd, Joseph C. *Eucharist as Meaning: Critical Metaphysics and Contemporary Sacramental Theology*. Collegeville, Minn.: Liturgical Press, 2014.

Nicholas Cabasilas, *Commentary on the Divine Liturgy*. Translated by J. M. Hussey and P. A. McNulty, 5th ed. Crestwood, N.Y.: St. Vladimir's Seminary Press, 2002.

O'Neill, Colman. *New Approaches to the Eucharist*. Staten Island, N.Y.: Alba House, 1967.

Nutt, Roger W. *General Principles of Sacramental Theology*. Washington, D.C.: The Catholic University of America Press, 2017.

Peter Lombard. *The Sentences, Book 4: On the Doctrine of Signs*. Translated by Giulio Silano. Toronto: Pontifical Institute of Medieval Studies, 2010.

Pohle, Joseph. *Lehrbuch der Dogmatik in sieben Büchern*. 7th ed. Vol. 3. Wissenschaftliche Bibliothek, Series 1: Theologische Lehrbücher 22. Paderborn, Germany: Ferdinand Schöningh, 1922.

Rahner, Karl. "Considerations on the Active Role of the Person in the Sacramental Event." In *Theological Investigations*, vol. 14, 161–84. Translated by David Bourke. New York: Seabury, 1976.

Roguet, Aymon-Marie. Notes to Thomas Aquinas, *Somme théologique, l'eucharistie*, vol. 1, *3a, Questions 73–78*, 281–423. Paris: Desclée et Cie, 1960.

Root, Michael, and James J. Buckley, eds. *What Does It Mean to "Do This"? Supper, Mass, Eucharist*. The Pro Ecclesia Series. Eugene, Ore.: Cascade Books, 2014.

Scheffczyk, Leo. *Die Heilszeichen von Brot und Wein: Eucharistie als Mitte christlichen Lebens*. Munich: Don Bosco Verlag, 1973.

Schmemann, Alexander. *The Eucharist: Sacrament of the Kingdom*. Crestwood, N.Y.: St. Vladimir's Seminary Press, 1988.

Sokolowski, Robert. *Eucharistic Presence: A Study in the Theology of Disclosure*. Washington, D.C.: The Catholic University of America Press, 1994.

Stevenson, Kenneth. *Eucharist and Offering*. New York: Pueblo, 1986.

Thomas Aquinas. *Commentary on the Gospel of John, Chapters 1–8*. Edited by the Aquinas Institute. Translated by F. R. Larcher. Latin/English Edition of the Works of St. Thomas Aquinas 35. Lander, Wyo.: The Aquinas Institute for the Study of Sacred Doctrine, 2013.

———. *Commentary on the Letters of Saint Paul to the Corinthians*. Edited by B. Mortensen and E. Alarcón, translated by F. R. Larcher, B. Mortensen, and D. Keating. Latin/English Edition of the Works of St. Thomas Aquinas 38. Lander, Wyo.: The Aquinas Institute for the Study of Sacred Doctrine, 2013.

———. *Commentary on the Sentences, Book IV, Distinctions 1–13*. Translated by Beth Mortensen. Latin/English Edition of the Works of St. Thomas Aquinas 7. Green Bay, Wisc.: Aquinas Institute, 2017.

———. *Scriptum super libros Sententiarum*. 4 vols. Edited by Pierre Mandonnet (vols. 1–2) and Maria Fabianus Moos (vols. 3–4). Paris: P. Lethielleux, 1927–47.

———. *Summa contra Gentiles*. Vol. 3. Edited by Ceslaus Pera, Petrus Marc, and Petrus Caramello. Rome: Marietti, 1961

———. *Summa theologiae*. 4 vols. Ottawa: Commissio Piana, 1953.

———. *Summa theologiae*. Translation by Fred Freddoso. https://www3.nd.edu/~afreddos/summa-translation/TOC.htm.

———. *Super Epistolas S. Pauli lectura*. 2 vols. Edited by Raphael Cai. Rome: Marietti, 1953.

———. *Super Evangelium Sancti Ioannis lectura*. Edited by Raphael Cai. Rome: Marietti, 1952.

Tillard, Jean-Marie Roger. *L'Eucharistie: Pâque de l'Église*. Unam sanctam 44. Paris: Cerf, 1964. English Translation: *The Eucharist: Pasch of God's People*. Staten Island, N.Y.: Alba House, 1967.

———. "Théologie, voix catholique: La communion à la Pâque du Seigneur." In *Eucharistia: Encyclopédie de l'eucharistie*, edited by Maurice Brouard, 397–438. Paris: Cerf, 2002.

Urfels, Florent. *La Pâque du Messie: Introduction à une théologie eucharistique du judaïsme*. Collège des Bernardins 20. Paris: Parole et Silence, 2013.

Vorgrimler, Herbert. *Sacramental Theology*. Translated by Linda M. Maloney. Collegeville, Minn.: The Liturgical Press, 1992.

Biblical Studies

Albertus Magnus. *Enarrationes in Joannem*. Borgnet Edition 24. Paris, 1899.

———. *Super Matthaeum, Capitula I–XIV*. Edited by Bernhard Schmidt. Cologne Edition 21.1. Münster, Germany: Aschendorff Verlag, 1987.

Aletti, Jean-Noël. "Romans." In, *The International Bible Commentary*, edited by William R. Farmer, 1533–1600. Collegeville, Minn.: Liturgical Press, 1998.

Anderson, Gary A. *Sacrifice and Offerings in Ancient Israel: Studies in their Social and Political Importance*. Atlanta: Scholars Press, 1987.

———. "Sacrifice and Sacrificial Offerings: Old Testament." In *The Anchor Bible Dictionary*, vol. 5, edited by David Noel Friedman, 870–86. New York: Double Day, 1992.

———. *Sin: A History*. New Haven, Conn.: Yale University Press, 2009.

Arletti, Claudio. "La manna, cibo rivelatore del patto tra YHWH ed Israele." In *Il Verbo si è fatto 'pane': l'Eucaristia tra Antico e Nuovo Testamento*, edited by Giacomo Violi, 27–39. Assisi, Italy: Cittadella Editrice, 2009.

Baumert, Norbert, and Maria-Irma Seewann. "Eucharistie 'für alle' oder 'für viele'?" *Gregorianum* 89 (2008): 501–32.

Benoit, Pierre. *Exégèse et théologie*. Vol. 1. Cogitatio fidei 46.1. Paris: Cerf, 1960.

Betz, Johannes. *Die Eucharistie in der Zeit der griechischen Väter*. Vol. 2.1, *Die Realpräsenz des Leibes und Blutes Jesu im Abendmahl nach dem Neuen Testament*. Freiburg im Breisgau: Herder, 1961.

Bock, Darrell L. *Acts*. Baker Exegetical Commentary on the New Testament. Grand Rapids, Mich.: Baker Academic Press, 2007.

Bornkamm, Günther. "Die eucharistische Rede im Johannes-Evangelium." *Zeitschrift für die Neutestamentlische Wissenschaft* 47 (1956): 161–69.

Braun, F.-M. "L'eucharistie selon saint Jean." *Revue Thomiste* 70 (1970): 5–29.

Brown, Raymond E. *The Gospel according to John*. 2 volumes. Anchor Bible Commentary 29–29A. New York: Doubleday, 1966–70.

———. *The Death of the Messiah: From Gethsemane to the Grave, a Commentary on the Passion Narratives in the Four Gospels*. 2 volumes. The Anchor Bible Reference Library. New York: Doubleday, 1994.

Bultmann, Rudolf. *Das Evangelium des Johannes*. Kritisch-exegetischer Kommentar über das Neue Testament. Göttingen, Germany: Vandenhoeck & Ruprecht, 1968.

Conzelmann, Hans. *First Corinthians: A Commentary on the First Epistle to the Corinthians*. Translated by James W. Leitch. Hermeneia: A Critical and Historical Commentary on the Bible. Philadelphia: Fortress Press, 1975.

Danielou, Jean. *The Bible and the Liturgy*. Notre Dame, Ind.: University of Notre Dame Press, 1956.

Dauphinais, Michael. "And They Shall All Be Taught by God: Wisdom and the Eucharist in John 6." In *Reading John with St. Thomas Aquinas: Theological Exegesis and Speculative Theology*, edited by Michael Dauphinais and Matthew Levering, 312–17. Washington, D.C.: The Catholic University of America Press, 2005.

Douglas, Mary. "The Eucharist: Its Continuity with the Bread Sacrifice of Leviticus." *Modern Theology* 15 (1999): 209–24.

Dumoulin, Pierre. "La manne dans le livre de la Sagesse: Synthèse de traditions et préparation au mystère eucharistique." Dissertation of the Gregorian University. Rome: Pontificia Universitas Gregoriana, 1994.

Dunn, James D. G. "John VI—A Eucharistic Discourse?" *New Testament Studies* 17 (1970–71): 328–38.

———. *Christianity in the Making*. Vol. 1, *Jesus Remembered*. Grand Rapids, Mich.: William B. Eerdmans, 2003.

Dupont, Jacques. "'Ceci est mon corps', 'Ceci est mon sang'." *Nouvelle revue théologique* 80 (1958): 1025–41.

Dupuy, Bernard. "Pâque juive et Pâque chrétienne: À l'origine de la différence herméneutique." *ISTINA* 48 (2003): 339–56.

Durwell, F.-X. *L'Eucharistie, présence du Christ*. Paris: Les Editions Ouvrières, 1971.

Feuillet, André. "Les thèmes bibliques majeurs du discours sur le pain de vie (Jean 6)." *Nouvelle revue théologique* 82 (1960): 802–22; 918–39; 1040–62.

Garuti, Paolo. "Espiazione." In *Dizionario teologico sul sangue di Cristo*, edited by Tullio Veglianti, 474–81. Vatican City: Libreria Editrice Vaticana, 2007.

Gese, Hartmut. *Sulla teologia biblica*. Biblioteca della cultura religiosa 54. Brescia, Italy: Paideia, 1989.

Grelot, Pierre. *Église et ministère: Pour un dialogue critique avec Edward Schillebeeckx*. Paris: Cerf, 1983.

Hahn, Scott. *The Fourth Cup: Understanding the Mystery of the Last Supper and the Cross*. New York: Image, 2018.

Hauke, Manfred. *"Versato per molti": Studio per una fedele traduzione del "pro multis" nelle parole della consecrazione*. Siena, Italy: Cantagalli, 2008.

Hengel, Martin. *The Atonement: The Origins of the Doctrine in the New Testament*. Philadelphia: Fortress Press, 1981.

Hengel, Martin, and Anna Maria Schwemer. *Jesus und das Judentum*. Tübingen, Germany: Mohr Siebeck, 2007.

Hofius, Otfried. "The Lord's Supper and the Lord's Supper Tradition: Reflections on 1 Corinthians 11:23b–25." In Meyer, *One Loaf, One Cup*, 75–115.

Jaubert, Annie. *The Date of the Last Supper*. Translated by I. Rafferty. Staten Island, N.Y.: Alba House, 1965.

Jeremias, Joachim. *The Eucharistic Words of Jesus*. 3rd ed. Minneapolis, Minn.: Fortress Press, 1966.

Jostein, Ådna. "Jesus' Meals and Table Companions." In *The Eucharist: Its Origins and Contexts: Sacred Meal, Communal Meal Table Fellowship in Late Antiquity, Early Judaism, and Early Christianity*, vol. 1, *Old Testament, Early Judaism, New Testament*, ed. David Hellholm and Dieter Sänger, 331–53. Wissenschaftliche Untersuchungen zum Neuen Testament 376. Tübingen: Mohr Siebeck, 2017.

Keener, Craig S. *The Gospel of Matthew: A Socio-Rhetorical Commentary*. Grand Rapids, Mich.: William B. Eerdmans, 1999.

———. *The Gospel of John: A Commentary*. Vol. 1. Peabody, Mass.: Hendrickson, 2003.

———. *The Historical Jesus of the Gospels*. Grand Rapids, Mich.: William B. Eerdmans, 2009.

———. *Acts: An Exegetical Commentary*. Vol. 1, *Introduction and 1:1–2:47*. Grand Rapids, Mich.: Baker Academic, 2012.

Klauck, Hans-Josef. *Hausgemeinde und Hauskirche im frühen Christentum*. Stuttgart: Verlag Katholisches Bibelwerk, 1981.

———. "Presence in the Lord's Supper: 1 Corinthians 11:23–26 in the Context of Hellenistic Religious History." In Meyer, *One Loaf, One Cup*, 57–74.

———. "Sacrifice and Sacrificial Offerings: New Testament." In *The Anchor Bible Dictionary*, vol. 5, edited by David Noel Friedman, 886–91. New York: Doubleday, 1992.

Klawans, Jonathan. *Impurity and Sin in Ancient Judaism*. Oxford: Oxford University Press, 2000.

Larcher, Chrysostome. *Le livre de la Sagesse ou La Sagesse de Salomon*. Vol. 3. Études bibliques, New Series 5. Paris: J. Gabalda, 1985.

Léon-Dufour, Xavier. *Le partage du pain eucharistique selon le Nouveau Testament*. Paris: Seuil, 1982.

Marshall, I. Howard. *The Gospel of Luke: A Commentary on the Greek Text*. The New International Greek Testament Commentary. Grand Rapids, Mich.: William B. Eerdmans, 1978.

Meier, John P. *A Marginal Jew: Rethinking the Historical Jesus*. Vol. 1, *The Roots of the Problem and the Person*. The Anchor Bible Dictionary Reference Library. New York: Doubleday, 1991.

Meyer, Ben F. "The Expiation Motif in the Eucharistic Words: A Key to the History of Jesus?" In Meyer, *One Loaf, One Cup*, 11–33.

———, ed. *One Loaf, One Cup: Ecumenical Studies of 1 Cor 11 and Other Eucharistic Texts*. New Gospel Studies 6. Macon, Ga.: Mercer University Press, 1993.

Milgrom, Jacob. *Leviticus 1–16*. The Anchor Bible 3. New York: Doubleday, 1991.

Moberly, R. W. L. *Old Testament Theology: Reading the Hebrew Bible as Christian Scripture*. Grand Rapids, Mich.: Baker Academic, 2013.

Moloney, Francis J. "'He Loved Them to the End': Eucharist in the Gospel of John." *Worship* 91 (2017): 43–64.

Montague, George T. *First Corinthians*. Catholic Commentary on Sacred Scripture. Grand Rapids, Mich.: Baker Academic, 2011.

Pitre, Brant. *Jesus and the Last Supper*. Grand Rapids, Mich.: William B. Eerdmans, 2015.

Ratzinger, Joseph. *Jesus of Nazareth, Part 2: Holy Week, From the Entrance into Jerusalem to the Resurrection*. Translated by the Vatican Secretariat of State. San Francisco: Ignatius Press, 2011.

Sanders, E. P. *Judaism: Practice and Belief, 63 BCE–66 CE*. Philadelphia: Trinity Press International, 1992.

———. *The Historical Figure of Jesus*. London: Penguin, 1993.

Schenker, Adrian. "Les sacrifices dans la Bible." In *Recht und Kultur im Alten Testament: Achtzehn Studien*, 7–21. Orbis Biblicus et Orientalis 172. Fribourg, Switzerland: Universitätsverlag, 2000.

———. *Anfänge der Textgeschichte des Alten Testaments: Studien zu Entstehung und Verhältnis der frühesten Textformen*. Beiträge zur Wissenschaft vom Alten und Neuen Testament 194. Stuttgart: Kohlhammer, 2011.

Schnackenburg, Rudolf, *Das Johannesevangelium*. Vol. 2. Freiburg im Breisgau: Herder, 1971.

Söding, Thomas. "Brot und Wein: Die Gaben beim Letzten Abendmahl." *Internationale Katholische Zeitschrift Communio* 42 (2013): 237–48.

Thiselton, Anthony C. *The First Epistle to the Corinthians: A Commentary on the Greek Text*. The New International Greek Testament Commentary. Grand Rapids, Mich.: William B. Eerdmans, 2000.

Thurian, Max. *The Eucharistic Memorial, Part 2: The New Testament*. Translated by J. G. Davis. Ecumenical Studies in Worship 8. Richmond, Va.: John Knox Press, 1961.

Vanhoye, Albert. *Prêtres anciens, prêtre nouveau selon le Nouveau Testament*. Paris: Éditions du Seuil, 1980.

———. *The Letter to the Hebrews: A New Commentary*. Translated by Leo Arnold. New York: Paulist Press, 2015.

Wright, N. T. *Jesus and the Victory of God*. Minneapolis, Minn.: Fortress Press, 1996.
———. "The Lord's Prayer as a Paradigm for Christian Prayer." In *Into God's Presence: Prayer in the New Testament*, edited by Richard N. Longnecker, 132–54. Grand Rapids, Mich.: William B. Eerdmans, 2001.
Zsengellér, József. "'The Taste of Paradise', Interpretation of Exodus and Manna in the Book of Wisdom." In *Studies in the Book of Wisdom*, edited by Géza G. Xeravits and József Zsengellér, 197–216. Supplements to the Journal for the Study of Judaism 142. Leiden, Netherlands: Brill, 2010.

Magisterial Teaching: Documents

Denzinger, Heinrich. *Compendium of Creeds, Definition, and Declarations on Matters of Faith and Morals*. Edited by Helmut Hoping, Peter Hünemann, Robert Fastiggi, and Anne Englung Nash. 43rd ed. San Francisco: Ignatius Press, 2012.
Flannery, Austin, ed. *Vatican Council II*. Vol. 1, *The Conciliar and Post Conciliar Documents*. Rev. ed. Dublin, Ireland: Dominican Publications.
Francis. *Amoris Laetitia, The Joy of Love: Post-Synodal Apostolic Exhortation*. Vatican City: Libreria Editrice Vaticana, 2016.
Hill, Christopher, and E. J. Yarnold, eds. *Anglicans and Roman Catholics: The Search for Unity*. London: SPCK/CTS, 1994.
Palmer, P., ed., *Sources of Christian Theology I: Sacraments and Worship*. London, 1957.
John Paul II. *The Encyclicals of John Paul II*. Edited by J. Michael Miller. Huntington, Ind.: Our Sunday Visitor, 1996.
———. *The Post-Synodal Apostolic Exhortations of John Paul II*. Edited by J. Michael Miller. Huntington, Ind.: Our Sunday Visitor, 1998.
———. *Ecclesia de Eucharistia*. Vatican City: Libreria Editrice Vaticana, 2003.
———. *Encyclicals*. Trivandrum, Kerala, India: Carmel International Publishing House, 2005.
Paul VI. *Mysterium Fidei*. In *The Papal Encyclicals*, vol. 5, edited by Claudia Carlen, 165–77. Ypsilanti, Mich.: The Pierian Press, 1990.
Pius XII. *Mediator Dei*. In *The Papal Encyclicals*, vol. 4, edited by Claudia Carle, 119–54. Ypsilanti, Mich.: The Pierian Press, 1990.
———. *Mystici Corporis Christi*. In *The Papal Encyclicals*, vol. 4, edited by Claudia Carlen, 37–63. Ypsilanti, Mich.: The Pierian Press, 1990.
Pontifical Council for the Promotion of the Unity of Christians. *Ecumenical Directory*. March, 1993.
———. "The Official Roman Catholic Response to the Final Report of ARCIC I (1991)." http://www.vatican.va/roman_curia/pontifical_councils/chrstuni/angl-comm-docs/rc_pc_chrstuni_doc_1991_catholic-response-arcici_en.html.

Magisterial Teaching: Studies

Bourgeois, Henri. "La constitution de la sacramentaire du XIIe au XVIe siècles." In Bourgeois, Sesboüé, and Tihon, *Les signes du salut*, 109–41.

———. "Les sacrements selon Vatican II." In Bourgeois, Sesboüé, and Tihon, *Les signes du salut*, 243–82.

Driscoll, Jeremy. "Sacrosanctum Concilium." In *The Reception of Vatican II*, edited by Matthew L. Lamb and Matthew Levering, 23–47. Oxford: Oxford University Press, 2017.

Gutierrez, C. *Trento: Un concilio para la unión (1550–1552)*. Vol. 3, *Estudio*. Corpus tridentinum hispanicum 4. Madrid: Instituto Enrique Florez, 1981.

Iserloh, Erwin. "Das tridentinische Meßopferdekret in seinen Beziehungen zu der Kontroverstheologie der Zeit." In *Il Concilio di Trento e la riforma tridentina: atti del convengo storico internazionale*, vol. 2, edited by Convengo storico internazionale 1963, 401–39. Rome: Herder, 1965.

Jedin, Hubert. *Geschichte des Konzils von Trient*. 5 volumes. Freiburg im Breisgau: Herder, 1951–75. English translation: *A History of the Council of Trent*. Translated by Ernest Graf. London: Nelson, 1957–61.

Mansini, Guy, "Lumen Gentium." In *The Reception of Vatican II*, edited by Matthew L. Lamb and Matthew Levering, 48–80. Oxford: Oxford University Press, 2017.

O'Malley, John W. *What Happened at Vatican II?* London: Harvard University Press, 2008.

Servigny, Gérald de. *La théologie de l'eucharistie dans le concile de Vatican II*. Paris, 2000.

Sesboüé, Bernard. "La doctrine sacramentaire du concile de Trente II: L'Eucharistie et le sacrifice de la Messe." In Bourgeois, Sesboüé, and Tihon, *Les signes du salut*, 158–70.

Wohlmuth, Josef. *Realpräsenz und Transsubstantiation im Konzil von Trient*. 2 vols. Bern: H. Lang, 1975.

Ancient Documents and the Church Fathers on the Eucharist

Ambrose of Milan. *De incarnationis dominicae sacramento*. Edited by Claudio Moreschini. Opera Omnia di Sant'Ambrogio 16. Rome: Nuova Città, 1979.

———. *De officiis*. Edited by Mauritius Testard. CCSL 15. Turnhout, Belgium: Brepols, 2000.

———. *Explanatio Psalmorum* XII. Edited by M. Petschenig. Corpus Scriptorum Ecclesiasticorum Latinorum 64. Vindobonae: Verlag der Österreichischen Akademie der Wissenschaften, 1999.

———. *Theological and Dogmatic Works*. Translated by Roy Deferrari. The Fathers of the Church 44. Washington, D.C.: The Catholic University of America Press, 1963.

Augustine. *City of God*. The Fathers of the Church 14. Washington, D.C.: The Catholic University of America Press, 1963.

———. *De civitate Dei*. Edited by Bernardus Dombart and Alphonsus Kalb. CCSL 47. Turnhout, Belgium: Brepols, 1955.

———. *Epistulae 56–100*. Edited by Kl. D. Daur. CCSL 31A. Turnhout, Belgium: Brepols, 2005.

———. *Expositions of the Psalms 73–98*. Translated by Maria Boulding. Works of St. Augustine 3.18. Hyde Park, N.Y.: New City Press, 2002.

———. *Homélies sur l'évangile de saint Jean, XVII–XXXIII*. Bibliothèque Augustinienne 72. Paris: Desclée de Brouwer, 1972.

———. *Letters 1–99*. Translated by Roland Teske. The Works of Saint Augustine 2.1. Hyde Park, N.Y.: New City Press, 2001.

———. *Sermons (184–229Z) on the Liturgical Seasons*. Translated by Edmund Hill. The Works of St. Augustine 3.6. Hyde Park, N.Y.: New City Press, 1993.

———. *Sermons (230–272B) on the Liturgical Seasons*. Translated by Edmund Hill. The Works of St. Augustine 3.7. Hyde Park, N.Y.: New City Press, 1994.

———. *Tractates on the Gospel of John, 11–27*. Translated by John W. Rettig. The Fathers of the Church 79. Washington, D.C.: The Catholic University of America Press, 1988.

———. *Tractates on the Gospel of John, 55–111*. Translated by John W. Rettig. The Fathers of the Church 90. Washington, D.C.: The Catholic University of America Press, 1994.

Basil the Great, "Letter 93." In *Letters 1–185*. Translated by Agnes Claire Way. Notes by Roy J. Deferrari. The Fathers of the Church 13. Washington, D.C.: The Catholic University of America Press, 1951.

Bradshaw, Paul F., Maxwell E. Johnson, and L. Edward Phillips, eds. *The Apostolic Tradition: A Commentary*. Hermeneia: A Critical and Historical Commentary on the Bible. Philadelphia: Fortress Press, 2002.

Brooks, Ernest Walter, ed. *The Sixth Book of the Select Letters of Severus, Patriarch of Antioch, in the Syria Version of Athanasius of Nisibis*. Vol. 2. London: Williams & Norgate, 1904.

Cyprian of Carthage. *Ceux qui sont tombés (De lapsis)*. Translated by Michel Poirier. Notes by Graeme Clark. Sources chrétiennes 547. Paris: Cerf, 2012.

———. *Epistularium: Epistulae 58–81*. Edited by G. F. Diercks. CCSL 3C. Turnhout, Belgium: Brepols, 1996.

———. *Letters 55–66*. Translated by G. W. Clarke. Ancient Christian Writers 46. New York: Paulist Press, 1986.

Cyril of Alexandria. *Commentary on the Gospel of John*. Vol. 1. Translated by David R. Maxwell. Edited by Joel C. Elowksy. Ancient Christian Texts. Downers Grove, Ill.: IVP Academic, 2013.

Cyril of Jerusalem. *Catéchèses mystagogiques*. Edited by Auguste Piédagnel. Translated by Pierre Paris. Sources chrétiennes 126bis. Paris: Cerf, 1966.

———. *Works*. Translated by Leo P. McCauley and Anthony A. Stephenson. The Fathers of the Church 64. Washington, D.C.: The Catholic University of America Press, 1970.

Gelston, Anthony. *The Eucharistic Prayer of Addai and Mari*. Oxford: Clarendon Press, 1992.

Gregory of Nazianzen. *Briefe*. Edited by Michael Wittig. Bibliothek der Griechischen Literatur 13. Stuttgart: Anton Hiersemann, 1981.

Hänggi, Anton, and Irmgard Pahl, eds. *Prex Eucharistica: Textus e variis liturgiis antiquioribus selecti*. Spicilegium Friburgense 12. Fribourg, Switzerland: Éditions universitaires Fribourg, 1968.

Ignatius of Antoch. *Letters to the Smyrnaeans*. In Kleist, *The Epistles of St. Clement of Rome and St. Ignatius of Antioch*.

Irenaeus of Lyon. *Against the Heresies*. Vol. 2. Translated by Dominic J. Unger and John J. Dillon. Ancient Christian Writers 65. New York: Paulist Press, 2012.

———. *Contre les hérésies, livre IV*. Edited by Adelin Rousseau. Sources chrétiennes 100.2. Paris: Cerf, 1965.

———. *Contre les hérésies, livre V*. Edited by Adelin Rousseau. Sources chrétiennes 125. Paris: Cerf, 1969.

Jenkins, Claude. "Origen on 1 Corinthians, part 3." *Journal of Theological Studies* 9 (1908): 500–514.

John Damascene. *On the Orthodox Faith*. Translated by Frederic H. Chase. The Fathers of the Church 37. New York: Fathers of the Church, 1958.

———. *Die Schriften des Johannes von Damaskos*. Edited by Bonifatius Kotter. Patristische Texte und Studien 12. Berlin: Walter de Gruyter, 1972.

Justin Martyr. *The Apology, The Second Apology, Dialogue with Trypho*. Edited by Michael Slusser. Translated by Thomas B. Falls. Revised by Thomas P. Halton. Washington, D.C.: The Catholic University of America Press, 2003.

———. *First and Second Apologies*. Edited and translated by L. W. Barnard. Ancient Christian Writers 56. New York: Paulist Press, 1997.

Kleist, James A., ed. *The Didache*. Ancient Christian Writers 6. New York: Paulist Press, 1978.

———. *The Epistles of St. Clement of Rome and St. Ignatius of Antioch*. Ancient Christian Writers 1. New York: Paulist Press, 1978.

Missel chaldéen: L'ordre des mystères avec les trois anaphores, selon le rite de la sainte Eglise de l'Orient. Edited by Francis Alichoran and P. Perrier. Paris: Eglise chaldéenne, 1982.

Niederwimmer, Kurt. *The Didache: A Commentary*. Translated by Linda M. Maloney. Hermeneia: A Critical and Historical Commentary on the Bible. Philadelphia: Fortress Press, 1998.

Schoedel, William R. *A Commentary on the Letters of Ignatius of Antioch*. Edited by Helmut Koester. Hermeneia. Philadelphia: Fortress Press, 1985.

Srawley, James Herbert. *The Catechetical Oration of Gregory of Nyssa*. Cambridge: Cambridge University Press, 1903.

Tertullian. *Opere Montaniste*, vol. 4.2. Edited by A. Capone, S. Isetta, S. Matteoli, A. Persic, R. Uglione. Scrittori Cristiani dell'Africa Romana. Rome: Nuova Città, 2012.

———. *Opera Montanistica*. Vol. 2. CCSL 2. Turnhout, Belgium: Brepols, 1954.
Theodore of Mopsuestia. *Katechetische Homilien*. 2 volumes. Translated by Peter Bruns. Fontes Christiani 17.1–2. Freiburg im Breisgau: Herder, 1994.
Theodoret of Cyrus, *Histoire ecclésiastique*. Translated by Pierre Canivet. Sources chrétiennes 501. Paris: Cerf, 2006.

Studies on the Eucharist and Liturgy in the Early and Medieval Church

Anatolios, Khaled. "Sacraments in the Fourth Century." In Boersma and Levering, *The Oxford Handbook of Sacramental Theology*, 140–55.
Barnard, Leslie William. "Notes." In Justin Martyr, *First and Second Apologies*, edited by L. W. Barnard, 97–201. Ancient Christian Writers 56. New York: Paulist Press, 1997.
Bellescize, Luc de. "L'eucharistie chez Ignace d'Antioche et Polycarpe de Smyrne." *Nouvelle revue théologique* 132 (2010): 197–216.
Betz, Johannes. *Die Eucharistie in der Zeit der griechischen Väter*. Vol. 1.1, *Die Aktualpräsenz der Person und des Heilswerkes Jesu im Abendmahl nach der vorephesinischen griechischen Patristik*. Freiburg im Breisgau: Herder, 1955.
———. *Eucharistie in der Schrift und Patristik*. Handbuch der Dogmengeschichte 4.4a. Freiburg im Breisgau: Herder, 1979.
Botte, Bernard. "Holy Orders in the Ordination Prayers." In *The Sacrament of Holy Orders: Some Papers and Discussions concerning Holy Orders at a Session of the Centre de Pastorale Liturgique, 1955*. London: Aquin Press, 1957.
Bradshaw, Paul F. *The Search for the Origins of Christian Worship: Sources and Methods for the Study of the Early Liturgy*. Oxford: Oxford University Press, 1992.
———. "Introduction: The Evolution of Early Anaphoras." In *Essays on Early Eastern Eucharistic Prayers*, edited by Paul F. Bradshaw, 1–18. Collegeville, Minn.: The Liturgical Press, 1997.
———. *Reconstructing Early Christian Worship*. London: SPCK, 2009.
Bradshaw, Paul F., and Lawrence A. Hoffman, eds. *The Making of Jewish and Christian Worship*. Notre Dame, Ind.: University of Notre Dame Press, 1991.
Camelot, P. Th. "Réalisme et symbolisme dans la doctrine eucharistique de s. Augustin." *Revue des sciences philosophiques et théologiques* 31 (1947): 394–410.
Daly, Robert. "Eucharistic Origins: From the New Testament to the Liturgies of the Golden Age." *Theological Studies* 66 (2005): 3–22.
Dix, Gregory. *The Shape of the Liturgy*. London: Dacre Press, 1945.
Giraudo, Cesare. "'In persona Christi' 'In persona Ecclesiae': Formule eucaristiche alla luce della 'lex orandi'." *Rassegna Teologia* 51 (2010): 181–95.
Hope, D. M. "The Medieval Western Rites." In Jones et al., *The Study of the Liturgy*, 264–85.
Jackson, Pamela. "Eucharist." In *Augustine through the Ages: An Encyclopedia*, edited by

Fitzgerald, Allan and John C. Cavadini, 330–34. Grand Rapids, Mich.: William B. Eerdmans, 1999.

Gy, Pierre-Marie. "Doctrine eucharistique de la liturgie romaine dans le haut moyen âge." In *La liturgie dans l'histoire*, 187–203.

———. *La liturgie dans l'histoire*. Paris: Cerf, 1990.

Johanny, Raymond. *L'eucharistie centre de l'histoire du salut chez saint Ambroise de Milan*. Théologie historique 9. Paris: Beauchesne, 1969.

Johnson, Maxwell E. "The Apostolic Tradition." In *The Oxford History of Christian Worship*, edited by Geoffrey Wainwright and K. B. Westerfield Tucker, 32–75. Oxford: Oxford University Press, 2006.

Jones, Cheslyn, Geoffrey Wainwright, Edward Yarnold, and Paul Bradshaw, eds. *The Study of the Liturgy*. Rev. ed. Oxford: Oxford University Press, 1992.

Jungmann, Joseph A. *The Mass of the Roman Rite: Its Origin and Development*. 2 volumes. Translated by Francis A. Brunner. Notre Dame, Ind.: Christian Classics, 2012.

Lang, Uwe Michael. "Eucharist without Institution Narrative? The Anaphora of Addai and Mari Revisited." In *Die Anaphora von Addai und Mari: Studien zu Eucharistie und Einsetzungsworten*, edited by Uwe Michael Lang, 31–65. Bonn: Nova & Vetera, 2007.

———. "Rhetoric of Salvation: The Origins of Latin as the Language of the Roman Liturgy." In *The Genius of the Roman Rite: Historical, Theological, and Pastoral Perspectives on Catholic Liturgy*, 22–44. Chicago: Hillenbrand Books, 2009.

Lienhard, Joseph T. "*Sacramentum* and the Eucharist in St. Augustine." *The Thomist* 77 (2013): 173–92.

Macomber, William. "The Ancient Form of the Anaphora of the Apostles." In *East of Byzantium: Syria and Armenia in the Formative Period*, edited by Nina Gargoian, Thomas Mathews, and Robert Thomson, 73–88. Washington, D.C.: Centre for Byzantine Studies, 1982.

Moll, Helmut. *Die Lehre von der Eucharistie als Opfer*. Cologne: Peter Hanstein, 1975.

O'Loughlin, Thomas. "Theologies of Intercommunion: Responding to a Recent Papal Request." *New Blackfriars* 97 (May 2016): 372–87.

Orbe, Antonio. *Teología de San Ireneo IV: Traducción y comentario del libro IV del "Adversus haereses."* Madrid: Biblioteca de Autores Cristianos, 1986.

———. *Introduction à la théologie des IIe et IIIe siècles*. 2 volumes. Translated by Joseph M. López de Castro, Agnès Bastit, and Jean-Michel Roessli. Patrimoines: Christianisme. Paris: Cerf, 2012.

Perler, Othmar. "Logos und Eucharistie nach Justinus I Apol. 66." *Freiburger Zeitschrift für Philosophie und Theologie* 18 (1940): 296–316.

Perrin, Michel-Yves. "Pratiques et discours eucharistiques dans les premiers siècles (des origines jusqu'à la fin du IVe siècle): Considérations introductives." In *Eucharistia: Encyclopédie de l'eucharistie*, edited by Maurice Brouard, 105–24. Paris: Cerf, 2002.

Rordorf, Willy. Introduction to *La doctrine des douze apôtres (Didachè)*, edited by W. Rordorf and André Tuilier, 11–135. Sources chrétiennes 248. Paris: Cerf, 1978.

———. *Liturgie, foi et vie des premiers chrétiens: Études patristiques*. Théologie historique 75. Paris: Beauchesne, 1986.

Russo, Nicholas, "The Validity of the Anaphora *Addai and Mari*: Critiques of the Critique." In *Issues in Eucharistic Praying in East and West: Essays in Liturgical and Theological Analysis*, edited by Maxwell E. Johnson, 21–62. Collegeville, Minn.: Liturgical Press, 2010.

Santogrossi, Ansgar. "Anaphoras without Institution Narrative: Historical and Dogmatic Considerations." *Nova et Vetera* (English Edition) 10 (2012): 27–59.

Sesboüé, Bernard. "Le témoignage de l'Église ancienne, des institutions sacramentelles II: La célébration des mystères, l'Eucharistie." In Bourgeois, Sesboüé, and Tihon, *Les signes du salut*, 66–81.

Sheerin, Daniel. "Eucharistic Liturgy." In *The Oxford Handbook of Early Christian Studies*, edited by David G. Hunter and Susan Ashbrook Harvey, 711–29. Oxford: Oxford University Press, 2008.

van der Lof, J. L. "L'eucharistie et présence réelle selon saint Augustin." *Revue des études augustiniennes* 10 (1964): 295–304.

Van Slyke, Daniel G. "The Study of Early Christian Worship." In *T&T Clark Companion to Liturgy*, edited by Alcuin Reid, 43–71. London: T&T Clark, 2016.

Wilson, Stephen B. "The Anaphora of the Apostles Addai and Mari." In *Essays on Early Eastern Eucharistic Prayers*, edited by Paul F. Bradshaw, 19–37. Collegeville, Minn.: The Liturgical Press, 1997.

Yarnold, Edward J. "The Liturgy of the Faithful in the Fourth and Early Fifth Centuries." In Jones et al., *The Study of the Liturgy*, 230–44.

———. "Anaphoras without Institution Narratives?" *Studia Patristica* 30 (1997): 395–410.

Zheltov, Michael. "The Anaphora and the Thanksgiving Prayer from the Barcelona Papyrus: An Underestimated Testimony to the Anaphoral History in the Fourth Century." *Vigiliae Christianae* 62 (2008): 467–504.

Medieval Theologies of the Eucharist: Studies

Colish, Marcia L. *Peter Lombard*. 2 volumes. Brill's Studies in Intellectual History 41.1–2. Leiden, Netherlands: E. J. Brill, 1994.

Cross, Richard. *Duns Scotus*. Great Medieval Thinkers. Oxford: Oxford University Press, 1999.

de Lubac, Henri. *Corpus Mysticum: L'Eucharistie et l'Église au Moyen Âge, étude historique*. Paris: Aubier, 1949.

———. *Corpus Mysticum: The Eucharist and the Church in the Middle Ages*. Translated by Gemma Simmonds and Richard Price. London: SCM Press, 2006.

Iserloh, Erwin. "Abendmahl III/2: Mittelalter." In *Theologische Realenzyklopädie*, vol. 1, edited by Gerhard Kraus and Gerhard L. Müller, 89–106. Berlin: Walter de Gruyter, 1977.

Levy, Ian Christopher. "The Eucharist and Canon Law in the High Middle Ages." In

A Companion to the Eucharist in the Middle Ages, edited by Ian Christopher Levy, Gary Macy, and Kristen Van Ausdall, 399–445. Brill Companions to the Christian Tradition 26. Leiden, Netherlands: Brill, 2012.

———. "The Eucharist in the Fourteenth and Fifteenth Centuries." In Boersma and Levering, *The Oxford Handbook of Sacramental Theology*, 235–48.

Macy, Gary. *The Theologies of the Eucharist in the Early Scholastic Period*. Oxford: Clarendon Press, 1984.

———. *Treasures from the Storeroom: Medieval Religion and the Eucharist*. Collegeville, Minn.: Liturgical Press, 1999.

Mangenot, E. "Eucharistie du XIIIe au XVe siècle." In *Dictionnaire de théologie catholique*, edited by E. Mangenot, vol. 5, cols. 1302–1326. Paris: Librairie Letouzey et Ané, 1939.

Montclos, Jean de. *Lanfranc et Bérengar: La controverse eucharistique du XIe siècle*. Spicilegium sacrum Lovaniense: Études et documents 37. Louvain: Spicilegium sacrum Lovaniense, 1971.

Morard, Martin. "L'eucharistie, clé de voûte de l'organisme sacramentel chez saint Thomas d'Aquin." *Revue Thomiste* 95 (1995): 217–50.

———. "Les expressions 'corpus mysticum' et 'persona mystica' dans l'œuvre de saint Thomas d'Aquin." *Revue Thomiste* 95 (1995): 653–64.

Murray, Paul. *Aquinas at Prayer: The Bible, Mysticism and Poetry*. London: Bloomsbury, 2013.

Oberman, Heiko Augustinus. *The Harvest of Medieval Theology: Gabriel Biel and Late Medieval Nominalism*. Cambridge, Mass.: Harvard University Press, 1963.

Tück, Jan-Heiner. *Gabe der Gegenward: Theologie und Dichtung der Eucharistie bei Thomas von Aquin*. Freiburg im Breisgau: Herder, 2009. English Translation: *A Gift of Presence: The Theology and Poetry of the Eucharist in Thomas Aquinas*. Translated by Scott G. Hefelfinger. Washington, D.C.: The Catholic University of America Press, 2018.

Vijgen, Jörgen. *The Status of Eucharistic Accidents 'sine subiecto'*. Quellen und Forschungen zur Geschichte des Dominikanerordens, Neue Folge 20. Berlin: Akademie Verlag, 2013.

Wawrykow, Joseph P. "The Sacraments in Thirteenth-Century Theology." In Boersma and Levering, *The Oxford Handbook of Sacramental Theology*, 218–34.

Wéber, Édouard-Henri. "L'incidence du traité de l'eucharistie sur la métaphysique de s. Thomas d'Aquin." *Revue des sciences philosophiques et théologiques* 77 (1993): 195–218.

The Institution of the Eucharist and the Eucharistic Signs

Bride, A. "Vin de messe." In *Dictionnaire de théologie catholique*, edited by É. Amann, vol. 15, cols. 3014–26. Paris: L. Letouzey et Âne, 1950.

Gaïse, Roger. *Les signes sacramentels de l'eucharistie dans l'église latine: Études théologiques et historiques*. Studia Friburgensia 89. Fribourg, Switzerland: Éditions universitaires, 2001.

Perrin, Bertrand-Marie. *L'institution des sacrements dans le Commentaire des Sentences de saint Thomas*. Bibliothèque de la Revue Thomiste. Paris: Parole et Silence, 2008.

Revel, Jean-Philippe, *Traité des sacrements*. Vol. 1, *Baptême et sacramentalité*, part 1, *Origine et signification du baptême*. Paris: Cerf, 2004.

Worship and Sacrifice

Cajetan, Thomas Vio. "The Celebration of the Mass." In Heiko Augustinus Oberman, *Forerunners of the Reformation: The Shape of Late Medieval Thought*, 256–78. Translated by Paul L. Nyhus. London: Lutterworth Press, 1967.

———. "De Missa Sacrificio et Ritu, adversus Lutheranos, ad Clementem VII," in *Opuscula Omnia*, 218–20. Venice: Apud Iuntas, 1712.

———. "Errors on the Lord's Supper (1525)." In Jared Wicks, *Cajetan Responds: A Reader in Reformation Controversy*, 153–74. Washington, D.C.: The Catholic University of America Press, 1978.

———. "The Sacrifice of the Mass: Against the Lutherans (1531)." In Jared Wicks, *Cajetan Responds: A Reader in Reformation Controversy*, 189–200. Washington, D.C.: The Catholic University of America Press, 1978.

Casel, Odo. *The Mystery of Christian Worship and Other Writings*. Edited by Burkhard Neunheuser. London: Darton, Longman & Todd, 1962.

Clark, Francis. *Eucharistic Sacrifice and the Reformation*. Oxford: Basil Blackwell, 1960.

Daly, Robert. *The Origins of the Christian Doctrine of Sacrifice*. Philadelphia: Fortress Press, 1978.

de la Soujeole, Benoît-Dominique. "La présence dans les saints mystères: Réflexions à propos du présent christologique de l'Eucharistie." *Revue Thomiste* 104 (2004): 395–419.

de la Taille, Maurice. *The Mystery of Faith: Regarding the Most August Sacrament and Sacrifice of the Body and Blood of Christ*. 2 volumes. London: Sheed & Ward, 1940–50.

Evans, Gillian R. "Opfer V: Mittelalter bis Neuzeit." In *Theologische Realenzyklopädie*, vol. 25, edited by Gerhard L. Müller, 278–86. Berlin: Walter de Gruyter, 1995.

Filip, Stepan Martin. "Imago repraesentativa passionis Christi: L'essenza del sacrificio della Messa nella sua parte formale secondo San Tommaso d'Aquino." Dissertatio ad lauream in Facultatae S. Theologiae apud Pontificiam Universitatem S. Thomae in Urbe, 2007.

———. "*Imago Repraesentativa Passionis Christi*: St. Thomas Aquinas on the Essence of the Sacrifice of the Mass." *Nova et Vetera* (English Edition) 7 (2009): 405–38.

Garrigou-Lagrange, Réginald. "An Christus non solum virtualiter sed actualiter offerat Missas quae quotidie celebrantur." *Angelicum* 19 (1942): 115–18.

———. *De eucharistia, accedunt de paenitentia: Questiones dogmaticae, Commentarius in Summam theologicam S. Thomae*. Paris: Desclée de Brouwer, 1943.

Geldhof, Joris. "On Interiorizing the Mystery of the Eucharist: A Reflection on *Sacrosanctum Concilium*, no. 48." *Questions liturgiques / Studies in Liturgy* 97 (2016): 123–40.

Girard, René. *Violence and the Sacred*. Baltimore, Md.: John Hopkins University Press, 1984.

Hart, David Bentley. "Thine Own of Thine Own: The Orthodox Understanding of Eucharistic Sacrifice." In *The Hidden and the Manifest: Essays in Theology and Metaphysics*, 191–216. Grand Rapids, Mich.: William B. Eerdmans, 2017.

Hauke, Manfred. "What Is the Holy Mass? The Systematic Discussion on the 'Essence' of Eucharistic Sacrifice." In *Celebrating the Eucharist: Sacrifice and Communion*, edited by Gerard Deighan, 108–34. Fota Liturgy Series 5. Wells, Somerset, Great Britain: Smenos/Carrigboy, 2012.

Hütter, Reinhard, and Matthew Levering, eds. *Ressourcement Thomism: Sacred Doctrine, the Sacraments and Moral Life*. Washington, D.C.: The Catholic University of America Press, 2010.

John Duns Scotus. *Quodlibet*. In *Opera omnia*, vol. 2.1, edited by Giovanni Lauriola. Bari, Italy: Alberobello, 1999.

Journet, Charles. *The Mass: The Presence of the Sacrifice of the Cross*. Translated by Victor Szczurek. South Bend, Ind.: St. Augustine's Press, 2008.

Margellidon, Philippe-Marie. "Satisfaction." In *Dictionnaire de philosophie et de théologie thomistes*, edited by Yves Floucat and P.-M. Margellidon, 478–80. Paris: Parole et Silence, 2011.

Marshall, Bruce D. "The Whole Mystery of Our Salvation: Saint Thomas Aquinas on the Eucharist as Sacrifice." In *Rediscovering Aquinas and the Sacraments: Studies in Sacramental Theology*, edited by Michael Dauphinais and Matthew Levering, 39–64. Chicago: Hillenbrand Books, 2009.

Masure, Eugène. *Le sacrifice du chef*. 7th ed. Paris: Beauchesne, 1944.

Matthiesen, Michon M. *Sacrifice as Gift: Eucharist, Grace and Contemplative Prayer in Maurice de la Taille*. Washington, D.C.: The Catholic University of America Press, 2013.

Pomplun, Trent. "Review of Charles Cardinal Journet, *The Mass: The Presence of the Sacrifice of the Cross*." *The Thomist* 73 (2009): 670–74.

———. "Post-Tridentine Sacramental Theology." In Boersma and Levering, *The Oxford Handbook of Sacramental Theology*, 348–61.

Poschmann, Bernhard. "'Mysteriengegenwart' im Licht des hl. Thomas." *Theologische Quartalschrift* 116 (1935): 53–116.

Rahner, Karl. *Die vielen Messen und das eine Opfer: Versionen 1949/1951 & 1966*. Sämtliche Werke 18: Leiblichkeit der Gnade, Schriften zur Sakramentenlehre. Freiburg im Breisgau: Herder, 2003.

Schenk, Richard. "*Verum Sacrificium* as the Fullness and Limit of Eucharistic Sacrifice in the Sacramental Theology of Thomas Aquinas." In Hütter and Levering, *Ressourcement Thomism*, 169–207.

Schlesinger, Eugene R. “Eucharistic Sacrifice as Anti-violent Pedagogy.” *Theological Studies* 80 (2019): 653–72.
Vaggagini, Cipriano. “Fundamental Ideas of the Constitution.” In *The Liturgy of Vatican II: A Symposium*, edited by William Barauna, translated by Salvatore Attanasio, vol. 1, 95–129. Chicago: Franciscan Herald Press, 1966.
Van Rooyen, Peter. “The Fruit of the Mass According to Maurice de la Taille: Concerning Regular Concelebration.” *Antiphon* 23 (2019): 185–97.
Zizioulas, John D. “Symbolism and Realism in Orthodox Worship.” In *The Eucharistic Communion in the World*, edited by Luke Ben Tallon, 83–97. London: T&T Clark, 2011.

The Substantial Presence of Christ, Transubstantiation, and Transignification

Adams, Marilyn McCord. *Some Later Medieval Theories of the Eucharist: Thomas Aquinas, Giles of Rome, Duns Scotus and William of Ockham*. Oxford: Oxford University Press, 2010.
Anscombe, G. E. M. “On Transubstantiation.” In *Faith in a Hard Ground: Essays on Religion, Philosophy and Ethics by G. E. M. Anscombe*, edited by Mary Geach and Luke Gormally, 84–91. Exeter, England: Imprint Academic, 2008.
Boeve, Lieven. “Thinking Sacramental Presence in a Postmodern Context: A Playground for Theological Renewal.” In Boeve and Leijssen, *Sacramental Presence in a Postmodern Context*, 3–35.
Boeve, Lieven and L. Leijssen, ed. *Sacramental Presence in a Postmodern Context*. Bibliotheca Ephemeridum Theologicarum Lovaniensium 160. Leuven, Belgium: Leuven University Press, 2001.
Brock, Stephen L. “St. Thomas and the Eucharistic Conversion.” *The Thomist* 65 (2001): 529–65.
Burr, David. “Scotus and Transubstantiation.” *Medieval Studies* 34 (1972): 336–60.
Chauvet, Louis-Marie. “The Broken Bread as Theological Figure of Eucharistic Presence.” In Boeve and Leijssen, *Sacramental Presence in a Postmodern Context*, 236–62.
———. “Le pain rompu comme figure théologique de la présence eucharistique.” In *Le corps, chemin de Dieu: Les sacrements*, 191–224. Paris: Bayard, 2010.
Hochschild, Joshua P. “Substance Made Manifest: Metaphysical and Semantic Implications of the Doctrine of Transubstantiation.” Version of a paper presented at the Metaphysics Colloquium of the Institute for Saint Anselm Studies, Saint Anselm College, Manchester, N.H., June 5–6, 2013. Available online at https://philarchive.org/archive/HOCSMM-2.
Hütter, Reinhard. “Transubstantiation Revisited: *Sacra Doctrina*, Dogma and Metaphysics.” In Hütter and Levering, *Ressourcement Thomism*, 21–79.
Jorissen, Hans. *Die Entfaltung der Transsubstantionslehre bis zum Beginn der Hochscho-*

lastik. Münsterische Beiträge zur Theologie 28.1. Münster, Germany: Aschendorff, 1965.

———. *Der Beitrag Alberts des Großen zur theologischen Rezeption des Aristoteles am Beispiel der Transsubstantiationslehre*. Lectio Albertina 5. Münster, Germany: Aschendorff, 2002.

Marion, Jean-Luc. *God without Being*. Translated by Robert A. Carlson. Chicago: Chicago University Press, 1991.

Marshall, Bruce. "The Eucharistic Presence of Christ." In Root and Buckley, *What Does It Mean to "Do This"? Supper, Mass, Eucharist*, 47–73.

McCabe, Herbert. *God Still Matters*. Edited by Brian Davies. London: Continuum, 2002.

McKenna, John H. "Eucharistic Presence: An Invitation to Dialogue." *Theological Studies* 60 (1999): 294–317.

Nutt, Roger. "Faith, Metaphysics, and the Contemplation of Christ's Corporeal Presence in the Eucharist: A Translation of St. Thomas Aquinas' Seventh Quodlibetal Dispute, Q. 4, A. 1 with an Introductory Essay." *Antiphon* 15 (2011): 151–71.

Rahner, Karl. "Die Gegenwart Christi im Sakrament des Herrenmahles." In *Schriften zur Theologie*, vol. 4, 357–85. Cologne: Benziger, 1960. English Translation: "The Presence of Christ in the Lord's Supper." In *Theological Investigations*, vol. 4, 287–311. New York: Crossroad, 1982.

Ratzinger, Joseph. "Das Problem der Transsubstantiation und die Frage nach dem Sinn der Eucharistie." *Theologische Quartalschrift* 147 (1967): 129–59.

Salkeld, Brett. *Transubstantiation: Theology, History and Christian Unity*. Grand Rapids, Mich.: Baker Academic, 2019.

Schillebeeckx, Edward. *The Eucharist*. London: Sheed & Ward, 1968.

Séjourné, P. "Rupert de Deutz." In *Dictionnaire de théologie catholique*, edited by É. Amann, vol. 14, cols. 169–205. Paris: L. Letouzey et Âne, 1939.

Sweeney, Conor. *Sacramental Presence after Heidegger: Onto-theology, Sacraments and the Moral Life*. Eugene, Ore.: Cascade Books, 2015.

Vonier, Anscar. *A Key to the Doctrine of the Eucharist*. Eugene, Ore.: Assumption Press, 2013.

Yarnold, Edward. "Transubstantiation." In *The Eucharist in Theology and Philosophy: Issues of Doctrinal History in East and West from the Patristic Age to the Reformation*, edited by Istvan Perczel, Réka Forrai, and György Geréby, 381–94. Ancient and Medieval Philosophy, Series 1, vol. 35. Leuven: Leuven University Press, 2005.

The Epiclesis and Consecration

Congar, Yves. *Je crois en l'Esprit Saint*. 3 volumes in 1. Paris: Cerf, 2002 (reprint). English Translation: *I Believe in the Holy Spirit*. 3 volumes in 1. New York: Crossroad, 1997.

de la Soujeole, Benoît-Dominique. "La forme de l'eucharistie." *Revue Thomiste* 103 (2003): 91–103.

Gill, Joseph. *The Council of Florence*. Cambridge: Cambridge University Press, 1959.

Gy, Pierre-Marie. "Prière eucharistique et paroles de la consécration." In *La liturgie dans l'histoire*.

———. "Le 'nous' de la prière eucharistique." *La Maison de Dieu* 191 (1992): 7–14.

Kappes, Christiaan. *The Epiclesis Debate at the Council of Florence*. Notre Dame, Ind.: University of Notre Dame Press, 2019.

McKenna, John H. *The Eucharistic Epiclesis: A Detailed History from the Patristic Era to the Modern Era*. 2nd ed. Chicago, Illinois: Hildenbrand Books, 2009.

Salaville, S. "Épiclèse eucharistique." In *Dictionnaire de théologie catholique*, edited by E. Mangenot, vol. 5, cols. 194–300. Paris: Librairie Letouzey et Âne, 1913.

Zheltov, Michael. "The Moment of Eucharistic Consecration in Byzantine Thought." In *Issues in Eucharistic Praying*, edited by Maxwell Johnson, 263–306. Collegeville, Minn.: Liturgical Press, 2010.

The Celebrant of the Eucharist and Con-celebration

Beauduin, Lambert. "La concélébration." *La maison de Dieu* 7, no. 3 (1946): 7–26.

Bernier, Réginald. "In persona Christi, in persona Ecclesiae." *Revue Thomiste* 113 (2013): 443–51.

Botte, Bernard. "Note historique sur la concélébration dans l'église ancienne." *La maison de Dieu* 35, no. 3 (1953): 9–23.

Butler, Sara. "*In Persona Christi*." *CTSA Proceedings* 50 (1995): 146–55.

———. "*In Persona Christi*: A Response to Dennis M. Ferrara." *Theological Studies* 56 (1995): 61–80.

———. *The Catholic Priesthood and Women: A Guide to the Teaching of the Church*. Chicago: Hillenbrand Books, 2007.

Cattaneo, Enrico. *I ministeri nella Chiesa antica: Testi patristici dei primi tre secoli*. Milan: Paoline, 1997.

Derville, Guillaume. *Eucharistic Concelebration: From Symbol to Reality*. Montreal, Canada: Wilson & Lafleur, 2011.

Donneaud, Henry. "La représentation sacramentelle du Christ Tête." *Revue Thomiste* 113 (2013): 615–44.

Ferrara, Denis. "Representation or Self-Effacement? The Axiom *In Persona Christi* in St. Thomas and the Magisterium." *Theological Studies* 55 (1994): 195–224.

———. "*In Persona Christi*: A Reply to Sarah Butler." *Theological Studies* 56 (1995): 81–91.

———. "*In Persona Christi*: Toward a Second Naïveté." *Theological Studies* 57 (1996): 65–88.

Joseph de Sainte-Marie. *The Holy Eucharist, The World's Salvation: Studies on the Holy Sacrifice of the Mass, Its Celebration and Its Concelebration*. Leominster, England: Gracewing, 2015.

Legrand, Hervé-Marie. "La présidence de l'Eucharistie selon la tradition ancienne." *Spiritus* 69 (1977): 409–31.

———. "Communion ecclésiale et Eucharistie aux premiers siècles." *L'année canonique* 25 (1981): 125–48.

———. "*Traditio perpetua servata?* The Non-Ordination of Women: Tradition or Simply an Historical Fact?" *Worship* 65 (1991): 482–508.

Logue, Damien. "Le premier et le principal du sacrement de l'ordre." In *Questions disputées autour du sacrement de l'ordre*, edited by Philippe-Marie Margelidon, 93–122. Sed Contra. Perpignan, France: Artège Lethielleux, 2018.

Mansini, Guy. "Representation and Agency in the Eucharist." In *The Word Has Dwelt among Us: Explorations in Theology*, 129–41. Naples, Fla.: Sapientia Press, 2008.

Mansini, Guy, and Lawrence J. Welch. "The Durable Synthesis of *Presbyterorum Ordinis*." In Guy Mansini, *The Word Has Dwelt among Us: Explorations in Theology*, 213–56. Naples, Fla.: Sapientia Press, 2008.

Marliangeas, Bernard Dominique. *Clés pour une théologie du ministère: In persona Christi, in persona Ecclesiae*. Théologie historique 51. Paris: Beauchesne, 1978.

McCusker, John. "Concerning Regular Concelebration in Seminaries and Religious Houses." *Antiphon* 22 (2018): 225–42.

Miquel Ciarrochi, Alejandro Blas. "Sponsus Ecclesiae, sicut Christus: Sobre il simbolismo nupcial del sacerdote dese Hugo de San Víctor hasta Santo Tomás de Aquino." Dissertation, John Paul II Pontifical Institute for the Study of Marriage and Family, Pontifical Lateran University, 2015.

Monléon, Albert Marie de. *Charismes et ministères dans l'Écriture, et l'expérience de l'Église*. Chemins ouverts. Paris, Desclée de Brouwer, 1995.

O'Loughlin, Thomas. "Are 'the Bishops … the "High Priests" Who Preside at the Eucharist'?: A Note on the Sources of the Text of *Sensus Fidei*." *New Blackfriars* 98 (March 2017): 232–38.

Schillebeeckx, Edward. *Ministry: A Case for Change*. London: SCM Press, 1981.

Schmitz, Rudolf Michael. "La concelebrazione eucaristica." In *Il mistero eucaristico*, edited by Antonio Piolanti, 501–20. Pontificia Accademia Teologica Romana. Vatican City: Libreria Editrice Vaticana, 1983.

Tihon, P. "De la concélébration eucharistique." *Nouvelle revue théologique* 86 (1964): 579–607.

Tirot, Paul. "La concélébration et la tradition de l'Église," *Ephemerides liturgicae* 101 (1987): 33–59.

Torrell, Jean-Pierre. *A Priestly People: Baptismal Priesthood and the Priestly Ministry*. Translated by Peter Heinegg. New York: Paulist Press, 2013.

Vagaggini, Cipriano, "Ancora sulla estensione della mano dei concelebranti al momento della consacrazione: Gesto indicativo o epicletico?" *Ephemerides liturgicae* 97 (1983): 224–40.

Welch, Lawrence J. "For the Church and within the Church: Priestly Representation." *The Thomist* 65 (2001): 613–37.

Wood, Susan K. "Holy Orders." In *The Oxford Handbook of Catholic Theology*, edited by Lewis Ayres and Medi Ann Volpe, 294–309. Oxford: Oxford University Press, 2019.

Communion and the Fruits of the Eucharist

Alphonsus Liguori. *Visits to the Most Holy Sacrament and to the Holy Virgin for Every Day in the Month*. London: T. Jones, 1849.

Bazelaire, Louis de. "Communion spirituelle." In *Dictionnaire de théologie catholique*, edited by E. Mangenot, vol. 3, cols. 1294–1300. Paris: Librairie Letouzey et Ané, 1908.

Blankenhorn, Bernhard. "L'eucaristia nella vita matrimoniale: Medicina dei peccatori o sacramento dei vivi?" In *Eucaristia e Matrimonio: Due sacramenti, un'alleanza*, edited by José Granados and Stefano Salucci, 127–49. Siena, Italy: Cantagalli, 2015.

———. *The Mystery of Union with God: Dionysian Mysticism in Albert the Great and Thomas Aquinas*. Thomistic Ressourcement 4. Washington, D.C.: The Catholic University of America Press, 2015.

Bonino, Serge-Thomas. "Saint Thomas Aquinas in the Apostolic Exhortation *Amoris Laetitia*," *The Thomist* 80 (2016): 499–519.

———. *Saint Thomas d'Aquin, lecteur du Cantique des cantiques*. Paris: Cerf, 2019.

Bria, Ion. "Intercommunion et unité." *ISTINA* 14 (1969): 220–50.

Buttiglione, Rocco. "*Amoris Laetitia: Risposte ai critici*." *Lateranum* 83 (2017): 191–240.

Corbett, John, Dominic Legge, Andrew Hofer, Kurt Martens, Paul J. Keller, Thomas Petri, Dominic Langevin, and Thomas Joseph White. "Recent Proposals for the Pastoral Care of the Divorced and Remarried: A Theological Assessment." *Nova et Vetera* (English Edition) 12 (2014): 601–30.

Dodaro, Robert, ed. *Remaining in the Truth of Christ: Marriage and Communion in the Catholic Church*. San Francisco: Ignatius Press, 2014.

Emery, Gilles. *Trinity, the Church and the Human Person: Thomistic Essays*. Naples, Fla.: Sapientia Press, 2007.

Francis de Sales. *Introduction to the Devout Life*. Translated by Allan Ross. Westminster, Md.: Newman Press, 1953.

Granados, José, Stephan Kampowski, and Juan José Pérez-Soba. *Amoris Laetitia: Accompagnare, discernere, integrare. Vademecum per una nuova pastorale familiare*. Siena, Italy: Cantagalli, 2017.

Kasper, Walter Cardinal. *Il Vangelo della Famiglia*. Giornale di Teologia 371. Brescia, Italy: Queriniana, 2014.

Leppin, Volker, and Dorothea Sattler, eds. *Together at the Lord's Table: A Votum of the Ecumenical Working Group of Lutheran and Catholic Theologians*. Freiburg im Breisgau: Herder, 2020.

Melina, Livo, ed. *Quale pastorale familiare dopo Amoris laetitia?* Studi sulla persona e la famiglia, Atti 36. Siena, Italy: Cantagalli, 2017.

Pérez-Soba, Juan José, and Stephan Kampowski. *The Gospel of the Family: Going beyond Cardinal Kasper's Proposal in the Debate on Marriage, Re-Marriage and Communion in the Church*. San Francisco: Ignatius Press, 2014.

Perrier, Emmanuel. "Le Pain de Vie chez Louis-Marie Chauvet et saint Thomas

d'Aquin: Représentation de l'inconnaissable ou terme de l'union spirituelle?" *Revue Thomiste* 113 (2013): 195–234.
Poschmann, Bernhard. *Penance and the Anointing of the Sick*. Translated by Francis Courtney. New York: Herder & Herder, 1964.
Schockenhoff, Eberhard, *La Chiesa e i divorziati risposati: Questioni aperte*. Giornale di Teologia 372. Brescia, Italy: Queriniana, 2014.
Spadaro, Antonio. "Struttura e significato dell'Esortazione apostolica postsinodale di Papa Francesco." In Pope Francis, *Amoris Laetitia*, edited by A. Spadaro, 5–42. Rome: Ancora, 2016.
Teresa of Avila. *Collected Works of St. Teresa of Avila*. Volume 2. Translated by Kieran Kavanaugh and Otilio Rodriguez. Washington, D.C.: Institute of Carmelite Studies, 1980.
Valuet, Basile. "*Amoris Laetitia*: Le chapitre VIII est-il une révolution?" *Revue Thomiste* 116 (2016): 585–618.
Wahlberg, Mats. "Cardinal Kasper's Proposal on the Meaning of Marriage." *Nova et Vetera* (English Edition) 13 (2015): 1003–8.
———. "The Two Faces of *Amoris Laetitia*." *First Things*, April 4 (2017), https://www.firstthings.com/web-exclusives/2017/04/the-two-faces-of-amoris-laetitia.
William of Saint-Thierry, *Lettre aux frères du Mont-Dieu (Lettre d'or)*. Edited, translated, and annotated by Jean Déchanet. Sources chrétiennes 223. Paris: Cerf, 1975.

Protestant Eucharistic Theologies

Allen, Michael. "Sacraments in the Reformed and Anglican Reformation." In Boersma and Levering, *The Oxford Handbook of Sacramental Theology*, 283–97.
Bayer, Oswald. *Promissio: Geschichte der reformatorischen Wende in Luthers Theologie*. Forschungen und zur Kirchen- und Dogmengeschichte 24. Göttingen, Germany: Vandenhoeck & Ruprecht, 1971.
Calvin, John. *L'institution chrétienne*. Geneva: Labor et Fides, 1958. English translation: *The Institutes of Christian Religion*. Translated by Henry Beveridge. Peabody, Mass.: 2008.
Ewerszumrode, Frank. *Mysterium Christi spiritualis praesentiae: Die Abendmahlslehre des Genfer Reformators Johannes Calvin aus römisch-katholischer Perspektive*. Reformed Historical Theology 19. Göttingen, Germany: Vandenhoek & Ruprecht, 2012.
Gerrish, Brian. *Grace and Gratitude: The Eucharistic Theology of John Calvin*. Eugene, Ore.: Wipf & Stock, 2002.
Hunsinger, George. *The Eucharist and Ecumenism: Let Us Keep the Feast*. Current Issues in Theology. Cambridge: Cambridge University Press, 2008.
Jensen, Gordon A. "Luther on the Lord's Supper." In *The Oxford Handbook of Martin Luther's Theology*, edited by Robert Kolb, Irene Dingel, and L'Ubomir Batka, 322–32. Oxford: Oxford University Press, 2014.

Levy, Ian Christopher. "Affirming Real Presence from a Historical Perspective." *Lexington Theological Quarterly* 38 (2003): 27–51.

———. "The Eucharist in the Fourteenth and Fifteenth Centuries." In Boersma and Levering, *The Oxford Handbook of Sacramental Theology*, 235–48.

Luther, Martin. *The Babylonian Captivity*, in *Church and Sacraments*, the Annotated Luther Study Edition 3, edited by Paul W. Robinson. Minneapolis, Minn: Fortress Press, 2016.

Mattox, Mickey L. "Sacraments in the Lutheran Reformation." In Boersma and Levering, *The Oxford Handbook of Sacramental Theology*, 269–82.

Morerod, Charles. *Ecumenism and Philosophy: Philosophical Questions for a Renewal of Dialogue*. Ann Arbor, Mich.: Sapientia Press, 2006.

Staedtke, Joachim. "Abendmahl III/3: Reformationszeit." In *Theologische Realenzyklopädie*, vol. 1, edited by Gerhard Kraus and Gerhard L. Müller, 106–22. Berlin: Walter de Gruyter, 1977.

zur Mühlen, Karl-Heinz. "Luther II: Theologie." In *Theologische Realenzyklopädie*, vol. 21, edited by Gerhard L. Müller, 530–67. Berlin: Walter de Gruyter, 1991.

Sacramental Theology in General

Blankenhorn, Bernhard. "The Instrumental Causality of the Sacraments: Thomas Aquinas and Louis-Marie Chauvet." *Nova et Vetera* (English edition) 4 (2006): 275–91.

———. "The Place of Romans 6 in Aquinas' Doctrine of Sacramental Causality: A Balance of History and Metaphysics." In Hütter and Levering, *Ressourcement Thomism*, 136–49.

de la Soujeole, Benoît-Dominique. "The Importance of the Definition of Sacraments as Signs." In Hütter and Levering, *Ressourcement Thomism*, 127–35.

Getcha, Job Ihor W. "La théologie sacramentaire byzantine: La synthèse de Nicolas Cabasilas et Syméon de Thessalonique." Habilitation Thesis, University of Lorraine, Department of Theology, 2012.

Langevin, Dominic M. *From Passion to Paschal Mystery: A Recent Magisterial Development concerning the Christological Foundation of the Sacraments*. Studia Friburgensia 121. Fribourg, Switzerland: Academic Press, 2015.

Schillebeeckx, Edward. *Christ the Sacrament of the Encounter with God*. Kansas City, Mo.: Sheed & Ward, 1963.

———. *L'économie sacramentelle du salut*. Translated by Yvon van der Have. Studia Friburgensia 95. Fribourg, Switzerland: Academic Press, 2004.

The Doctrine of God and Christology

Balthasar, Hans Urs von. *To the Heart of the Mystery of Redemption*. Translated by Anne Englund Nash. San Francisco: Ignatius Press, 2010.

Dodds, Michael J. *The Unchanging God of Love: Thomas Aquinas and Contemporary*

Theology on Divine Immutability. Washington, D.C.: The Catholic University of America Press, 2008.

———. *Unlocking Divine Action: Contemporary Science and Thomas Aquinas*. Washington, D.C.: The Catholic University of America Press, 2012.

Gaine, Simon Francis. *Did the Saviour See the Father? Christ, Salvation and the Vision of God*. London: Bloomsbury, 2015.

Journet, Charles. *L'Église du Verbe Incarné: Essaie de théologie spéculative*. Vol. 2, *Sa structure interne et son unité Catholique*. Saint Maurice, Switzerland: Éditions Saint-Augustin, 1999.

Levering, Matthew. *Christ's Fulfillment of Torah and Temple: Salvation according to Thomas Aquinas*. South Bend, Ind.: University of Notre Dame Press, 2002.

Morard, Martin. "Une source de saint Thomas d'Aquin: Le deuxième concile de Constantinople (553)." *Revue des sciences philosophiques et théologiques* 81 (1997): 21–56.

———. "Thomas d'Aquin, lecteur des conciles." *Archivum Francisanum Historicum* 98 (2005): 211–365.

Perrier, Emmanuel. "L'enjeu christologique de la satisfaction (I)," *Revue Thomiste* 103 (2003): 105–36.

———. "L'enjeu christologique de la satisfaction (II)," *Revue Thomiste* 103 (2003): 203–47.

Ocáriz, Fernando, Lucas F. Mateo Seco, and José A. Riestra. *The Mystery of Jesus Christ: A Christology and Soteriology Textbook*. Translated by Michael Adams and James Gavigan. Portland, Ore.: Four Courts Press, 2011.

Ramelow, Anselm. "Not a Miracle: Our Knowledge of God's Signs and Wonders." *Nova et Vetera* (English Edition) 14 (2016): 659–73.

Torrell, Jean-Pierre. "La causalité salvifique de la résurrection du Christ selon saint Thomas." In *Recherches Thomasiennes*, 214–41. Bibliothèque Thomiste 52. Paris: Vrin, 2000.

———. *Encyclopédie Jésus le Christ chez saint Thomas d'Aquin*. Paris: Cerf, 2008.

———. *Christ and Spirituality in St. Thomas Aquinas*. Translated by Bernhard Blankenhorn. Washington, D.C.: The Catholic University of America Press, 2011.

Tschipke, Theophil. *Die Menschheit Christi als Heilsorgan der Gottheit: Unter besonderer Berücksichtigung der Lehre des heiligen Thomas von Aquin*. Freiburger theologische Studien 55. Freiburg im Breisgau: Herder, 1940.

White, Thomas Joseph. *The Incarnate Lord: A Thomistic Study in Christology*. Thomistic Ressourcement 5. Washington, D.C.: The Catholic University of America Press, 2015.

Miscellaneous

Blankenhorn, Bernhard. "Implicit Philosophy and Hermeneutics: Metaphysics and the Historicity of Thought in Light of *Fides et Ratio*." *Angelicum* 95 (2018): 201–18.

Blowers, Paul M. *Maximus the Confessor: Jesus Christ and the Transfiguration of the World*. Christian Theology in Context. Oxford: Oxford University Press, 2016.

Congar, Yves. *La foi et la théologie*. Le mystère chrétien: Théologie dogmatique. Paris: Desclée de Brouwer, 1962.

de la Soujeole, Benoît-Dominique. *Introduction to the Mystery of the Church*. Translated by Michael J. Miller. Thomistic Ressourcement 3. Washington, D.C.: The Catholic University of America Press, 2014.

Elders, Leo J. *La métaphysique de saint Thomas d'Aquin dans une perspective historique*. Bibliothèque d'histoire de la philosophie. Paris: Vrin, 1994. English translation: *The Metaphysics of Being of St. Thomas Aquinas in a Historical Perspective*. Leiden, Netherlands: Brill, 1993.

Emery, Gilles. *The Trinitarian Theology of St. Thomas Aquinas*. Translated by Francesca Aran Murphy. Oxford: Oxford University Press, 2007.

Feser, Edward. *Scholastic Metaphysics: A Contemporary Introduction*. Heusenstamm, Germany: Editiones Scholasticae, 2014.

Finnis, John. *Moral Absolutes: Tradition, Revision, and Truth*. Washington, D.C.: The Catholic University of America Press, 1991.

Galot, Jean. *La nature du caractère sacramentel: Étude de théologie médiévale*. Paris: Desclée de Brouwer, 1956.

Gardeil, Henri-Dominique. *Introduction to the Philosophy of St. Thomas Aquinas*. Vol. 2, *Cosmology*. Translated by John A. Otto. Eugene, Ore.: Wipf & Stock, 2009.

———. *Introduction to the Philosophy of St. Thomas Aquinas*. Vol. 4, *Metaphysics*. Translated by John A. Otto. Eugene, Ore.: Wipf & Stock, 2012.

International Theological Commission. *In Search of a Universal Ethic: A New Look at the Natural Law*. London: Catholic Truth Society, 2012.

Léthel, Fr.-M. *L'amour de Jésus: La christologie de sainte Thérèse de l'Enfant Jésus*. Jésus et Jésus-Christ 72. Paris: Desclée, 1997.

Mansini, Guy. "The Development of the Development of Doctrine in the Twentieth Century." *Angelicum* 93 (2016): 785–822.

———. "The Historicity of Dogma and Common Sense: Ambroise Gardeil, Reginald Garrigou-Lagrange, Yves Congar, and the Modern Magisterium." *Nova et Vetera* (English Edition) 18 (2020): 111–38.

Meszaros, Andrew. "Yves Congar and the Salvation of the Non-Christian." *Louvain Studies* 37 (2013): 195–223.

Rosier-Catach, Irène. *La parole efficace: Signe, rituel, sacré*. Paris: Éditions du Seuil, 2004.

Sullivan, Francis A. *Salvation Outside the Church? Tracing the History of the Catholic Response*. New York: Paulist Press, 1992.

Torrell, Jean-Pierre. *Initiation à saint Thomas d'Aquin: Sa personne et son œuvre*. 2nd ed. Paris: Cerf, 2015.

INDEX OF NAMES

GENERAL INDEX

ALSO IN THE SACRA DOCTRINA SERIES

Ecclesiology
Guy Mansini, OSB

An Introduction to Vatican II as an Ongoing Theological Event
Matthew Levering

Fundamental Theology
Guy Mansini, OSB

John Henry Newman on Truth and Its Counterfeits
A Guide for Our Times
Reinhard Hütter

The Godly Image
Christian Satisfaction in Aquinas
Romanus Cessario, OP

The One Creator God in Thomas Aquinas and Contemporary Theology
Michael J. Dodds, OP

Bread from Heaven: An Introduction to the Theology of the Eucharist was designed in Garamond, with Scala Sans and Garda Titling display type, and composed by Kachergis Book Design of Pittsboro, North Carolina. It was printed on 60-pound House Natural Smooth and bound by Sheridan Books of Chelsea, Michigan.